Praise for

Keepin' On

"You can feel deep in your soul the actual struggles of single parents who live in poverty. If ever there is documentation to support the need to expand Early Head Start and Head Start, this book not only captures it but also provides concrete evidence of the programs' effectiveness. Great, inspirational reading for advocates and people working in the programs."

—**Sarah M. Greene**
President and CEO
National Head Start Association

"In *Keepin' On: The Everyday Struggles of Young Families in Poverty*, Drs. Ispa, Thornburg, and Fine have given us a significant view of the lives of young families struggling with poverty in America. Although there are examples on television of the lives of such families, those depictions are usually quite superficial. . . . The value of this book is that it gives the reader a real idea of who these people are and why they frequently react the way they do. I believe it will make it easier to interact in a positive manner with such individuals and perhaps improve society for everyone."

—**Benjamin S. Carson, Sr., M.D.**
Director of Pediatric Neurosurgery
Professor of Neurological Surgery, Oncology,
Plastic Surgery, and Pediatrics
Johns Hopkins Medicine

"Grounded in relevant theoretical perspectives and carefully using a mix of data collection and interpretive methods, the authors provide a description of the collection of challenges facing these young women, their children, the men in their lives, and the communities in which they live. The information and perspectives included in this book are invaluable to those who train teachers and service providers and to policy makers and program developers from local to federal levels. These are lives tenuously sustained by a weak and shifting support system that often provides contradictory and confusing resources and constraints. It is critical that we understand the dynamics of poverty at this level, where it intersects with and dominates family life, if we are ever to build systems effective at helping these families achieve their goals, which, as we are reminded by this volume, are our goals as well."

—**Robert C. Pianta, Ph.D.**
Director, Center for Advanced Study in
Teaching and Learning (CASTL)
University of Virginia

D0993204

"This is a wonderful book. On every level—the voices of the young women participants in Early Head Start, the careful attention to theoretical frameworks, and the practical and policy implications—this book succeeds."

—Carollee Howes, Ph.D.
Professor
Director, Center for the Improvement
of Child Care Quality
UCLA

"Evaluations of early interventions rarely capture the life stories of individuals involved in such programs. Using case study and narrative approaches, the authors delve deeply into the lives of low-income women as they make the transition to motherhood. Their powerful stories will inform early childhood professionals, interventionists, and policy makers of the extraordinary resilience of the human spirit, even when surrounded by persistent risk."

—Hiram E. Fitzgerald, Ph.D.
University Distinguished Professor
Michigan State University

"*Keepin' On* does a phenomenal job of capturing the challenges, anguish, and triumphs of young, single African American mothers living in poverty. This is a must read for Early Head Start teachers, home visitors and directors, and others working within zero to five programs across the United States. Andreya's story, and the portrayal of her courage and love of her children, in spite of incredible hardship, is worth the read alone!"

—Helen Raikes, Ph.D.
Professor, Family and Consumer Sciences
University of Nebraska–Lincoln

Keepin' On

Keepin' On

The Everyday Struggles
of Young Families in Poverty

by

Jean M. Ispa, Ph.D.
Kathy R. Thornburg, Ph.D.
Mark A. Fine, Ph.D.
University of Missouri–Columbia

with invited contributors

·P A U L·H·
BROOKES
PUBLISHING CO.®

Baltimore ▪ London ▪ Sydney

Paul H. Brookes Publishing Co.

Post Office Box 10624

Baltimore, Maryland 21285-0624

www.brookespublishing.com

Typeset by Integrated Publishing Solutions, Grand Rapids, Michigan.
Manufactured in the United States of America by
Versa Press, Inc., East Peoria, Illinois.

The situations described in this book are real, as are the names of the
researchers, but the names of the participants and the Early Head Start
staff, as well as details about the location in which the study took place,
have been changed to protect confidentiality.

Library of Congress Cataloging-in-Publication Data

Ispa, Jean.
   Keepin' on : the everyday struggles of young families in poverty /
   by Jean M. Ispa, Kathy R. Thornburg, Mark A. Fine ; with invited
   contributors.
       p.   cm.
   Includes bibliographical references and index.
   ISBN-13: 978-1-55766-781-6 (alk. paper)
   ISBN-10: 1-55766-781-0 (alk. paper)
   1. African American poor families—Longitudinal studies.   2. Early Head
   Start (Program)—Evaluation.   3. African American mothers—Social
   conditions—Longitudinal studies.   I. Title: Keepin' on.   II. Thornburg,
   Kathy R.   III. Fine, Mark A.   IV. Title.
   HV699.I87 2006
   305.5'6908996073—dc22   2006004227

British Library Cataloguing in Publication data are available
from the British Library.

Contents

About the Authors

Jean M. Ispa, Ph.D., Professor, Department of Human Development and Family Studies, University of Missouri–Columbia, 314 Gentry Hall, Columbia, Missouri 65211

Dr. Ispa has been on the faculty of the University of Missouri–Columbia since 1978. She has taught courses on child development, early childhood education, the history of the family in Russia, and, most recently, on the causes and consequences of poverty for U.S. children and families. Her research interests include the implications of culture for parenting and child development, children's social development, and child-rearing and family relationships in families with low income. Her previous book, *Child Care in Russia: In Transition* (Bergin & Garvey, 1994), described child-rearing philosophy and practice in six Moscow child care centers shortly before the collapse of the Soviet government. Dr. Ispa also is the author of journal articles on African American, European American, Latino, and Russian parents' and teachers' child-rearing ideas and behaviors and their implications for children's development.

Kathy R. Thornburg, Ph.D., Professor, Department of Human Development and Family Studies, and Director, Center for Family Policy and Research, University of Missouri–Columbia, 1400 Rock Quarry Road, Columbia, Missouri 65211

Dr. Thornburg has been teaching and working in the area of early childhood education for 40 years. Her experience includes teaching preschoolers and third graders and directing early childhood programs for children ranging in age from 6 weeks to 10 years. She taught child development and child and family policy courses at the Universities of Kentucky and Missouri for 36 years. Dr. Thornburg serves on numerous state, regional, and national boards, councils, and commissions. From 2000 to 2002, she was president of the National Association for the Education of Young Children. She has published more than 100 research articles, book chapters, and books. Her research has appeared in journals such as *Early Childhood Education Journal, Educational and Psycho-*

logical Measurement, Early Childhood Research Quarterly, and *Educational Research Quarterly,* and she currently serves as a consulting editor to several major professional journals. Her research interests include public policy issues relating to early childhood programs, early childhood teacher training, and teacher turnover.

Mark A. Fine, Ph.D., Professor, Department of Human Development and Family Studies, University of Missouri–Columbia, 310 Gentry Hall, Columbia, Missouri 65211

Dr. Fine was Editor of *Family Relations* from 1993 to 1996 and Editor of the *Journal of Social and Personal Relationships* from 1999 to 2004. His research interests lie in the areas of family transitions such as divorce and remarriage, early intervention program evaluation, social cognition, and relationship stability. He was co-editor, with David Demo and Katherine Allen, of *Handbook of Family Diversity* (Oxford University Press, 2000). He has published almost 200 peer-reviewed journal articles, book chapters, and books. He co-authored, with John Harvey, *Children of Divorce: Stories of Hope and Loss* (Lawrence Erlbaum Associates, 2004), and he co-edited, with John Harvey, *The Handbook of Divorce and Relationship Dissolution* (Lawrence Erlbaum Associates, 2005). In 2000, Dr. Fine was selected as a Fellow of the National Council on Family Relations.

About the Contributors

Gina Barclay-McLaughlin, Ph.D., Associate Professor, College of Education, Health, and Human Sciences, A414 Claxton Complex, Knoxville, Tennessee 37996-3442

Dr. Barclay-McLaughlin is an associate professor at the University of Tennessee, Knoxville, in the College of Education, Health, and Human Sciences. Her research has focused on child development, education, parenting, and the dynamics of race, culture, and class. She is the founding director of the Beethoven Project, an early intervention program that served the Robert Taylor Homes, the country's largest public housing project and the program model for Early Head Start.

Sheila J. Brookes, Ph.D., Assistant Professor, Family and Consumer Sciences Department, Northwest Missouri State University, 800 University Avenue, Maryville, Missouri 64468

Dr. Brookes, an assistant professor at Northwest Missouri State University, teaches courses in child and family studies. She also is director of the University's Child Development Lab. Her research interests include poverty and young families, child care quality, and the impact public assistance policies have on families and children.

Gayle Cunningham, Executive Director, Jefferson County Committee for Economic Opportunity (JCCEO), 300 Eighth Avenue West, Birmingham, Alabama 35204-3039

Ms. Cunningham directed the Head Start and Early Head Start programs at the JCCEO Community Action Agency from 1986 to 2004. She has been Executive Director of that agency for the past 18 years. JCCEO offers a wide range of services for low-income families.

Linda C. Halgunseth, Department of Human Development and Family Studies, University of Missouri–Columbia, 314 Gentry Hall, Columbia, Missouri 65211

Ms. Halgunseth is working toward a doctorate in Human Development and Family Studies at the University of Missouri–Columbia. Her dissertation focuses on parenting beliefs and practices in Mexican American families.

Deborah A. Phillips, Ph.D., Professor, Department of Psychology, Georgetown University, 37th and O Streets, NW, Washington, DC 20057

Dr. Phillips is professor of psychology and public policy at Georgetown University and co-director of the Center for Research on Children in the United States. Her research has focused on early childhood programs and children's development, including on-going studies of child care and prekindergarten programs. She has held numerous policy positions, most recently as Director of the Board on Children, Youth, and Families at the National Research Council and Institute of Medicine.

Elizabeth A. Sharp, Ph.D., Assistant Professor, Human Development and Family Studies, Texas Tech University, Box 41162, Lubbock, Texas 79409

Dr. Sharp's current research focuses on young women's close relationships and feminist pedagogy. She teaches classes on gender role development, family theory, and qualitative methods.

Foreword

This impressive book is an extremely welcome birthday present for our nation's Early Head Start (EHS) program, which turned 10 in 2005. It will be a wonderful companion piece to Lombardi and Bogel's *Beacon of Hope* (2005), which presents a comprehensive history and description of this younger version of Head Start. EHS currently serves some 60,000 families and children from conception to age 3. Like its older and larger sibling, Head Start, which serves more than 900,000 impoverished 3- and 4-year-olds and their families, EHS was mounted to reduce the well-known achievement gap in school performance between children reared in poverty and those reared in more affluent circumstances.

One half of this later achievement gap has been found to exist at school entry, and a considerable portion is measurable even before children start preschool (Groark, Mehaffie, & McCall, in press). In fact, soon after the birth of Head Start in 1965, the program's conceptualizers and practitioners realized that starting at age 3 was intervening too late. Too many children were arriving at Head Start already seriously behind what one would expect of a 3-year-old. To address this problem, a demonstration program called the Head Start Parent–Child Centers was mounted in 1966 to serve children from birth to age 3. However, these centers did not have the performance standards or quality controls that Head Start had, and they were never rigorously evaluated. Perhaps because the idea was so sound, they continued to be funded until the model was folded into Early Head Start.

A great impetus for the birth of Early Head Start was a report issued by the Carnegie Corporation (1994) titled *Starting Points*. The authors emphasized how little programmatic attention was being given to the critical foundation years between conception and age 3. *Starting Points* highlighted research showing how quickly the human brain develops during the first 3 years of life, and the great importance of the environment in determining the actual physical structure of the brain (Shonkoff & Phillips, 2000; Zigler, Finn-Stevenson, & Hall, 2002).

Fascination with the early brain development research exploded through the national consciousness. Cover stories appeared in magazines such as *Time* and *Newsweek,* and myriad media reports proclaimed the importance of the environment experienced in the first 3 years in shaping a child's total life course. (For a strong caveat to this view, see Bruer, 1999.) This emphasis on the earliest years of life was consonant with the discussions that inspired the Parent–Child Centers and eventuated in the legislation that authorized Early Head Start in 1994. Rather than being launched as a new intervention, however, Early Head Start was funded out of a small percentage of the Head Start appropriation. Thus, we pay for Early Head Start by taking needed money away from the preschool Head Start program. This *stealing from Peter to pay Paul* approach is damaging to both efforts. If Early Head Start is to prosper and grow as it should, these two programs should each be a boat with its own bottom. Each should be funded independently based on merit and the needs of the populations served.

The study in this book offers a rare glimpse of participants in the Early Head Start program and the nature of growing up in poverty. Although studying how poverty affects child development has been something of a cottage industry, it has been many years since a book took readers directly through the war zone trenches. The authors examine the daily lives of nine poor, young, African American mothers in a major urban city (with one described thoroughly in a detailed case study). This approach is unusual in many ways. It is refreshing to find scholars who eschew the usual mask of objectivity and openly admit that they honestly care about the participants in their study as breathing, feeling human beings. They openly note how their interactions with these nine women changed their own lives and behavior. For example, when the program was faltering, they dropped their evaluative role and used their expertise to teach the staff in the off-site child care settings the children attended the skills to provide quality care that promotes healthy growth and development. Although a hard-nosed methodologist would have thrown up his or her hands in despair ("You contaminated your independent variable!"), this aging scholar has nothing but admiration for the authors and their awareness that the ultimate end of a piece of research is not a publication but improving the life course of the children they study.

The authors display this awareness in the conceptual framework in which they view research, practice, and policy as closely connected (a view I have held for decades). Although the book is about Early Head Start families, it also conveys the authors' warmth, empathy, and, although they deny it by quoting Kozol, physical courage necessary to conduct a study inside the troubled homes of parents in neighborhoods characterized by crime and violence. Also worthy of praise is the authors' decision to use a combination of Bronfenbrenner's bio-ecological formulation and feminist theory as the theoretical framework for their study.

The study of human development is essentially the study of change over time and the concerted effort to discover the processes mediating these changes (Zigler, 1963). Thus, developmentalists are badly in need of longitudinal studies. This 5-year longitudinal study is an important exception to the current preference for rigorous but essentially cross-sectional studies. In the current *publish or perish* culture of the university, it is the rare and dedicated scholar who would spend 5 years studying nine individuals.

This study raises an old controversy over the nomothetic (investigating large groups of individuals in the search for some commonality among them) approach versus the idiographic (investigating individuals in depth to achieve a unique understanding of the person) approach. There is no question that in the behavioral sciences the nomothetic approach is currently in the ascendancy. We compare groups of individuals (e.g., those who received an intervention versus those who did not). This approach has produced what I refer to as the "tyranny of the mean" (Zigler & Styfco, in press) in which the mean value is treated to represent equally each member of the group, and the variation within each group is essentially ignored. We know that some individuals profit from an intervention, while others do not. Likewise, some members of the control group fall behind while others in the same group succeed without the intervention. With the nomothetic approach, we continue to pursue the question, "Do interventions work?" The more important questions are "For whom does the intervention work?" and "For whom does the intervention not work?" The case history approach allows us to generate hypotheses that can be tested regarding the last question.

Although champions of the nomothetic approach would be unconvinced, scholars in the field of human development should be cognizant of the impressive and highly developed theoretical edifice that Piaget built on the basis of his longitudinal study of his own three children. In my view, the dichotomy between the nomothetic and idiographic approaches is a false one, because when conceptualized properly, these two approaches are synergistic rather than conflicted. The understanding that accrues from case studies often leads to experimental investigations of phenomena of interest.

There are many roads to truth, and those interested in human behavior should travel them all. I mourn the fact that in our current popular methodological practices, we have become farther and farther removed from individual lives. I think here of our now common practices of meta-analyses and secondary analyses of large-scale data sets. There is an agreement today that the penultimate evaluation of the effectiveness of an intervention is a cost–benefit analysis (Zigler & Styfco, in press). At this level, there are no individuals involved, and the entire matter becomes one of dollars and cents. Although I agree that such an evaluation has great value for policy makers, it is far removed from our primary task of understanding human behavior.

Actually, the Ispa et al. study is in a direct line of descent from Robert White's landmark study *Lives in Progress* (1952). Like White, the present authors attempt to achieve understanding of a phenomenon (i.e., young mothers living in poverty) by a hermeneutic analysis of individual 5-year life histories. This approach has been utilized effectively by other leaders in our field. One thinks here of Glen Elder and his study of children of the Great Depression, as well as the work of Elder's mentor, John Claussen.

To demonstrate the synergy between the idiographic and nomothetic approaches, this study illuminates a major finding of the rigorous, random-assignment evaluation study of Early Head Start. A consensus has now been reached that the greater the number of risk factors and the lower the number of protective factors a child has, the greater the threat to his or her developmental course and the need for intervention. The Early Head Start study used a number of risk indices and discovered a curvilinear relationship. Children with a moderate number of risks displayed the greatest benefits of the intervention. Those having few or a great many risks derived fewer benefits from participating in Early Head Start. This finding is not difficult to interpret. Those with few risks do not need the intervention and therefore do not profit from it. The problems of children with a great number of risks overwhelm the efficacy of the intervention. What are these problems, and how must we adjust our programs so that they will be effective with these very needy individuals? We can gain insights into the answer to this question by carefully reading this volume. This book contains the best, close description of very high-risk, impoverished individuals since Pavenstedt's classic study *The Drifters* (1967), published some four decades ago.

Although I feel that this is an important book that merits wide readership, I take issue with the authors on one point. They recommend that Head Start should expend its energy in training and improving the quality of the child care poor children attend. The evidence presented in this book convinces me that the children of these nine parents and other Early Head Start children need high-quality care provided in freestanding child care settings run by Early Head Start. In many cases, the poor child care so many impoverished children receive is part of their problem rather than a road to a solution (Vandell & Wolfe, 2001). Early Head Start should take on the responsibility of providing child care directly, as some sites are doing now, rather than depending on an incoherent child care system that is known to have an average quality that is somewhere between poor and mediocre. Our national Head Start program is a direct provider of quality preschool education. Early Head Start should adopt the same role by providing child care that meets the needs of these high-risk children and their families. The need has become more desperate under the provisions of our nation's welfare policy embodied in the Temporary Assistance for Needy Families legislation.

Edward Zigler, Ph.D.
Sterling Professor of
Psychology, Emeritus
Yale University

REFERENCES

Bruer, J.T. (1999). *The myth of the first three years: A new understanding of early brain development and lifelong learning.* New York: Free Press.

Carnegie Corporation. (1994). *Starting points* (report). New York: Author.

Groark, C.J., Mehaffie, K., & McCall, J. (in press). *Evidence-based programs, practices and policies for early childhood care and education.* Thousand Oaks, CA: Corwin Press.

Lombardi, J., & Bogel, M. (Eds.). (2005). *Beacon of hope.* Washington, DC: ZERO TO THREE.

Pavenstedt, E. (Ed.). (1967). *The drifters: Children of disorganized lower-class families.* Boston: Little, Brown.

Shonkoff, J., & Phillips, D.A. (Eds.). (2000). *From neurons to neighborhoods.* Washington, DC: National Academies Press.

Vandell, D., & Wolfe, B. (2001). *The economic rationale for investing in children: A focus on child care.* Retrieved January 6, 2006, from http://aspe.hhs.gov/hsp/cc-rationale02/ConferenceSummary.htm

White, R. (1952). *Lives in progress.* New York: Holt, Rinehart & Winston.

Zigler, E. (1963). Metatheoretical issues in developmental psychology. In M. Marx (Ed.), *Theories in contemporary psychology* (pp. 341–369). New York: Macmillan.

Zigler, E., Finn-Stevenson, M., & Hall, N.W. (2002). *The first three years and beyond: Brain development and social policy.* New Haven, CT: Yale University Press.

Zigler, E., & Styfco, S.J. (in press). In N. Watt, C. Ayoub, R.H. Bradley, J. Puma, & R. Lebeouf (Eds.), *The crisis in youth mental health: Critical issues and effective programs. Early intervention programs and policies.* Greenwich, CT: Praeger.

Preface

Keepin' On: The Everyday Struggles of Young Families in Poverty explores the experiences and perspectives of nine young, African American mothers with low incomes who participated in an inner-city Early Head Start (EHS) program during the years just after the passage of the Personal Responsibility and Work Opportunity Reconciliation Act of 1996 (PRWORA), commonly referred to as *welfare reform*. In addition to signing up to participate in EHS, the young women accepted our invitation to join a 5-year research project that would allow us to visit them and their families several times a year, attend meetings with them, keep in touch between visits via telephone, observe their children in early childhood programs, talk to their parent educators and their children's teachers, and meet with romantic partners and extended family members. We told them that we simply wanted to get to know what life was like for them. As the title of our book suggests, we came away from the project with a deep appreciation of the difficulties that infuse so many aspects of the young women's lives and a respect for their determination to nevertheless "keep on" doing the best they could for their children and for themselves.

At the start of the project, we divided ourselves into three teams, each consisting of a professor and a graduate student. Each team was to get to know three mothers and their family members. The professors—Jean M. Ispa, Kathy R. Thornburg, and Mark A. Fine—had either conducted major research projects with African American families or taught in shelters, in early childhood programs, or in schools in which most of the children were African American and living in poverty. Elizabeth A. Sharp, the student interviewing with Dr. Ispa, had a concentration in family studies. Michelle Mathews, the graduate student interviewing with Dr. Thornburg, focused her doctoral studies on child development and early childhood education. Miriam Wolfenstein, the student interviewing with Dr. Fine, was in a doctoral program in clinical psychology.

Joanne Perry, a social work graduate student with many years of experience working with families in low-income communities, helped develop interview questions, interviewed community leaders and the EHS staff about community issues, and conducted a series of interviews with some of the mothers about their views on the effectiveness of the EHS program. Sheila J. Brookes, whose doctoral studies focused on state and federal policies relating to children and families, joined our project a year after it began and accompanied us on several interviews. Much of her work entailed coding page after page of seemingly endless interview transcripts. Se-Kyung Park, a doctoral student studying child development and parenting, managed a massive amount of quantitative data that also helped inform this book. (The role of quantitative data in this project is explained in subsequent chapters.) Linda C. Halgunseth, a doctoral student focusing on multiculturalism in parenting and child development, contributed greatly to our analysis and writing efforts.

All of the interviewers (the three professors and the graduate students) are European American and from middle-income backgrounds. Although we wanted to include on our teams graduate students who were from low-income backgrounds and/or were African American, the reality was that none were available to us the year the project began. Once we had established friendships and rapport with the families, we wanted to keep our interviewing teams stable. We acknowledge that there may be aspects of the families' lives that we did not tap into or that we did not fully understand because of our racial, cultural, and socioeconomic differences. Yet there was a positive side to this: Our interviewees understood that there were words, experiences, and expectations that they needed to explain to us in detail—concepts that they would probably have thought unnecessary to explain had we shared their backgrounds. Throughout the years of the project, we also welcomed the insights of African American family scholars and practitioners concerning our emerging understandings—inviting them to engage in discussions about sample transcripts.

Getting to know our research participants well often meant sharing emotions with them. Sometimes what we witnessed saddened us, as when mothers told us that they were pregnant again and wished they were not, or when they informed us that young men we had gotten to know through them had been killed. We knew the grim murder statistics for young African American men, but it is a different experience to know the individuals personally. We came to realize how many forces converge to create the struggles that are entailed in the everyday lives of young parents in poverty. By no means were all of our lessons unhappy, however. Many of the articles and books we had read previously about adolescent, single mothers living in poverty pointed out their deficits relative to older, more socioeconomically advantaged mothers. In contrast to the expectations those readings might have created, we often came away from interviews impressed by the mothers' insightfulness and strength as they grappled with child-rearing issues and with other relationships and responsibilities.

In each chapter of this book, we describe the many transitions that the mothers and their children experienced during the 5-year study. As a result of knowing those families, we, too, made changes in our personal and professional lives: the development of a new university course on children and families in poverty, increased advocacy for change in federal and local policies that affect families with low incomes (see Chapter 16), decisions to join a campus discussion group on race-related issues, awakened interest in (and understanding of) the lyrics of soul and rap music and discussions, and sometimes arguments with friends and relatives about the roots and consequences of poverty and racism.

We hope the result of our research is a volume in which the presentation of personal stories integrated with scholarly analyses promotes understanding and encourages thoughtful application by students, social services providers, and policy makers whose work gives them the power to influence the lives of families with low incomes. We hope, too, that our work stimulates further research that will enhance knowledge of human development in the context of poverty.

Acknowledgments

A project of this scope depends on the support of many people. To all who made contributions, whether they were large or small, we want to convey our most sincere gratitude.

In the preface, we mentioned the graduate students who participated in many aspects of our work. Here we would also like to thank the transcribers and the others who helped us along the way. First among them are individuals whom we do not name to preserve their anonymity—the mothers, family members, and Early Head Start staff and administrators who were at the center of our work. Their contributions, needless to say, were invaluable, and we thank them profusely.

We are grateful for the support of members of the Early Head Start Research Consortium. Esther Kresh, our Head Start Bureau Project Officer, had the vision to see value in *local* projects complementing the national evaluation of Early Head Start and, until her retirement, oversaw our funding. Other consortium leaders, John Love of Mathematica Policy Research, Inc., and Helen Raikes and Rachel Chazan Cohen of the U.S. Department of Health and Human Services, Administration for Children and Families, also warmly encouraged us and provided the necessary administrative support. Jean Ann Summers and Carol McAllister gave us needed guidance regarding qualitative research methods. Mark Spellmann introduced us to the small-sample Q-sort methods that contributed to our understanding of the mothers' child-rearing goals (see Chapter 10). Others in the consortium—too many to name individually—wholeheartedly encouraged us, bolstering our confidence in the importance of our work.

We look back to a 2-day workshop we organized on culture and qualitative research methods. Gina Barclay-McLaughlin, an expert on African American culture and qualitative research methods and author of one of this book's commentaries, now at the University of Tennessee–Knoxville; Nina Jones, Assistant Project Director of the Community Development Institute, Quality Improvement Center in Kansas City; and Erma Ballenger, a University of Missouri–Columbia School of Social Work faculty member, met with us on our campus to read sample transcript pages (with names altered, of course) and to join in a discussion about emerging themes and their relations to poverty and/or African

American culture. We came away from that workshop with valuable insights that were especially important during the launching period of the project.

The work that goes into the final preparations of a book like *Keepin' On: The Everyday Struggles of Young Families in Poverty* is enormous. We are much indebted to Heather Shrestha, then Acquisitions Editor and now Editorial Director, who immediately saw promise in our work and arranged to have it published by Paul H. Brookes Publishing Co. Trish Byrnes was a gem of a book production editor, catching everything that could possibly confuse the reader or that was worded awkwardly and respectfully and cheerfully guiding every step of the revision process. We owe her tremendous thanks.

Finally, we each offer a note of gratitude to our families.

I want to thank my husband, Nelson, and my children, Simone, Zachary, and Alexander, for their support and interest during all the years of this project. Nelson's willingness and ability to maintain a happy and stable home during my out-of-town research trips was essential. Our children also made important contributions. Simone, now a doctoral student in sociology, suggested additional readings that enriched the analysis of several chapters. Zac good-naturedly helped me understand some important aspects of contemporary youth culture and slang. His fiancée Corey helped with final editing. And it was Alex who, when we were struggling to come up with a subtitle for this book, easily suggested the perfect one.

—*Jean M. Ispa*

I thank my husband, Jim, who supported me and believed in me through the time-consuming work on this book and the many projects of the past few years—and decades. Our children, Scott and Matt, kept me grounded in the importance of children's development as they grew up. Today I thank them and their wives, Kelly and Susie, and many colleagues and friends who supported me personally and professionally. And, as all grandparents know, there is nothing like a grandchild to keep the spirit and desire alive to fight for the needs and rights of ALL children. Thank you, Jake (Matt and Susie's 2-year-old), for reminding me of what all children need and deserve.

—*Kathy R. Thornburg*

I express appreciation to all of those individuals who supported me both during the time-consuming data-collection phase of this project and in the actual writing of the book. In particular, I thank my children, Aubrey and Julia, and my wife, Loreen, for their continual support and understanding.

—*Mark A. Fine*

To the mothers and children described in this book—
and to the countless others like them with similar struggles

The Context

Early Head Start and Our Research

1

The Background

Jean M. Ispa and Kathy R. Thornburg

It was a Monday morning in November of 1996 when Anita, Roneeka's Early Head Start (EHS) home visitor, finalized plans to have two researchers, Kathy and Michelle, meet Roneeka and her 5-month-old daughter Regina in their home. (Early Head Start is an intervention program that provides child and family development services to low-income pregnant women and families with infants and toddlers. A more complete description follows below.) According to Anita, Roneeka was excited about being one of nine EHS mothers who would be part of a special research project that would last for several years. She had been told that two researchers from the university would visit her several times a year, call her occasionally, ask lots of questions—and watch Regina grow. A research grant would allow the researchers to pay Roneeka $50 each visit. The first visit was scheduled for 4:00 P.M. the next day at Roneeka's house.

Kathy and Michelle also were eager to get started. When they pulled up in front of the house and saw couches, lamps, dishes, and other household items on the curb, however, they wondered what was happening. When no one answered the door, they decided to drive several blocks to where Roneeka would be moving in a couple of weeks, but that house was empty too. For the next hour, Kathy and Michelle knocked on neighbors' doors, hoping that someone could help them. Finally, they found a neighbor who told them that the family had moved the afternoon before. The neighbor was sure that they would be coming back for their belongings, so Kathy and Michelle decided to wait.

About 20 minutes later, a man and a woman arrived at the house and started piling the items on the curb into their van. Thinking that they might know Roneeka, Kathy and Michelle introduced themselves and found that the woman was Roneeka's mother, Sylvia, and the man was Sylvia's boyfriend. Sylvia explained that their house had just been condemned and their new home would not be available for another two weeks. Sylvia, 19-year-old Roneeka, and Roneeka's daughter, Regina, were temporarily staying at a house 12 miles away with Roneeka's brother's girlfriend and her child. Roneeka's brother was in prison. It was growing dark as Kathy and Michelle followed the van across town to find Roneeka.

When they got to the house, they found a living room stacked high with trash bags filled with the belongings of the three people who had no home. Roneeka and Regina were in a small room with a bed, a dresser, and a television. Because there were no chairs in the room, Kathy settled on the bed with Roneeka, and Regina and Michelle sat on the floor. The three women talked for more than 2 hours. A relationship had begun that was to last for the next 5 years, through many more moves and other changes in Roneeka's life.

PURPOSE OF THE STUDY

The research project that brought Kathy and Michelle together with Roneeka and her family had been initiated by the authors of this book with two goals in mind. First, we wanted to trace the development of the new EHS program in this midwestern urban core in which most families were African American and living in poverty. (We have been assured by our Black/African American colleagues and friends that the terms *Black* and *African American* are equally acceptable, and so we have used them interchangeably.) Second, we also wanted to provide insights into individual, family, community, and program factors that appeared to facilitate and/or constrain the program's effectiveness. Our plan was to conduct longitudinal qualitative research describing the lives of nine young EHS mothers and their families. (See Chapter 3 for a discussion of how we selected the mothers.) From the fall of 1996 to the fall of 2001, we used a variety of techniques to gather information about the mothers and their children, family members, friends, romantic partners, EHS home visitors, and various service providers and community leaders. Our main objective was to further understanding of the strengths and challenges of inner-city families that daily face the tribulations of young single parenthood, racial minority issues, and poverty.

We were meeting the mothers at critical junctures in their lives—shortly before or after the births of their first children. It was also a pivotal time from the standpoint of federal policy: The beginning of our study in 1996 coincided with the enactment of the Personal Responsibility and Work Opportunity Reconciliation Act (PRWORA; PL 104-193), commonly referred to as *welfare reform*. This law limited the number of years a person could receive cash assistance and required most recipients to be gainfully employed or to be in job-related training.

HEAD START AND EARLY HEAD START

The school performance of children living in poverty consistently lags behind that of children from more advantaged families (Bradley & Whiteside-Mansell, 1997). One way in which the U.S. government has responded to the opportunity and achievement inequalities that divide children of different socioeconomic strata is through the funding of early childhood intervention programs. Head Start, founded as part of the Economic Opportunity Act of 1964 (PL 88-452), is probably the best known of these efforts.

The founders of Head Start inaugurated their program based on a hope that providing children from impoverished families with educationally stimulating preschool activities, nutritious meals, and medical care, and their parents with child-rearing information, would give them the preparation they needed to succeed in school. Unfortunately, the results of evaluation studies of Head Start programs and other interventions for preschoolers living in poverty have been mixed. Some studies indicate that such programs truly give children a boost in social and cognitive skills relevant for future school achievement (Lee, Brookes-Gunn, Schnur, & Liaw, 1990; U.S. Department of Health and Human Services, 1994); others show initial benefits but no lasting advantages to Head Start attendance (Cicirelli, Evans, & Schiller, 1969).

Early Head Start

In 1994, Congress acted on the growing belief (fueled in part by new research on the human brain) that Head Start was a valuable program but that intervention beginning at age 3 or 4 comes too late for many children. Accordingly, funding was allocated in the 1994 reauthorization of Head Start for a new, comprehensive two-generation program that would provide child development and family support services during the prenatal period and through the child's first 3 years of life.

Early Head Start Mission and Goals   The first 68 EHS programs were launched in 1995. The program's rapid expansion is evidenced by figures showing that in 2003, EHS served more than 61,500 children under the age of 3 in 708 community-based programs across the nation (Administration for Children and Families, 2003). The program's primary focus is prenatal health and optimal infant and toddler physical, social, emotional, and cognitive development. A primary long-term goal is to prepare the child to be ready to succeed in school.

To reach these goals, EHS programs must implement intensive strategies that strengthen four *cornerstones*: child development, family development, staff development, and community building. Outcomes in terms of *child development* include enhancement of child health and social, emotional, cognitive, and language development. Progress in terms of *family development* involves access to social services; improvements in the home environment and family functioning; physical and mental health for all family members; and, for parents, job training and job attainment. *Staff development* involves ongoing training of EHS staff members so that they can better meet the needs of the children and families they serve. *Community building* requires staff to work with community leaders, agency personnel, and care providers to strengthen community collaboration and the integration of services for families with pregnant mothers and young children (U.S. Department of Health and Human Services, 1994). Although every program must address all four cornerstones, child development is the most important one; it is the one most closely monitored by federal program officers because the child's welfare is the ultimate goal of the EHS program.

There is no single EHS program model. Some sites offer a *center-based* approach to intervention in which high-quality early childhood education is provided to all infants and toddlers. Other sites use a second model called *home-based*, which relies primarily on home visits to provide parents with support, information, and modeling. The *mixed* model has been adopted by sites that tailor their services to the needs of individual families, providing home-based services and/or center-based services to families, and working with community child care programs in which some parents have enrolled their infants and toddlers.

Early Head Start Research and Evaluation Mandate Sensitive to criticisms that Head Start had operated for many years without the benefit of a strong evaluation component, the architects of Early Head Start included funding for evaluation in the initial master plan. The evaluation arrangement was unique and revolutionary in that it included both a national comparison between randomly assigned program and non-program children and families and opportunities for local research to be carried out by research teams in conjunction with their program partners. Researchers from 15 universities partnered with 17 new EHS sites across the country to help plan the national study and to facilitate data collection. Each of the 15 research teams was responsible for data collection at its site or its partner sites. Mathematica Policy Research, Inc., and Columbia University's Center for Children and Families at Teachers College provided coordination and a central location for all of the national data collections and analyses. In addition, each re-search team carried out studies at its local program site. The local stud-ies were meant to add depth to the national study and to answer ques-tions that the national study did not address.

Early Head Start as Partner The EHS site with which we were partnered was located in the inner core of a large midwestern city. Re-flecting the neighborhoods it serves, almost all of the families who en-rolled in the program during its first 2 years were African American and headed by young, single mothers. At the outset of the program's oper-ations, we used a home-visiting model to deliver services to parents and children. With time, as more mothers responded to the changed welfare system by going to work and placing their children in child care, the program evolved into a mixed-model approach.

Part of our work as researchers and evaluators at the local level in-volved describing the processes that the administration and staff under-went as they built their fledging EHS program. During the first years, some of the greatest difficulties stemmed from a lack of clarity regard-ing the relative importance of child, family, and staff development and community building. Staff at the agency with which we partnered thought that as long as programs addressed all four of these cornerstones, EHS directors could determine the relative emphasis placed on each. They firmly believed that child development could not be a priority for parents who face basic shortcomings in their physical home environ-ments, in their close peer and adult relationships, and in their readiness for economic self-sufficiency. Accordingly, in the EHS proposal the agency submitted to the Administration on Children, Youth and Fami-lies (ACYE), special emphasis was placed on family development. When the proposal was approved, the newly appointed director hired home visitors whose backgrounds were in social work. The training they re-ceived had prepared them to work toward the goals of the family de-velopment and community building cornerstones. It had done less to equip them for work supporting child development. Despite their lack of specific training in child development, the home visitors were ex-pected to teach young mothers about effective parenting and assist com-munity child care administrators and providers in raising the quality of their infant and toddler care. Understandably, these were difficult tasks.

Initially, the program addressed this problem by dividing up tasks. EHS home visitors would attend to the family development and com-munity building cornerstones. Another organization, Parents as Teach-ers, would attend to the child-development content via monthly home visits to families. The director of the site would be responsible for the staff development cornerstone. This arrangement proved to be unworkable for a variety of reasons, including staff problems within both organizations.

Changes in Early Head Start   About a year after the program began, ACYF clarified that child development was to be preeminent among the four cornerstones. Staff members were told that family and staff development and community building were to be pursued in the service of child development, not simply because they were important in their own right. A 1998 revision of the Head Start Performance Standards, which included goals for EHS, made explicit the centrality of children's development (the Performance Standards are available at the Head Start Bureau's web site: http://www.acf.hhs.gov/programs/hsb/performance/).

In addition, standards regarding the frequency of home visits were modified to accommodate the fact that, as a result of the passage of the PRWORA in 1996, many mothers in low-income families could no longer stay home with their children. Faced with a state-imposed, 2-year deadline for involvement in work or work activities (such as job training or subsidized employment), a federal 5-year lifetime limit for receipt of cash assistance, and sanctions if they were not currently in school or at work at least part time, young mothers were placing their children with relatives, with neighbors, or in child care centers and homes so that they could progress toward self-sufficiency. Monitoring and improving the quality of the child care sites attended by EHS children therefore took on heightened importance. Whereas the initial program requirements had included weekly home visits to each mother, the new performance standards stipulated that families whose children were in child care were to be visited at home a minimum of twice a year. Staff were to help child care providers raise the quality of their programs. Staff members' knowledge of both child development and early childhood education had become essential, and previous attempts to adequately train them in these areas (e.g., all home visitors had to pass the Parents as Teachers training) were now considered to be insufficient.

One administrator and two home visitors stayed in the local program throughout these changes (out of the two administrators and five home visitors who were hired during the startup months). The contract with Parents as Teachers was terminated, and a new director and three new staff members were hired. Intensive training in child development milestones, effective parenting strategies, and developmentally appropriate practices for child care was instituted for staff members who needed additional education in these areas. Some of the training was conducted by us in our capacity as continuous improvement consultants, and some by consultants from ZERO TO THREE: National Center for Infants, Toddlers and Families and local child development professionals. A noticeable improvement in services to children and families followed the extensive training. In 2005, the program served 279 children and their families with a combination of state and federal dollars.

Our Early Head Start Research Foci

As researchers/evaluators, we took notes documenting the course of the development of EHS. We paid special attention to the implications of the program's growing pains for the relationships that were developing between EHS home visitors and the mothers. Chapter 13 describes, for example, the tensions that home visitors experienced as they tried to adjust their priorities between helping parents with their teen- or adult-related issues and helping them learn more about child development. The chapter also documents the confusion and frustrations of some parents when introduced to the program. At the same time, we want to clarify that a number of home visitors were tremendously helpful to families even during these first few challenging years. In our chapter on raising children (Chapter 10), we describe another source of tension connected to the EHS program, namely, the disconnect some mothers experienced as they tried to integrate the information they were receiving from EHS about effective parenting (especially regarding discipline) with the sometimes differing beliefs and practices of their relatives, neighbors, and friends.

HOW THE BOOK IS ORGANIZED

Our book is separated into five sections. Section I comprises three chapters providing background information on the history and goals of EHS, the research methods and theory that guided our work, and some details about the study itself. Section II contains a rich holistic case study of one mother, Andreya, and her family. We consider this to be a central feature of the book because it allows the reader an up-close view of one family's life with all of its aspects intertwined. In Sections III and IV, we share our own voices and perspectives as well as those of our participants in a series of chapters centered on issues that emerged as salient for our families. Section III focuses on individual characteristics and interpersonal relationships within the family (e.g., the mothers' relationships with their parents, with their children's fathers, and with other romantic partners; child-rearing beliefs and practices; fatherhood issues). Section IV focuses on important relationships outside the family (e.g., with friends, neighbors, EHS home visitors) and on cultural and societal forces that support or impinge on the families' well-being. Brief vignettes—portraits that illustrate and give a human face to major themes—appear in Sections III and IV. In Section V, we summarize and integrate common themes and consider the lessons they imply for researchers, practitioners, and policy makers. At the end of the book, we include commentaries by Dr. Gina Barclay-McLaughlin, a researcher and national consultant on race, culture, and child development; Gayle Cunningham, who is widely respected for the leadership she provides to Head Start and Early Head Start at the state (Alabama) and federal levels; and Dr. Deborah Phillips, an accomplished child development and early education researcher who is also well-known for her work in the policy arena.

REFERENCES

Administration for Children and Families. (2003). *Head Start information folder.* Retrieved October 27, 2005, from http://www.headstartinfo.org/infocenter/ehs_tkit3.htm

Bradley, R.H., & Whiteside-Mansell, L. (1997). Children in poverty. In R.T. American & M. Heroines (Eds.), *Handbook of prevention and treatment with children and adolescents* (pp. 13–58). New York: Wiley.

Cicirelli, V.G., Evans, J.W., & Schiller, J.S. (1969). *The impact of Head Start: An evaluation of the effects of Head Start on children's cognitive and affective development* (Vols. 1–2). Athens, OH: Westinghouse Learning Corporation and Ohio University.

Economic Opportunities Act of 1964, PL 88-452, 42 U.S.C. §§ 2701 *et seq.*

Lee, V., Brookes-Gunn, J., Schnur, E., & Liaw, F. (1990). Are Head Start effects sustained? A longitudinal follow-up comparison of disadvantaged children attending Head Start, no preschool, and other preschool programs. *Child Development, 61,* 495–507.

Personal Responsibility and Work Opportunity Reconciliation Act of 1996 (PRWORA), PL 104-193, 42 U.S.C. §§ 1305 *et seq.*

U.S. Department of Health and Human Services. (1994). *The statement of the Advisory Committee on Services for Families with Infants and Toddlers.* Washington, DC: U.S. Government Printing Office.

2

Introducing the Mothers

Jean M. Ispa, Sheila J. Brookes, Kathy R. Thornburg, and Mark A. Fine

Whereas one goal of our work was to learn about various aspects of Early Head Start (EHS), our primary interest was much broader. We wanted to learn about the lives of young African American families living in poverty, and we wanted to do so in a way that would give voice to their perspectives as well as to our own.

Table 2.1 summarizes the demographic characteristics of the nine mothers who were at the center of our study. Marital status and race are omitted from the table because there was no variation—all mothers were single and all identified themselves as African American (although two mothers were biracial). The paragraphs following the table provide additional short descriptions of the mothers and some of the issues each faced over the course of our 5-year study. In subsequent chapters, readers will learn much more about Andreya, who is the subject of the case study in Section II of the book, and about the other mothers, whose experiences and opinions informed Sections III and IV. We expect that readers will refer back to Table 2.1 and the descriptive paragraphs that follow as they try to keep track of "who is who" in the remainder of the book.

Andreya was 19 and living with her 1-year-old son Lavell, her mother Patricia, her 16-year-old brother Tony, and her 12-year-old cousin Kalia when we first met her in 1996. Her older brother Quintus was in jail on drug-related charges. Like her mother and grandmother before her, Andreya left school when she discovered that she was pregnant. However, she demonstrated a desire for a better life and enrolled in Job Corps, a program that would give her a high school degree and training as a certified nursing assistant. She also had the support of a very capable EHS home visitor. For a number of years, Andreya remained in love with William, a man 11 years her senior, who continued to seek her affections while living with another woman. Complicating Andreya's life further were problems with asthma—she and her children were chronically affected.

Table 2.1. Demographic characteristics of the nine mothers in the study

Mother's name	Age at birth of first child	Age when study began	Living arrangement at beginning of study	Number of housing moves during 5-year period	Employment/school status when study began	Educational level 5 years after study began	Employment history during the 5 years of study	Number of children 5 years after study began
Andreya	18	20	Living with her son, mother, brother, and cousin in her mother's house.	1	Dropped out of high school in 11th grade due to pregnancy. Now enrolled in Job Corps, a high school and job-training program.	Completed high school and training to be a certified nursing assistant through Job Corps.	Worked briefly in construction and as a nursing assistant. Longest employment has been as an early childhood teacher.	3
Breanna	15	15	Living with her daughter in the home of fictive grandparents, mother, and siblings.	No permanent living arrangement. "Stayed with" numerous relatives.	Attending an alternative school for pregnant teens and new mothers. Not employed (student).	Some college	Worked briefly in construction and fast-food restaurants. Longest employment was as early childhood teacher.	1
Chandra	17	17	Homeless; staying with her son at the home of a female friend.	No permanent living arrangement. "Stayed with" friends and relatives until last year of study when she obtained an apartment of her own. Lived there 11 months, and then moved in with relatives.	Dropped out of high school in 10th grade. Now caring for infant full time.	Took but did not complete GED classes.	Worked intermittently in fast-food restaurant, chain discount store, and clothing store.	1
Kyierra	20	20	Living with daughter and boyfriend in her own apartment.	5	Completed high school and a semester of community college. During early pregnancy worked as an assistant in a nursing home. Now pregnant and not employed due to doctor's orders.	Completed career-training program.	Held several jobs in medical offices—filing, drawing blood, and so forth. At end of study completed training to become a medical assistant.	2

Maria	19	19	Living with son and parents in parents' home.	5	Completed high school and one year of college.	Same	At beginning of study, worked for 2 years in a telephone sales office. Later held a variety of jobs (e.g., hotel desk clerk, office assistant, 9-1-1 operator).	1
Roneeka	19	19	Living with daughter, mother, and brother in her mother's home.	5	Dropped out of high school in 11th grade; unemployed.	Took but did not complete GED classes.	Worked intermittently in fast-food restaurants.	3
Shardae	22	22	Living with daughter, mother, and brother in her mother's home.	6	Completed high school and 2 years of college. Dropped out during pregnancy. Now caring for infant full time.	Needed approximately 30 credit hours more for B.S.	Worked in different phone sales offices, each time changing jobs for higher pay. At last interview, attending college and working as a work-study student.	1
Sherryce	23	24	Living with son in own apartment.	6	Completed high school and medical assistant training. Completed 1½ years of college. Now employed as a nursing assistant.	Same	At beginning of study, worked as nursing assistant in nursing home. Worked in medical offices as a file clerk during most of study. At last interview, had taken a job as an early childhood teacher.	2
Tanisha	18	18	Living with daughter and boyfriend in her own apartment.	5	Dropped out in 11th grade. Now taking GED classes.	Took but did not complete GED classes.	Changed jobs frequently (approx. every other month). Held jobs such as phone solicitor, sales clerk, fast-food worker.	1

Breanna stands out as the youngest of the mothers in our study and as one who viewed the EHS services as especially helpful. She became pregnant at 14; the father of her baby was 21 years old. Despite her youth, numerous moves, and exposure to some of the most challenging environmental and community experiences, Breanna took parenting and her own education very seriously. While mothering Corinna, she obtained a high school diploma, completed training for technical employment, and attended some college. Although family members gave her considerable support, Breanna remained Corinna's primary caregiver and was successful in convincing Corinna's biological father as well as her subsequent boyfriends to play important positive roles in Corinna's life. When she was 19, Breanna began work as an early childhood teacher and held this job for nearly two years. The following year, one tragedy followed another. First, her brother was murdered, and, devastated, Breanna quit her job. Several months later, Corinna's social father, Breanna's former long-term boyfriend, was also murdered. At the time of the last interview, Breanna, still very upset, was not working.

Chandra told us that she was 3 months old when her father kidnapped her from her mother, whom she never saw again. She surmised that her father was motivated by his desire for Aid to Families with Dependent Children (AFDC) checks more than by love for her. He showed little interest in her, and at times was verbally abusive, deriding her appearance and intelligence. Two stepmothers were kind to her and maintained relationships with her even after they divorced her father. Chandra considered these women and their relatives to be her relatives. We met Chandra when she was 17 years old, homeless, and jobless. Her son Patrick was 10 months old. Patrick's father, Patrick Sr., seemed to be in love with Chandra and came to see her and his son fairly often. Chandra, however, was skeptical about his faithfulness. Much to his sorrow, she broke up with him when Patrick Jr. was 4. During the years of our study, she held a variety of low-wage jobs in chain stores and fast-food restaurants. An attractive young woman, she cared a great deal about her appearance, and much of the money she earned was spent on clothing, hairdressing, and manicures. Over time, we came to see that her strongly expressed desire for independence was mixed with low self-efficacy. She depended on others to arrange for the resources she needed, and for 2 years an EHS home visitor fulfilled that role. Tensions between Chandra's love for Patrick and her longing to go out and have fun were palpable throughout the years of our interviews. When Patrick was 4, Chandra's yearning for an unfettered adolescence led to a decision to arrange for an ex-stepmother to take temporary custody of her son. This arrangement lasted a year, after which Chandra took Patrick Jr. back.

Kyierra became pregnant during her first year at a community college. She identified herself as African American—her father was African American and her mother was European American. She had a tumultuous adolescence involving rebellion and attempts by her mother to restrict her activities. The parent–adolescent conflict was exacerbated by shared housing arrangements with her mother's lesbian partners. Despite these struggles and episodes of severe depression for which she was hospitalized, Kyierra did graduate from high school. Shortly after she became pregnant at age 19, Kyierra was evicted from her mother's home because of conflicts surrounding Kyierra's boyfriend. Soon after that, Kyierra's boyfriend beat Kyierra severely and she ended the relationship. While still pregnant, Kyierra reestablished a relationship with Tejon, a young man she had known in high school. By the time her daughter Jalisa was born, Tejon had committed to helping to parent the baby. Two years later, they had a daughter, Ciera. Kyierra resumed her education after this birth and completed training to become a medical assistant. For several years she worked intermittently in low-wage jobs she did not enjoy. Toward the end of our study she began work as a medical assistant and seemed very pleased with her new position. Tejon had a goal of entering the military when he and Kyierra were first together, but this was never really pursued. For a while he provided full-time child care for Jalisa. At our last interview, Tejon told us that he had been working for a carpet-cleaning business for several months and was trying to establish a new apartment-cleaning business with a friend. A noteworthy aspect of Kyierra's relationship with Tejon was its stability; they had been together for approximately 9 years and planned to marry.

Maria grew up in a middle-class neighborhood and was the only child of still-married parents. She had attended a parochial elementary school and an all-girls' college preparatory high school. She dropped out of college at the end of her first year when she discovered that she was pregnant. Maria identified herself as African American. Her father was African American and a college graduate. Her mother was a Mexican American whose educational background included some coursework in medical assistance at a community college. Despite what might look like an advantaged background, Maria was eligible for EHS services because her own earnings ($3,000 the year she enrolled) placed her below the poverty line. (Eligibility determination is based solely on the applicant's income.) During her son Bryce's first 3 years, Maria worked nights and weekends so that she could share child care with her mother, who worked during the day. When Maria did place Bryce in an early childhood program, her goal was to expose him to peers and additional developmental stimulation, not to obtain additional child care support. Maria's first two attempts to live independently ended in her returning to her parents' home because she found living alone with Bryce lonely, frightening, too expensive, and logistically inconvenient (she had to bring Bryce to her parents' home every evening so that they could care for him while she worked). At our last interview, Maria was again living in an apartment alone with Bryce.

Roneeka became pregnant at 18 after she had been suspended from school for involvement in a fight. Up until that time, she had enjoyed school and intended to graduate. Roneeka's home life was chaotic due to heavy drug involvement by several brothers. Two were in jail or prison for serious crimes during the years of our study. Every interview with Roneeka brought surprises, as her plans and circumstances changed frequently. She had attempted to get a General Educational Development (GED) degree (a high school equivalency testing program), but had not completed it. She worked at a number of fast-food jobs that did not give her full-time hours or a sustainable wage. Roneeka spent several years dating a married man, hoping that he would leave his wife for her, but she came to realize that this was not likely to happen. Roneeka's difficulties in attending sensitively to her oldest child's needs increased with the birth of two additional children. Toward the end of the study, she met Lonnie, a hard-working, stable young man. They became engaged and, together with her children, moved to another state in which his family lives.

Shardae had completed 2 years at a private college on scholarships when she became pregnant with Alexis, her daughter. The relationship with Alexis's father ended early in the pregnancy. Shardae deferred her education until Alexis was 4 years old. At that point, she found a way to return to college. Shardae's education and skills enabled her to obtain jobs that paid considerably more than minimum wage. Over the course of the study, she was usually employed full time and able to maintain an apartment for herself and her daughter. Nonetheless, largely because of the high cost of child care and car payments, she struggled to make ends meet, incurring credit card debt during her pregnancy, after the birth of her daughter, and during short periods between jobs. Although she considered the EHS program to be potentially supportive, she felt it offered her little because her home visitor did not make regular visits and the parent meetings were typically held during days and times when she was working.

Sherryce, unlike most of the mothers we came to know, had completed five semesters of post-high school training before becoming pregnant, and did not have her first child Michael until she was 23. After leaving school, she was gainfully employed for several years in the Army

Reserves and at various low-wage positions. She and Michael's father had been romantically involved and even engaged for many years; she had not expected him to leave her when she became pregnant. During the first 3 years of our study, Sherryce conveyed a sense of alienation and hopelessness. During many of our conversations, she complained that federal, state, and local social service systems are unfair because they ignore the needs of the working poor. Fortunately, her spirits improved greatly after she joined a nondenominational church. The members of that church became her friends and provided her with a great deal of emotional support and help meeting instrumental needs (e.g., stocking her kitchen when they discovered that it was bare, including her in clothing swaps, doing her laundry when she was recovering from childbirth). Spirituality is very important to Sherryce, and the church fulfilled that need as well. A second child, Ariana, was born when Sherryce was 27. Ariana's father was a former boyfriend whom Sherryce had started seeing again. About a year after our last interview, she and this man married.

Tanisha was raised primarily by relatives rather than by her parents. In her view, none of the family members responsible for her, including those who raised her, showed her much affection or cared what she did. She readily recognized that her involvement and attachment to Davian, her baby's father, derived from her need to be cared for. She was 17 and pregnant with Tierra when Davian was killed in an automobile accident. Still pregnant, she became involved with Dwayne. She had received some financial assistance and benefited from periodic weekend child care from the deceased boyfriend's mother. Overall, however, Tanisha preferred to do things on her own; she would rather not depend on anyone. Tierra was born prematurely and was in a neonatal intensive care unit for the first month of her life. She was a year old when Tanisha enrolled in EHS. Because Tanisha tended to rely on herself and on Tierra's grandmother, and because many of her perceived needs were met, she made only minimal use of the program's services, not seeing them as worthwhile. The program terminated her after about 18 months because she did not keep appointments. We were able to follow her for an additional 6 months.

TRANSITIONS

When we began the study, we did not know that eventually we would look at thousands of pages of interview transcripts and other data and find one overarching theme in the lives of the families we had studied—transition. We were often amazed at the frequency and number of changes that occurred in the lives of our research participants. Somehow it was fitting that in their first interview, Kathy and Michelle landed right in the middle of one of those transitions (see Chapter 1).

Transitions, we were to learn, touched many aspects of the families' lives. Often we came away from telephone calls and interviews in awe of the many changes the mothers experienced in housing, shifts in jobs and social service usage, school attendance, additions and losses of household members, new and ended romantic interests, telephone connections and disconnections, exposure to violent crime, and the incarceration of loved ones. After becoming familiar with the recording "This number is no longer in service," we learned to keep the telephone numbers of the mothers' friends and relatives handy. We also came to understand that changing addresses and telephone numbers reflected deeper issues. Over the course of our study, three of the houses the families lived in were condemned due to structural problems and lead contamination. Another two fell victim to arson. One mother, Chandra, was essentially homeless, moving from one relative or friend to another. In several cases, the mothers wanted to move out of their own mothers' homes but found it difficult to maintain a separate residence. The result was a series of revolving doors in which the mothers would move back into their mothers' homes and then back out again. Disconnected telephone numbers were not always rooted in an inability to pay, however. Andreya, for example, occasionally changed telephone numbers to avoid calls from her brother in prison and harassment by a former boyfriend's current girlfriend.

Most dramatic and unsettling, however, were the adjustments the families had to make as their households and family compositions changed. The mothers shared their thoughts with us as they adjusted to pregnancies, shifting romantic attachments, incarceration of loved ones, and, worst of all, the murders of cousins, brothers, and former boyfriends.

During the years of our study, not only were there ongoing transitions in the lives of the EHS mothers, there also were far-reaching changes in the federal and state policy landscape. Policies governing the receipt of public assistance were reformed by PRWORA in 1996. Chapter 1 explained the further tightening in 1998 of federal EHS policies concerning the program's focus and home-visiting standards. These reformulations had significant impacts on the local programs and families we studied. In this book, we explore our insights and those of the mothers regarding the transitions that took place at the personal, family, and policy levels. The next chapter briefly describes our theoretical perspectives and explains how they informed our research foci, our data-gathering procedures, and our analytic approach.

3

Theoretical Perspectives and Research Methods

Jean M. Ispa, Mark A. Fine, and Elizabeth A. Sharp

Throughout this book, we draw conclusions and inferences about the young mothers in our sample from the rich data we collected. Underlying he quality of our conclusions are two key ingredients: our theoretical perspectives and our research methods.

THEORECTICAL PERSPECTIVES

Researchers are always influenced by their theoretical perspectives. These perspectives prompt them to ask certain kinds of questions and guide them in selecting their data-collection and analysis approaches. Our guides were Bronfenbrenner's ecological systems theory (or, as he later renamed it, the bioecological model of human development) and feminist theory. This chapter begins by briefly describing these theoretical perspectives and explains how they framed our interview foci, our data-gathering procedures, and our approaches to analyzing the wealth of data we gathered.

Bioecological Theory

The *bioecological model* (Bronfenbrenner, 1979, 1986; Bronfenbrenner & Morris, 1998) ties human development to its biological, social, cultural, political/historical, and economic contexts, seeing interactive, reciprocal paths of influence among children, close family members, and the societal systems in which families live. Its focus on the interdependence of child competence, family functioning, community resources, cultural values, and social policy make it particularly useful as a theoretical framework for understanding life within the context of urban poverty in the opening years of both the Early Head Start (EHS) program and welfare reform in the United States.

Microsystems   Figure 3.1 depicts the bioecological model from the perspective of an infant boy whose unmarried mother receives cash assistance from Temporary Assistance to Needy Families (TANF) while studying for her high school degree at a Job Corps program. As denoted by the double-headed arrows pointing to and from the child (at the center of the figure), his individual physical, cognitive, and social characteristics influence and are influenced by the various physical and social settings in which he has face-to-face contact with other people. These settings, termed *microsystems,* may include patterns of interrelationships and events that occur in settings such as the child's mother's home, his father's home (if he spends time there with his father and paternal relatives), his child care center, and even the grocery store. In Figure 3.1, three of these common microsystems are represented by ovals bordered by dotted lines.

The bioecological model of human development adopts a basic assumption of family systems theory—that the whole is greater than the sum of its parts and that changes anywhere in the family system are likely to affect other members or units within the family. Accordingly, within a microsystem, individuals are thought to change in response to influences from all others; thus, characteristics of one member of a microsystem have implications not only for that individual but also for all the others in that microsystem. If all members of each microsystem in Figure 3.1 were included, there would be double-headed arrows connecting every member to every other member. Direct and indirect paths of influence and chain reactions that magnify the eventual consequences of personal characteristics and experiences make it a complex picture. *Direct influences* tend to be reciprocal and occur when two people (e.g., a mother and her child) affect each other through their interactions with each other. *Indirect influences* occur when one person brings to a relationship feelings or thoughts arising from his or her relationship with another person. For example, a young mother who is upset over an argument with her own mother may be harsh later that day toward her children. Chain reactions may lead to the magnification of children's early temperamental characteristics (such as a propensity to react strongly and negatively to even mildly aversive events) as others respond with behaviors that elicit more of the same. In Andreya's family, for example, we observed that 2-year-old Lavell's tendency to become aggressive

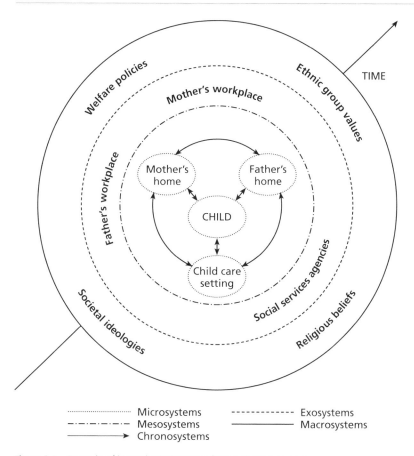

Figure 3.1.   Example of bioecological systems from a child's perspective.

when frustrated seemed to evoke retaliation from his adolescent uncle. This resulted in an escalation of Lavell's aggressiveness.

Mesosystems   Understanding the psychological and interpersonal patterns that characterize lives at home has been central to our research endeavor. At the same time, even for infants and very young children, the sources of influence are not limited to the home. Most of the participants in our study regularly spent time in other microsystems as well. Moreover, no microsystem stands alone because nearly all of its members move from microsystem to microsystem during the course of most days, bringing thoughts and feelings from one setting to the others. Bronfenbrenner (1979) called the interconnections among microsystems in which a person is actively engaged *mesosystems;* these are represented in Figure 3.1 by an oval with dashed lines around the microsystems and double-headed arrows connecting each microsystem with every other microsystem. Mindful of the importance of mesosystem influences, we tried to learn about conditions in the various settings in which family members regularly participated; we often asked mothers and other family members how events in one setting seemed to affect events in other settings.

Exosystems   The next-to-last concentric circle represents the *exosystem*. An exosystem is a setting in which a person does not actively participate but one that nevertheless has power over him or her. Often this occurs because someone with whom the individual is directly connected spends time in that other setting. An example of a child's exosystem is the mother's workplace. What happens there can have major implications for the child, as when praise from a supportive colleague or supervisor improves the mother's self-concept and sense of mastery, which in turn leads to a more positive child-rearing style at home. In Figure 3.1, the exosystem is depicted as including the workplaces of the mothers and fathers and the social services agencies to which parents may apply for benefits such as food stamps. Although the child may not accompany the parent to these agencies, he may feel the agencies' influence through the economic support given to his family and/or the feelings the parent brings home after having met with either a sympathetic or an unsympathetic caseworker.

Macrosystems   The *macrosystem*, symbolized by the outermost circle of Bronfenbrenner's (1979) nested model, results from and reflects the overarching ideologies of the larger society. Examples include religious beliefs, national economic philosophies, and societal positions regarding race and gender. The macrosystem influences people's values and goals and their interpretations of situations and events. For example, in the United States, personal independence tends to be valued, and therefore many Americans frown on mothers sleeping with their infants. For members of low-income, minority groups, dominant societal ideologies may present significant obstacles to personal fulfillment, as when individuals with little preparation for well-paying jobs are expected to "pull themselves up by their bootstraps," or when landlords deny that they have vacancies because they do not want tenants of color. Macrosystem influences on the lives of those who participated in our study are presented in each chapter. Readers will note that although many of these beliefs are consistent with dominant U.S. ideologies, some are not.

Chronosystems   We also knew to expect change. Figure 3.1 shows an arrow cutting through the diagram, suggesting movement of all systems through time. Ways of thinking, feeling, and behaving are not static. For children, change occurs because of age-related cognitive and physical shifts and because of new experiences, such as entry into new child care arrangements or the introduction of a new father figure. Bronfenbrenner (Bronfenbrenner & Morris, 1998) developed the notion of a *chronosystem,* which he proposed as important for the understanding of change in people and environments over time.

The bioecological perspective thus calls for sensitivity to a rich array of influences at multiple levels of context. It alerted us to take note of individual traits and histories, the interpersonal connections among microsystems that have significance for each family, and the impacts of community-level resources and issues. The model's emphasis on reciprocal causation, and on indirect as well as direct effects, prompted attention to the interplay among many variables with complex paths of influence. We were careful to note, for example, that not only did parents affect children, but also that children affected mothers. In addition, the influences of fathers on their children were sometimes indirect, through the fathers' impact on the mothers (see Chapters 10 and 11). Gaining an understanding of the role played by ideology demanded consideration of the meanings each individual attached to specific relationships, events, and opportunities. In Chapter 9, for instance, we consider the mothers' commitment to the ideal of marriage despite their negative feelings about their past and current boyfriends.

Concepts from the life-course perspective (Elder, 1998; Hareven, 1996) adopted in Bronfenbrenner's reformulation of his theory (Bronfenbrenner & Morris, 1998) suggested that we should be attentive to the ways in which mothers managed to combine their several roles (e.g., parent, daughter, aunt, friend, student). It also suggested that we should examine what happens when major life events are experienced "out of order" (i.e., at ages and in sequences that conflict with societal ideals). For example, we asked how parents, grandparents, and friends reacted when adolescent girls became pregnant before finishing high school and outside of marriage. Life-course ideas alerted us to pay attention to transitions in general—how mothers negotiated and gave meaning to new circumstances such as housing moves, welfare and job changes, shifts in friendships, and the loss of EHS support when their children graduated from the program.

We were not able to address every possible influence that the bioecological model suggests—even if that were possible, our resources could not have stretched that far. That said, the theory was an essential piece guiding our approach. In particular, as indicated earlier, it provided a framework for the questions asked and for the way we organized and grew to understand our rich data.

Feminist Theory

Feminist theory, similar to bioecological theory, embeds human development and family relationships in their wider social, political, and economic contexts (Thompson, 1992; Wuest, 1995). This theory supplements
the bioecological perspective through its emphasis on understanding the
complexities and contradictions inherent in women's ordinary experiences and through its explicit acknowledgment that cultural construc-
tions of gender are centrally implicated in people's everyday interactions
and decisions. Feminist scholars advocate for an activist research agenda
aimed at helping women and men understand the societal context of
their personal life experiences and encouraging them to adopt a vision
of nonoppressive relationships inside and outside the family (Thompson, 1992).

For this to happen, researchers must recognize that their research
participants are the real authorities on their lives. The voices of women
and other members of marginalized groups must be heard and conveyed. Furthermore, researchers must expect heterogeneity; division
always exists even within samples of demographically similar people.
(Readers of our book will see that, despite the existence of common
themes, the differences among the participants in our study are substantial.) Moreover, feminists contend that by listening to the perspectives
of the oppressed, we learn about them as well as about those whom the
dominant culture privileges. This is because, unlike advantaged citizens,
oppressed individuals are in positions that require them to attend not
only to those whom society favors but also to those whom it marginalizes.

Feminist theory has been criticized by African American scholars
and activists for focusing too narrowly on issues of Caucasian women
from the middle class (e.g., hooks, 2000). Nonetheless, as pointed out
by hooks (2000) and Kelly (2001), the theory clearly has the potential to
spark research on (and advocacy for) women who face discrimination
based not only on gender but also on race and socioeconomic status. This
framework alerted us to consider how the young women in our study
made sense of, adapted to, and/or resisted the various roles and behaviors expected of them by virtue of their membership in four inter-
secting, marginalized groups—they were poor, they were female, they
were African American, and they were unmarried mothers. As members of groups that face discrimination from many different sources,
they were likely to experience particular burdens (Collins, 1990; Elise,
1995; Kelly, 2001).

Our inquiry built on our awareness of these issues by including
questions designed to elicit information and opinions related to the participants' social location. For example, using gender as an organizing

construct, we asked about household and workplace divisions of labor and about participants' relationships with their mothers, sisters, fathers, brothers, and romantic partners. Which sorts of situations did they perceive as fair and unfair, and how did they handle them? How did their perceptions of male–female roles influence their goals for their sons and daughters? What did they make of the risks faced by young, urban African American men and women? Did concerns about the prevalence in their communities of school disengagement, crime, and early pregnancy affect their child-rearing decisions? If so, how? As we thought about their answers, we worked toward looking past Eurocentric, middle-class, taken-for-granted assumptions about the reasons and consequences of behavior. For example, putting aside the assumptions that young adolescents will seldom be good mothers allowed us to see that Breanna, who was only 15 when her daughter was born, was in fact a devoted and capable mother.

Most of our past research experiences had been guided by the notion that the researcher must maintain objectivity and eliminate subjectivity as much as possible. Feminist theory, on the other hand, holds that the intertwining of objectivity with subjectivity is a valid and desirable research pursuit. The theory also explains that an expectation of emotional distance between the people being studied and the researchers is unrealistic—and that such emotional distance could not ensure objectivity even if it were possible. Therefore, what the study needed most was honest reflection about the feelings, biases, and thoughts flowing from all parties (including ourselves) both during and after the interviews. In addition, the theory reminded us to be aware of the biases and expectations that might be engendered by the differences between *our* "social location" (i.e., White, older, middle class, well-educated) and that of the participants (i.e., African American, in their teens and early 20s, with low incomes, without a higher education). Consequently, not only did we pose questions and listen, but we also shared some of our interpretations with them so that they could tell us if we had accurately captured their perceptions. For example, in one of our last interviews with Sherryce, we asked if she agreed that her involvement in the church she had joined 2 years earlier accounted for the fact that she was much happier now than when we first met her. She agreed. We then shared our impression that the church had been important because of the very supportive friendships she had made there. She agreed that the friendships were important to her, but she disagreed that this was the main reason the church had been helpful. Spirituality, she said, was the church's main gift to her. Her analysis then became integrated with our own.

Finally, we were mindful of feminists' watchfulness concerning the ethics of research. We gave careful consideration to the ways in which our relationships with the participants might empower and/or encumber them. We also considered how research could be used politically. We hope that, in telling the stories of the nine families we have come to know, we will have contributed to a sympathetic understanding of young African American single mothers living in the circumstances of urban poverty. That knowledge, we trust and hope, will be used for their benefit by social services providers, policy makers, and the general public.

RESEARCH DESIGN AND DATA-GATHERING PROCEDURES

On the following pages, we explain how we conducted our research. We describe how we selected the nine families in our study, the procedures we used to gather data, the nature of our interview protocols, and how we organized and analyzed our data.

Selecting the Families

We selected our qualitative sample on the basis of *theoretical sampling*. In theoretical sampling, participants are chosen to fulfill a particular research purpose and focus (Strauss & Corbin, 1998). In this case, we were interested in understanding the experiences of young mothers and children in poverty from a variety of demographic circumstances. Thus, we decided to identify nine mothers from our larger quantitative study of approximately 90 pregnant women and first-time mothers who had been randomly assigned to receive EHS services. (A total of 193 pregnant women and first-time mothers of infants had initially applied for the program. For national evaluation purposes, approximately half were assigned to receive EHS services while the other half were assigned to a comparison group.) We chose participants on the basis of a variant of a stratified random procedure. We randomly selected participants until we had a mix of mothers who were diverse in terms of age (early teens, late teens, and early 20s) and parity status (pregnant and postpartum).

We established three teams of interviewers, each consisting of a principal investigator and a graduate student, who would have responsibility for following three of the mothers and their families. (Our grant allowed us to pay the mothers $50 for each interview in which they participated.) We conducted one interview with each of the nine mothers who agreed to participate. After the first interview, however, despite repeated attempts to contact her, we lost track of one mother who had moved several times without leaving any forwarding information. We quickly replaced her with another participant—a first-time pregnant woman—who was chosen because we wanted greater representation of women who had not yet given birth. After seven interviews, and again after many unsuccessful attempts, we were unable to locate another participant. Thus, we have data on a total of 10 mothers, including complete data on 8 mothers, partially complete data on one mother, and very limited data on another. We analyzed the data only from the nine mothers for whom we have at least partially complete data.

Data-Gathering Procedures

Consistent with the bioecological model's emphasis on multiple, layered influences on human development, we planned to interview not only the mothers but also as many other individuals as possible who were influential in the lives of the mothers and their children. We were able to interview at least one parent of most of the mothers in our sample, the romantic partners of several mothers, and a range of other influential individuals in the mothers' lives (e.g., great-grandmothers, brothers). These individuals were interviewed in a variety of places—in the mothers' homes, in their own homes, and in a number of other locations (e.g., restaurants, prison).

We conducted 12 interviews with eight of the mothers. Most of the interviews took place in the mothers' homes approximately every 4 months, with short telephone interviews conducted in between the longer in-person ones. (A few interviews were conducted over meals in restaurants, in relatives' homes, or at the EHS center.) After the interviews, often on the way home, we wrote field notes describing observations we knew would not be captured in the transcriptions of the tapes (e.g., participant's emotional reactions; children's behaviors; the physical condition of the home; our own feelings, thoughts, and impressions). The research team met on a biweekly basis throughout the first 2 years of the study and then monthly for the remainder of the study to discuss progress, to review preliminary findings, and to plan subsequent interviews. We also had several longer *theme meetings* during which we attempted to identify a focused set of themes or patterns that would provide guidance in the planning of later interviews. As is often the case in qualitative studies (Morse, 1998), the interview protocols (i.e., the specific set of questions asked in each interview) were flexibly developed as the study progressed.

Interview Protocols

We saw several clear trends in the nature and content of the interview protocols. First, over time they became progressively less structured and, paradoxically, more focused. In initial interviews, based on our desire to gather data on a variety of systems in Bronfenbrenner's model, we accumulated a wealth of information from each mother pertaining to her family background, experiences with EHS, attitudes toward child rearing, romantic relationships, interactions with and support from extended family and friends, work and educational experiences, and much more. Thus, the initial interviews were lengthy (2–4 hours on average) and broad (but not deep) in coverage. Because these initial interviews provided extensive background information and the preliminary data analyses yielded guidance regarding salient issues on which to focus, subsequent interview protocols were less broad and more focused. The extensive information gathered in early interviews allowed us to ask for brief updates on life changes (e.g., new romantic relationships, changes in employment or residence) before delving into the in-depth topics planned for particular interviews. These later interviews were less similar across mothers, as the unique circumstances of each mother led us to pursue somewhat different lines of questioning.

Two overlapping organizational schemes guided the development of our interview protocols. First, guided by Bronfenbrenner's model, we identified six areas that we thought comprehensively described the various dimensions important in the lives of the young mothers and their children, namely: 1) *intrapsychic factors* (e.g., their maturity, their degree of autonomy versus dependency on parents or home visitors); 2) *interpersonal factors* (e.g., past and current romantic relationships, relationships with extended family and friends); 3) *parenting* (e.g., beliefs about appropriate discipline of children, parenting behaviors); 4) *experiences with EHS* (and other social services programs); 5) *extrafamilial factors* (e.g., schools, churches, employment settings, neighborhoods); and 6) *cultural and societal factors* (e.g., larger cultural influences such as consumerism, racism, and sexism). Accordingly, we regularly asked about each of these key aspects of the lives of the mothers and their children.

Second, we noticed in our preliminary analyses of the early interview data that social support—received and given, helpful and less helpful—was a key organizing element in the lives of the mothers. As a result, we asked participants in a number of different ways for information pertaining to their social networks. For example, not only did we directly ask about supportive and nonsupportive interactions with family and friends, but also we asked participants on two occasions to construct a *Support Wheel* that involved placing individuals who were essential to their children's lives and well-being in an inner circle very near to the child, placing those with moderate amounts of influence in a concentric circle farther out, and placing those with little or a negative influence in an outer circle or outside the support circle. The participants then told us why the individuals were placed where they were and described the influence of those individuals (both positive and negative) on the lives of the children. In addition, after asking the mothers to complete the Support Wheel with their children as the focus, we asked them to complete the activity with themselves as the focus. By engaging in this activity twice, we were able to track changes in support networks and to ask the participants to reflect on these changes.

We also engaged in data-gathering techniques other than the formal interview. For example, consistent with a *participant observation* approach, we regularly attempted to interact with participants in the natural course of their daily lives. In many instances, we took the mothers out for a meal, drove them to a store to purchase Christmas presents for their children, or took them to a picnic sponsored by the EHS program. We *shadowed* each mother and child by having a trained observer (typically the graduate student who was a member of the interviewing team) watch the mother as she interacted with her child in their home for a few hours. We did this to obtain reasonably naturalistic data about the mothers' parenting styles and daily activities.

Finally, we used some quantitative data from questionnaires and assessments collected from all available and willing EHS program and comparison mothers and children as part of the national evaluation of EHS and as part of our local research. (These instruments are identified in the chapters in which their use is described.) Other measures were administered only to the nine mothers participating in the case study portion of our research. We used some quantitative measures for the purposes of methods triangulation, which involves using more than one research method (e.g., interviews and questionnaires) to determine if they identify the same patterns (Patton, 1990) and to determine how a given individual compared with the larger sample of African American, EHS-eligible families who were involved in the EHS program in our area. For example, we found ourselves frequently applying the code *alienation,* or tendency to be pessimistic and to expect betrayal, to the statements of one of the mothers (Sherryce) (coding is described in more detail in the next section). After concluding from the qualitative data that alienation was an organizing principle in Sherryce's life, we looked at her scores and at sample averages on the Multidimensional Personality Questionnaire (Form NZ; Tellegen, 1982), the personality inventory we had administered to 128 mothers. We saw that Sherryce's score on the Alienation subscale was in the top 13%. The impression that emerged out of our analyses of qualitative data was confirmed by the quantitative data. Other instruments, such as the modified Maternal Child-Rearing Values and Behaviors Inventory (MCR-VBI; Lausell-

Bryant, Gonzalez-Ramos, Zayas, & Cohen, 1998), were completed by the case study mothers only. These were useful in helping us understand individual mothers' positions on various issues.

Managing and Coding a Wealth of Data

A fine-grained coding and analysis of interviews and field notes was essential to our search for themes. After field notes were typed and interviews transcribed, we began our analyses with the aid of QSR NUD*IST NVivo (Version 1.3), a software package that assists in the management and analysis of qualitative data. In the first step, broad categories were assigned to every topic of conversation recorded in the transcripts and to every issue discussed in our field notes. Codes were developed to mark statements according to the person(s) and issue(s) to which they pertained. For example, Andreya's complaint that "As soon as Lavell do something, William wants to hit him, but I told him, 'No, you can't do that because you don't be around all the time,'" was initially assigned the broad codes *child's biological father* and *discipline*. These codes marked the statement as pertaining to Andreya's reactions to the disciplinary strategies of her son's father.

Toward the end of the data-collection period, we divided into workgroups according to the list of planned chapters for this book. Each chapter had a different workgroup. Each workgroup chose the broad categories (or the intersection of categories) that held promise for its chapters and closely read the material coded as pertaining to those categories. Our second data-analysis step involved the creation of new categories—subcategories of the initial broad categories—using the *constant comparative method* (Strauss & Corbin, 1998). This meant comparing each instance of a concept or category in the text with previous data to determine if it should be assigned an already-developed code or if a new code should be created. For instance, the Chapter 10 ("Raising Children") workgroup recoded the statement by Andreya quoted above to indicate that it reflected feelings related to *corporal punishment* and *being there* as well as to *child's biological father*. As this example illustrates, it was not unusual to attach more than one code to a single conversational turn.

The third step involved bringing together all the passages assigned the same code (or intersection of codes) and looking for themes. For example, in examining passages coded as *mother's mother* in Andreya's transcripts, we saw how, over time and after she moved out of her mother's home, Andreya's anger vis-à-vis her mother was transformed. She began acknowledging that her mother had often been "right," and their relationship took a dramatic turn for the better. We developed a theme that we called *Mama was right,* which became a category in and of itself. The next step involved examining text to determine if, and under what circumstances, *Mama was right* was a valid theme. In other words, we looked for evidence confirming our insight that *Mama was right* reflected Andreya's post–moving-out attitude toward her mother. As a result of this process, we became aware of the events and situations over time that elicited Andreya's negative and positive evaluations of her mother's intent and correctness.

Ongoing discussions about coding and theme-building provided checks on reliability. Disagreements about the coding of particular passages and the validity of emerging themes were resolved after careful rereading of the text and discussion among authors. On many occasions, co-researchers working on other chapters were also consulted. Moreover, as soon as chapter authors completed a chapter, other members of the research team read it and offered feedback that was incorporated into subsequent revisions. Each chapter received at least two such readings.

Although our analytic approach was based on inductive procedures, it is important to consider our roots in the theoretical principles described at the beginning of this chapter. These principles were influential because they helped direct our search for themes. Bronfenbrenner's concepts regarding mesosystem influences, for example, guided our reading of text concerning the quality of the child care centers attended by the children of the families. As we read these passages, we thought not only about the direct impact that child care quality might be having on children, but also about the ways in which children's child care experiences came home with them to influence the family climate. Awareness of the possibility of mesosystem influences also made us take special note of mothers' comments about their relationships with their children's teachers.

The Biographical Approach   For the case study of Andreya and her family (Section II of this book), we used a biographical approach. Miller (2000) wrote that most modern biographical researchers are eclectic in their methodologies; our approach was not an exception. Although our basic approach was closest to the neopositivist stance (use of semistructured interview schedules and the belief that respondents' answers represent aspects of reality), we also used analytical concepts developed by both the realist and narrative schools of analysis. These schools require a *bottom-up* approach—determining concepts from data (rather than beginning with theory and interpreting data accordingly). They also require an awareness that participants' narratives about past, present, and anticipated events reflect the meanings they have given to their experiences. Using the NVivo software, we developed themes that reflected our understanding of the organizing principles that seemed to undergird the experiences and day-to-day choices of Andreya, her mother, her children, her romantic partners, her brothers, and the other major figures in her life. The case study was then written around these themes. Mindful of a precept of feminist theory, we also wanted to share Andreya's voice. We were therefore committed to weaving direct quotations and other rich illustrations into the story. We believe that Andreya's story captures themes that are common in the daily lives of young, single African American mothers living in poverty in our urban centers.

Basically, the same methods were used to create the vignettes that appear in most chapters. For each vignette, we focused either on a parent for whom chapter-relevant themes were well demonstrated or on a parent whose situation and circumstances illustrate a particularly meaningful point made in the chapter. The main difference between the vignettes and the case study of Andreya is that the latter presents a holistic portrait in full context, whereas the scope of each vignette is limited to a theme or two that is salient to that person's story.

CONCLUSION

Because we used multiple theoretical orientations and a combination of qualitative and quantitative methods, we were able to develop rich descriptions of the young mothers' experiences, challenges, successes, and frustrations. Bioecological systems theory encouraged us to look for multiple levels of influence on the ideas, feelings, and behaviors of the mothers and their family members. Some of these influences were direct, some indirect, and some multidirectional. The feminist perspective, which easily complements the bioecological model because of its emphasis on the importance of context, led us to be especially sensitive to gender, racial, and social class issues.

Qualitative methods were our most important tools for data collection and analysis. However, we also used some quantitative methods to help us obtain additional detail and to check the stability of our qualitatively derived emergent patterns and inferences.

REFERENCES

Bronfenbrenner, U. (1979). *The ecology of human development: Experiments by nature and design.* Cambridge, MA: Harvard University Press.

Bronfenbrenner, U. (1986). Ecology of the family as a context for human development: Research perspectives. *Developmental Psychology, 22,* 723–742.

Bronfenbrenner, U., & Morris, P.A. (1998). The ecology of developmental process. In W. Damon (Series Ed.) & R.M. Lerner (Vol. Ed.), *Handbook of child psy-*

chology: Vol. 1. Theoretical models of human development (5th ed., pp. 993–1028). New York: John Wiley.

Collins, P.H. (1990). *Black feminist thought.* Boston: Unwin Hyman.

Elder, G. (1998). The life course as developmental theory. *Child Development, 69,* 1–12.

Elise, S. (1995). Teenaged mothers: A sense of self. In B.J. Dickerson (Ed.), *African American single mothers* (pp. 53–79). Thousand Oaks, CA: Sage Publications.

Hareven, T.K. (1996). Life course. In J.E. Birren (Ed.), *Encyclopedia of Gerontology, 2.* San Diego: Academic Press.

hooks, b. (2000). *Feminist theory: From margin to center.* Cambridge, MA: South End Press.

Kelly, E.M. (2001). Female, young, African American and low-income: What's feminism got to do with her? *Feminism & Psychology, 11,* 152–156.

Lausell-Bryant, L., Gonzalez-Ramos, G., Zayas, L., & Cohen, E. (1998). *Maternal Child-Rearing Values and Behaviors Inventory.* Unpublished manuscript, New York University, New York.

Miller, R.L. (2000). *Researching life stories and family histories.* Thousand Oaks, CA: Sage Publications.

Morse, J. (1998). Designing funded qualitative research. In N.K. Denszin & Y.S. Lincoln (Eds.), *Strategies of qualitative inquiry* (pp. 56–85). Thousand Oaks, CA: Sage Publications.

Patton, M.Q. (1990). *Qualitative research and evaluation methods* (2nd ed.). Newbury Park, CA: Sage Publications.

Strauss, A., & Corbin, J. (1998). *Basics of qualitative research: Techniques and procedures for developing grounded theory* (2nd ed.). Thousand Oaks, CA: Sage Publications.

Tellegen, A. (1982). *Brief manual for the Multidimensional Personality Questionnaire.* Unpublished manuscript, University of Minnesota, Minneapolis.

Thompson, L. (1992). Feminist methodology for family studies. *Journal of Marriage and the Family, 54,* 3–18.

Wuest, J. (1995). Feminist grounded theory: An exploration of the congruency and tensions between two traditions in knowledge discovery. *Qualitative Health Research, 5,* 125–138.

Andreya

An In-Depth Case Study

4

From Birth to Age 16

Jean M. Ispa and Elizabeth A. Sharp

I sat in Rickie's pickup truck, nervous. Rickie was Andreya's Early Head Start (EHS) child and family development specialist. A couple of weeks earlier, I had reached in a bag and picked out a piece of paper with Andreya's name on it—thus randomly choosing her as someone I would try to get to know. All I knew about her were some demographic facts—19 years old, African American, single, living with her mother and her 12-month-old son. I had asked Rickie to see if Andreya would be willing to participate in our project. I had also asked him to explain that I was one of a team of researchers who wanted to learn about the lives of EHS families. He had described our process to her—that we planned to interview each mother at least three times a year for 5 years, with occasional telephone calls in between visits to see how each participant was doing. He had explained to Andreya that she would be paid $50 for each face-to-face interview. When Rickie called back to tell me that Andreya had said yes, I asked if I could accompany him on a home visit so that he could introduce us.

Now, as we neared her house in a rundown neighborhood of small, detached homes, I was worried. First, I worried about how I, a middle-age, Caucasian professional, would establish a relationship with an African American low-income 19-year-old. Would we like each other well enough to sustain a 5-year relationship? Would she feel comfortable talking to me about the very personal things I wanted to know and understand? How would I word my questions, and how would I respond to hers? Second, I worried about safety—after all, this was the section of the inner city that was often featured in newspaper crime stories. And, finally, that day there was a more immediate, though less serious, worry: Would Andreya be home when we got there? Her telephone had been disconnected, so Rickie had not been able to confirm the 4:30 appointment.

We arrived at the house, a relatively well-maintained, two-story frame building. Rickie knocked on the door. A minute or two passed. Sensing my concern, Rickie muttered a plea, "Oh, please, Andreya, be home." The door opened, and a tall, heavyset young woman told us to come in. Rickie greeted her cheerfully and warmly, "Hi, Andreya!"

Rickie and I waited in the living room while Andreya went upstairs to get her son. As I looked around, I thought to myself that the two rooms in view, the living and dining rooms, were cozily furnished and quite clean. I wondered, however, about the glass figurines on the coffee table: It surprised me that a family with a toddler kept breakables in easy reach. I also wondered if the family was religious: Near the door was a knee-high statue of the Virgin Mary. Just one detail marked the family's financial need: Only one light was turned on, and when it was time to read a Consent to Participate in Research form to Andreya, I had to strain to see the typed words in the dim lighting.

Rickie and I stayed for a little more than an hour. Over the course of that hour, I became increasingly relaxed and even happy. Though Andreya had talked in a monotone and smiled little at the beginning of the visit, she had gradually warmed up and started telling me a bit about herself. Her obvious delight in her child had been heartwarming to see. Before Rickie and I left, I asked if it would be okay if I brought my research assistant Elizabeth, a graduate student, along on future visits, and if she would mind if we taped our interviews. She answered that she had no problem with either; she said she had nothing to hide.

On my return to the university the next day, I reported to Elizabeth that I thought we were lucky to have drawn Andreya's name— that she seemed like a person we would enjoy knowing. What I didn't know was how much we would learn from her, or how much she would touch us, or even simply how deeply fond of her we would become.

What follows here and in the next few chapters is a holistic portrayal of Andreya's life (and the lives of the people significant to her) until she reached the age of 22. Our presentation of the story conveys Andreya's perspectives regarding the personal and relationship characteristics, values, and events that are important to her and her children. Our research voice is perhaps not as apparent but nevertheless undergirds the story's telling by virtue of the choices we made about what to include. These choices reflect our desire to illustrate the organizing principles that we believe direct Andreya's day-to-day experiences and that color the meanings she gives to past, present, and anticipated events (Miller, 2000). Occasionally, we make statements that reflect our analysis of particular situations, but most of our explicit analyses are saved for sub-

INFLUENTIAL PEOPLE IN ANDREYA'S LIFE

Andreya Bradley:	The central figure of the case study
Lavell Jones:	Andreya's older son
Kevon Bradley:	Andreya's younger son
Patricia Bradley:	Andreya's mother
Roy:	Andreya's father
Grandma Dorothy:	Patricia's mother (Andreya's maternal grandmother)
Grandma Laverne:	Roy's mother (Andreya's paternal grandmother)
Lucia:	Andreya's aunt (Patricia's older sister)
Quintus Bradley:	Andreya's older brother
Tony Bradley:	Andreya's younger brother
Julius:	Tony Bradley's father
George:	Andreya's uncle, who was killed by Julius (Tony's father) when Andreya was 3
Kalia:	Andreya's young cousin who is being raised by Patricia
James:	Andreya's abusive "stepfather"
Sam:	Andreya's later "stepfather" (of whom she speaks fondly)
Tyrone:	One of Andreya's first boyfriends in early adolescence
Jimmy:	A suitor whom Andreya brushes off
Lamar:	The boy (later killed) whom Andreya liked when she was 9
William Jones:	The father of Andreya's children
Ms. Russell:	William's mother (Lavell and Kevon's paternal grandmother)
Tessa:	William's sister
Sonya:	William's girlfriend after Lavell's birth and for the next several years
Ms. Moore:	Andreya's Job Corps counselor
Dr. Gates:	The pediatrician for Andreya's children

sequent chapters. We start with Andreya's childhood and continue in roughly chronological order, building the narrative around the themes we believe to be central to Andreya's life.

—Jean M. Ispa

CHILDHOOD AND ADOLESCENCE

One day we asked Andreya, "What do you remember about your childhood?" "I didn't have no bad childhood. I had a good childhood," she answered, eyes smiling. "I was never deprived of nothing. I was never short Easter or Christmas. My mama always had for us. If we wasn't able to have new clothes, we wore our best clothes. You know, it was always good."

She went on to list the toys she had, item by item. It was a long list. Memories of toys and holidays were intertwined with stories about family members, especially her mother, paternal grandmother, aunts, and cousins. Andreya described each toy and piece of clothing bought by a relative who cared enough to spend scarce dollars on something for her. "I had two birthdays in one year," she told us. We asked what she meant. "My mother would give me a party and I would get clothes and stuff from my mama's people," she explained. "And then my daddy's mother would give me a party. I would have presents, cake, cookies, potato chips, everything. I mean, balloons, everything. Grandpa would come in with a big ol' cake. And my cousins on that side and my aunties and my mama's little sister and brother would come to that party. And whenever I want something, I'll call my grandmother. I'll be like, 'Grandma, I want such, such and such.' She'd be like, 'Okay.'"

Andreya thought that this was the way childhood should be: a time to enjoy toys, to feel nicely dressed, and to bask in the love of relatives. When her 1-year-old's father complained that it was wasteful to spend money on Christmas presents for a child too young to understand the meaning of the holiday, she objected that a child should not be punished for not knowing what Christmas really is. She wanted her child to have the pleasures she had. "So I'm not going to deprive him of nothing, even if he don't know the meaning of it," she said. "If he enjoys it—fine." Providing that kind of childhood for her children was more than difficult, she had discovered, but she was determined to try.

Over the years of the study, we asked Andreya many times about her childhood. Almost all of the stories were happy ones, and they almost all involved her mother or paternal grandmother. Many also involved her maternal grandmother, aunts, cousins, brothers, and one of her uncles. She told stories of a neighborhood in which almost everyone she loved lived within a child's walking distance. So when she "got tired of my mama," she could just go visit her grandmother or an aunt. She spent more time with her father's mother than with her mother's, but her maternal grandmother was there for her too. "My mother's mama, she kept us at times, like when she felt my mama wanted to party, she would keep us."

Andreya was "under the orders" of her mother and grandmother, but she liked the way they required respect and obedience. She had chores, but as a child, washing dishes felt like play. She hardly ever saw her father, and when she did it was not pleasant. Still, there were other males in her life—in particular, her step-great-grandfather, her uncles, and her two brothers. The family moved a lot as her mother Patricia struggled with her own independence and boyfriend issues, but with one exception (a move to a disliked uncle's house), Andreya did not mind. After all, none of the moves took her away from her grandmothers or her aunties. Her mother warned her not to walk past a certain block—it was "not safe for Black folk" over there—but she was a child and the restriction did not yet carry a larger meaning.

Such was the flavor of the stories we heard during the first 2 years of knowing Andreya. But as time went on, we learned that there were other sides to her childhood. Was she covering up when she told us that her childhood was good? On reflection, we do not think so. Her happy assessment did not change after she confided some terrible things. In her mind, what had been good seemed more important and powerful than what had been bad.

Andreya's mother Patricia was 15 when her first child Quintus was born. Andreya, who had a different father, was born 2 years later. Dorothy, Patricia's mother, was not pleased and told Patricia that enough was enough. If she was going to have a second child, she had to move out. But there was nowhere else for Patricia to go, so as she struggled to find her way over the next 10 years, she would move herself and her children in and out of her mother's home, her older siblings' homes, her paternal grandmother's home, and a boyfriend's home.

As a child, little Andreya was frequently ill; she was particularly prone to pneumonia. Her mother told her that as a baby, she seemed to spend more time in the hospital with pneumonia than at home. (Home, at the time, was Grandma Dorothy's.) By the time Andreya was 5, there had been six hospitalizations with that disease alone.

During one of those times, the nurses made comments indicating that they suspected Patricia of neglect. "Once they told my mama if she brought me to the hospital with pneumonia again, they were going to put her in jail, but it wasn't her fault that I was sick." It wasn't until she was 12 that Andreya was diagnosed with asthma, but asthma may have played a role in the earlier illnesses as well.

In addition to bouts of pneumonia, Andreya had bad eczema—her skin was so dry and itchy that her mother and grandmother had to cover her with Vaseline and tie socks on her hands to keep her from scratching and infecting herself. When they did that, Andreya would rub her face on the wall. It was years before her grandmother found a lotion that gave Andreya relief.

When Andreya was 3, Patricia fell in love with a young man named Julius and pinned her hopes on their relationship. According to Andreya, when Julius moved in with the family, things seemed to be going well, except for his complaints about George, Patricia's 22-year-old brother. Julius accused George of harassing him, taking his things, and demanding money.

One day an argument between the two got out of control, and Julius pulled out a gun and shot George, killing him. "I lost two people I loved," Patricia told Andreya when she was old enough to discuss that horrible day.

Two weeks later, her brother dead, her boyfriend in jail, her family in mourning, and her brothers and sisters angry at her for bringing Julius into their lives, Patricia discovered that she was pregnant. Appalled, her brothers and sisters insisted that she have an abortion and pooled their money to pay for it. They did not want a child in their midst who reminded them of Julius, but Patricia did not believe in abortion. Andreya remembers her mother hiding in the bathroom for hours on end, weeping. Grandma Dorothy stood by Patricia's side and told Patricia that she could keep the baby.

Patricia named the baby Julius after his father. Her mother immediately accepted the infant, but her brothers and sisters never did. One day, when little Julius was 2, one of his uncles tied him up with electrical wiring, screaming, "If it wasn't for your damn daddy, my brother could still be alive." Dorothy advised Patricia to change the boy's name. She did not blame the child for what his father had done, but the name Julius was just too hard to say. Patricia started calling the toddler Tony. Still, Andreya told us, "My mama was like the black sheep of the family for a long time. Every now and then when her brother start drinking or come over for dinner he'd throw it up in my mama's face, but that wasn't my mama's fault. And everybody threw it in Tony's face: 'That little bastard' [they called him]."

Andreya is grateful that her mother was a homebody, spending all her time before and after work with her children. Patricia emphatically confirms her daughter's impression. "I was always around my kids. I grew up with my kids. I mean, you know, I never really let nobody babysit my kids outside my mama. My mother kept my kids and Andreya's [paternal] grandmother kept *her*. Outside of them, nobody kept my kids. I was constantly with my kids."

When asked about discipline, Andreya told us that her mother required obedience. "I remember the time that we couldn't even say no to my mama," she recalled approvingly. Yet "whuppings" were only occasional, like the time Andreya did not come straight home after school. She says she herself "wasn't the type" to do something that would warrant a whupping, but even her brothers were usually spared. Andreya thinks that her mother was stricter with her than with the boys. In retrospect, looking at where her brothers are now, she thinks this was a mistake.

Andreya liked kindergarten and the first five grades even though her mother's moves meant that she went to three different elementary schools. She also enjoyed the summer day camps she attended at the nearby community center. She remembers caring teachers, school plays, wearing pretty dresses to special events, and the activities and field trips these schools and programs provided.

At home, she looked up to her older brother Quintus and fought with her younger brother Tony. "I mean, Tony was my fighting partner every day. I mean, he would get me sometimes and scratch on my neck, and sometimes I'd get him and just bite up his fingers." Now that she has children of her own, she understands why her mother used to get so upset about those fights. Yet, the fighting did not stop her from loving her little brother. Besides, she was a tomboy and there were many good times playing with both brothers and their friends.

The children didn't see their fathers much. Quintus's father moved to Iowa and was rarely heard from. Julius was released from prison when Tony was 5 but would come by to see his son only once in a while. Roy, Andreya's father, showed even less interest. Soon after Andreya's birth, Roy enlisted in the army and left for boot camp followed by a 6-year tour of duty in Japan. Andreya is a strong believer in the importance of fathers, but she doesn't think she missed much not having this particular one around. Even after Roy's return when she was 6, he showed her little affection. Andreya's main memories of Roy relate to his attempts to teach her to count in Japanese and his annoyance when she could not do it. Roy's father (Andreya's paternal grandfather) was another potential father figure, but that relationship was strained too. Andreya thinks her grandfather, whom she described as "a gambler and a dope peddler," did not like her. The feeling was mutual. It scared her how her grandfather would sit at the top of the stairs, teasing her by swinging an open pocketknife as she tried to get by. Andreya and her grandmother both told her grandfather to stop doing that, but he persisted, insisting that he was just playing. As for her maternal grandfather, Andreya said that he had been behind bars "for robberies and all kind of stuff" during most of her childhood, and when he got out, he was not welcome in their home. For one thing, he had a drug problem. For another, Patricia would never forgive him for attempting to molest her when she was a teenager.

When Tony was 2, Andreya 5, and Quintus 7, 22-year-old Patricia moved the family in with James, her new love. Unbeknownst to her, however, James was a pedophile. As she was to find out later, he had made advances toward his younger sisters, and now he repeatedly attempted to touch Andreya. At first, he succeeded, but as she got a little older, she found ways to protect herself. At night she would creep into the bed of her older brother Quintus, finding comfort in sleeping right next to him. She made sure that her arm was under him so that if anything happened, Quintus would wake up too. On weekends when her mother was out working, Andreya stayed at Grandma Laverne's house. Andreya's success at evading James inflamed him. When Patricia was at work, James would feed only the boys. Andreya would be denied food and forced to stay in her room. Sometimes she escaped by climbing out of her window and sliding down a porch pole. Sometimes James was cruel to Patricia as well, hitting her and threatening her when he was angry.

Andreya told her mother that she did not like James, but she didn't say why. Patricia countered Andreya's complaints with reminders that James was giving her money that helped support them. It was not until Andreya was 9 years old that she told her mother she was being sexually abused. Why did Andreya wait 4 years? Why didn't she admit it to the aunts whom James had also propositioned, and who asked her point-blank if James had been bothering her? According to Andreya, the reason was that James had warned her that he would kill both her and her mother if she told about his advances. And, indeed, when Andreya finally did tell her mother, and Patricia confronted James with questions, he assaulted Patricia. Andreya had to call her uncles to come stop the fight.

Andreya had another reason to keep the abuse a secret: She worried that her mother would hate her for being a rival for James's affections. Fortunately, this concern did not materialize. Patricia's retort to James after he denied doing anything wrong—"You capable of it"— shows that she believed Andreya. Patricia moved the family out of James's house. In the years that followed, James stalked both Patricia and Andreya.

When Andreya listed the men who had been important to her, she did not mention James. When we wondered aloud if James should be on the list, Andreya dismissed his significance in her life. She did not want James on the list because she hated him. But during another visit, she reflected on James's impact on her relationship with William, the father of her children. She couldn't help but associate sex with memories of James. "When I was pregnant with Lavell, I pushed William completely out from me. And he never understood. He thought he did something to me or something. But I mean, it was eating me up. He didn't know what it was inside of me. But it was that."

The household grew once again when Andreya was 12. Kalia, her 7-year-old cousin, came to live with them. The daughter of one of Patricia's sisters, Kalia had been neglected and abused by both of her parents when she was an infant. For the next several years she lived with another aunt and her husband in Milwaukee. Things had not been good for Kalia there either. She finally told her aunt that her uncle had been raping her about twice a week—as punishment, he said, for things she had and had not done. Patricia agreed to give her niece a home.

Another change for Andreya was the transition to middle school and then to junior high school. Although she had fond memories of elementary school, her middle and junior high school stories depicted insensitive teachers and herself as a sincere but unyielding adolescent. Many of the stories were about respect. "My attitude really started getting bad in sixth or seventh grade," she said, "to where I'd cuss out teachers if I felt they disrespected me."

She described herself as having been "nosy," wanting explanations for scientific facts and for rules. She asked "why" and "how" a lot. One way in which she believed her teachers showed their disrespect was by not answering her questions and telling her to be quiet instead. Her mother was willing to explain her rules, and Andreya expected teachers to do the same. Talking about the teacher with whom she had the most trouble, she said, "When you don't know nothing, you ask. And I always asked, 'How do you do this, and why you can't do it like this?' And you know, the teacher didn't like that. She started hollering at me and I told her she's not my mama, 'Don't holler at me.'"

Very often (Andreya said it was every day), a teacher would call her mother at work. One day Andreya came home to find her mother distraught. "Whatever you doing?" Patricia demanded. "And I said, 'Mama, well, I go in there and I just, when I don't know nothing, I ask her [the teacher] a question. She gets mad at me.'" Patricia tried to make her daughter understand that some teachers do not like questions, and you just have to live with it. Her mother explained that there could be serious consequences for the whole family. That morning, Patricia's boss informed her that if Patricia got one more call from Andreya's school, she would be out of a job.

Telephone calls were not the end of it; there were also frequent suspensions, sometimes for fights with other kids, sometimes for talking back to teachers. After some of her outbursts, Andreya tried to apologize to her teachers, "'I don't realize what I doing,' but it's just like they didn't never give me a chance." Teachers started to expect bad things from her. One time Andreya said a word that a teacher mistook for an obscenity. The teacher suspended her, not believing Andreya's protestations that she had said something different.

Andreya continued to visit her paternal grandmother Laverne often. "I was always under her, always, always, always." (Andreya's use of the expression "under her" conveys the sense that her relationship with her grandmother was a positive one. The expression signifies that she spent a lot of time by her grandmother's side, that she felt comfort in her presence, and that she felt connected to her.) In fact, it seems that her relatives on her mother's side were a little jealous. Grandma Dorothy and an uncle complained to Patricia, "You need to keep her around *us* sometimes."

When Grandma Laverne became a Jehovah's Witness, she started reading Bible stories to her granddaughter. Andreya liked the stories and believed in them, but she was not interested in going to church. One of the uncles whom she and her mother and brothers had lived with for a while was a Baptist preacher. He had given Andreya a distaste for organized religion. Although he had tried to get her and her mother to attend church, they had rarely gone, and that was fine with Andreya. "He was just trying to, like, more or less tell us how to live our lives. I didn't like that too much."

It was her uncle's hypocrisy that really bothered Andreya. First, he had tried to get her to sit on his lap. After Andreya's experiences with James, she was not about to sit on any man's lap. Second, it bothered her that her uncle did not want to spend money on his own children. Andreya knew that he had tried to get her mother to buy his children the things they needed. A decade later, her skepticism about the morality of religious leaders would still stand in the way of Andreya's willingness to join a church.

Not all of Andreya's experiences with men were negative. For example, around that time, Patricia met a man named Sam and began a 4-year romance with him. For Andreya, as well as for Patricia, this was a good thing. When Andreya first started talking to us about Sam, the "stepfather" she had had in middle adolescence, we asked for clarification. Had Patricia been married to him? Had he lived with the family? The answer was no on both counts. In fact, Sam was married to someone else, but, according to Andreya, "his wife wasn't into him."

Andreya talks fondly about Sam. He had earned her love and respect. "Yeah, only reason why I call him 'Daddy' is because—the times that my father wasn't there—*he* was there. I called him 'Stepdaddy' or 'Daddy' because he was taking care of me. It wasn't because my mama went with him and I *had* to call him 'Daddy.' Sam supported me in a lot of ways. Everything I wanted to do, he supported me in it. He gave me whatever I wanted. If I did good, he rewarded me." Andreya tells of activities she wanted to try such as sewing, and places she wanted to go with her friends such as the skating rink, and of Sam's willingness to either pay the entire cost or split it with her 50/50. Andreya also remembers Sam being good to Patricia, checking on her when she was sick, and going to the drugstore to get her medicines when she needed them. "He is a good man," Andreya said, although she rarely saw him anymore.

Andreya's stories about her early adolescence are also about pride in her own self-sufficiency. She surprised us with a declaration that "I have been independent since I was 12." A favorite story—Andreya has told it to us several times—is about how she handled "coming into womanhood." Andreya was at her grandmother's house when her first period started. "I came home and I said, 'Mama, I need to count out, like, 500 pennies.' And she's like, 'Why you count out all them pennies? You been saving all them pennies for a long time.' I said, 'Because I'm going to the store to get me something. I'm coming right back home, Mama.' And when I came back and she saw what I had, she just looked at me like, 'What are you doing with those?' I'm like, 'Mama, I started over at Grandma's house.' And she just started crying. She said, 'Why didn't you tell me? I could of gave you the money.' And then she's like, 'Well, I'm glad you did what you did 'cause I didn't think you knew what to do. I thought you'd be too scared."

After this day, Andreya's mother and grandmother began giving her an allowance, but a month or so later, Andreya also began baby-sitting for her mother's sisters and friends. "You know, I felt independent all the time. I mean, you know how some girls come into woman-hood and they always expect, 'Mama, Mama, Mama, give me this.' I never felt that way. I mean from the time I even started womanhood, I always had my own everything from deodorant to soap to comb and brush. All my personal hygiene. Always felt that way. And everybody was like, 'You too young to be so independent.' And I was like, 'That's the only way to be.'"

All through her adolescence, Andreya used her allowance and baby-sitting money to buy her own clothing as well as personal care prod-ucts. She liked babysitting. "It didn't make me grow up no faster like most people say. My cousin—she did grow up too fast because she was actually raising her younger brothers. It was like she was the mama. Babysitting's different because you don't always have to be there. It's not like a mandatory thing, like a mama thing. You know how mamas have to be mandatory to their kids? It's nothing like that."

Andreya contrasts her independence and frugality with her broth-ers' behavior. They wore only expensive name-brand items and asked their mother for the money to buy them. Andreya saw that her mother was proud of the way Andreya paid for a lot of her things, and that, she says, caused a positive shift in their relationship. It made Andreya feel closer to her mother and braver about asking for freedoms. "That's what really brought us closer for me to talk to her and stuff because most of the time I was scared to ask my mama if I could spend the night over at my friend's house, you know, little stuff. 'Can I go to the store with my friends?' And 'I just met this person. . . . '"

There was one kind of friend Patricia was firmly opposed to when it came to her daughter—boys. Patricia was determined that her daughter not become a pregnant high-school dropout like she had been. Making her expectations very clear, Patricia told Andreya that if she ever thought about having sex, she should first talk to Patricia. Moreover, she forbade Andreya to speak to older boys and men she did not already know. Still an obedient child (especially regarding her mother), Andreya complied, "At first I wouldn't even dare to talk to a boy." Andreya remembers how she reacted when a cousin encouraged her to talk to some boys who were walking down the street past the house. Andreya told her cousin, "My mama does not let me have boyfriends." Her cousin wondered at this, "You can't even go off the porch when it get dark?" Andreya replied that this was correct. The cousin was amazed. "Your mama too strict," she said.

Andreya did like one boy at school. Lamar was neither older nor a stranger, so Andreya figured a friendship with him was permissible. Sometimes, starting when they were about 9 years old, they walked home together. Suspicious, Patricia demanded, "Did you kiss him?" and pronounced him "an ugly boy." Andreya refused to agree that Lamar was ugly, so in further attempts to discourage the budding romance, Patricia not only threatened to "whup" Andreya if she continued talking to him, she also asked her sisters to back her up by confirming that Lamar was ugly. When a couple of years later it turned out that Lamar was dealing drugs, Patricia told her daughter that if Lamar loved Andreya, he would stop that business right away. Their relationship, in fact, had never been intimate, and Andreya and Lamar eventually drifted apart. When she was 15, Andreya heard that Lamar had been killed by older drug dealers with whom he had become entangled.

Quintus had long been his little sister's protector—as when at night he had provided Andreya a safe haven from James. Now, aware that his little sister was maturing, Quintus started warning her to stay away from his friends. One day Quintus knocked Andreya out of a tree that she had climbed because he was afraid that his friends might come by and look up her skirt.

Quintus also tried to protect Andreya from his own nighttime activities, which, by the time he was 16, included drug dealing. Andreya described her attempts to hang out on street corners with Quintus and his determination to save her from that scene, "Before I had kids, I smoked weed. I ain't gonna lie, I did. The reason why I did it was because I thought it was so cool. My brother and them was doing it, and I wanted to be with him. Quintus was like, 'My little sister ain't supposed to be standing outside with me on no corner.' He would call me a cab to go home—give me cab fare. I would tell the cab to let me off at my cousin's house right up the street, and I'd come right back down there and he would do it again, only this time he'd go with me. He would make sure I would go to sleep before he would leave to go back out. 'Cause see that's how bad he didn't want me to be out there. I was like, 'Well, I wanna stay out there with ya.' Well, one day he was like, 'Look young lady, I'm doing bad stuff.'" Fortunately, after a while Andreya realized that the drug scene was not for her. She was not hooked, so it was easy to stop. "But I stopped myself way before I had Lavell. It's just not me, you know. It's up to the person. It's not up to the drugs."

The attempts of her mother and brother to keep Andreya from harm were not foolproof. They might have been more effective if Patricia's working hours had not taken her away from home at crucial after-school hours. At the grocery store in which Patricia was a cashier, she was scheduled to work from 2:30 P.M. to 11:00 P.M. She entrusted Quintus with the care of his younger siblings and cousin. All four were to come home right after school and stay there under Quintus's supervision. Quintus, however, was not up to the responsibility. He would come home, make sure Andreya, Tony, and Kalia were indoors, lock the door, and, defying his mother's orders, leave to see his girlfriend and his buddies.

Tyrone, the 16-year-old brother of Quintus's girlfriend, started asking Quintus for the key to the house so that he could use the bathroom. Tyrone said he was afraid that if he went to his own home, his mother would not let him out again. One night 13-year-old Andreya woke up thinking she was wetting the bed. Tyrone was lying on top of her. When she asked him what he was doing, he replied that he was having sex with her. Andreya liked Tyrone, but she was not prepared for this. Tyrone told Andreya that they were boyfriend and girlfriend, and so that was what they were supposed to do.

Over the course of the next several months, Tyrone kept borrowing the house key from Quintus, and he and Andreya kept having sex. Sometimes Andreya was willing, sometimes she was not. Sometimes when she told him she did not want to have sex, Tyrone would repeat the line that they were boyfriend and girlfriend. Other times, he would grab her hard enough to bruise her arm. Andreya discovered that the only way to get him to stop was to threaten that she was going to tell her brother. Finally, one day Quintus noticed a particularly bad bruise on Andreya's arm. Putting two and two together, he confronted Tyrone, accusing him of having hurt Andreya. Though Tyrone denied guilt, Quintus broke off the friendship. They never spoke to each other again. Tyrone, however, kept coming by, and Andreya would usually let him in.

Andreya says that ever since the beginning of her relationship with Tyrone, she had wanted to tell her mother about it. (Recall that her mother had told her to come talk to her if she ever contemplated having sex.) She just couldn't find the right time. Either her mother was at work or other relatives were around. It was not that Andreya did not want her aunts to know; it was just that she knew her mother would want to know first. Also, she had another dilemma—how to present Quintus's complicity. Andreya did not want to tell her mother that Quintus had lent Tyrone the house key. And, finally, Andreya knew her mother would take strong measures if she found out that her daughter was sexually active. "I was scared to tell her, 'cause I knew she was going to whup me, or I was gonna be on punishment or living with my daddy, and I didn't want to live with my daddy at the time, because he had this girlfriend. Then he had this drug problem. I didn't want to be around my daddy." Another possibility, Andreya thought, was that her mother would make her live at Grandma Laverne's where she could be more closely supervised. Andreya loved her grandmother, but she did not want to burden her. "I mean, 'cause she would do stuff for me regardless, but I didn't want her to feel like I'm always her responsibility. So, I just tried to just like deal with it and ignore it. And then the more and more I ignored it, the worse it got."

Patricia finally found out about her daughter's sexual relationship with Tyrone not from Andreya, but from her niece Kalia. One evening Kalia woke up to go to the bathroom, heard some "goings on" from Andreya's room, and figured out what was happening. Although only 9 years old, she had been exposed to enough to understand. Kalia told her Aunt Patricia, "Andreya been doing it in her bed with that boy."

Patricia was very upset. She called Tyrone, demanding that he come over at once. As soon as he appeared, Patricia lit into him, telling Tyrone that it was "awfully low" of him to have taken advantage of an innocent 13-year-old, that if it turned out that Andreya was pregnant, she would "kick his ass," that she really should have him put in jail, and that he better not show his face around her house ever again. He never did. Patricia also stormed at Andreya and Quintus, telling both that they were "not right." More drastically, Patricia called juvenile authorities, asking for help. She thought that perhaps it would be best to have her children taken into a supervised living arrangement where they would be monitored more closely than she could manage, given her working hours. Andreya was checked by a doctor and offered counseling, but she was too afraid to talk to the professionals because she thought they might take her away from her mother. After "juvenile" refused to take the children, Patricia got a prescription for birth control pills and, for the next several years, made sure that Andreya took one every morning—even though she had extracted a promise from Andreya not to have sex anymore. She didn't want to take any chances.

She also "put down a lot of rules" and told her two teenagers that they would be shipped off if they disobeyed. Quintus would be sent to Iowa to live with his father, and Andreya would have to live with Grandma Laverne. They would see their mother only occasionally, whenever she could manage it. More than anything, the thought of losing daily contact with her mother scared Andreya.

For the next 3½ years, until she was 16, Andreya kept her promise to forego sex. It took some inner strength to fend off peer pressure—not only from boys but also from her girlfriends. Andreya explained that "My friends have kids. They was having kids like at 12, 13, 14." The independence with which she prided herself helped Andreya resist. "I mean, I never felt because they was doin' something, I had to do it. And they was like, 'Girl, you just don't know. Babies are so cute.' I was like, 'I don't want no babies right now. I got baby cousins and they cute. I can play with them and I can give them back to their mamas.' And they was like, 'Well, you need to have your own.' And I never ever said, 'Okay, I'm gonna have a baby because you got one.'"

At this point in her adolescence, Andreya was determined to make her mother proud by finishing high school, getting a job, and building a stable relationship with a responsible man—and only then becoming pregnant. Chapter 5 takes Andreya to a series of turning points when all of that changed.

REFERENCE

Miller, R.L. (2000). *Researching life stories and family histories.* Thousand Oaks, CA: Sage Publications.

5

Becoming a Mother

Jean M. Ispa and Elizabeth A. Sharp

Although Patricia did not tell Andreya that she needed to find work, Andreya was sensitive to the fact that it was not easy for her mother to support the family, and she also wanted to supplement her babysitting earnings. When she was 15, Andreya got a summer job through the Full Employment Council at a nearby community center, assisting in their preschool program. Some days she'd work there from 8:00 A.M. to 3:00 P.M. and then go to babysitting jobs. During the following school year, she worked for an after-school program run by the Camp Fire Girls. She put her whole heart into it, thinking up activities for the children and worrying about their welfare. With the money she earned, she started buying shoes and clothing for herself. Her mother, understandably, was amazed and proud of her daughter's self-sufficiency. "My mama was like, 'Gosh! Buying your own socks and everything! I didn't think you would be like this.' I said, 'Yeah!'"

Another opportunity to learn how to make money came in the form of a Housing Authority entrepreneurship program for community teenagers. The program gave each participant $500 to start an account for a small business. Andreya, now 16, wanted to start a sewing and a candy business and used some of the money to buy a sewing machine, material, and thread. The African-style dress she produced was exhibited at a show featuring African American handiwork, won an award, and sold for $75. Inspired, she created a skirt and vest, which she also sold. She also bought candy in bulk from a wholesale club and sold it to her friends and neighborhood children for more than she had paid but less than the stores charged. Though she would continue having a "candy store" off and on for many years, her interest in sewing was short-lived. Grandma Dorothy told us that she thought Andreya was too lazy to keep it up. Andreya offered a different explanation: She was discouraged, she said, when the director of the entrepreneurship program was arrested for embezzling money from the teens' accounts (including Andreya's).

Andreya suffered a serious emotional blow when Grandma Laverne (her paternal grandmother) died. Apparently Grandma Laverne had been ill for several years, but because a doctor was never consulted, Andreya didn't know what the illness was. The symptoms Andreya listed (blindness, incontinence, fatigue) suggest diabetes. Andreya blamed her grandfather for never taking his wife to a doctor or the hospital. When we asked why he didn't, she replied simply, "Being evil." She also told us that her grandmother had been under a lot of stress during the last years of her life. One of her daughters, who was mildly disabled, had run off and gotten pregnant. A son who was homosexual had disappeared for good after telling friends he couldn't listen to his mother's disapproving remarks any longer.

WILLIAM

Andreya began a new chapter in her life at 16 when she became involved with William, 11 years her senior and the father of three girls. William lived next door with his mother, sister, and one of his daughters (his mother had legal custody of this daughter). He'd struck up a friendship with Patricia, dropping by to play cards and dominoes with her and Sam. At first, Andreya didn't pay much attention to him except to ask for occasional rides to Wal-Mart. On one of those trips, William insisted on paying for a dress she wanted. Patricia was immediately suspicious. "My mother, she was like, 'You went to Wal-Mart with $35 and you still got $35 left.'" Andreya's response was to lie and tell her mother that she'd taken more than $35 with her. That trip was followed by other outings with William and more gifts of jewelry and clothing. Andreya was enchanted. Looking back 7 years later, she said,

"I mean at first I was at the point where, you know how you have somebody that really, really likes you and they going out they way for you but you don't have no feelings for them. I mean he took me places. He gave me stuff. And by me being 16, I was like in the materialistic excitement. I knew I could babysit so much and my mama gonna give me so much and half the time I knew I still couldn't get everything I want. He was giving me everything that I wanted so I liked that."

Another way in which William made himself desirable was by assuring her that although he would like to have sex with her, there was no problem waiting until she was ready. Patricia's misgivings about William show that she had no illusions regarding where things were heading. "Don't let him buy you," she warned her daughter.

Two weeks before her 17th birthday, Andreya agreed to have sex with William. She takes full responsibility for what happened, "It was my choice to do it. Like I told my mama, he didn't force me to do nothing I didn't wanna do. I mean he told me he'll wait and that's what he did. I wasn't pressured. He didn't ask me every day. I mean I got treated with respect." Moreover, she was falling in love with William and thought they would always be together. "After a while, I thought this is the person that's gonna really be here," she said. "I thought nothing was gonna ever get in the way of this relationship."

Patricia confronted her daughter time and again with accusations and questions stemming from her suspicions that Andreya was "messing around" with William. Each time, Andreya denied the charges. Then the day came when she realized she was pregnant. She was terrified. What would she tell her mother and grandmother? "It was like, how can I tell my mama? They was like, 'Well, we got plans for you and you got dreams.'" She thought about how her mother would have felt at the high school graduation that now might not happen.

"I'll be the first to graduate out of my mother's three, and she'll be happy for me and, you know, I made her happy, I made her satisfied, she proud of me. I thinkin' like that. It was like I cannot tell her and I actually freaked out at the doctor's. I had them do the test at least three times. I mean I had to find a way to go to her without her thinking the worst of me. You know. I mean, I knew that they was thinking highly of me and I couldn't just find a way to just say, 'I'm pregnant.'"

For the next nine days Andreya stayed at a cousin's house in order to avoid her mother, "I tried to stay away 'cause I couldn't find the words." Remembering the scene when she finally did confess, she describes her mother as "laughin' and cryin' at the same time. And I was like, she is kinda unhappy and kinda happy." Mostly, however, her mother was deeply upset. Her voice dropping, Andreya recalled, "It's like when I got pregnant, seemed like I let everybody down." Not only were her grandmother and aunts dismayed that she was pregnant, they also predicted that now that she'd started having babies, she wasn't going to stop. "A breeder," they called her. "They made me feel like I was just gonna keep on havin' babies. And I didn't feel that way."

We questioned Andreya on three different occasions in an effort to understand whether the pregnancy was accidental or intentional, but we were never sure what the answer was. We finally concluded that our confusion reflected Andreya's ambivalence about having a baby at that time. She said that she thought the birth control pills she was taking would prevent a pregnancy, and sometimes she even required William to supplement the birth control pills by using condoms. Yet, when she didn't conceive for a few months, she started worrying that she might be sterile, even going so far as to ask her doctor what she could do to get pregnant. Alarmed, the doctor told her it would be a big mistake to get pregnant when she had just a year left before high school graduation. But Andreya was in love, and she loved babies and children and knew that she wanted to have some of her own.

Furthermore, even though she was still in school, she felt the time was right. She'd managed to wait until "a decent age"—past the age when her friends had started giving birth and past the age when her mother had Quintus. Her one worry was about her mother and grandmother's desire that she graduate from high school. She kept thinking about how much they wanted her to break the family tradition of teenage motherhood, and she didn't want to disappoint them.

For a few weeks, Andreya refused to tell her mother who the father was. She pretended that it was a boy with whom she'd had a brief fling a few months prior to becoming involved with William. She knew her mother disapproved of her seeing a man so much older than she, and she knew that her mother would be angry that she'd been having sex in the house. She also knew that the news would destroy the friendship that had developed between her mother and William. When she finally admitted to Patricia that William was "the daddy," her mother said she'd known all along "'Cause I knew ain't nobody gonna come around and bring you no fruit and vegetables for nothin'. And constantly comin' over here." When William's mother asked who the father was, Andreya told her the truth, "And she was like, 'Well, William's just gonna have to take care of this responsibility.'"

Andreya's teachers, her social worker, and some of her relatives referred to the pregnancy as a "mistake," but Andreya refused to see it that way because that would mean taking no responsibility for it. "My baby's no mistake, because if it was a mistake I wouldn't have laid there and did it. And, you know . . . it's girls go to my school, they be like, 'My first one was a mistake,' and I say, 'How can your first one be a mistake? It was your responsibility. You knew what you was doin'.'" To the people who asked her how this could have happened even after she'd passed a school sex education course, she replied that she'd done well to wait so long before having her first child. "Well, I was in the ninth grade when I took sex education, and I came this far without being pregnant and you know, all my friends—they was tryin' to influence me and I didn't." Her friends marveled that she was 18 when she had her first child. "They was like, 'You waited 'til you was 18! *Daaaaaang!!*'

Everybody was sayin', 'You so *late*. You so *late.*' I think I did good to be 18 and have my baby. I don't feel no guilt. I don't feel like I just did it because I seen everybody else with a baby. I don't feel that way."

William, meanwhile, showed every sign of being happy about the pregnancy. Not only did he bring Andreya fruits and vegetables so that she and the baby would be healthy, he ate extra garlic so that he would be a healthy father for his son. He was sure Andreya, unlike his previous girlfriends, would produce a boy. He let Andreya know he was hurt when, out of fear of her mother's wrath, she at first told her that someone else was the father. "He was like, 'I can't believe you tellin' your mama this is somebody else's baby.'" For a while, he worried that it might *really* be someone else's baby, but Andreya assured him that there was no way it could be.

When we asked Andreya if their arguments ever turned violent, she answered that William was not an aggressive man, that the only time there was physical contact during a disagreement was when he admitted to working some evenings as a stripper for additional income. She'd hit him with a frying pan, furious that he would stoop so low. He'd shaken her to stop her talking, but that, she said, was the only time there was violence between them.

After Andreya admitted that William was the father, Patricia grudgingly allowed him to spend evenings and even nights at the house. In the summer, when William was doing construction work, he would come over in the evening, muddy and tired. Andreya would prepare his dinner and wash his clothes. When William occasionally proposed marriage, Andreya felt pressured. She didn't think they should get married until she'd finished school and she and William could support themselves. "I'll say, 'I can't marry you because my career ain't off the ground. I don't want to be married and you living with your mama and I'm living with my mama and we only see each other half of the time.'"

Morning sickness and doctors' appointments added up to a lot of missed school days. Finally, Andreya told the school counselor that she was pregnant. The counselor strongly recommended that she transfer to Stanton School. Andreya agreed to transfer to what she referred to as "the pregnant school," but she wasn't happy there. For one thing, she had to take two buses, and sometimes the second bus left before the first one arrived at the transfer spot. But even more important, the classes didn't seem serious to her. She was taking eleventh- and twelfth-grade English and math, but the rest of the time was spent learning about parenting and money management. "Like I told my mama," she said, "that's not no kind of school." Andreya contemplated asking for a transfer back to her old school but didn't think that they would accept her. After a while, frustrations with bus problems coupled with her disdain for the school led her to drop out altogether.

No longer in school, Andreya started working full time at the community center preschool and after-school program where she'd worked summers before, but she found that working there full time was emotionally draining. As she got to know the children and their family situations, she hurt for them. She'd never before imagined that an afternoon juice-and-crackers snack provided by the center might be dinner for a preschooler, that 8-year-olds might have to cook for themselves and their younger siblings because no one else would, or that mothers might sell their children's shoes to buy drugs. "You know it was like me going home knowing I'm gonna eat a full-course meal and this kid ain't." Sometimes she spent her own money to buy them treats. Often, she would come home grumpy, and then find herself crying in the shower. Though not meaning to, she took her feelings out on her family. Her mother accused her of "having an attitude" and told her, "You don't take your problems at home to work, and you don't bring your problems from work home." "I never understood that," she told us, meaning that her mother was right, but she wasn't old enough at the time to appreciate it.

In general, after the initial storm over her pregnancy died down, Andreya's relationship with her mother returned to the way it had been before except that Patricia expressed her feelings of closeness to her daughter in a new way—she developed pregnancy symptoms. "My mother, she had most of my morning sickness"—waking up dizzy, vomiting, and, in later months, with a huge hunger. Andreya asked Grandma Dorothy if it was possible that "someone you close to can get your morning sickness." Her grandmother answered, "Yeah, my mama got my morning sickness all the time." Andreya swears that her mother started having those symptoms even before Andreya confessed that she was pregnant. This is just one of the examples Andreya has given of her mother's sixth sense when it comes to her children. "She know each one of us like the back her hand." There were times when Andreya thought that she could outsmart her mother, but she was always wrong. Her mother had told her, "Girl, you will never out-beat me. Never. Not in a million years."

"She just like a mile ahead of me," said Andreya. "And then I'm thinking I'm doing something slick, because I know she asleep. I be like, I come in and lay down, take off my clothes like I've been in the house since, like, 9:00. She like, 'Girl, you just came in here off that porch and it's 11:30.' 'How do you know? You're asleep!?' I ask her. 'I know, she say.'"

Birth of Lavell

William was sure the baby would be a boy, and Andreya was sure it would be a girl. What money she could muster went toward lacy socks and other infant-sized "pink stuff." William was right—the baby was a boy. You couldn't say she was disappointed—her feelings for her son were so strong and so loving that "disappointment" is too strong a word to describe the twinge of regret she felt about the cute girl clothing she'd have to give away.

She named the baby Lavell Iman Jones. A couple of months before the birth, William had told her he wanted to name his son Iman, an African name his brother had suggested. Andreya had never heard of this name and didn't like it. She had agreed to it offhandedly, without really considering it, just to end the conversation. When the nurse asked her for the baby's name, Andreya said it was Lavell. She liked the sound of it and she knew a couple of nice men her mother's age named Lavell. When William came to the hospital and found out that his son's name wasn't Iman, he was angry. "What did you mean it's not Iman?" he demanded. A nurse came in and asked them to quiet down. "He said, 'I'm gonna walk away from here and when I come back his name better be Iman.' He left for three hours. He came back and Lavell's name was Lavell. Lavell Iman Jones." She'd compromised by using the African name for the baby's middle name. Though her mother didn't want her to, she'd also given Lavell William's last name, not hers. In the back of her mind was the thought that William might feel more responsible for a child who had his last name. William told her that if they had another son, his first name had better be Iman.

Andreya was confident in her mothering abilities. After all, she'd learned a lot about babies during her babysitting years. She figured she would stay home with Lavell for one school year. He would be 16 months old when the next September came around and she would go back to school. Making her mother and grandmother proud was still a goal. She didn't want just a GED. It needed to be a bona fide high school degree. In the meantime, she applied for Aid to Families with Dependent Children (AFDC), for which she was approved ($232 per month); the Special Supplemental Nutrition Program for Women, Infants, and Children (WIC), for which she was also eligible; and food stamps, which she was denied because, as an 18-year-old living in her mother's home, she didn't qualify. Instead, her mother's food stamps were increased to cover her, Tony, Kalia, and Lavell. After paying her mother $50 for household expenses, she had just enough for baby items, a few things for herself, some food to supplement what her mother bought, and bus fare.

Soon after Lavell was born, Andreya got a phone call from her father. His sister had told him that Andreya had had a child, and he was excited about the prospect of being a grandfather. He wanted to come over to see Andreya and his grandson. Andreya told him he wasn't welcome. "I told him, 'You can't really be a grandpa and you wasn't a father.'" Dismayed, her father pleaded for a visit. He told her she was making him angry. "How could I make you mad?" she asked him. "I should be mad at *you*. I shouldn't even *talk* to you. I mean, you left my mama and it was really hard because I had pneumonia the first 6 years of my life. I was in and out of hospitals. You never came to see me." Explaining her hard stance to us, she summarized her position, "His mother always be there for me. Always was around, his mother. *He* was never there for me."

She absolutely delighted in her baby and wanted him to have the best of everything, including all the stimulation her mother and her Parents as Teachers educator[1] said he needed. She had talked, sung, and even read to Lavell during her third trimester. Now she kept it up, even out in public. Sometimes it took an unusual measure of certainty and courage. When she was pregnant, her mother had told her she was silly; a baby couldn't hear you from inside the womb. Andreya was sure she was wrong. Now, out on the street, strangers thought she was odd—talking to a baby who couldn't talk yet. "People be thinkin' I'm talkin' to myself. They say, 'That's a shame. No offense but you're at a bus stop and you're talking to this little baby and the baby don't know how to talk and he don't understand.' I'm like, 'He do understand but that's none of your business. He not your child. You just mind your business. Keep your mind on the bus stop or whatever.'"

There was no problem getting her mother to accept the baby. Patricia was second only to Andreya in loving Lavell. "He's my heart. He's my idol," she replied when we asked her if she enjoyed her grandson. Many nights she took him to bed with her so he wouldn't cry. As for William, at first "he was always under me," Andreya recalls. He continued coming over many nights a week, and Andreya continued giving him dinner and washing his clothes. Sporadically, on no particular schedule, he gave her money. He told her she was doing the right thing, staying at home to take care of her baby and her man. He didn't want her to go back to school.

As devoted as she was to her child and to William, however, on many days Andreya felt cooped up. Some days she went over to her grandmother's apartment to help her with laundry, vacuuming, and

---

[1]Parents as Teachers provides in-home parenting education to parents of children under 3. A parent educator visits the parent(s) and child once a month to discuss child-rearing issues and to suggest developmentally appropriate activities. Andreya signed up for the service in the hospital right after she gave birth to Lavell.

dusting. Other days she sat at home. "It was just like he wanted me *not* to go back to school. He wanted me to always wait on him, depend on him. It was like I was bein' bored just sitting at home. I wasn't bored by my baby. I was just bored of sitting at home waiting on William."

William's visits were becoming more and more irregular. Many evenings she didn't know where he was. "And then he wouldn't come half the time. It was just like, if I wait here to wait on him, I'm gonna lose out a long life. And I knew if I set at home with a baby I wasn't gonna get nowhere without a education." The situation really worried her mother's oldest sister, Auntie Lucia. "Every time she came around I was just sitting at home watching TV. She said, 'Do you even go *outside?*' I mean, she got real upset with me. I said, 'Yeah, I go outside.' She was like, 'Well, I'm tired of looking at your face like that 'cause you not happy.'" Auntie Lucia went on to lecture Andreya about William. "She was telling me, 'Andreya, he's not right for you because a man wouldn't want you to sit. A good man would want his woman to look better than what she do, or to have more life, better things, a better jump on things in life.' And she made me look at things real different."

As the months wore on, other problems cropped up or became magnified. Lavell, it turned out, was seriously asthmatic—to the point where it was life-threatening. Andreya found herself running back and forth to the hospital, just as her mother had once done with her. Each time Lavell had an episode of gasping for breath, she would call William, and sometimes he would drive them to the hospital or meet them there. Sometimes it took a whole day of waiting in the emergency room or the clinic before Lavell was actually seen. But much more terrible than that was the fear that Lavell might die. Andreya almost never went to church, but she did a lot of praying every time her son had an attack. She begged her mother to stop smoking in the living room because she was sure the cigarette smoke exacerbated the child's breathing problems. When her mother wouldn't stop, Andreya started staying in her bedroom with the infant, towels pressed under the door so the smoke couldn't enter.

That wasn't the only reason she started hiding in her room: Another reason was that the emotional climate in the house was acrimonious. She thought of herself as grown, but Tony and Kalia were teenagers. "They think they know *everything*. Can't tell 'em nothing. There's always arguin' in the house about something." In addition to the strain of her relationships with these two, was the growing irritability of her mother. Andreya understood why: Patricia was exhausted from her night job at a 24-hour gas station, and her sons were breaking her heart. She had painful ulcers that she blamed on worry over their "doings." Quintus had just been sentenced to a 6-year term for drug dealing, and it was almost a relief to have him off the streets. In the past couple of years he'd been in two fights serious enough to require hospitalization. And it seemed that Tony was set to follow in his older brother's footsteps. He'd been suspended from school for assaulting a teacher, and it wasn't clear where he was getting the money he was spending on CDs and expensive shoes. Patricia just couldn't believe her "baby" was stealing or selling drugs and blamed it on the friends he'd been hanging out with. Andreya feared that Tony was either consciously or unconsciously trying to live up to the low expectations the family had of him because of what his father had done. She thought that if his father were around, Tony wouldn't identify so much with that negative image. In her view, Tony was acting out the behaviors imputed to his father in an attempt to feel close to him. (Listening to her, we wondered if she had ever read psychoanalytic theory. She hadn't.)

Rickie thought there was an additional reason for Patricia's mood swings. Once when he came over, the smell of marijuana was strong enough to make his eyes water. Andreya and Patricia blamed it all on Tony, but Rickie's social work experience gave him grounds to think otherwise. Andreya had told him that the first time Patricia caught Tony smoking pot, she was extremely angry and threatened him with all sorts of punishment. But later she had decided to tell him exactly what her own mother had told her and her siblings: If he was going to do it, he had better do it at home, in the basement, not outside and not in anyone else's home. Andreya knew he invited friends over to do just that. "I don't know very many moms that allow their kids to smoke marijuana in the house if they themselves don't already do it too," Rickie reasoned, adding that he thought marijuana withdrawals might well be "why there're arguments so much." Alcohol may also have played a role. On a couple of our visits, we saw whiskey bottles and beer cans in the dining room trash can.

A letter informed Patricia that there was a spot for Tony in "a school for bad kids" (she saw no use for euphemisms), but it was in a suburb and she didn't know how he could get there. She didn't have a car and, even if she'd had one, she got off work right at the time he needed to be leaving the house. "I'm barely living," she told us one day to express her anguish. And, Kalia, too, was a handful—skipping school, refusing to pick up after herself, staying out late, and always dressing like a boy. Andreya understood how much all this bothered her mother, but she still didn't think it was fair that she was taking it out on *her.*

Besides, she deeply resented the way her mother treated her differently than she treated Tony and Kalia. She complained that her mother was far too lenient with her brothers and cousin, and far too demanding of her. It wasn't fair that she, the good child, was made to do chores and they weren't. She couldn't understand why her mother put up with all the disrespect—"talking bad" and refusing to do as they were told. She knew her mother would never have stood for it if *she'd* acted that way. Reflecting on the situation several years later, Andreya made it clear how much this imbalance had bothered her. "And it was just like that was my biggest problem with my mama. That's why we always used to argue, because she'll come down on *me*. She'll make me wash Tony's dishes, make me clean up the bathroom when it's *his* week. If it's my week to clean up the kitchen, it's his week to clean the bathroom, but he didn't have to. I had to do both of them, and I didn't like it because I didn't think it was fair. She should have been twice as hard on Tony. He wouldn't be like he is today."

Patricia was well aware of Andreya's bitterness on this score, but she was not about to change how she was handling things. "I feel like you have to be tougher on the girl than on the boys," she told us one day when we were alone with her. We asked her why. "I had my first child when I was 15," she reminded us. "I want Andreya to be *better* than me. I mean I am a strong African American woman, but I want her to be *stronger*. Her friends was running around having babies at 14, 15. I mean lives was being ruined. I didn't want her to hang around those kids. And I wanted her to learn responsibility." When her children were little, Patricia ruled the household with an iron hand, but she didn't think she could *force* Tony to do the right things now that he was 16. Teenage boys, she said, would "go wilder" if you tried to "tame" them. "Boys will be boys," she said. "They have to learn from they mistakes."

As if all this weren't enough, Lavell was turning out to be quite a handful. He'd always been very active, afraid of little, and more than typically tolerant of pain. As an infant, for example, he'd continued to want to be held up to the birdcage even after the parakeet had pecked at his finger. And when Andreya took him to the hospital after he'd burned his finger on the iron, the nurses had remarked on how little the pain seemed to bother him. Now, as he grew into a toddler, he was happily getting into everything—taking handfuls of dirt out of flower pots to sprinkle on the floor, pushing glass dishes and figurines off the coffee table to shatter on the floor, "carving his teeth" into ornamental candles, and putting cigarette butts and empty beer bottles he found in the trash into his mouth. Sometimes Andreya caught herself wishing he were a little baby again. She'd been so anxious then for him to grow up, but now it seemed like it had been so much easier before he'd turned 1.

The steroids prescribed to control his asthma seemed to make matters worse. Andreya described him as "hyper" and uncontrollable after every dose, and decided that she wouldn't give him nearly as much as the doctor had prescribed. She also begged her mother to babyproof their home, but her mother insisted that this was *her* house and she was going to keep things out even if they were fragile because she wanted to enjoy them. And she didn't bother to dispose of trash right after she'd been smoking and drinking with her friends. "I hurt when my mama and her friends do that, and they know he gonna dig in the trash," Andreya said. Here was another reason for her to stay in her room with Lavell. It was the only way to keep him from breaking things her mother valued, making messes, and putting things he shouldn't into his mouth. Her mother didn't seem to understand. "Get him out of that prison," she would admonish Andreya.

During one of our visits with the family, Patricia justified her stance by pointing to two problems with Andreya's notions about babyproofing: First, they proved that Andreya was allowing her child altogether too much freedom and, second, they demonstrated her desire to have too much say in household matters. "You know, you just *ain't* going to rule my household, 'cause this is *my* home. I've been a parent this long, I've been that single parent, and just because you got a child, you're not going to do it. I'm still trying to build something and Lavell come down here breaking up little things, gifts I get from different people. I believe in *cherishing* stuff. I got stuff 28 years old in this house that I have been keeping. I've got a lot of memories in this house, and gradually he is breaking my memory stuff. You know he got a tendency to test the limits. *All* little kids do, you know. But you got to stop the child. Because I broke mine at an early age, I really did. My kids didn't touch *nothing* on *no* table." When we asked her how she got them not to touch, she chuckled and explained, "How'd I do that? 'Do-not-do-that' (spoken in evenly measured separate words). You can hit a kid, to a point, not bruise them, but let them know that it's a no-no. You know, you ain't got to hit a kid to make it hurt; you can hit them just to hurt they feelings. Let them know you don't do that, you know." She hoped that Andreya understood that she wasn't putting her and Lavell down when she told her all of this and that she wasn't "kicking them to the side or nothing like that." She just didn't want her things ruined.

Andreya *didn't* understand. She started dreaming of moving out. William suggested that they get an apartment together, but when she told her mother of her plans, her mother wouldn't hear of it. Repeatedly, she let Andreya know that she had no faith in the man or the relationship, "She's like, 'Ya'll staying *here.*' She didn't want me to get an apartment with him. She said, 'Andreya, you're gonna be right back here. You ain't gonna last or nothin'. He's gonna take you for everything you got.'"

A letter came telling Patricia that her house was being condemned. They'd lived in it for seven years and loved its spaciousness. They'd gotten "real tight" with some of the neighbors. There'd been yard sales and barbecues with them. One couple was always ready to babysit Lavell for free because they loved him so much. Patricia found another house just a mile away, but it would never be as good. For one thing, it was smaller. For another, although the block on which the house stood was quiet, something was always happening on the big avenue just two blocks away. "You can hear gunshots. Ambulance constantly. Police constantly. Fire trucks constantly. It's always something happening at the store."

Moreover, the "neighborhood thing" the family had enjoyed at the old place never happened at the new one. Even a year after moving into the new house, Patricia hardly knew her neighbors. "I don't mess around with nobody in this neighborhood. 'See you, hi.' 'See you, bye.' I mean, I go to work, come in, get somethin' to eat, and go to sleep. Rise, go to work, come back in, and I'm here. I ain't trying to meet nobody, see nobody or nothing like that. Not in this neighborhood." On the other hand, she also had reason to be glad they'd moved. A week after they'd vacated the old house, the second floor bathroom gave way, falling into the bedroom that had been Andreya's. The bathtub had fallen right where Lavell's crib used to be.

About a month after the move, Andreya made arrangements to go back to school. She had decided that the Job Corps was the right choice for her; she could get a high school diploma plus training for a job.[2] She thought training to become a certified nursing assistant (CNA) might be good. At the Job Corps orientation, she told the counselor that she was very serious about getting a degree, but that her son occasionally had life-threatening asthma attacks, so she might have to miss school some days.

Going back to school meant that she had to find child care. Holding Hands, a center within walking distance, seemed good and had an opening. Andreya started visiting it with Lavell for a couple of hours a day so that he would get used to it. She wanted to make the transition as easy as possible for him. As for transportation, William said that he would drive her and Lavell to the center every morning, and then drive her to school. He would also pick them up. He'd gotten a job in an auto parts store, and the hours would permit him to give her rides.

---

[2]Job Corps is a federally funded program that provides a high school education as well as job training. In order to earn a high school degree, students must complete all high school requirements in addition to all requirements for their "trade"—the job-specific training.

It was soon after she'd arranged everything so that she could attend Job Corps that Andreya found out about Early Head Start (EHS). The program was recruiting at a required meeting for Temporary Assistance for Needy Families (TANF) recipients on the new welfare reform rules. William drove her and Lavell to the meeting and said he'd wait to take them home. While standing in line to sign in, she was approached by Rickie, an Early Head Start home visitor. "How you doin'?" he asked. She answered that she was fine. "What's your name?" he asked. She didn't know many White men, but he seemed nice, so she told him her name. "That's a cute name," he noted. "Have you heard about Early Head Start?" "No," she answered. "Are you interested in early childhood?" he asked. Of course she was. "And he was like, 'Is it okay if I come do home visits?'" She told him, "I don't mind." She thought she knew a lot about babies from having babysat for 7 years, but she also figured that there was a lot more to know.

After she'd given Rickie some information on how to reach her, she told him that her boyfriend had brought her, but apparently William had already left. She needed to call him to come get her, but she only had a dime in her pocket. Rickie offered her a quarter. She accepted and walked down the hall to find a phone. On the way, she saw William, who hadn't left after all. She returned to the spot where Rickie had been so that she could return his quarter. She'd had a positive feeling about Rickie when she first met him, and what followed left an even better impression. "I said, 'I'm sorry. I gotta give you your quarter back.' He said, 'Oh, no. Don't worry about it.' I said, 'That was so nice!'" If he was so nice to a stranger, he probably did other good things, she thought. She decided to tease him a little. "And I was like, 'Do you cook for your wife?' And he was like, 'Yeah.' And I started laughing because usually men don't cook. He was like, 'What's so funny, Andreya, Miss Bradley?' I was just crackin' up. I said, 'You cook! I can't believe you cook!' You actually cook for your wife and your daughter?' He said, 'Well, I cook, yeah.' I was like, 'That is so *sweet!*' I said, ''Cause men don't cook! They don't even want to take out they trash. I never seen this! I haven't. Not a whole meal. They probably cook some hamburger—call it a day. No French fries, no side or nothin'.' He was like, 'You are really going all out to rag on me cooking!' I said, 'That is so *sweet!*'"

Rickie came over a week later for the first home visit. They chatted as he helped her prepare dinner. Watching a man cook put her in a very good mood. It was so odd yet so wonderful that she couldn't help laughing. He told her a little about his wife and infant daughter, and she told him about her life—about the fact that she was "a dedicated mother" and a "homebody," about her strong desire to move into her own apartment so that she could get away from the conflicts with her mother and younger brother and cousin, and about her plans to return to school. Over the course of the next several months of weekly home visits (every Tuesday at 5:00), Rickie and Andreya established a warm relationship. A sensitive observer of people, Rickie understood that he should go easy, never pushing her to talk, but being ready when she was ready. As she opened up, he was charmed by her sincerity and insight-fulness, by her huge love for Lavell, and by how appreciative she was of the child development ideas and explanations he shared. She was so open to new ideas, so reflective and willing to reexamine habitual ways of doing things.

She started telling him about interactions she'd had with people who "disrespected" her, such as the caseworker who had grilled her about William's whereabouts and threatened to cut off her payments if she didn't reveal why William's mother had custody of his daughter. In Andreya's stories, Rickie heard about real wrongs, but he also thought her tendency to react strongly and aggressively to every slight was counterproductive. He thought she would be happier and more suc-cessful if she could control her temper, let some things go, and speak politely even to people who upset her—especially if they were people in positions of authority. It would also help her as a mother.

As was characteristic of Rickie, he approached the issue directly and with humor. "You know," Andreya told us one day, "I used to get an attitude about everything, the way people do me, the way they talk to me, and I actually would go off on you." Quoting Rickie, she ex-plained how he'd helped her see a better way. "Andreya," he'd told her, "I'm not trying to be in your business but you need to just let it *ride* sometimes; let it *go*." Smiling, she recalled how she started to get mad at his comment. "And then I kind of *eased* up off of it. He's like, 'See, you about to get mad at me, wasn't you?' I *was!* I was about to tell him off and it's like, hold your tongue, Andreya. And he's like, 'Just *cope* with it.' He said, 'I know some people that can really drive you to the limits. You need to just lighten up a little bit.' And I started doin' that." Sometimes Rickie used teasing to check on how she was doing. "Have you got in any fights at school?" he asked her one day after she'd started attending Job Corps. "And I was like, '*Nooo!*' And he's like, 'Are you sure?' I'm like, 'Yeah! Why you ask me that?' He said, 'Because you got a *baaad* attitude.'"

He also told her that he didn't think she should be popping Lavell on the hand when he disobeyed—even if her mother had told her she should. Andreya listened attentively. Rickie's message that corporal punishment leads to increased aggressiveness in children made sense to her. She resolved to desist. It wasn't easy. "Oh, there's days I'm about to pull my hair out. I mean, it's like Lavell know what I'm sayin' and it's like, he don't pay attention to what I say. I be wantin' to hit him and it's like I gotta hold it in and I'll be holdin' my hand sometimes. I have so much problems in his behavior and I try not to pop him on his hand even though he needs it."

Her mother made it especially hard to follow Rickie's advice. In fact, Andreya partially blamed her mother for Lavell's "rowdy" behavior. When Lavell was tiny, her mother had taken him to bed with her whenever he cried at night. "My mama used to come and get him all the time. He'd sleep all night for her. With me he wouldn't sleep all night. I think the spoiledness started then." Even more troublesome to Andreya, however, was her perception that her mother and brother were needlessly hitting Lavell and calling him "bad." Andreya could understand tapping a toddler on the hand if he did something unsafe, such as touch a curling iron, but her mother was hitting him for "little minor stuff" such as rumpling her bed when he climbed on it. "You know it's teaching him to hit back. And he hits her back now. I really want my own place because I'm gonna have to start all over from scratch with him. This hitting, it's from her hitting him."

It wasn't just the hitting; Andreya also worried about the inconsistencies in the messages Lavell was getting. "Yeah, my mama might be grown. She might be my mama. She might be his grandma. But I can say no and she telling him yeah. And that's why he's like he is. He go to her every time I tell him don't do something. Or he can spit at me, and one time I hit him in his mouth and it's like he'll go run to her and she, 'Oh, we gonna get your mama.' And he smile. He knows if he go to Grandma, he not gonna get in trouble." What she seemed not to notice as she told this story was the fact that she was giving Lavell a mixed message—that hitting was not acceptable and yet that she would do it herself if sufficiently peeved.

Tony's influence was even worse. Love didn't seem to temper his violent behavior toward his nephew. The 15-year-old found the inquisitive child annoying and insisted that, in his role as uncle, he had the right to punish Lavell. Once he went so far as to push the toddler down the stairs. Often he slapped him. Andreya tried to convince Tony to use time-out instead—the way Rickie had suggested. "I'm his uncle. I can hit him," he replied. Andreya countered, "Wait a minute. He got one parent in this house, and one parent only." Her arguments fell on deaf ears.

The time came to begin her classes at Job Corps. She had been looking forward to getting out of the house on a regular basis, and she knew finishing high school was important not just for the sake of making her mother proud but, even more critically, so that she could get a steady job that would allow her to take care of herself and Lavell. She thought she'd try CNA training for a month, then the business clerical track, and then make up her mind between the two. Five weeks into the CNA program, she asked to switch to the business–clerical program but was told it was too late. She resigned herself to sticking out the CNA program even though her mother, who had worked for a while as a cook in a nursing home, had told her about the ways in which patients and staff mistreated each other. The more she thought about it, the more she didn't want to be part of that scene, but the training would at least result in a high school diploma. After graduation, she could decide if she really wanted to work in a nursing home.

Going to school was very difficult. Just getting there on time was a challenge. William had told her he would use his mother's car to come pick her up in the morning, but many mornings he didn't show up. That meant she had to take one bus to the child care center to drop Lavell off, then two more to get to the Job Corps building. Sometimes, even though she managed to get to the child care center on time, it was hard to leave in time for the next bus because Lavell would cry when he realized she was about to go. She took to waiting until he was focused on a toy or activity, and then sneaking out.

In addition, it was hard to keep up with all the assignments. Though Andreya loved reading to Lavell and she enjoyed magazines such as *Jet*, the reading level of the schoolbooks was higher, "It's kinda hard. You got a big ol' booklet with the three rings. And it's about this big. And the books be this thick and there be five of them. And it's a whole bunch of work. You gotta do the chapter, remember all the stuff, and then turn around and take a test. Some of the stuff you do forget 'cause it's a lot of stuff. It's like chapters, and it goes all the way to number 53, one of 'em. Turn around—take a test. If you miss it you have to pay for your next one."

To make matters worse, for several months the school could not provide books for everyone, and students were not allowed to use the photocopying machine. They had to take notes during class to take home to study.

Coping with schoolwork on top of the demands of caring for an active and often-sick child (not to mention her unhappy interactions with her mother and brother and her growing anxiety about William's on-and-off attentiveness) exhausted Andreya. "I'm working my tail off," she told us after detailing her daily routine: rising early, dressing, readying a reluctant Lavell for child care, rushing to be on time for school, running to pick Lavell up in the afternoon, making time to play with him at home, doing the housework her mother required, completing schoolwork, and getting Lavell's things prepared for the next day. Some days she was so tired, she didn't bring her books and notes home. Studying in the evening when she was so tired gave her migraines.

In addition, Andreya didn't find the teachers and counselors very helpful. One teacher urged students to ask for help when they needed it, but when Andreya asked for additional explanations, the teacher was likely to tell her to please wait and she'd get back to her, and then she would forget. Andreya understood that the teacher was overworked with too many students, but a lot of the material was hard for her, and she really needed some assistance. One time when she got stuck, Andreya asked a student who was ahead of her for help. The teacher told her not to talk in class.

What made things most difficult, however, was that the Job Corps faculty really didn't seem to understand what it meant to have an asthmatic child, or to be asthmatic oneself. She really didn't like to miss school, but sometimes she had to because she had to take Lavell to the hospital. She had a breathing machine for him at home and she knew how to use it, so she only took Lavell in when it was a true emergency. Unfortunately, that was fairly often. Sometimes while in class, she would get a note from the office that someone from the child care center had called because Lavell was having trouble breathing. When that happened, she ran out of the school as fast as she could. She didn't always stop to tell someone where she was going. One day, the director called Andreya into her office to talk about her attendance. The school counselor Ms. Moore also was present. Ms. Moore started the conversation, "It's really starting to be a bother because it's like every week you're at the hospital. This is like an everyday thing for you, huh?"

Andreya tried to explain. "I said, 'Well, if I could stop my son from getting sick, I would. You know, my son has asthma, and my son's life is more important than school. I can always come back to school, but I can't always have a son like the one I got.'" The director told her she should find a family member who could take him to the doctor so that she could come to school whether or not he was ill. "It's not that easy," Andreya told her. Her mother could take him some days, but not always, and all her aunts worked during the day. There really was no one else who could take him.

After listening to the two, Andreya began to realize that the director and the counselor just didn't understand what a child's asthma means to a mother.

"I said, 'Wait a minute. When I first started Job Corps and I was just in orientation, I made it clear to everybody that the only reason why I wasn't going to be here if I had some important business to take care of or if my son is sick. I can-

not stop him from getting sick. I can give him all the medicine in America—that don't mean he going to be well.' I mean, they act like I just make him as the excuse, because some of them girls do that, you know. My son's life is nothing to play with, and when they say his asthma is acting up, I'm running. It's not like I'm going to sit there and wait for my counselor to sign me out. I'm gone. What I supposed to do? I supposed to be, 'Oh, while I was at school, my son died.' No. 'You know, I was waiting on my counselor to give me a pass and my son died.' No. I don't look at it the way they look at it. They look at it like school should be more important than life itself, and I don't feel that way. I told her, 'I can always come back to school, but I can't always have a son that's going to be laughing and playing because asthma, it's like, when you have asthma attack, it's like breathing out of a straw. You know, a straw has a very small hole, and you don't get very much air out of it blowing in or out of it.' I said, 'Have you ever had a pop and you was through with your pop and still be sucking on the straw, but you never get nothing in your straw, and you notice there's just not very much air coming through that straw?' She was like, 'Well, I did that several times.' I said, 'Well, you try breathing through a straw for like 10 minutes, or even 3 seconds, and you tell me how you will feel afterwards.' I said, 'I know his chest hurt 'cause when my asthma acts up, my chest hurts, and he be crying.'"

Ms. Moore interjected, "Andreya, girl, you act like you're real upset." Andreya answered, "I am." She told us,

"I didn't have no attitude, but if I'd have had an attitude, I probably would have cussed her out. I took like a deep breath, and I said, 'I'm going to tell you something.' I said, 'My son is more important than Job Corps could ever be to me in life.' I said, 'Can't nobody give me back the same little boy I had at first.' And she's, 'Well, you really. . .' I said, 'No, wait a minute, listen to me.' I said, 'You think asthma is just like getting a cold, and getting a cold you take some medicine and the cold gone.' I said, 'Asthma is there with you all your life. It can trigger any time of the day, night, morning.' I said, 'And you don't think me staying up, running back and forth to the hospital and they keep telling you the same old thing, but every time you take your son home, it get worser and worser; you don't know when you fall asleep, you don't know if he's going to stop breathing in his sleep.'"

Andreya, thinking that the director had a skeptical look on her face, became angry. She told us, "And she thought I was just making a joke, clowning, and I was getting upset, because, here I am, I'm trying to work hard to get him to day care, go to school, and it's like she think I'm playing with her." Andreya got up to leave. At the door, she turned around. "'Job Corps will play a big part in my life. I'm not going to say it's not, but my son plays a more bigger role in my life than anything. I know I need my education. But right now my son, he's my first and main priority. I can't be here when he's sick. That's all.' And I just walked out."

Andreya started bringing in signed doctor's excuses with the exact times she arrived at and left the hospital. She brought in Lavell's medication as further proof. She even asked the doctors to call the school to verify that Lavell had been seen that day, and they complied. One morning Andreya called the school to say that her son was sick so she wouldn't be coming in. "Take him to the day care, tell them to give him his medicine, and you come on to school," the counselor instructed her. Andreya was appalled, and not only for her son's sake. She didn't think it was fair to take a sick child to the center where he could infect other children. She knew other parents did it, but she didn't think it was right.

Around this time, we called Andreya to arrange a visit. Thinking that we could save her the hassle of bus travel that one day, we offered to pick her up at Job Corps when it let out at 3:15, drive her to the child care center to pick up Lavell, and then drive them both home. She agreed to it. She told us to wait for her just inside the front door. We arrived a few minutes before the bell rang. A teacher came by. We explained that we were waiting for Andreya. A wave of students, mostly female, passed by. Andreya was not among them. Trying not to worry, we waited until the last student had left. The same teacher we'd talked to before came by again. She told us that Andreya must have left school early. "Well, you know Andreya," she said. "She dances to her own music."

We didn't think Andreya would stand us up, so we waited longer. Finally, a man who was in a little office by the door came out and asked if we were waiting for Andreya. "She left a message for you that she had to leave early," he said. We called Andreya's house. Kalia told us that Andreya was at the child care center. We drove there, certain that Lavell was ill. Sure enough, Andreya had gotten a call from the child care center, but the person who called her had gotten two names mixed up. It was Latelle who was sick, not Lavell. The incident perfectly illustrated Andreya's complaints about the school–family strains engulfing her.

There were days when she seriously considered dropping out, but Rickie reminded her how big the stakes were. She resolved to stick it out.

Though she tried to talk herself out of it, Andreya was still in love with William. On the days when he didn't come or call, she was sad. On the days when he did come, she was torn between resentment and joy. A few years later, reflecting on that time, she told us, "It was just like he was a piece of candy that I always craved for. I just . . . if I got to see him, I was happy." Sometimes she had sex with him, succumbing to her loneliness and wishful thinking that the relationship was righting itself. And it wasn't just for herself that she wanted him to come over; she strongly believed that her son needed a father in his life.

William wasn't one to talk about feelings much, but she could tell something was really bothering him. One big problem, she knew, was that he'd been fired. She was fairly certain that she had caused him to lose his job. Lavell had recently had an asthma attack. She'd tried the breathing machine twice, and then called the hospital when he started turning blue. The nurse had told her to bring him in immediately, so she'd called the shop where William was working. "This is an emergency," she'd told the manager. "William needs to come home. His son is very sick. He's having an asthma attack." The manager told her to stop calling or William would lose his job. Distraught, Andreya turned rude. She cussed him out. He hung up. She called again, crying and pleading. William got the message and left work to give her a ride to the hospital. The next day the manager told him he was fired.

He got a job in a discount store stockroom, but it wasn't the kind of work he wanted. In addition, it was only 7 months before the store closed down. At the employment agencies he went to, he was told there would probably be no hiring in the industrial or contracting sector until the summer. He started collecting unemployment compensation, but didn't feel good about it. He felt like it was "free money"—money he hadn't earned and didn't deserve.

"He be upset half the time," Andreya told us. Acknowledging the complexity of the situation and her own possible contributions to it, she continued. "And sometimes *I* just can upset him. Just 'cause, you know, when he don't come around, it pisses me off. And when he come around it's like me going off on him, and I know he's not ready for that, and I see the more and more I do that, the farther and farther he stay away. It's just that I'm so used to doing it that I just automatically do it. It's like it's always some argument." Sometimes William would call in the evening and ask what Lavell needed. She'd tell him she was nearly out of diapers. He might bring some by, play a little with Lavell, and leave. Many days, however, she didn't see or hear from him at all.

Lavell enjoyed roughhousing with his father during his sporadic visits as long as Andreya was also around. He would begin crying the minute Andreya left them alone together. Andreya understood that he didn't feel secure with his daddy and blamed it on his unpredictable mix of visits and absences. As the next chapter reveals, things weren't about to become any easier.

6

Mother of Two

Jean M. Ispa and Elizabeth A. Sharp

When she was 20 and Lavell was 20 months, Andreya realized that she was pregnant again, although she didn't want to admit it. Her grandmother Dorothy knew and just shook her head at her granddaughter's denials. "I can see the heartbeat right now and I feel it," she said. "Old people know what they talking about."

Andreya was afraid to tell her mother, who she was sure would point out the folly of having another child with a man who wasn't taking care of his first with her. During one of our phone conversations with Andreya at this time, she told us that she was so depressed her hair was falling out. Deeply distressed, she asked Rickie what he thought she should do. Maybe she should run away, she said. Take Lavell with her and move to another state. Rickie offered four pieces of advice: 1) She should tell her mother right away because she was probably hurting her more by not telling her. Besides, he said, her mother probably already knew but was waiting to hear it from Andreya. 2) She shouldn't move away because there were too many people in town who loved her, even if she couldn't see it now, and she needed their support. 3) She should keep going to Job Corps because she really needed her education. 4) She should carefully examine her relationship with William. Did she really think he'd be there for her in a year? In two years? In four?

That evening, Andreya confessed to her mother that she was pregnant. To her surprise, Patricia's reaction was nothing like her reaction to the first pregnancy. "You went back to school which I didn't think you was gonna go back to school," she said. "You in a job training that guarantees you a job. So I ain't mad at ya." She did, however, point out that Andreya was responsible, too, for what had happened. She couldn't just blame William. "It's not just his fault. It's your fault too." Patricia still did not approve of William; her hostility toward him was palpable. She couldn't stand his on-again, off-again support of Andreya and Lavell.

Although she was relieved by her mother's reaction to the pregnancy, Andreya could not shake her depression. She didn't want another child right now. And although William told her that he was excited by the news, she knew that he would not be the partner or father she wanted him to be. Her doctor and a friend mentioned abortion, but William told her not to do it. He wanted this baby, he told her. One day she got her courage up and called the abortion clinic. When the receptionist answered, however, Andreya panicked and told the woman that she had the wrong number and hung up. When she talked about the possibility of abortion with her mother, Patricia was shocked. "You're going to do *what?*" she asked in disbelief. Patricia thought that abortion was morally wrong, and she and her sisters told Andreya to have the baby and then get her tubes tied. Andreya prayed for a miscarriage, but when it didn't happen by the end of the third month, she decided that "this baby is *meant.*"

Things did not look up during the rest of the pregnancy. Tony was arrested for stealing and had to live in a halfway house. Grandma Dorothy said it was a relief to have him there. Patricia's ulcers flared, and she was fired for missing too many days of work. Andreya knew her mother was unhappy but found it hard to reach out to her when she herself hurt so much. Besides, she was upset that even though she thought she acted like an adult, her mother treated her like a little kid. "I don't act like no kid and I feel I'm taking on a very big responsibility," she said. Andreya thought the fact that she was buying things for the entire family like detergent and doing all her own laundry and Lavell's, showed that she was an adult. Why should she also have to clean up after Kalia? Why wouldn't her mother help more with Lavell? "You know, she just want too much from me," she told us.

Financial issues also came between Andreya and Patricia. For a couple of months, Patricia paid the bills using her "income tax money."[1] The employment agencies she went to kept telling her about jobs in the suburbs, but without a car she had no reliable way to get there and back. Finally, she found a job in the stockroom of a downtown drugstore. She liked working days instead of nights, but she didn't know if she could keep the job long because something in the drugstore base-

---

[1] Andreya, like the other mothers we interviewed, calls the Earned Income Tax Credit (EITC) "income tax money." The EITC was created in the 1970s by President Ford and expanded in the 1990s by President Clinton. It is meant to help low-wage workers with one or more children get back some or all of the federal income tax withheld from their paychecks. Some families, such as Andreya's, are eligible to receive more money from the IRS than they put in. Grandparents (like Patricia) caring for their grandchildren may claim the credit if their children do not. One of the few antipoverty programs with bipartisan support, it lifted 4.8 million people, including 2.6 million children, above the poverty line in 1998.

ment, where the stockroom was, aggravated her allergies. Anticipating that she might have to quit this job and knowing there would soon be another mouth to feed, Patricia told Andreya that after her baby was born, she would have to increase her contribution to the household from $50 to $100 a month. Andreya was upset not only by this greater demand, but also by the fact that very often her mother did not include her in decision making about purchases. When they went grocery shopping together, Patricia nixed many of Andreya's choices, saying they were junk food. Andreya didn't think pudding, fruit cups, Jell-O, and cheesecake ingredients were junk food. And Patricia would buy Lavell candy even though Andreya didn't want him to have it. Often Patricia went to the grocery store when Andreya was in school; Andreya took this as a deliberate attempt to do the grocery shopping without her input. It really bothered her that the government sent her food stamp allotment ($190 per month) to her mother instead of directly to her. (When both parents and their children under the age of 22 qualify for food stamps and live together, food stamps are issued in the parents' names.) Sometimes Andreya was so broke that she had to swallow her pride and ask her mother for money to buy diapers. Her mother often responded with a question: "Where's his daddy?" Andreya thought her mother should understand that she had tried to call William but couldn't find him. Her mother's words exacerbated the pain she already felt because of William's neglect of her and Lavell. She stopped telling her mother when William did come around and give her something for Lavell because she knew her mother would then say that she didn't need her help.

In the heat of some of their arguments, Patricia told Andreya that she should kick her out of the house the way her mother had kicked her out. She would always take it back, but Andreya worried that one day she'd really make her leave. Rickie had told her that although in the past homeless people had priority in obtaining Section 8[2] or public housing, in the spirit of Welfare Reform, priority was now going to people who were in school or working. He thought something might come through for her soon and took her to see some apartments that had Section 8 approval. There was one complex she liked, and she was willing to take the available one-bedroom apartment, but the Section 8 regulations stipulated that families with two children could only rent two-bedroom apartments. No two-bedroom apartments were vacant. The only two-bedroom apartment she was offered was in a crime-infested housing project she'd be afraid to live in. She contemplated moving into a homeless shelter, but decided that the atmosphere there would be even worse for Lavell than the atmosphere at home.

---

[2]Section 8 provides government rent subsidies for low-income families.

Moving in with other relatives or with friends was out of the question because no one had the room. Andreya resented the fact that she helped her aunts and friends by babysitting for them and even lending them a dollar here and there, but they hardly ever reciprocated. Sometimes she felt that her aunts favored their nieces over Lavell and their other nephews. The nieces got all sorts of gifts of clothes and toys, but the boys didn't.

Perhaps the worst thing, however, was her discovery that William had another woman. She'd suspected as much but tried to deny the evidence. There had been signs such as a woman's shoes in William's car and crumbs in Lavell's car seat—as though another child was using it. And when William did spend the night with her, he'd leave two hours before he was due at his new job at a used car lot, saying that he was afraid to be late. One time, however, his boss called to ask why he hadn't been showing up. In addition, someone had started calling the house and hanging up if Andreya answered. "Andreya, why can't you see it?" her mother asked. Two years later, Andreya would explain her blindness, "When I seen what my mama was really actually saying to me all this time, I realized that I couldn't see past love."

She found out for sure about William's infidelity during the eighth month of her pregnancy. She went to his house to pick up some diapers she had left in his car. When she arrived, Tessa, William's sister, was in the living room braiding a woman's hair. Nervously, Tessa introduced the woman as her friend Sonya. Then Andreya noticed something covered with receiving blankets. When it moved, she asked what it was. Tessa took away the blankets and Andreya saw a 1-month-old baby—Sonya and William's baby.

Andreya left abruptly, forgetting why she had come. A block away, she realized that she'd forgotten to get the diapers but she didn't want to go back. She decided to walk to Grand Street, where the stores were. She'd buy diapers with the few dollars she had in her pocket. At the street corner, the light turned green and she stepped out into the street in a despondent daze. A car running a red light flew by, missing her by an inch, and then slowed down. "What the hell? Was you gonna hit me?" she yelled after it. "Black bitch," the driver, who was White, yelled back. Suddenly a full soda can hit her. Turning around, she saw a group of skinheads smirking at her. "You black nigger," they taunted.

She went home crying. When her mother asked why her head was bleeding, Andreya was surprised; she hadn't realized she was bleeding. As her mother tended to her, Andreya asked, "Why a lot of people still hate? I don't hate nobody. I mean I thought the purpose of Black history, the purpose of Dr. Martin Luther King, I thought all this had stopped." Her mother didn't have an answer.

Andreya told us this story in response to our question about her experiences with racism. We also wanted to know what she planned to teach her children about Black–White relations. "I'm gonna tell them they shouldn't hate," she said, and then she told us that she saw the problem of stereotyping very broadly—not confined to prejudice about race and not limited to Whites' negative assumptions about Blacks. She'd listened to Blacks make fun of Whites for adopting Black styles and tastes and didn't think that was right either. "I'm gonna tell my kids don't disrespect or misjudge somebody because of race or clothes or hairstyles. How could I say, 'Oh, Jean got a Black girl hairstyle. What is she doing with that?' I can't judge you for how your hair is or how you dress. That's like if you see me in a T-shirt and some sweatpants and you say, 'Oh, that's a project girl.' You can't say that. It's to each his own."

When Andreya went into labor, she called Tessa, hoping against hope that she would locate William and that William would drive her to the hospital. That didn't happen. Tessa drove her to the hospital but didn't stay. The baby was another boy. Andreya's first reaction was to cry from disappointment—she had so much wanted a daughter. As was the case after Lavell's birth, she'd have to give away the girl clothes she'd bought (after a false sonogram reading indicating that it was a girl). But, also like the first time, her heart melted when she saw her newborn son. She asked that he room-in with her and wouldn't let the nurses take him away except for diaper changes and bathing. His name would be Kevon Bradley. This child would have *her* last name, not William's. The doctor, an African American woman, didn't think she should name him Kevon. She suggested a more mainstream name like Jordan, but Andreya preferred Kevon. She understood that the doctor thought a name like Kevon might make life a little harder for the boy, but she thought he would be able to handle it. Besides "Jordan" didn't sound like a part of her.

When a nurse asked her when she thought she'd be coming back to the maternity ward, Andreya told her, "Never. I ain't having no more kids. . . . I have my two I want." "Oh, you can have another one," the nurse offered, "you don't have a little girl." Andreya replied, "Oh, well, life is done. I got two boys. Evidently, it wasn't meant for me to have no girl." The nurse shook her head, "Are you sure about this?" Andreya was sure. In fact, she wanted to have her tubes tied, but when she called to schedule the procedure, she was told she was too young, that tubal ligations are not performed on women under 25.

On the third day after Kevon's birth, the doctor told Andreya she could go home, but Kevon had to stay because he was breathing too fast. They suspected asthma and needed to monitor him. Andreya couldn't bear the thought of leaving him behind. She'd had to leave Lavell at the hospital for several days after he was born, and she remembered how anguished she'd been at the separation. She pleaded with the doctor to let her stay too. Two more days went by, and the doctor told her he would have to discharge her even though Kevon should stay. Again she begged, this time for permission to take Kevon home with her. She explained that she'd had asthma since she was 12, and that her older son was asthmatic; she knew how to deal with it. The doctor relented, telling her to make sure to watch her son closely.

Her bedroom was cramped now with her bed, a toddler bed, a crib, and a dresser. Some of Lavell's toys were kept under the crib and others had to go down to the basement. Things were better now with her mother but they weren't perfect. Patricia had been taking care of Lavell while Andreya was in the hospital, and now fully accepted her new grandson, just as she had accepted Lavell. Tensions over smoking, child-rearing philosophies, chores, and money, however, were always just below the surface. Her room was where she and the boys spent a lot of their time.

Lavell would say to Kevon, "I love you, brother," but Andreya worried about the rough way he handled the newborn. Once, for example, he picked Kevon up by the head and carried him to his grandmother. Andreya was sure he meant no harm; he was just too young to understand how to be gentle. She decided to buy him a baby doll. She encouraged him to pick the doll up and carry it around instead.

She told her caseworker that she now had two children, and her monthly Temporary Assistance for Needy Families (TANF) allotment was raised to $292. She steeled herself every time she had to talk to the caseworker. She'd had to sit in the waiting room for almost 5 hours the first time she'd applied for cash assistance, and then she'd had to endure questioning about William and his mother. She felt bad, knowing how she was perceived. "They said we must come sign this thing saying we work or do something with our time. I mean they complain if we do set at home with our kids and take care of them. They complain when we don't. It's hard and, you know, I'm entirely occupied with my kids. I mean, if I work *and* go to school, I be harmin' my kids. You know what I'm sayin'; it's people who abuse welfare, but most people don't. They really need it. And you know, if you just give people a chance and let them get on they feet, they find a job. It'll be okay." Rickie's lessons on taking things more calmly helped. Despite usually being "the type of person if you don't show me no respect, I'm not going to show you none," she maintained her composure with the caseworker.

For 2 months, William neither visited nor called. When he finally called to say he'd been in jail, Andreya wondered if it was for drug activity. When he came over, he played a little with Lavell but wouldn't touch Kevon. The baby wasn't his, he said. This hurt Andreya; she challenged him to a blood test. William agreed to it, but on the appointed day, he didn't show up. Over the course of the next several weeks, Tessa would occasionally pick up Lavell so he could spend some time at his father's, but she wouldn't take Kevon. Maybe her brother had convinced her that the baby wasn't his, or maybe she didn't want to ruin her relationship with Sonya. Then one day Andreya told Tessa that this wouldn't do: "There's no more come and get one and don't come and get the other. Because they brothers. They have the same father and I'm not about to go through 'I think this is my nephew and this is not my nephew.'" Her complaint didn't do much good; Tessa continued to ignore Kevon.

Andreya, now 21, tried to convince herself that she no longer had any romantic interest in William—that the only reason she wanted to maintain contact with him was to give her boys a father. Her efforts didn't seem to be working. When we visited her 4 months after Kevon's birth, she seemed depressed and alienated. When we asked her to fill in a social "Support Wheel,"[3] a form on which she was to put people close to her in the center of a series of concentric circles, she said that only her sons, her mother, Rickie, and we (the researchers) could go in the middle. She wrote William's name near the edge of the paper, indicating that he was someone who hurt her. Later that day, over dinner in a restaurant, she told us that another young man, Jimmy, was showing interest in her. Lavell liked him and he was good at making her laugh, but she just didn't trust men enough to develop another relationship. Besides, romance wasn't what was important right now. "I'm trying to get on my feet, to be working at my career. I'm trying to not let anything distract me."

A couple of months after Kevon was born, Tony returned home from the halfway house. His presence in the house made life much more difficult. He had not reformed. Andreya told us that he left the house every morning, but that she wasn't at all sure he was going to school. When we asked Patricia about it, she said, "He better go. Education is everything." In truth, however, she wasn't sure either. Then there was the continuing issue of marijuana use. Tony had gone back to using the basement as a smoking spot for himself and his friends.

Even more troubling to Andreya was Tony's behavior with 2-year-old Lavell. Sometimes he would deliberately teach his nephew cusswords, instructing him to repeat them after him. Then he would threaten him saying, "Man, you better stop cussing or I'm gonna whup you."

---

[3]See Chapter 12, Figure 12.1.

Andreya would tell him he had no right to whup her son, and that it was he who was teaching him the cusswords in the first place. Moreover, didn't he realize that Lavell was at an age when children imitate everything they hear, so he should really watch his language around the child? Her words were to no avail.

Meanwhile, Lavell's behavior was becoming more of a problem. Not only was he very active; he was becoming increasingly destructive and aggressive. Sometimes his pinches, hits, and bites seemed to come out of nowhere. He might be perfectly pleasant one minute, and then without warning strike whoever was nearby. His expression was often gleeful during these episodes; it seemed he thought that it was fun to hurt other people. Andreya found herself feeling annoyed with him and helpless. When we'd first met her, when Lavell was barely 1, we'd been impressed by their relationship. Though there'd been lots of "No, don't do that" in response to his explorations, there also had been many playful, loving exchanges. Now things seemed to have soured a great deal. She hated feeling this way about her child. She blamed her mother's and Tony's whuppings and mixed messages, William's absence, and the bad examples Lavell had seen in child care. She also wondered if the steroids she was supposed to give him when she saw an asthma attack coming on contributed to his out-of-bounds behavior.

She was disturbed especially because one of her goals as a mother was to raise children who were polite. In answer to our question, "What do you want your kids to be like when they're older?" she had replied without hesitation, "Very respectful. Very mannered, because that's a big turn-off to me, kids that are not respectful. I'm steady trying to teach Lavell, 'yes ma'am,' 'no ma'am,' 'sorry,' 'can I please have some water,' 'thank you,' stuff like that." One way she was accomplishing this, she said, was by showing *him* respect. "Give kids respect and you get it back," she told us. We indeed saw that she often prefaced commands with "please" and thanked Lavell when he complied. She also insisted that he say "please" when he asked for something and "I'm sorry," or "excuse me" when he did something wrong. In addition, she thought it important that she apologize for her own infractions. "Because if I don't do that then he's gonna be like, 'Well, my mama said it so I can say it, it's okay.'" Clearly, however, the emphasis on politeness wasn't making him respectful in the true sense of the word.

Calling Lavell "rambunctious," Rickie suggested that the boy needed more consistency in the messages he was getting about appropriate behavior. Rickie had noticed that Andreya was overusing words like "no" and "stop," and that she often threatened Lavell with a variety of consequences (e.g., having to take a nap, not getting to watch a favorite video), but that she rarely carried them out. Lavell might be prohibited from doing something one minute yet allowed to do it another. Reflecting on a conversation they'd had on this issue, Andreya recalled something Rickie had said to her, "Lavell was your firstborn and you probably didn't discipline him right on time all the time. He's more used to you telling him to do something and not following through than he is to your following through. And to him the rules change every day."

Rickie realized that it would be hard to refrain from corporal punishment when Tony and Patricia were not to be deterred, but he told Andreya it would be so much better if Lavell weren't whupped or even popped; he was learning that the way to get what you want is through force. He assured her that alternatives to corporal punishment—redirecting, offering choices between two equally acceptable behaviors, praising good behavior, giving reasons for her requirements, using "positive language" (wording commands so that the focus is on what the child *should* do instead of what he was not allowed to do)—would work if consistently applied. He told her that these strategies took time, that they were not quick fixes, and that they needed persistence. He gave her a pamphlet discussing the fact that sometimes parents, like toddlers, have tantrums and suggesting ways to maintain self-control.

Andreya agreed with Rickie. In fact, one time when we asked her what she'd gotten out of Early Head Start, she told us that Rickie had given her good strategies for dealing with children. "Most single parents, they cuss they kids out and whup them all the time for little petty stuff. He just give me better ideas than what I already been doin' and it help me out more than anything." But sticking to those good ideas was difficult. Her emerging understanding of effective "positive guidance" techniques sometimes conflicted with her immediate visceral reactions to Lavell's misbehavior. During one home visit she started crying, and when Rickie asked what was wrong, she sobbed, "I'm sitting up here whupping him for hitting somebody and I ain't doing nothing but teaching him how to hit."

A year or so later, talking about Andreya's approaches to discipline, Rickie told us,

"She's like a sponge. I mean any information that I share with her, she retains it. It may not be practiced, but she can think back on what she should have done in a situation. Like instead of positive reinforcement or giving choices, she'll give Lavell the swat on the behind and sit him down forcefully. Then once we talk about it, she can let you know what she could have done instead. It's just that split-second decision making that she does. It's, you know, that Band-Aid approach. Lavell is such a force to be reckoned with. We talk about how a lot of

that comes from inconsistency. About how, you know, she deals with it one way
for a while and then decides that she'll try something else. She tries it, but it's
always back to the swatting or slapping the hands or raising the voice real loud."

Rickie acknowledged that the home environment presented a significant obstacle. Andreya's confidence in gentler techniques was under-
mined when almost everyone around her was telling her and showing
her the opposite.

It wasn't just family members whose ideas conflicted with Rickie's.
During one of her visits to the hospital, Andreya turned to her pediatrician for advice on behavior management. Like Rickie, Dr. Gates was
a believer in the importance of consistency in rules and follow-through.
She differed with him, however, on the subject of corporal punishment. She told Andreya that she needed to discipline Lavell—to use
spankings in conjunction with time-outs. Saying "don't listen to Tony"
and "please" over and over with no consequences for disobedience was
teaching Lavell that she was just playing a game. According to Dr. Gates's
philosophy, you "Say it one time, hit him on his bottom, and say, 'Here,
sit down.'" The doctor demonstrated that Lavell could be made to sit still
until told to get up. Andreya was impressed. "She did that, 'Lavell, sit
down' and he didn't get up until she told him to get up," she said. "So,
I started trying it and Lavell started doing what I asked."

Money was another large issue. Out of her $292 per month TANF
money, she had to give her mother the $100 she now required. The
$192 that was left had to cover diapers, clothing, toddler books and
toys, personal care products, food not covered by the family's food
stamps, bus fare, occasional video rentals, and medical needs. Medicaid
paid for most of their health care bills, but not all. For example, one
month an inhaler that was supposed to last a month didn't. By the end
of every month, she was strapped. She asked Rickie to give her a ride
to a discount store so that she could buy candy for her "candy store."
Rickie gave her the ride, but just once; he didn't want her to start expecting him to take her places. Andreya made a little money selling
candy to neighbors and relatives.

William told Andreya that he wasn't working, but his sister Tessa
told her that he *was*. Andreya wondered if he was selling drugs or if
he was just lying to her so she wouldn't ask for child support. In any
case, the only time he gave her money during the 6 months after
Kevon's birth was when he came over unexpectedly while she was
bringing in groceries, helped her bring them in, gave her $40, and sug-
gested that they might have sex again. She refused. "I laid my laws
down with William. I told him simply we couldn't have no relationship
far as me and him." However, she left the door open for him to come

over to be a father to their sons. "I still have to talk to him for his kids," she told us. "I'll be his associate for life but only reason why is because of my kids. It wouldn't be nothing farther." When she told him that, he replied with two warnings. The first was that if she felt that way, he saw no need to take care of Lavell. The second concerned her potential relationships with other men. "Don't you ever mess with nobody else and let my son call him daddy," he said. "If I can't have you, nobody can."

Nevertheless, William started coming over some evenings, taking Lavell over to his home, and bringing him back to her by bedtime. Andreya was glad Lavell was getting to spend some time with his father, but she didn't want him to spend the night at his place. She suspected Sonya wasn't very nice to him. It also continued to bother her that William would barely look at Kevon.

Tension with her mother over resources continued. In addition to the ongoing problems, a new one surfaced when Patricia claimed Andreya, Lavell, and Kevon on her Section 8 application. Patricia wanted to qualify for a large house like the one they'd had before, but Andreya wanted the right to apply for public housing or a housing subsidy on her own. She wanted to live apart from her mother and brother, not with them. That would be impossible if her mother claimed her as a dependent.

The Job Corps counselor had told Andreya that she could take a maximum of 6 months maternity leave after Kevon's birth, but she wanted to take only 2 so that she could graduate as soon as possible. To do that, she had to face the problem of child care. She'd become dissatisfied with Holding Hands; she didn't think they kept the place clean enough. Some days it even smelled, she told us. She also feared for Kevon's safety if she were to enroll him there because a baby cousin of hers had come home from Holding Hands with scratches on her face. Infants and toddlers were together in one room, and in general there didn't seem to be good monitoring of the children or adequate activities to keep them busy. Andreya thought that Lavell's aggressiveness was in part a result of the poor quality of the care he'd received at Holding Hands. We had to agree. When we went there to observe, we saw a room full of wandering children and teachers who paid little attention except when one of the children cried.

A new child care facility was opening in the building that housed Early Head Start, and Rickie strongly suggested that Andreya enroll her children there. Between funding provided by the state and some additional help from Early Head Start, she wouldn't have to pay anything and the care would be so much better than what she could find in her neighborhood. Andreya seriously considered the offer but then declined. Taking her children to that center would mean standing at two bus stops (she'd have to transfer once each way) and she feared the consequences.

"I wanna go to that center, don't get me wrong, but I can't afford to take my kids out in this weather; they have asthma. I'll be at the hospital every day. I can't keep on getting on the bus with them and getting off and getting on and they all wrapped up, and then they gonna have a cold 'cause when you're wrapped up and you sweat you get a cold. Like I told Rickie, I'm taking a big chance on my kids getting pneumonia. It's not that I'm making excuses not to go, but I can't take no risks like that because I don't have nobody to help me. Yeah, my mother'd help me from time to time, but she's not supposed to be their everything, everything."

The center, unfortunately, was not providing transportation, and she certainly couldn't afford cab fare.

Patricia had quit her job at the drugstore because her allergies had been acting up there. She had gotten a job at a nearby child care center, and Andreya decided to enroll her children there. After all, they'd have their grandma close by.

Andreya returned to school 3 months after Kevon was born. The baby's illnesses made it impossible to return after 2 months, as she'd planned, but at least she hadn't taken the full 6 months that Job Corps allowed. She'd actually finished the requirements for her high school diploma before she'd had Kevon. She'd wanted so much to graduate then, but the rules were that you had to finish both the high school requirements and "the trade" (certified nursing assistant [CNA] requirements, in her case) before you could get your diploma. So now she took only CNA classes even though that wasn't the kind of work she wanted. It was lucky that she'd completed the high school requirements before Kevon was born. Shortly after she re-enrolled, a wall in the room used for the high school classes collapsed and the program was suspended until it could be repaired.

As before, going to school was hard—even harder now that she had *two* frequently ill children. Twice in one month Kevon was diagnosed with pneumonia. That was on top of all the asthma attacks. Even when both children were healthy, mornings were a scramble getting them to child care and herself to the Job Corps building on time. Every school morning, she'd wake up at 5:30 and quickly get herself ready. Then she'd change and dress Kevon and give him a bottle so that he wouldn't be fussy before he was fed at the child care center. At 6:00 she'd wake Lavell up. Often he was sleepy and didn't want to get up; she'd have to struggle with him. Then she'd fill the diaper bag with bottles and baby food and give Lavell breakfast because he didn't like the breakfasts served at the center. Some days she was so tired she could hardly keep her eyes open. She told us about a time when a teacher told her to listen carefully because what she was about to say was very important, but she fell asleep anyway.

Evenings also were hectic. She'd come home to a full house, make dinner for herself and her children (and anyone else who asked for food), eat and then feed the children, wash dishes and mop the kitchen floor, wash soiled clothes, pack clothing changes and diapers for the boys to have at the center the next day, watch some TV, study, read to the boys and play with them, and then put them to bed. Lavell's bedtime was unpredictable—if he hadn't slept during naptime that day, he'd be ready for bed at 7:00. If he had slept, it might be 10:00 when he went to bed. Often it was a struggle to get him in bed. Andreya noticed, however, that on the nights when William was over, Lavell went to bed without a fuss.

Frequently Andreya stayed up until 1:00 A.M. finishing chores and catching a few moments to herself. Rickie suggested ways to manage her evenings so she could get the sleep she needed. He brought her some recipes for quick dinners. Simplifying meal preparation and cleanup would surely help. She agreed that setting an earlier bedtime for herself should be a goal. Rickie had taught her the value of short-term, attainable, "everyday" goals. Before, she used to set herself grand goals but would never meet them. Rickie commented to us that he couldn't imagine coming home to all the hubbub in that house and having to get children fed and settled down. (The hubbub was from Tony and Patricia and their various friends and relatives.)

Andreya felt that she deserved some acknowledgment at school for the fact that she was "running here, running there, don't hardly get no sleep." Instead, she said, her counselor and the teachers "had an attitude" toward her. They wouldn't say "hi" to her in the hall. They wouldn't believe her when she told them that the buses weren't following their posted schedules—not until the counselor called the bus company and was told that it was true. Worse yet, she said, they still didn't understand her situation as the mother of two asthmatic children. There were even financial repercussions. Bus tokens were given out first thing in the morning on Wednesdays. If she was late or absent on a Wednesday because either she or one of her children was sick, she didn't get her tokens at all. She couldn't understand why they wouldn't hold her tokens for her. Her mother called the counselor to try to explain that Andreya really did have sickly children, but nothing seemed to change. Patricia told her daughter to try not to take it so hard, to let it go.

Then things came to a head. One morning Andreya woke up to Lavell's heavy wheezing. When she saw that he also had a fever, she called Job Corps to say that she'd have to miss school again. Lavell's condition alarmed even Patricia who took the day off so that she could accompany Andreya to the hospital. The diagnosis was asthma and bronchitis. They had just returned home from the emergency room, when Ms. Moore, the Job Corps counselor, came to their house. She told them that she was about to give Andreya five more penalty points and proceed with a meeting to have her expelled if it weren't true that Lavell was sick. Andreya gave her the hospital papers and showed her the tag around Lavell's wrist. Both had that day's date on them. Despite the corroborative evidence from the hospital, Ms. Moore was unconvinced; she continued talking about what she was going to do to have Andreya permanently dismissed for poor attendance.

We knew that Patricia could criticize Andreya up and down to her face, and even to others, but she would rush to her daughter's defense if she saw her attacked by outsiders. As Ms. Moore continued talking about the meeting she was about to call, Patricia snatched the hospital papers out of Andreya's hand and hurled them onto the floor. "If you want them, you pick them up," she dared the counselor. "My mama was getting mad," said Andreya. "Ms. Moore was acting like I was just lying, like we had just been out having fun all day." Emboldened by her mother's reaction, Andreya looked Ms. Moore in the eye. "Well, Ms. Moore, I ain't got no reason to lie and I wouldn't lie on my kid anyway if he wasn't sick."

"When are you coming back to school?" Ms. Moore asked. "When my son get better," Andreya replied. And then she said what she had said before, "I can always come back to Job Corps but I can't always have another son, not like this one. So therefore Job Corps ain't important to me right now." Patricia turned to Andreya and said, "You just tell her you be at school when your son gets well, and I'm going upstairs." Andreya ended this story with an insight into her mother. "My mama turned red and she got mad. And I know when she mad, but when she get red, she's just *pissed* off."

The threatened meeting never took place, but Ms. Moore's suspiciousness weighed on Andreya. Finally one day she went to Ms. Moore's office in tears. She told the counselor that she was continually upset by her and didn't understand why her [Andreya's] respectful attitude was not reciprocated. "I said, 'Ms. Moore, can I ask you a question?. . . I don't mean to be mean, but I've noticed you have been real hostile with me. I don't holler and I don't talk smart to you and you still treat me like this.' I told her, 'Most of these people talk to you like you ain't nothing and I give you the utmost respect and you still talk to me the way you do.' And I said, 'Well, this is how I feel. Ya'll want us to act like adults. I'm gonna treat you the same way you treat me. If you want respect, I only give it where it is due.'" Then she left the office. There was no contact between the two for a week. Finally, Ms. Moore called Andreya back down to her office. "Andreya, I want to know why you stepped up for yourself," she said. "'Cause I really got tired of you doing me like that," Andreya answered.

Things changed after that and we don't really know why. Perhaps Andreya speaking up for herself had made a difference. Perhaps Rickie's intervention helped. We do know that he called Ms. Moore around this time, explained his role in Andreya's life, told Ms. Moore that it was absolutely true that Andreya's children suffered from very fragile health, and assured her that Andreya was doing everything in her power to complete the CNA training. Andreya was serious about earning that diploma, he said, and was not making up excuses. Perhaps it was Ms. Moore's visit to the home that allowed her to better understand Andreya's situation. Whatever it was, her attitude and that of the other Job Corps staff took a dramatic turn for the better.

Ms. Moore started giving Andreya her bus tokens even if Andreya couldn't come in on a Wednesday. She told her not to worry if she had to be at the hospital and made efforts to buoy up Andreya's spirits. Andreya's account reflects her commitment to school, her stress, and Ms. Moore's new support. "And I just keep on thinking about what it was gonna be like if I didn't get up and go to school every day. It really irked me when my kids got sick and I couldn't go to school and it was like it put me more behind. And I felt like the more and more I try to go forward, I'm being pushed back, or I'm going in a circle and Ms. Moore was like, 'You need to stop putting yourself down like that. I think you make yourself depressed by saying that. If you stop telling yourself that, you can get ahead.'" One day after Andreya told her that she needed diapers but neither she nor her mother had the money, Ms. Moore went out and bought her a box.

The CNA teacher, Ms. Johnston, especially went out of her way to help. Concerned about Andreya's living situation, Ms. Johnston drove her to the Housing Authority to find out about available public housing, and then drove her to look at a housing project that had some vacancies. She worried about Andreya's transportation problems and started giving her cab money from her own pocket. Ms. Johnston told Andreya to use this money to get the children to their child care center. She would pick her up there and drive her to school, she said. Andreya tried several times to return the cab money, but the teacher insisted she keep it. She told Andreya that she was praying for her and every day asked Andreya how she and her children, and even her mother, were doing. This personal touch meant a lot to Andreya. Perhaps it was critical in moving her toward her graduation day. The next chapter takes us to that happy day and to the events of the year that followed.

7

After Moving Out

Jean M. Ispa and Elizabeth A. Sharp

Four months after Andreya told us about her confrontation with Ms. Moore and its aftermath, we arrived for our next scheduled visit. Andreya greeted us with good news: She had signed for an apartment in a new housing project and was very close to finishing school. The apartment was ready, but she hadn't moved in because there was no phone yet and she couldn't risk not being able to call the hospital in a medical emergency. During the following visit, she was the happiest we had ever seen her. She and the boys had moved into the apartment, a two-story, two-bedroom townhouse in a clean, attractive public housing project. For now, because she'd been a full-time student, she was living rent-free. When we asked her if she'd like to be upstairs or downstairs for the interview, she told us it didn't matter because she was happy in any room. "I'm just so happy!" she exclaimed while telling us about the move.

Not only had she moved, but she also had graduated. We'd known since our first meeting that Andreya is a wonderful storyteller, but the description of her graduation stands out in its animation and joy. Because of all the missed days, it had taken a couple of months longer than originally planned to complete all the certified nursing assistant (CNA) requirements. But now, just a few months shy of her 22nd birthday, she'd done it and she'd walked across that stage with justifiable pride. She'd gotten her hair and nails done and worn her best dress and high heels. When her friends saw her, they'd teased, "We thought you was going to come to the graduation in jeans and a T-shirt!" She'd shot back, "Yeah, right! This is the NEW IMPROVED ANDREYA!!"

An aunt, a great-aunt, her grandmother, and her friend Jimmy had come, but the main person in the audience as far as Andreya was concerned was her mother. To our question, "Is your mother really proud?" Andreya nodded, "She is. That's all she tells me: 'I'm so proud of you and that day at graduation.'" Andreya had to get to the building early to get her cap and gown. She knew her mother would be getting a ride from an aunt. As she sat with the other graduates at the front of the auditorium, she kept looking back over the sea of people, eyes searching for her mother. Three times the Job Corps director called her name to come to the stage to get her diploma, and each time, Andreya didn't budge because she hadn't spotted her mother yet. "They called my name three times and they said ANDREYA! I just sat there and I kept looking at the door. I got teary-eyed 'cause I couldn't see my mama. And then the girl sitting next to me, she's like, 'Ain't that your mama over there?' And I said, 'HI, MAMA! HI, MAMA!!' I'm waving to my mama and the girl was like, 'Girl, they calling your name! Go up there!' I didn't even hear them calling my name 'cause I was still hollering, 'HI, MAMA! I'm glad you here!' I was happy."

Much to Andreya's surprise, Lavell had accepted Ms. Moore's invitation to sit with her. He had sat quietly up to this point, but when he saw his mother get up and walk toward the stage, he ran up too. The two walked across hand in hand while the audience chuckled and cameras flashed. Everyone's excitement over Andreya's accomplishment was infectious. "Lavell was happy hisself, and he kept on saying, 'Mama, I love you! I love you, Mama!'" Afterwards, Ms. Moore came over to tell Andreya that Lavell was so cute. She wanted to take a picture before they left. Andreya could hardly believe her ears.

Photographs mean a lot to Andreya, and so in appreciation of Ms. Johnston's support, she gave her a framed picture of herself holding Lavell and Kevon. On the frame were written the words "To My Favorite Teacher" with an apple painted on the edges. In her own apartment, on a living room shelf, Andreya displayed two new photographs. One was of herself in cap and gown. Next to that stood a group photograph of all the students who had graduated with her. The face of one young woman had been rubbed out. It was a friend of Sonya's.

The next thing Andreya had to do was find a job. She worried that the jobs available to her in the inner city paid only a minimum wage ($5.15 an hour). Her achievement in finishing Job Corps, she discovered, didn't get her as far as she had hoped. It seemed that you needed two years of college to qualify for jobs that paid a living wage. "I mean you not gonna make no money unless you've got some degrees behind what you got already. And it's like, instead of winning, you losing." Working as a certified nursing assistant in a nursing home would bring her $6.00 an hour, a little better than minimum wage, but how could she support herself and two children, especially because she'd have to start paying rent once she was earning a salary? Ms. Moore told her there were better-paying jobs in the surrounding counties, but transportation would be a problem, especially because many entry-level positions required work in the evening hours after the buses stopped running. Besides, who would take care of her children on a consistent basis during evening hours? And even though her new neighborhood looked pleasant enough, and there was a security guard on patrol at all times, it was after all a public housing project. She didn't want to be coming home late at night. How could she be sure she wouldn't be attacked while the guard was on another block? Her mother agreed, "You can't let anything happen."

Soon after she started looking for a job, Lavell came down with chicken pox. Then it was Kevon's turn. According to the welfare reform laws, a person was eligible for a full Temporary Assistance to Needy Families (TANF) benefit only if he or she was in school or actively looking for a job. Andreya called her caseworker to explain her dilemma. She also wanted to apply for food stamps in her own name now that she was living apart from her mother. The caseworker seemed not to understand. He kept insisting that she immediately make appointments for job interviews. He told her that he should impose sanctions, cutting her TANF payments to $133 per month because she wasn't actively job searching. When she told him that she couldn't look for a job at that time because her sons were sick and no one else could care for them, he called that an "excuse." Andreya explained that she couldn't ask her mother or aunts to take off from work—it would be too much to ask. She persisted that she needed both food stamps and the full TANF benefit because she could not otherwise afford food, diapers, and utilities. The caseworker retorted that he did not believe that she had utility bills in her own name to pay, and went on to accuse her of working and receiving money under the table. He asked her to send him her EBT[1] card and PIN number so that he could check to see how much money was still on it. She refused, citing instructions she had received with the card not to release the number to anyone. (Also she could not afford to be without it.)

Keeping her cool ("I was trying to be sooooo nice") but defending herself against these insults, Andreya addressed the caseworker's suspicions about mothers like herself. In her words to him (as recounted to us), we see her beliefs that 1) caseworkers do not understand the hard realities of poverty, 2) caseworkers distrust the intentions of welfare recipients, and 3) some welfare recipients do abuse the system, but she did not and should not have to pay for the sins of a few.

---

[1]The federal Electronic Benefits Transfer (EBT) program issues food stamp recipients an electronic debit card with which to buy groceries.

"Y'all don't compromise with us. Y'all don't understand what we go through from month to month. Y'all think we got a welfare check and we gonna blow it on this or blow it on that. I can understand if I was one of these mothers that go give my check to the dope man or go give my check to anybody and then I calling 'I need more money because I did this and I did that,' but I'm not like that. Y'all told me I had to go to find a job or go to school. I went to school. I could see if I'm just sitting at home watching the stories all day. [Stories was the word the mothers used for soap operas.] The situation I'm in now is not because I want to be there. It's because my sons are sick. I can't do nothing about them getting chicken pox. I can't make it go away. If I had somebody else to watch them I would let them watch them. I would agree to it, but I don't have that. I can't take them to the day care 'cause other kids would get exposed to it. It's contagious. I'm following my procedures. What is wrong? Y'all don't want to work with us. Y'all don't agree with what we're doing. If we sit at home with our kids, y'all complain about that. If we send them to the day care and work or go to school, y'all complain about that. I mean, I'm a dedicated mother—stay home with my kids. I don't, you know, go out and do what my other friends do. What more can y'all want us to do?'"

On a day when a cousin could watch the boys, Andreya and her grandmother (Dorothy) went to the Division of Family Services to give the caseworker some papers he required (Social Security card, proof of graduation, and utility bills). Dorothy had come for moral support; she sat in the waiting room while Andreya went into the caseworker's office. After accepting the papers, the caseworker went to the waiting room to question Dorothy. He suspected that Andreya was living with her or with William instead of independently as she claimed.

Andreya's efforts to preserve her benefits worked. She was not sanctioned and received a letter assuring her that she would begin receiving food stamps in 30 days. In the meantime, however, her situation became close to desperate. With very little food left in the refrigerator but a strong reluctance to ask her family for help, she finally forced herself to "beat around the bush" in a conversation with her mother. "Andreya, what do you want?" Patricia asked, picking up on her daughter's hints. Andreya told her mother how little food she had left. Patricia's reaction surprised us. Rather than being proud of her daughter's consideration and independent spirit, she was hurt. "Why didn't you say this a long time ago?" she asked. "Because I waited until I just didn't have anything," Andreya replied. "I don't care what you don't have. Ask me for it. You don't ask me for nothing anyway," her mother returned. "I don't like asking nobody for nothing. I just don't like to do it," Andreya defended herself. "Well, do you need anything?" her mother asked. "No," Andreya said. "And my mama said, 'You should of said yeah. If someone ask and you need something, you say yeah, Andreya.'" Andreya promised she would.

A few hours later, Patricia brought over several bags of groceries. But all she would say was, "I'm mad at you. You need something to eat." When Andreya called later, Patricia told Tony to say she wasn't home. Finally, Andreya used humor to break the ice. She called and in a fake voice asked for Ms. Bradley. She said she was Sharlene at the Catering Place and wondered if Ms. Bradley could come in next weekend to work at a wedding. Patricia guessed who it was, "Andreya, I don't want to talk to you." Laughing, Andreya begged her, "Mama, don't hang up on me. I'm sorry." "Whose daughter do you think you are?" her mother asked. "Yours," Andreya assured her. "Mama, I don't like asking you for money. It's not your business to take care of me." "Y'all are my responsibility still," her mother answered.

"But we've been getting along real good," was the way Andreya ended this story. Moving out and graduating had made a tremendous difference in their relationship.

Andreya accepted a job as a certified nursing assistant at Rosemont Nursing Home. It wasn't her dream job and the pay wasn't very good ($6.00/hour), but it was on a direct bus line and she was promised daytime hours. Because she had to work alternate Saturdays, she arranged with a teenager who lived a few doors down to babysit her boys on Saturday afternoons. Her mother could be with them Saturday mornings.

Perhaps because she wasn't living with her mother, William started coming over more often and giving Andreya money to contribute to the children's upkeep. He said he'd been having a hard time. His younger brother had been shot to death in an argument over a girl. He and Sonya had broken up. And now "child support" was after him. He demanded to know why Andreya had reported him. Andreya snapped that he should have been paying all along; if he had, she wouldn't have had to be on welfare. As things stood, the Child Support Enforcement Agency was about to start garnishing back pay as well as his current obligation from his salary.[2]

On the positive side, William no longer denied that he was Kevon's father. (Indeed, it was hard to deny—they looked so much alike.) They had been back and forth about the possibility of Kevon going for visits to William's home. At first, William declined to take him, saying that he was too little and that he cried when left alone with William. He blamed Andreya for having turned his son against him and turning him into a

---

[2]Andreya explained to us that as long as she was receiving cash assistance, she would not benefit directly from William's child support payments to the state. After she started working, however, money garnished from his wages would supplement her salary.

crybaby. Andreya countered that Kevon cried only because he wasn't used to William—and couldn't get used to him until William spent more time with the child. Yet when William finally did offer to take both boys to his place for an overnight visit, Andreya would only let him take Lavell. She was afraid he wouldn't know what to do if Kevon got sick.

Patricia didn't think William should be allowed to take either child out. When we first met her, she'd told us, "It is best for children to know they fathers even if they choose not to do for them." She'd also told Andreya, "William better cherish them kids 'cause one day he'll need them," to which Andreya had replied, "One day gonna be too late." More recently, however, Patricia's anger at William's treatment of her daughter and grandsons had led to a change of heart. Now she argued that he hadn't earned the privilege of having his sons at his place.

Andreya, however, was firm and consistent in her belief that her boys needed their father. She'd noticed that Lavell listened better to William and to Rickie than to her. "See, it's a man thing," she'd said once when Lavell had immediately complied with Rickie's order to sit down. During the months when William had hardly ever come around, it had hurt her to think that he didn't want to be part of the boys' lives. She had anticipated that one day he would wake up and want to be involved, but that by then it would be too late: The boys would not accept him because he hadn't been there for them when they were little. (In this regard she was her own example, having rebuffed her father when he had wanted to be a grandfather to Lavell.) Besides, she didn't want her sons to blame her later on for denying them access to their father. "I don't want them to say, 'I hate you; you didn't let me see my daddy.'" A sense of "who knows what might happen later" was also at work: William might disappear entirely someday and it was important that the boys have contact with him while they could. "Them are his sons, too, and I can't forgive him myself for what he done, but I mean, life goes on. Them still his kids and he want to spend time with them and one day he might not be here to spend this time with them. I say it's better now than never."

Ironically, although Patricia objected to William having a role in her grandsons' lives, Andreya's beliefs about the importance of a father's involvement were also fueled by her mother's analysis of the reasons behind Tony's difficult behavior. According to Andreya, "He [Tony] ain't listening to nobody. And he wanna bond with his daddy but he don't know where he's at. His daddy used to come around. That was when he was a whole lot younger. Now he older and his daddy's nowhere to be found. My mama said that's the problem. And I feel that's part of Lavell's problem. I mean, I think every male need a man figure especially when they little like Lavell's age." For Tony, the "stepfathers," even Sam who'd been so good to the family, had not fully substituted for his biological father. Andreya remembered a time when Sam had told Tony about the importance of school. Tony had retorted that Sam wasn't his real father so he didn't have to listen to him.

Two other people Andreya really wanted involved in her children's lives were Ms. Russell, William's mother, and Tessa, his sister. Andreya's own paternal grandmother and her aunt had meant so much to her when she was growing up; perhaps she especially had in mind how her Grandma Laverne's home had been a refuge during the years her mother was involved with James. It pained her that her boys did not have much of a relationship with Ms. Russell. Ever since Kevon was born, Ms. Russell had stopped calling, saying she'd heard rumors that Kevon wasn't really her grandson. Andreya wanted to rectify the situation, but when she called to talk to Ms. Russell, she was told not to call the house. Andreya answered, "I'm gonna call as long as I got kids by him and you need to accept them because they a part of him." She also pointedly told Ms. Russell that she should realize that if she weren't there for her grandsons when they were young, they would not be there for her when she wanted their company and help in her old age. Reflecting on this difficult conversation (and others like it), Andreya added, "Because if somebody say something to me and I don't like it, I'm gonna tell them just how I feel. I'm not gonna hold it in. I tell 'em just how I feel. Because I'm straightforward."

To Patricia's comment that it's not a good idea to "run to no in-laws; let them come to you," and that she couldn't stand that family anyway, Andreya countered,

"If you don't like them, you don't have to like them. But that's still they auntie and that's still they grandma no matter what happen between me and William. Still, they are family. Just like my sons know my side of the family, they got to know they daddy side of the family because y'all might not be here for my kids all the time, and I have to turn to them because my kids have to have a grandma, have to have other aunties besides your sisters and your mama. Your sisters got kids of they own. They ain't gonna mess with them [Lavell and Kevon] like a grandma would. And if I don't ever let Lavell and Kevon know this side of the family, if they haven't seen them, they wouldn't want to be around them because they don't know who they are."

We were touched by the reasoning behind Andreya's determination to keep William's relatives (especially his mother and sister) in her children's corner. One reason clearly was that she viewed these relationships as insurance policies. If in good order, they would provide shelter for her children in hard times. Also, as reflected in her comments to Ms. Russell, adults who take the time to "be there" for children are making an investment for their own old age.

Two months after she started working at the nursing home, Andreya was fired. They told her she'd called too many times to say she couldn't come in because her children were sick. They couldn't keep someone they couldn't rely on, they told her. Andreya couldn't understand why the world was so cold. Why couldn't people in positions of power understand that she was trying hard? Why wouldn't they work with her?

She consoled herself that she hadn't really liked being a nursing assistant anyway. Also, working Saturdays, when the child care center was closed, had presented a real hardship. One Saturday she'd come home to discover that the babysitter had been watching lewd videos in front of the boys and had had her boyfriend over.

A week later, Andreya responded to a sign in the housing project office advertising on-the-job training for construction workers. She learned how to install insulation. The work appealed to her and it paid well, but it was seasonal; she didn't see how she could make a life for herself and her boys on work that wasn't year-round. Also, it was hard to be a woman in a man's world. "They made me feel like nothing 'cause 'This is a man's job.'" Plus one of the workers started coming on to her. Nevertheless, she resolved to stick it out.

William had gotten a car and asked Andreya if she'd like him to pick her and the boys up after work and drop them off at home. She accepted the offer. Lavell had talked about Sonya doing this and doing that, so Andreya knew Sonya was back in William's life, but she told herself that she was merely encouraging contact between the boys and their father. Clearly, however, William had other feelings. On one occasion, when he came to pick Andreya up at a construction site, she was talking to one of the other workers. William was so angered at the sight that she feared he would hit the man. And then, abruptly, he stopped giving her rides. She wouldn't see him for another 9 months.

Lavell, now 3½, was at times a loving and joyful child, and he still liked listening to his mother read to him. At other times, however, he seemed out of control. His child care teachers complained that he was now not only aggressive, but also displaying inappropriate sexual behavior and language. Andreya assured us that she had never so much as kissed a man in view of her children. She told Lavell that the words he was saying were "grown-up words" and that he shouldn't say them. Our impression on our visits was that he enjoyed repeating the prohibited words and watching his mother get upset. Andreya blamed William and Sonya for this development. One day Lavell had come home from their place saying he'd seen "something nasty." She thought he'd seen them having sex. She also wondered what had gone on when she'd left her boys with the teenage babysitter.

Lavell also seemed to be dragging Kevon into his troublesome behavior. Little Kevon, now almost 2, seemed to have been born with a much calmer temperament than Lavell, but he, too, was hitting and pinching and laughing about it.

Andreya was frustrated by her inability to quench her boys' out-of-bounds behavior. She'd told us many times that it was important to teach and discipline children when they were very young. Parents shouldn't wait until children were older and "think they have they own mind," she once told us. "You don't just start disciplining a kid when they get 10 and 11. And some parents, 'Well, since he wanna start stealing and being out on the street, I'm gonna start whupping him.' You should have been whupping him a long time ago." On the other hand, she had to admit that her own whuppings and attempts at using time-out and reasoning were not having as much impact as she wished. She felt that forces beyond her control were overwhelming her efforts at child rearing. It made her empathize with her mother. "My mama got a friend and he say it's the parent's fault for how the boys [referring to Tony and Quintus] is. I don't feel that way 'cause Lavell—it's not my fault he act like that. You raise a child one way and they go another way . . . they fall on a crowd."

Our conversation about her sons segued into talk about her brothers. Quintus was still in jail, but she had had some phone contact with him recently. He had told Andreya that he regretted that all three of them hadn't listened to their mother more. "Mama was trying to tell you [about William] and you wouldn't listen and you tried it for yourself and you see now. 'That's the way I did y'all.'" He said he felt "as dead" knowing that Tony was now using and dealing drugs as he'd felt when he himself was doing those things.

Andreya didn't feel as hostile toward Tony as she had during those last years of living in the same house with him. She was glad that his relationship with Lavell had improved. It had become much more playful and less antagonistic. At the same time, her brother's lack of interest in school and his involvement in the drug world worried her. She'd been trying to talk some sense into him. She prefaced her account of a lesson she'd tried to impart to him by letting us know that "I love my brother deep down in my heart but I can't stand his ways. And I tell him, 'I hate your *ways.*' I don't say I hate *him.* He's not a bad person." She believed it was his "so-called friends" who were pulling him into the life he was leading. She wished he understood that if he got in trouble, it would be Mama, not his friends, who would try to rescue him—do everything possible to get him out of jail. "I hate to see Tony out there because I think Black males—I'm not separating it from nobody, but it's nothing but the truth—they don't have no future in getting no job because they out here killing and selling drugs. They wanna live in the fast lane. You can't achieve nothin' unless you helping yourself and you working. It might be hard; you might feel you being set back some, but that's the only way. Once you get out there on the fast lane and you go sell drugs, you always gonna go down. You gonna get put in jail. You gonna have a record. You won't wanna be 30 and the police come up to you when you with your kids having a good time, 'Hey, Mr. Bradley, are you still selling drugs?' And your kids be like, 'Daddy, you sell drugs?'"

Andreya was still getting home visits from Rickie and she started going to the monthly evening parent meetings. Her mother would come over to watch the children and Rickie would give her rides both ways. At school, she told us, she'd always been too shy to run for class office or to read in front of others. She credited Early Head Start with helping her overcome her reticence. During the first parent meetings she attended, she sat quietly, too shy to say anything. Then came a holiday party. A man had been invited to speak on holiday customs from various religious traditions. Then he put on music and said it was time for some dancing. "I really didn't want to do it. Rickie was like, 'Andreya! You act up at home!' I'm like, 'That's not home,' and everybody started laughing. And I was like, 'Okay, so let me see, float like a butterfly and all that,' so all us started dancing and they said, 'Girl, you know how to boogie, don't ya!' I said, 'A little bit.' Rickie said, 'Naw, you know how to boogie!' And so after the program was over and everybody was going home, I said, 'Rickie, I ain't shy to dance in front of people no more.'"

Even more important was her speech. Rickie told her that at the next parent meeting, parents would be asked to talk about their thoughts regarding child rearing. Would she get up and talk about her struggles and fears as a single parent? She couldn't imagine talking to a group like that, and told him no. He persisted, offering to make it easier by preparing some speaking notes for her. Reluctantly, she agreed. She was to surprise herself. Walking up to the podium at the appointed time, she made a split-second decision to abandon Rickie's notes. She spoke with feeling.

"My name is Andreya Bradley and I'm a parent of two and I'm a dedicated mother. My biggest fears are about my kids—I have two Black males and in our environment Black males don't last long. The generation before my kids—they in jail or dead or they in a bad environment. And they don't have nothing else to turn to, and I want to better that because the generation of my kids is going to be in that environment if we don't put a stop to it."

A mother in the audience called out, "Look at your kids; they just babies, and you thinking like that." Andreya answered, "Yeah, I think like that because that's my biggest fear. I mean because everywhere you go, it's that environment. You move south, it's there. You move east, it's there. You move west, it's there. . . . It's nowhere to run, but you got to deal with it. And they start as early as 5, you know. It gonna come to where I'm gonna have to deal with these situations. Other kids encouraging them 'cause they all got jewelry and all these name-brand clothes and my kids want the same and I probably won't be able to afford them at that time. They will want them faster than what I can afford."

A parent got up to compliment her, "That was a good speech! You wasn't scared!" Andreya responded, "I said I was, but I said stuff from my heart."

Nine months later, Andreya had incredible news to tell us. William had suddenly come over after a long absence and proposed to her. He'd told her he'd always loved her and that he'd stayed away only because Sonya had threatened that she would hurt Andreya and the boys if he went back to them. He wouldn't put it past her. He wanted Andreya to marry him. He had a diamond ring for her. They would move far away where they could start living as a family, safe from Sonya. He'd been tearful about his neglect of her and his sons. "He was like, 'Man, I messed up. I messed up.' And I'm like, 'Yeah, you did but it is better to fix it now than try to fix it later because at 7 or 8, Lavell's not gonna wanna hear this, 'Man, I'm sorry Daddy been gone.' And I told him, 'I don't want you to think you can just keep walking in and out of our life. I mean even if you just called and, 'Can I speak to Lavell and Kevon?' I mean that'd be reassuring them that you not leaving."

Lavell had asked him why he hadn't been over for so long. William had answered his son that he'd made some bad choices. He'd repeated to Andreya that he was so sorry for what he'd done. He was amazed by her strength, that she hadn't been driven to drink or drugs by him. He'd told her he admired her for not cussing him out. She'd responded that she wasn't the important one; what was important was his relationship with their sons. He disagreed; she was important, too, and he wanted the relationship back.

We asked Andreya how she felt about the marriage proposal. She said that at first she'd laughed in William's face, but now she didn't know what to do. Her mother was counseling her against it and reminding her that, "He shouldn't have been lyin' in the first place." Every day Andreya was praying for guidance, wishing for a sign telling her what to do.

We called two weeks later. William had moved in. The boys were better behaved than ever. She was getting more rest because William was letting her sleep while he took care of them. But when we called in another 6 weeks, we learned that for 3 weeks in a row, William had disappeared every Thursday without even a call, then reappeared the following Monday. And then we heard that he had completely gone back to Sonya.

Andreya was very upset. She kept asking herself why she'd taken him back again. It seemed to her that every time she let her defenses down and let William know how she felt about him, he decided things between them were fine so he could safely return to Sonya. "Every time he wanted to come back, I thought it was so much better, but it wasn't. It turned out to be the same thing. It's a big old game to him. And out of it, the kids are getting hurt and I'm getting hurt. I keep asking myself *why* and I pray about it. Why do I keep on taking him back after I know what he's gonna do?" Rickie had been asking her the same question.

She tried to keep a stiff upper lip, saying that she was upset not so much for her own sake as for her children's, especially Lavell's. "And it's just like, I can ignore my feelings but seeing them hurt or to have a 4-year-old to ask you, 'Mama, I be bad? Did my daddy like me?' I mean that would just tear you apart. I want to say no to him, 'No, he don't care. No, he don't wanna be here.' But I gotta look at how he feeling about this. I told William, 'You are hurting me because I'm hurting for them.'" She felt like he treated his other three children better than hers. "Out of all of his kids, mine are just like stepkids, and his stepkids [Sonya's two children from a previous relationship] get treated better than my kids." Her tears, she said, were mostly out of sorrow for her children.

The children's distress was making it almost impossible for her to get to work on time. They had started wetting themselves, refusing to get dressed, and deliberately spilling juice and raw eggs on the kitchen floor in the mornings. Andreya figured that they were trying to punish her for their father's unpredictability. She couldn't bear to leave home knowing that the floor was dirty; it seemed like every morning she had some major mess to clean up before she could leave for work. "I get the bad part of it," she said. "I have to hear from them."

It wasn't just the absences that hurt the children, she thought. Even worse was the fact that William sometimes told them that he would be coming over, and then did not show up. Andreya said, "I told him, 'Don't tell them nothing that you're not gonna do because they look forward to it. Then it don't happen and it's all on me; it's my fault. They don't know no better. If you choose not to be in their life, stay away because it's making it bad in so many ways. They upset and they take it out on me. And I mean I try to work with them more than anything.'"

At least there was one good thing concerning William. He'd gotten a job with a company that made metal handles and locks, and she had started getting child support. She was promised $589 monthly.

Lavell had started going to an afternoon Head Start program and Andreya reported that he was adjusting to it very well. However, it was a different story at the child care center attended by Lavell in the mornings and by Kevon all day. Both children cried and threw toys when it was time for her to say goodbye. When a teacher asked her where they'd learned to hit so much, Andreya was insulted. Although she had liked the center at first, after a favorite teacher had resigned, she'd become more and more critical of the care the boys were receiving. For one thing, staff turnover was huge. It seemed that no sooner would the boys get used to a teacher than she'd leave. She saw that misbehavior was simply ignored for the most part. Time-out, when used, was misused. The center rules stated that no single time-out event could last longer than 4 minutes, but she'd seen teachers leave children there much longer because they'd forgotten about them. Worse yet, Lavell told her that a teacher had hit him.

Also, she thought the children weren't given enough to do. There weren't nearly enough toys or books for them. And the teachers didn't pay enough attention to the children or offer them a variety of interesting activities. "Kids gonna be kids regardless," said Andreya. "I mean they need to do different things, 'cause they get bored with the same thing every day. A day care that don't interact with the kids is not teaching them anything." Interesting activities would do more than stimulate learning. They would help reduce the amount of aggression. "Kids gonna fight in day care, but give them something to do and they won't do it [fight]," she said. She told a teacher to use redirection, "When he about to hit somebody, take him away from it. You don't snatch him away but you be like, 'Lavell, come over here and play with this.'"

Andreya believed firmly in the importance of giving children plenty to do and respecting their choices. Perhaps if her children had access to acceptable activities they enjoyed, they would stay out of trouble even when they were older. "I prefer my sons to have an active life, you know. I mean I know people around here can turn you around, but hopefully I'll have them hooked up into activities and different things that they like. I don't want to make them do something they don't want. I want them to do stuff they choose to do. I mean, even if it's just goin' to the movies every week or something like that, I would want my sons to do that if they like that." Parents shouldn't force their own activity preferences on their children: "You know, I'm not gonna make them bored with what *I* want in life, what *I* wanted to accomplish when I was little." People had told her that Lavell had the physique of a future football player, but "I'm not gonna say, 'Hey, you got to play football, Lavell. You big enough.' And he'd be like, 'Well, Mama, that ain't nothing I wanna do.' Okay, I'm gonna respect that and say, 'Okay, well, what do you want to do?'"

Now that Lavell was 4, they could have conversations about his preferences.

"We have time where I just turn off the TV and we just talk. I'll let him tell me what he want, what he'd like, because if I get to know what he like to do, then I can do it. I can't just be doing all the time what I want to do. Then he'd be like, 'I'm tired. I don't wanna do this. Just leave me alone.' So I sit down and I ask him, 'Lavell, what you like?' And he be, 'Mama can we go to the park?' And I'll compromise with him, say, 'Lavell, when your brother wake up, sure, we can go to the park, no problem.' "

Self-awareness helped her accept her son's changes of mind. "And I mean if he change it or switch it, that's fine. I mean, you know, just like I got in CNA and it's something that I wanted to do, but then I changed my mind."

Cold weather came and Andreya and her co-workers were laid off. They were told to look for hiring notices in the spring. She couldn't wait that long and was once again looking for a job. Thinking about the jobs she'd enjoyed most since she first started working as an adolescent, she decided to try working in a child care center. She lined up a job as a teaching assistant in a toddler classroom. If not for the Welfare-to-Work program, she would have been earning only minimum wage, the typical beginning pay at this center. Instead, she would be earning $6.00/hour. The Full Employment Council would reimburse the center for her salary for 6 months. The director had signed an agreement that after the 6 months had passed, she would continue to pay Andreya $6.00 per hour. After she had worked 9 months, Welfare-to-Work would give her vouchers worth $1,800. She planned to use some of the money to buy clothes and pay off utility bills. She wished the money could be used to buy a car, but that wasn't allowed.

When Andreya found out that William had quit his job, she was sure it was because he'd decided it wasn't worth working if so much of his pay went to child support. He'd told her that after child support was garnished from his paycheck, he only had $167 a month to live on.

Andreya said, "I told my mama the other day, I said, 'If I went back, I don't think I would have any kids, to be honest.' I mean, I waited 'til a decent age to have kids, but . . ." her voice trailed off. We asked her to elaborate.

"Like I told my mama, I don't regret my kids at all. I don't regret them. But I just hate that I had somebody to just really use me. And you know all I got out of it was my kids and being hurt. He took a lot away from me. I gave him my youth. I didn't graduate when I was supposed to. I didn't go to none of the pep rallies or to the games or none of that. I didn't get to go to the prom. I didn't get to enjoy that. I was pregnant and I was sick. I didn't get to go to the family re-union. William was like, 'I don't want you to go.' And I thought anything he wanted me to do, okay, I'm gonna do. He loves me. That's all I thought about."

She went on to talk about how William was "a different person" when she first knew him. He was considerate and he didn't "cover" [hide his feelings] so much. Perhaps convincing herself that he used to be a better person helped her rationalize her continuing, as well as her past, willingness to involve herself with him.

She talked about crying and about needing some time to herself. Making it clear that she loved her children, she also made it clear that her situation was very hard. "It gets hard. When I get home I'll be so tired and then it's one problem after another, to where I'll be so stressed out all I can do is just sit there and cry. I still cook, but I just cry because I just feel like I don't have nothing but my kids. I don't have no fun. I don't have fun like I used to. I mean it's not that it's the kids but it's just that I need to get out some more." Then, after a silence, she added, "You know I'm trying real hard, I'm just really trying. I'm a keep on keepin' on. I can't stop. Because of my kids."

She thought it might help to start going to church. One of our very first conversations with Andreya 3 years earlier had been about how much she enjoyed taking Lavell to a church playgroup for 1-year-olds. She'd talked with delight about a Christmas party in which he'd been dressed up as Santa Claus. She hadn't gone to church since then. That didn't mean she didn't believe in God. Her God was someone she could turn to for help and support in easing life's burdens. When upset, she would "pray at concerns"—for her children to recover from their illnesses, for Tony and Quintus to shape up, for the strength to "keep on keepin' on," for wisdom to do the right thing about William, for self-esteem, and for the material items she needed, such as adequate clothing for her children. She told God she'd been trying so hard. Once when Kevon was 2 months old and would not stop crying, she'd coped by leaving the room and praying for forgiveness for even thinking she wanted to hit him. Usually she prayed alone, but sometimes she found it helpful to call a church prayer line. And when things went well, she thanked God.

Recently she'd started reading the Bible and listening to religious music on the radio. She found this calming. The Bible on the coffee table, we noticed, was open to Psalms. She said she read and reread them many nights after the boys were in bed. On the inside front cover was a handwritten inscription, "to Patricia from Mama." Patricia had passed it down to her. Andreya wasn't sure reading by herself was good enough though. She decided to formally join a church. "I think that's one of my biggest problems—not going to church. I need to start going back."

She called a church that was nearby. The woman who answered told her that she was welcome to come to a Wednesday evening Bible study group as well as to Sunday services. Andreya accepted the invitation, but the next Wednesday Lavell was sick. She called the church to say she couldn't come and to apologize. Her sincerity shone through in her rendering for us of the conversation that ensued.

"I said, 'I'm sorry, I didn't promise you but I told you I would come and that was my word, and I was coming but my son, my older son, is sick and I know there's gonna be kids there and I don't want nobody to catch what he's got.' And she was like, 'Don't come on account of me. You come because you ready to be accepted by God. Come because you ready, this is what you want. You just can't come 'cause your kids are sick or you can't come 'cause you want something to happen right now, and then you stop going in a couple of weeks.' And I realize what she was saying because most people will get in church because, 'Oh, God bless me with a house. God gonna bless me with a car. God gonna get me a hus-band.' It's stuff like that. And I realize what she's saying. Don't come unless I'm committing myself to this; this is gonna be in my life every day. I'm kinda scared. I know I'll probably turn back and I don't want to get in church for 2 or 3 weeks and then don't go no more. I wanna be dedicated to it. I'm not gonna go 'til I'm ready because most people don't do that. Like on Mother's Day, 'Ain't you going to church?' I haven't been going; why should I go because today is Mother's Day? Why should I go 'cause today is Easter?"

We wondered, but at the moment didn't want to ask, if childhood memories of her preacher-uncle also figured in her hesitations.

Deciding not to join the church did not mean that she had stopped believing. If anything, it seemed that she was becoming *more* religious not less. To people's comments that she was lucky to have as many things as she had, she had taken to replying that she was blessed, not lucky, to have furniture, pots and pans, clothing, toys for the children, low rent, and subsidized child care. She was sure that God was looking out for her. Prayer took her to another level: "Every time I just be praying in silence and kids can be screaming to the top of their lungs and I'll just be thinking about praying and, you know, saying things in my head." She told us that sometimes she cried while she prayed. The com-bination of tears and prayer reduced tension and helped her refrain from displacing her stress on loved ones. "The more and more I hold it in, it might come out the wrong way. And I don't wanna hurt one of my kids. I don't wanna hurt none of my family members or nothing like that. So basically I cry it out and I talk it out. I talk to God. I know He hear me. It helps me. I feel relieved and not so stressed."

Praying wasn't her only coping strategy. She'd also done some prob-lem solving; she'd figured out a way to make the mornings easier. In-stead of trying to rouse the children by yelling "get up" and clapping her hands, she'd taken to singing to them. She'd sing "Good morning, good morning, good morning, sleepyheads." And she'd tell them that cartoons were on. They could watch for half an hour if they got up right away. This was making mornings so much better.

Three months passed before our next call. Andreya answered the phone, her voice flat. There was something she had to tell us. She was pregnant again. The baby was due in 5 months.

She named her daughter Aisha and, a couple of months later, had her tubes tied. William agreed that Aisha was beautiful, but he insisted that she was not his. Four years later, a court-ordered blood test would confirm Andreya's claim. William was Aisha's father.

Family and Romantic Relationships

8

Mothers' Relationships with Their Parents and Parent-Figures

Mark A. Fine, Linda C. Halgunseth, and Jean M. Ispa

This chapter analyzes the relationships that young mothers in poverty have with their parents. Understanding the nature and quality of these relationships is important because

1. The stressful nature of raising children in poverty requires considerable emotional and instrumental support, and parents may provide that support (Burton, 1996).

2. The relationships that mothers have with their parents provide templates that influence how the mothers parent their own children (Benoit & Parker, 1994).

3. Mothers' emotional well-being is often to some degree contingent on the past and current quality of their relationships with their own mothers (and sometimes fathers; Umberson & Slaten, 2000).

Accordingly, this chapter examines how the young mothers in our study related to their own mothers and fathers. For clarity, when multiple generations are referred to at the same time, we refer to children (the youngest generation), mothers (the second generation), and grandmothers/grandfathers (the oldest generation).

The source of our information came first from regular interviews with the young mothers. Second, whenever possible we gathered information from interviews with maternal grandmothers and grandfathers; we interviewed six of the nine grandmothers, two ex-step-grandmothers, and several grandfathers. Third, we were able to collect informal observational data during some interviews with the mothers because grandmothers interacted with their daughters (the mothers) during some of the interviews. Finally, we obtained information on these relationships from the Early Head Start (EHS) program director and home visitors, who worked closely with the mothers and occasionally with the grandmothers. By integrating information from these various sources, we developed the list of themes described below.

RELATIONSHIP BETWEEN YOUNG MOTHERS AND THEIR MOTHERS

The nine mothers in our sample were unanimous in believing that their mothers should "be there" for them and their children. "Being there" meant being available during good and bad times, with special emphasis on providing emotional and instrumental support when times were tough. For the most part, the grandmothers agreed with this norm. Breanna's mother Penny expressed this sentiment when, after lamenting Breanna's relationship with her baby's father, she concluded, "I'll just have to be there to be like the cushion, to catch her." Recall also Patricia's hurt when Andreya did not call on her for help when she was struggling to put food on the table (Chapter 7).

At the same time, as was reflected in Andreya's initial reluctance to ask her mother for help, the young mothers wanted some degree of autonomy from their mothers. This is to be expected given the mothers' youth. Adolescents and young adults often want to avoid being controlled by their parents (Frank, Avery, & Laman, 1988; Holmbeck, 1996). Some of the grandmothers understood the tightrope they had to walk in this regard. Penny shared her way of resolving this tension, "I can't force her. I know she has to be allowed to make [her own decisions] and I know that there are emotions that she's gonna have to learn how to deal with, and the only thing I can do is give my opinion. If I think it's too wrong, I will step in. . . . If I really do see something hurting her, then it would be no problem. But other than that I am trying to keep an open mind."

There were both positive and negative qualities in the mother–grandmother relationships, with the balance tilting toward more positive than negative aspects. Sometimes feelings of closeness and frustration fluctuated from interview to interview, and sometimes positive and negative feelings were expressed within the same interview.

Positive Aspects of the Mother–Grandmother Relationship

Below, we present the themes representing the positive aspects of the mother–grandmother relationship. As noted above, the mothers talked about the positive aspects of this relationship more frequently than the negative aspects.

Closeness Between Most of the Mothers and Grandmothers

The prevailing sentiments among the young mothers were that they were close to their mothers and that their mothers were their main supports. For some, these feelings were reflected in their depiction of the relationship as a friendship. Maria, when asked how she got along with her mother, replied, "We get along, we're like best friends now. When I was growing up, we fought a lot. . . . When high school started, that's when a lot of kids start rebelling and you know, saying no, and [I decided] I'm not going to do that [anymore]. I really regret a lot of the things I did to her, but we're like best friends now. We talk about everything, anything."

The "friend" label was not restricted to the young mothers. Shardae's mother said of her relationship with her daughter, "We probably are friends first. And we are really close. . . . Because I've raised them [her two children] by myself and I'm basically all they know."

As these quotations imply, a primary way that closeness or friendship was manifested lay in the mothers' sense that they could confide in the grandmothers about troubling issues that they wanted or needed to discuss. Breanna explained, "We've got a good relationship. If I need anything, I tell my mom, or if I got a problem, I can come and talk to her. Our communication is very open and honest toward each other. She knows everything [about Breanna]."

An interesting feature of some of the mother–grandmother relationships involved both parties' belief that the older women had a sort of sixth sense about their daughters—that they "knew" how they were doing (or what they were doing) even when they were not told. We understood the mothers' and grandmothers' accounts of such "knowing" to be expressions of the closeness they felt toward one another. Several such instances involved the younger mothers' pregnancies. The mothers of Andreya, Kyierra, and Sherryce, for example, said that they knew their daughters were pregnant weeks before they were told, and Maria's mother described a dream about having a grandson even before Maria admitted that she was pregnant. Recall also Andreya's contention (Chapter 5) that her mother knew her children "like the back of her hand" and could tell if they had done something "slick."

Grandmothers' Pride in Their Daughters

One prevailing sentiment that emerged from interviews with the grandmothers was pride in their daughters. Breanna's mother Penny, for example, told us that "I kiss her every day and tell her I'm proud of her because she gets up, she goes to school, and as soon as she comes home she takes over the responsibility of her baby." (Breanna was only 15 at the time.) Three years later, Penny again told us how proud she was that Breanna was a responsible and flexible mother, "She's a good mother. I think she's a good parent 'cause she's open-minded. You know, she listens to constructive criticism." In addition to expressing pride in their daughters' child-rearing competence, some of the grandmothers were glad to see that their daughters were hard-working in general. Kyierra's mother Elise reflected this feeling when she commented, "Kyierra's a worker. She's not a lazy person. . . . She would rather work than get paid by AFDC."

Mothers' Respect for Grandmothers' Strength, Dedication, and Wisdom   Most of the mothers returned the grandmothers' respect, admiring them for being hard-working, strong, and dedicated. As Roneeka put it, "She's a strong woman. . . . I look up to her because you know, she's been our mother and daddy for a long time. 'Cause my daddy he just stay in and out of jail. That's where my brothers get it from. From him, you know. She's worked all her life. . . . And, shoot, she's just, she's a good woman."

When Breanna was asked to think of a female friend or relative to whom she looked up, she quickly replied, "My mother. I look up to her. She's a big role model for me. She's a good person." Breanna later explained that she admired her mother for "all she's been through" and for overcoming many difficulties.

Similarly, Shardae and Maria said that their mothers were the most influential people in their lives. Echoing a pattern that we found for several of the mothers, Maria, Breanna, and Roneeka all said that their mothers were the people they looked up to most. They also thought that they shared their mothers' most admirable characteristics. Maria provided an example when she told us, "My mom is a hard worker like me. She's the type of person that will work two jobs and will exhaust herself to do what needs to be done. And she still has a smile on her face when she does it. And she doesn't complain too much. And I think that's where I get my energy to do these two jobs."

The mothers were clear in stating that as they matured, their appreciation and respect for their own mothers increased. Reflecting this trend, toward the end of our study, some of the young mothers acknowledged that their own mothers had been right about issues and situations that had caused friction in the past. Recall Andreya's belated appreciation of her mother's warnings about William (described in Chapter 7). After Andreya moved to her own apartment, she told us several times that she had been wrong to resent her mother's advice when she was an adolescent, "I felt that I was grown and she couldn't tell me nothin'. And I was wrong, 'cause I still needed her to tell me stuff."

Grandmothers Support of Their Daughters   Although not all of the grandmothers provided instrumental support, they were as a group supportive of their daughters. For example, some of the mothers reported that they depended on the grandmothers to help with child-rearing issues that came up for the first time. As Breanna explained, "It's just maybe like the unexpected things of when [her baby] falls and start bleeding too bad and I need some help. What am I supposed to do?" Similarly, Roneeka asked her mother for help when her daughter appeared to be getting her first cold.

The grandmothers also provided physical support such as caring for their daughters when they were ill, providing transportation, baby-sitting grandchildren when the mothers were working or in school, and offering financial assistance. The mothers of Shardae and Maria regularly dropped off and/or picked up their grandchildren at child care. At times, Shardae's mother would take Shardae's daughter Alexis with her to visit relatives in the South so that Shardae could rest. (Instead, Shardae used the time to work more hours at her job.) The grandmothers who lived with their daughters were more likely to engage in these activities.

On the other hand, several mothers reported that the grandmothers either did not help them financially or helped only in a limited way. Tanisha, Kyierra, Shardae, and Sherryce all said that they did not receive any financial support from their mothers, but both Shardae and Sherryce moved back with their mothers for brief periods when they were having financial difficulties. Moreover, Shardae once told us, "Always if I need money for like [diapers] or something, my mother's always there." The mothers may have interpreted our questions about financial help from the grandmothers as relating only to gifts of cash, not to a willingness to provide no-cost housing for their daughters or necessities such as diapers. An example of helping in a limited way is Roneeka's mother, who helped pay for certain of Roneeka's needs such as a bedroom dresser and her wedding. Other than that, however, she was clear that she would pay only for things for her grandchildren. Roneeka explained, "No. She don't give me money. I don't ask for money. She used to give me money. Now she say, 'It's my grandkids' time,' so I don't even ask her for no money [for things for myself]."

Negative Aspects of the Mother–Grandmother Relationship

Not all of the mothers were close to their mothers. Tanisha had limited contact with her mother, who had a recurring drug problem (see below), while Chandra had never met her mother (see p. 122). Even among the mothers who did have regular or semiregular contact with grandmothers, at least two, Andreya and Kyierra, reported having frequent periods when they were upset with their mothers. Kyierra, who had deep-rooted and frequent conflicts with her mother that are described in more detail below, summarized her situation when she said, "I talk to her every day, but I'm not real close to my mother."

Moreover, and as might be expected given the ages of the young mothers, even in those mother–grandmother pairs characterized by closeness, both parties complained about each other. For the mothers, the complaints centered around the grandmothers being unreliable and unfair and, in several instances, abusing drugs and/or alcohol. The grandmothers' concerns tended to focus on their perceptions that their daughters were not sufficiently caring toward them, were not independent enough, and had chosen irresponsible boyfriends. Differences in child-rearing approaches also fed some mother–grandmother tensions.

Mothers' Complaints About the Grandmothers   The mothers' grievances concerning the grandmothers' unreliability often seemed to revolve around broken promises to provide child care. Shardae complained, "I've had a few times where my mother have said she was going to keep Alexis for me and she waits 'til that night and tell me she's not going to watch her the next morning. And that's hard. Because I have to call up everybody I know and see if they'll do it. It just happened this past weekend." Kyierra echoed that complaint when she said, "She says she'll do it and then the next day I'll call her and ask her if she's going to do it and she says, 'Well, we have to do this and do that.' And they don't do anything but sit on their rump roast."

Several mothers felt that they had been treated unjustly and had, for example, been required to do more housework than their brothers. From our observations, their perceptions were generally accurate. For example, consistent with what Rickie (Andreya's home visitor) had heard from other African American families—"We love our sons, but we raise our daughters"— Andreya reported, "Only two people cleaned and that was me and my mama. . . . And it's like, you know, me and my brother had no choice but to do it [when we were younger]. Since Tony's 16 and he thinks he's grown, he can say and do what he wants to. He disrespects my mother more than I ever did."

A tendency for African American mothers to be more directive and restrictive with daughters than with sons is well documented in the literature (Cauce et al., 1996; Hare & Castenell, 1985; Smetana, 2000; see also Chapter 15).

Grandmothers' Complaints About the Mothers   Some grandmothers were upset that their daughters did not help them enough when they needed assistance. On several occasions, Andreya's mother Patricia had health problems that made it difficult for her to work or do housework. She was upset with Andreya for not helping more around the house, particularly given that Andreya knew about her mother's limiting health conditions. Similarly, Kyierra's mother Elise, who at the time was unable to walk on her own because of hip replacement surgery, lamented that Kyierra would not help her if she needed it, "I mean she don't come over now to see how I'm doing or to see if 'Mama do you need something to eat?' or 'Mama, can I give Alice [mother's partner] a break?' You know, 'I have today day off. I can do something for you today. Let Alice get out and do what she wants to do.' What's wrong with that? She don't think of those things."

As illustrated in Andreya's case study, several grandmothers worried that their daughters needed to be more goal-oriented and persistent. Often these concerns were combined with strong desires that their daughters finish school and disappointment when they dropped out instead. Roneeka's mother looked to a future when she would no longer be around and Roneeka would have to manage without her help.

"So, I'm trying to get her together, before I get out of here, you know. Right now that's the only thing, that my main problems—her and the baby. You know, about getting them settled. Then I stay on her about being independent, have some motivation about yourself, 'cause I'm not going to be around here all the time, you know. I'm trying to learn her . . . so I told her you need to stay in school, do something with yourself. Like I tell them, 'Mama ain't going to be around all the time, you know.'"

Similarly, Kyierra's mother Elise worried that Kyierra was not sufficiently self-reliant. "I'll never grow away from Kyierra. I'll always love her and Jalisa," said Elise. "But she's not able to take care of herself hardly, besides taking care of me." In her mind, preparation for adulthood required self-restraint and persistence in two (related) realms. "There was only two things I really asked from Kyierra is to finish high school and watch her virginity," Elise told us. Kyierra did graduate from high school, but disappointed her mother by completing only one semester of college before becoming pregnant. Kyierra, in a separate interview, confirmed Elise's distress when asked about the kinds of things that her mother worries about, "Oh, the only two things she asked of me was to keep my virginity and to graduate. That was her biggest worries. And I drove her crazy."

Another area of conflict revolved around the mothers' sexuality and choices of boyfriends. Grandmothers were generally negatively disposed toward the fathers of their grandchildren. While they understood that it "takes two to tango," they tended to blame these men for derailing their daughters from continuing their education and/or for not waiting to have children until they were established in a job and married. They also criticized them for not being there for their daughters and/or grandchildren. In most cases, the fathers of their grandchildren were older than their daughters and were therefore seen as particularly guilty of having taken advantage of the young women. In a conversation about the fact that Breanna was still a child while the person who fathered her child was an adult, Breanna's mother reflected these themes when she told us, "I just let him know recently that I may not know him personally, but from what he's done to my child, and how he's treated her, what I know of him, I do not like."

Conflicts over Child-Rearing Philosophies and Practices   It was clear that the grandmothers and mothers had similar core goals for the children. Both generations wanted the children to be respectful, bright, and well-behaved. There were, however, disagreements regarding appropriate strategies for helping the children reach these goals. At one point, we asked the mothers how their parenting behavior compared with their own mothers' approaches to parenting. As might be expected for a relatively young group of new mothers, several wanted to be different from their mothers. Andreya said that she wanted to be "very different, very." She planned to treat all her children equally and to monitor her boys more closely than her mother had. When Shardae was asked to speculate about how parenting her daughter would be different from the way her mother parented her, she replied, "I'll be more open with her." A desire to be different seemed to be due in large part to persistent tensions between mothers and grandmothers around issues of spoiling and discipline. In a few cases, grandmothers also worried that their daughters were not careful enough with their children. However, in most cases, the tensions were periodic and not reflective of an underlying weak mother–grandmother relationship.

The mothers who complained about spoiling were especially upset when grandmothers' greater lenience created mixed messages for the children. Maria provided an example when she said, "I think he's spoiled. Not by myself, well, by myself, but his grandmother too. If it is something he's reaching for and it doesn't look like it will choke him or he's crying, Grandma will come and rescue him from me. Or if I spank him, if I say no and he's crying, Grandma will come and rescue him from me. Like 'Come here, Bryce, Mommy's mad.' And she'll take him out of the room and spoil him somewhere else in the house."

Showing the same pattern, when asked how her two girls got along with their grandmother, Kyierra replied, "Good. Except for the baby, she gets by with everything. They told me not to correct the kids when I'm in their house. My mama don't think that we should discipline the kids, so Jalisa [Kyierra's older daughter] feeds on that and that drives me crazy."

Disagreements regarding discipline were thus intertwined with disagreements about what constituted spoiling. Divisions regarding babyproofing provided a case in point. As illustrated in the case study of Andreya, the mothers tended to see the wisdom of the practice while the grandmothers were more likely to believe that it was possible to use discipline to teach toddlers to stay away from breakable or dangerous objects. The grandmothers thought toddlers who did not keep their hands off forbidden objects were spoiled. Also along these lines, some of the mothers and grandmothers disagreed about the frequency with which one or the other used (or should use) corporal punishment. (See Chapter 10 for more on the mothers' perspectives on these issues.)

In a few cases, the grandmothers criticized their daughters for lack of attentiveness, or for not being careful enough with their children. Kyierra's mother Elise and her partner Alice, for example, thought that Kyierra and her boyfriend should be more gentle with and attentive to little Jalisa. On one occasion, they threatened to call protective services. Alice told us,

"Jalisa was like 3 months old and I guess she was asleep. They [Kyierra and Tejon] both got in the car and went to Taco Bell. They brought it [the food] back home, but they left her [Jalisa] in the apartment by herself. And periodically my son's girlfriend stops in now that she's seen her [Jalisa] without shoes and socks on. . . . She [Kyierra] was honest about it [leaving the baby at home alone]. She didn't even think nothing was wrong with it. And I said, 'In that instant, she could of choked to death, being a baby.' And, yes, there was a big fight about that. And, that's when Elise said, 'I'm telling you, Kyierra, to your face, if I hear of any of this again, I'm calling Social Services.' And it hasn't happened since then."

Maria and her mother were much closer and much more appreciative of each other's child-rearing practices than were Kyierra and Elise. Nonetheless, they disagreed about some child-rearing issues, such as how late it was appropriate to take Bryce out of the house and spoiling him. During one of our visits, Maria commented on the subtle (or sometimes not so subtle) pressures that created what she perceived to be a "no-win" situation for her, "I always had this voice in the back of my head like, 'Okay. I have to ask them, should I take Bryce to the doctor? He's rubbing his ear.' I feel like I've got to ask their permission, ask them what they think because if I don't, well, [they would say] 'You didn't have to take him. I knew what that was.' And then if I didn't take him, they are like, 'Why didn't you take him to the doctor?'"

Grandmothers' Substance Abuse   We have some evidence that problems in six of the mother–grandmother pairs were exacerbated by the older women's drug and/or alcohol use. For reasons that may have been related to her mother's drug abuse, Chandra had not seen her mother since she was 3 months old. Tanisha saw her mother occasionally, but said she could not regularly depend on her, "She kind of comes in and out of my life, but when we're around her, she's really sweet, you know. She just has a drug problem, but she's pretty good with my daughter. . . . She asked me, 'Has she did this?' 'Is she walking?' She's trying to get herself together."

Andreya's mother Patricia used marijuana and alcohol, which may have contributed to her mood swings and conflicts in their relationship. Kyierra also reported that her mother used to drink too much, and Roneeka disapproved of her mother drinking beer in front of Regina.

The complaints that some mothers and grandmothers had about each other reflect one key difference between mother–grandmother relationships and friend relationships. Friends certainly have their spats from time to time, but seldom could their relationships withstand the frequent conflicts that characterized the relationships between Kyierra and Elise and Andreya and Patricia. Further, even those mothers and daughters who had better relationships still tended to argue more than typical friends, perhaps because parent–child relationships are generally assumed to be permanent, and friendships often end when the friends argue frequently and complain about each other (Fehr, 2000).

Changes Over Time in Mother–Daughter Relationships

The relationships between the mothers and grandmothers did not follow a linear course. There was an ebb and flow to them. First, there were frequent periods of relatively little overt conflict along with shorter periods of regular conflict. These conflicts were fueled by persistent tensions that sometimes bubbled to the surface and sometimes did not. Second, there was a movement between a desire for closeness and a desire for distance, as the mothers strove to establish some independence from their parents.

Third, and related to the second tension, was a movement between autonomy and dependence, which is normal in this stage of human development. Cohen, Kasen, Chen, Hartmark, and Gordon (2003) found that most of the young people in their sample had periods of great independence followed by periods when they functioned in a more dependent manner—at least in some domains. Cohen et al. found that African American young adults were more independent immediately after high school, "but did not subsequently increase their independence and responsibility to the same extent as did White participants" (p. 668). The mothers in this study wanted to establish their autonomy and sense of independence from their mothers (and other caregivers). On the other hand, financial circumstances and the need for assistance often resulted in their needing to remain at least somewhat dependent on the grandmothers. Six of the nine mothers moved out of their parents' home, and then for a variety of economic, psychological, and interpersonal reasons, temporarily moved back within months. The ebb and flow of the mother–grandmother relationship is illustrated by Shardae's experience.

Shardae and Her Mother

Shardae's parents divorced when she was 3 years old, and she and her brother were raised primarily by their mother. As Shardae tells it, "She was really our main, our only parent for a long time." Whenever she was upset, nervous, or depressed and needed someone to talk to, Shardae turned to her mother first. Shardae calls her mother the most influential person in her life, a person who had taught her values such as respecting elders (e.g., staying out of "grown folks' business") and being a stable parent. Shardae also recognized the close relationship that her mother had with her daughter Alexis. "She loves Granny," she told us.

Shardae's relationship with her mother has not been without its problems, however. Shardae sometimes felt that her mother was unreliable, such as when she agreed to provide child care for Alexis when Shardae was scheduled to work weekends but then cancelled at the last minute. Shardae also did not like her mother's habit of gossiping or spreading news, especially news given to her in confidence. "Well, if you tell my mama something, it will get to everybody. You can tell her it's supposed to be a secret and it will get out some kind of way." Furthermore, when she moved back into her mother's home, while she was in between apartments, Shardae found it difficult to follow the house rules. These feelings of frustration may have influenced Shardae's initial desire to move with Alexis to the state where her father lived (a move that never took place). When we asked if she would miss her mother if she moved, Shardae replied, "By then, I'll be ready for a break from her. I'll miss her but being apart will be good for us."

Shardae loved her mother and father and has maintained close relationships with both of them. She leaned more on her mother than her father for both emotional and instrumental support, but there were times when Shardae felt that her mother was "not all there" and said that she "gets on my nerves."

The Importance of Fictive Grandmothers

Chandra was unique among the mothers in our study in that since the age of 3 months she had had no contact with her biological mother. She did, however, receive continuing maternal-like support from other women, most notably two of her father's ex-wives and a paternal aunt. Her story, described in the vignette below, illustrates the well-known pattern in the African American community for fictive kin and extended family members to step in to compensate for absent parents (Hill, 1999).

Chandra and Her Mother

Chandra last saw her mother when she was 3 months old. The reason given for her biological mother's absence varies depending on the person asked. According to Chandra, she was kidnapped by her father as an attempt to "get back" at her mother for trying to put a stop to his physical abuse and thefts of her welfare checks. Chandra thought that her mother had tried to rescue her but could not because her father outmaneuvered her. Edith, one of Chandra's step-grandmothers, told a different story. According to her, Chandra was taken away because her mother was a "dope addict" and an unstable mother. Despite different versions of the story, however, there are two consistent components in all of the stories. First, Chandra was sent to live with her uncle and aunt in an adjoining state shortly after being separated from her mother, and, second, Chandra never saw or heard from her mother again.

Chandra's father remarried twice. He was married to Sharon for approximately 9 years and then to Cecelia for approximately 5 years. A strong supporter of parental responsibility, Cecelia insisted that Chandra be reunited with her father and come live with them in their home. Chandra was 12 and excited about the move because she was ready to get away from her uncle, whom she perceived as too strict. Although physically abused by Chandra's father, Cecelia endured life with him until she felt that Chandra was old enough to take care of herself.

During the years we knew Chandra, Aunt Eileen (Chandra's father's sister), Grandmother Rita (Cecelia's mother), and Chandra's two stepmothers continued to be sources of shelter, food, empathy, and much unsolicited advice. Although both Sharon and Cecelia experienced abuse from Chandra's father and divorced him, they both empathized with Chandra's history and continued contact with her. Smiling, Chandra told us that Cecelia was there during the birth of her son Patrick. Whenever Chandra needed last-minute child care for Patrick, she knew she could count on Aunt Eileen. When she was evicted from her apartment, she leaned on Grandmother Rita for shelter and support. With regard to Cecelia, Chandra explained, "I get along with her, we're real close, it's like she's my real mother because she was there for me and that's who he [Patrick] calls his grandma, and I'm not going to tell him that it's not his grandma."

The statement that Cecelia "was there" for Chandra is not an overstatement. When she turned 20, Chandra decided that she could not properly raise her son. She did not feel like she had her "life together" and craved the freedom to be "young" and to "kick it." She turned to Cecelia, asking if she would consider taking over legal guardianship of Patrick. Cecelia agreed and did everything she could to make sure Chandra's son was safe and healthy (see vignette in Chapter 13 for more on this situation).

For at least six of our mothers, other women played key roles as mother figures. Four of the mothers indicated that their grandmothers were significant figures in their lives. For example, Shardae's grandmother, a retired nurse, provided her with important information on health-related issues. For two other mothers, maternal aunts played mother-like roles for at least a limited period of time. Kyierra told us, "When I first got pregnant, my mother was in Kentucky. . . . Now they're [her mother and her mother's partner] back [but] my aunt and them are closer to me than my mom is." Responding to a question about whom she confides in about important things, Shardae said, "Sometimes my mother. Mostly my aunt. I go to her with things more than I do my mother."

Effects of the Mother–Grandmother Relationship on Mothers and Children

The mothers' relationships with the grandmothers seemed to have at least two direct effects on them and, consequently, indirect effects on their children. First, relationships with their mothers seemed to affect the younger women's functioning. Consistent with previous research (Umberson & Slaten, 2000), we suspect that the mothers' mental health and ability to cope with stress were likely related to the quality of their relationship with their mothers (and, to a lesser extent, their fathers). Andreya's home visitor Rickie, for example, could accurately anticipate how Andreya would sound on the phone by the way her mother Patricia answered his call. He observed that Patricia's moods greatly affected Andreya. Of course, the mothers' level of functioning was determined by a large number and wide variety of interacting factors, not only the nature of their relationships with their mothers, but there seemed to be a link between the mother–grandmother relationships and the mothers' sense of well-being.

Second, the younger mothers' parenting behavior seemed to be affected by their relationships with their mothers. Those who had good relationships with their mothers and who were in close contact with them seemed to function better as parents. Like Burton (1996), we saw that the mothers who lived with their mothers benefited to some extent from the grandmothers' supervision and guidance regarding parenting responsibilities. However, it should be noted that there is some inconsistency on this issue in the literature. McLoyd, Cauce, Takeuchi, and Wilson (2000) concluded that "the impact of grandmother involvement, especially when mother and grandmother are coresiding, coparenting, or both, is decidedly mixed . . . . Studies of Black and White urban or high-risk families have also suggested that coresidence and high levels of grandmother involvement can predict lower quality parenting by adolescent mothers" (p. 1083). In our sample as well, there was at least one mother, Roneeka, who was close to her mother but who struggled with parenting skills. More research is needed regarding the circumstances under which grandmothers' involvement in the parenting of their grandchildren is beneficial for young mothers and children.

MOTHERS' RELATIONSHIPS WITH THEIR FATHERS

The mothers in our study had far less contact with their fathers than with their mothers—a phenomenon certainly not limited to young mothers in poverty (Amato, 2000; Umberson & Slaten, 2000). Nevertheless, most had multiple father figures in their lives—for example, a stepfather, a grandfather, or even a neighbor. In this section, several themes related to these relationships are discussed.

Presence of Multiple Father Figures in the Mothers' Lives

Three mothers—Chandra, Breanna, and Maria—lived with their fathers at least some of the time. Shardae also had considerable phone contact with her father and saw him twice a year. The remaining mothers had very little contact with their biological fathers. This pattern is illustrated in the following vignette:

Kyierra and Her Father

Kyierra never knew her father. As a child, she would ask her mother Elise questions such as "Who was he?" "How did you and he meet?" and "Where is he now?" But these questions seemed to irritate Elise and were either ignored or responded to with brief answers such as "I don't know his name. I barely even knew him." The only thing back then that Kyierra really knew about her father was that he and Kyierra's mother had never married.

Growing up, Kyierra said that her concept of a father's role mainly stemmed from watching television programs and seeing certain friends interact with their fathers. She believed that real fathers were "always there" for their children, always willing to play and interact with them, and would never leave them. Kyierra saw how one friend's father would "watch out" or "check up" on his daughter and would "adore" her. Kyierra deeply wanted a father–daughter relationship just like her friend had and just like the ones she had seen on television. She wanted to know her "real dad."

Kyierra had had a positive relationship with her maternal grandfather. She appreciated how he would make time for her and make her laugh by calling her silly names. However, she did not see him as a substitute father. She did not feel that he could fulfill her needs like a father could because he was old and in poor health. Before he died, she recollected that he smoked a lot and was constantly coughing. Elise had had a conflicted relationship with her father (Kyierra's grandfather) and always had bad things to say about him; however, Kyierra never agreed with her mother's opinions. To Kyierra, he was always "a good man."

It was when Kyierra was pregnant with her daughter Jalisa that she became particularly interested in learning more about her father. One evening, Elise had had too much to drink and accidentally revealed that "Harold" was the name of Kyierra's father. After Elise realized what she had done, she said that she barely knew the man and that it was just a chance engagement. Several weeks later, Kyierra came across a card signed by a man named Harold in her mother's apartment. The card was received on the day Kyierra was born. Equipped with evidence, Kyierra confronted her mother and wanted to know, "Why had she lied all this time?" Kyierra's mother defended herself by saying that Harold "beat the crap out of" her and sold dope. When Kyierra asked where her father was currently, her mother explained that he had died from an overdose of heroin and alcohol.

Kyierra could not believe that her mother was just now telling her this and that her dreams of one day meeting her father were shattered. Kyierra's mother, on the other hand, felt that the matter had been out of her control. According to Elise, Harold "drank and took pills you know. He beat me. I didn't want Kyierra to follow [in his footsteps]."

Since the birth of her first child, Kyierra came to believe that she and her life would have "turned out better" if she had had a father. She believed that there were things that a father would have done to make sure that she was safe and "did right." According to Kyierra, these expectations of a father expanded after meeting her current fiancé. She is a strong believer in two-parent families and that children benefit from having father figures in their lives. As for her own father, Kyierra mentioned that she hoped to find his family one day.

Other Male Figures in the Mothers' Lives

Some of the mothers had males such as brothers who played significant roles in their lives. Roneeka exemplified those mothers:

Interviewer: Are there any other men who were important in your life?
Roneeka: Uh, my grandma's boyfriend. And I guess my brothers since I was growing up.

For these mothers, fatherhood was determined more by function than by blood. According to the mothers, fathers were men who provided for them, guided them, assisted them, and supported them regardless of whether or not they were their biological fathers. In some instances, the fathers were the biological fathers of the mothers, but other men were considered fathers because of what the mothers felt they had done for them. Some men who were involved on a long-term basis with a mother or grandmother were referred to as "stepfathers," "daddies," or "grandpas," suggesting that their kinship status was based on the functions they performed rather than on the existence of a legal marriage or genetic ties.

> Tanisha: I had a father figure. My mother married this one guy who I thought was my father clear up until I was 8.
>
> Roneeka: And I mean, he [her mother's ex-husband] was like more like a father, I really, I mean, my daddy he did little stuff like on Christmas, but you know you need more than that from a father, you know. . . . They can bring and drop off stuff all they want but it ain't like them being there with you, so, I mean, Terrance, he was really like my father. Not biologically but. . . ."

Recall that Andreya's biological father was minimally involved in her growing-up years and that her mother's boyfriend of 12 years, Sam, served the role of a supportive father figure. Andreya called him "Daddy" because he was there for her. When talking about him to us, she called him her stepfather, probably to distinguish him from her biological father. This man, according to Andreya, was generous to her, giving her everything she wanted (or paying half if she would pay the other half).

Mothers' Expectations of Their Fathers

What did mothers expect from their fathers or the male figures in their lives? Overwhelmingly, they reported that their fathers should "be there" for them when they needed help. Breanna described a father as "Somebody that if I need anything I could go to somebody to talk to, somebody to love and care for me. And love me for who I was or who they thought I was gonna be or like standing behind me 100% regardless if it was good or bad."

Tanisha provided the following image of what a father should be, which goes beyond just being there for his children: "I think that being a good father would be to provide for the child. Quality time more than just spending money on the child. More quality time to gain a relationship with that particular child. If you spend quality time . . . then at that point you have a bond with the child."

When the fathers were not perceived as being there for their children, the mothers became angry and withdrew from them. Recall that Andreya's bitterness over her father's lack of involvement with her during her childhood resulted in her refusal to allow him to play a grandfather role vis-à-vis her son (see Chapter 5). In another example, Tanisha noted, "No support. Uh, he didn't call me and ask me how I'm doing or what I'm doing. [He did not ask me] 'Is everything all right? Do you have anything to eat?' He did not give emotionally or financially or anything to help me out in any way. So I figure I shouldn't even associate with him. Evidently those are signs that he don't care so I don't talk to him anymore."

Tanisha clarified that her father did occasionally help her, but only if she "begged." Had he been more forthcoming on his own, she might have had a more positive attitude toward him, "He has been helping out as far as when my phone bill was high he gave me money. I mean one time I didn't have food and he brought me some food over. Yeah, he's helped. He helps out if he could, you know if possible he'll help me out if I'm really begging or if he has it, he'll help me."

Lower Expectations for Fathers than for Mothers   The mothers expected their fathers to "be there" for them, which included but was not limited to providing financially when they were able to and occasionally doing things with their daughters. Their mothers, by contrast, were expected to care for their daughters, which required a great deal more time, attention, and contact. These lower expectations for fathers seemed to help some of the mothers feel more satisfied with the small amount of contact they had with their fathers. The expectation that mothers would do more for them than their fathers perhaps also explained in part why there was more conflict with mothers than with fathers—more contact is likely to be associated with more conflict.

Mothers Forgiving Their Fathers

Shardae and Roneeka told us that their fathers had turned their lives around and were showing renewed interest in them and/or their babies. The mothers were willing to accept their fathers and their new romantic partners. For example, when asked if there were men in her life whom she admired, Roneeka (contradicting her earlier statement when she did not include her father as an important male in her life) answered,

"My daddy. I look up to him also because he done turned his life around a whole lot. . . . 'Cause he used to be on drugs, this and that. But now he work every day. He's got a nice car, nice home now. He has a nice woman. A nice young thing. He has, I mean, he done been through a lot. He used to be in and out of jail. Now he just working every day and taking care what he gotta take care of. So I look up to him for that. And whenever I need something, he, you know, 'cause I'm the baby girl anyway."

Others, however, felt that it was too late. In two cases, lack of forgiveness may have been connected to the fact that the fathers were not perceived to have changed much for the better. As indicated above, Andreya provided one example. Chandra provided another.

"I would pretty much get to do what I want to do [when I was a child], and I didn't have nobody telling me what I can and couldn't do, so I was really by myself . . . and like when somebody would try to tell me something, I would get mad, because you know, I feel as if I don't have no parents. So I figured, you know, he ain't been there for me. So that's why there's no feelings toward me and my father, I really don't, I've been on my own so it doesn't worry me."

FINAL REFLECTIONS

In this section, we speculate about how the relationships that the mothers in this study had with their mothers and fathers seemed to differ from the comparable relationships that middle-income mothers have with their parents.

Comparing Young Mothers from Low-Income Families with Young Mothers from Middle-Income Families

From a qualitative study of only nine mothers, all with low incomes, it is of course impossible to learn how low- and middle-income young mothers' relationships with their parents compare. Nevertheless, we share some thoughts based on our study and past research on this issue. The mothers in this study seemed to be similar to more economically advantaged teenage and young adult daughters in the sense that they were generally close to their mothers, but had periods of conflict and areas of disagreement (Smetana, 1989; Smetana, Daddis, & Chuang, 2003). Mother–daughter conflict is certainly not restricted to young mothers living in poverty.

The young mothers in our study differed from most middle-income and older mothers in that they were closer in age to their mothers because their mothers were teenagers when they gave birth to their daughters. A mother who has her daughter when she is 15 years old will be a 30-year-old grandmother if her daughter follows in her footsteps. Both the younger age of the grandmothers and the smaller age discrepancy may partially explain why these young mothers often considered their mothers to be their "friends" or even their "best friends." Women who are both young and of somewhat similar ages may be more likely to consider themselves to be peers than mothers and daughters who are from clearly different generations. As Andreya's mother said, "I grew up with my kids." This relatively small age discrepancy may be detrimental for children, however. Burton (1996) found that children's outcomes were better when there was a larger age difference between the mother and grandmother because these mothers and daughters were better able to establish a hierarchical role structure. This finding may explain why the mothers in this study emphasized the importance of discipline and respecting elders. Explicit values may be necessary in families where there is a small age discrepancy between mothers and grandmothers.

Comparing Low-Income and Middle-Income Father–Daughter Relationships

The mothers in our study seemed to be less involved with their fathers than may be the case in typical middle-income families (Furstenberg, Nord, Peterson, & Zill, 1983; Seltzer, Schaeffer, & Charng, 1989). The extent of this potential difference should not be exaggerated, however, as there is compelling evidence that fathers from all socioeconomic strata, after divorce and/or relationship termination, typically have reduced involvement with their children over time (Demo & Cox, 2000; Stephens, 1996). Nevertheless, most of the young women in our study did not have regular and sustained contact with their biological fathers, even though three of them lived with their fathers occasionally (Maria, Breanna, and Chandra). We found that some of the young mothers in our study were fortunate enough to have other men who, in limited ways, acted as fathers. We need more research that explores how involvement with other men in the community can compensate for daughters' lack of involvement with their biological fathers. We also need basic information on the specific strategies that father figures use to support young mothers or their children—to which degrees they offer tangible financial assistance, advice and guidance, assistance with child care and child rearing, and emotional support. We know very little about the daily ways in which fathers or father figures of young mothers offer them help.

IMPLICATIONS FOR POLICY AND INTERVENTION

The grandmothers of the young children in our study were (and probably still are) integrally involved in their daughters' lives. Most of the mothers lived with their mothers, at least periodically. Thus, policies and interventions designed to improve the lives of young mothers and their children would seem to have a greater likelihood of success to the extent that they involve the grandmothers. Involving the grandmothers is consistent with a family systems approach that served as the foundation for the later development of the ecological model discussed in Chapter 2. The family systems approach posits that to effect positive changes among some individuals within the family requires some attention to all the individuals in the family and the entire family as a unit. We also would advocate involving the grandfathers, but that seems less realistic given that they are often less involved in their daughters' (or grandchildren's) lives.

In which ways would involving the grandmothers in low-income households be helpful? First, and most important from the standpoint of Early Head Start, is for the children's grandmothers to have a considerable amount of direct contact with their grandchildren. To the extent that the grandmothers receive some of the educational services of programs like Early Head Start, their grandchildren are more likely to receive program benefits. Second, the mothers' receptivity to programs like Early Head Start is likely to be greater if the grandmothers "buy in" to the utility of such programs. Mothers are more likely to listen carefully to home visitors, to be responsive to suggestions from their children's teachers and child care providers, and to follow through on recommended interventions when their own mothers are also clearly invested in and believe in the value of the program. Third, in some instances, particularly when grandmothers and mothers live in the same household, it may be helpful for practitioners to help mothers develop good relationships with grandmothers. In cases of extreme conflict that is harming the mother's ability to care for her child, it may be useful to help mothers and grandmothers carefully define the nature of their relationship, determine who is responsible for fulfilling which tasks, delineate the boundaries around their relationship, and decide how they will relate to the child; for example, the grandmother will help enforce rules set by the mother but will not set her own rules.

CONCLUSIONS

We have learned that young mothers' relationships with their parents can and often do play an important role in their lives and the lives of their children. In the best of situations, the grandmothers provided instrumental (e.g., helping care for children), educational (e.g., suggestions for child rearing), emotional (e.g., caring and love), and financial (e.g., help purchasing food and diapers) support for their daughters and granddaughters. However, this support was not uniformly provided to all nine mothers in the study; some of the mothers felt that their mothers' help was either too sporadic, too restrictive, and/or came "with strings attached." As a result, it was not uncommon that occasional conflicts arose as the young mothers negotiated their relationships with their own mothers.

These parental relationships were not the only ones that were important to the mothers in our study. Romantic relationships, too, were very salient. The next chapter turns to those relationships.

REFERENCES

Amato, P.R. (2000). Diversity within single-parent families. In D.H. Demo, K.R. Allen, & M.A. Fine (Eds.), *Handbook of family diversity* (pp. 149–172). New York: Oxford University Press.

Benoit, D., & Parker, K.C.H. (1994). Stability and transmission of attachment across three generations. *Child Development, 65,* 1444–1456.

Burton, L.M. (1996). Age norms, the timing of role transitions, and intergenerational caregiving among aging African American women. *Gerontologist, 36,* 199–208.

Cauce, A.M., Hiraga, Y., Graves, D., Gonzales, N., Ryan-Finn, K., & Grove, K. (1996). African American mothers and their adolescent daughters: Closeness, conflict, and control. In B.J. Ross Leadbeater & N. Way (Eds.), *Urban girls: Resisting stereotypes, creating identities* (pp. 100–116). New York: New York University Press.

Cohen, P., Kasen, S., Chen, H., Hartmark, C., & Gordon, K. (2003). Variations in patterns of developmental transitions in the emerging adulthood period. *Developmental Psychology, 39,* 657–669.

Demo, D.H., & Cox, M.J. (2000). Families with young children: A review of research in the 1990s. *Journal of Marriage and the Family, 62,* 876–895.

Fehr, B. (2000). The life cycle of friendship. In C. Hendrick & S.S. Hendrick (Eds.), *Close relationships: A sourcebook* (pp. 71–82). Thousand Oaks, CA: Sage.

Frank, S.J., Avery, C.B., & Laman, M.S. (1988). Young adults' perceptions of their relationships with their parents: Individual differences in connectedness, competence, and emotional autonomy. *Developmental Psychology, 24,* 729–737.

Furstenberg, F.A., Jr., Nord, C.W., Peterson, J.L., & Zill, N. (1983). The life course of children of divorce: Marital disruptions and parental contact. *American Sociological Review, 48,* 656–668.

Hare, R.B., & Castenell, L.A., Jr. (1985). No place to run, no place to hide: Comparative status and future prospects of Black boys. In M.B. Spencer, B.K. Brookins, & W.R. Allen (Eds.), *Beginnings: The social and affective development of Black children* (pp. 201–214). Mahwah, NJ: Lawrence Erlbaum Associates.

Hill, S.A. (1999). *African American children: Socialization and development in families.* Thousand Oaks, CA: Sage.

Holmbeck, G.N. (1996). A model of family relational transformations during the transition to adolescence: Parent–adolescent conflict and adaptation. In J.A. Graber, J. Brookes-Gunn, & A.C. Petersen (Eds.), *Transitions through adolescence: Interpersonal domains and context* (pp. 167–199). Mahwah, NJ: Lawrence Erlbaum Associates.

McLoyd, V.C., Cauce, A.M., Takeuchi, D., & Wilson, L. (2000). Marital processes and parental socialization in families of color: A decade review of research. *Journal of Marriage and the Family, 62,* 1070–1093.

Seltzer, J.A., Schaeffer, N.C., & Charng, H. (1989). Family ties after divorce: The relationship between visitation and paying child support. *Journal of Marriage and the Family, 51,* 1013–1032.

Smetana, J.G. (1989). Adolescents' and parents' reasoning about actual family conflict. *Child Development, 60,* 1052–1067.

Smetana, J.G. (2000). Middle-class African American adolescents' and parents' conceptions of parental authority and parenting practices: A longitudinal investigation. *Child Development, 71,* 1672–1686.

Smetana, J.G., Daddis, C., & Chuang, S.S. (2003). "Clean your room!" A longitudinal investigation of adolescent–parent conflict and conflict resolution in middle-class African American families. *Journal of Adolescent Research, 18,* 631–650.

Stephens, L.S. (1996). Will Johnny see daddy this week? *Journal of Family Issues, 17,* 466–494.

Umberson, D., & Slaten, E. (2000). Gender and intergenerational relationships. In D.H. Demo, K.R. Allen, & M.A. Fine (Eds.), *Handbook of family diversity* (pp. 105–127). New York: Oxford University Press.

9

Matters of the Heart

Romantic Relationships

Elizabeth A. Sharp and Jean M. Ispa

In recent decades, African American romantic relationship patterns have elicited considerable attention, with researchers citing higher divorce rates, lower rates of marriage, and higher nonmarital birth rates among African Americans than among members of other U.S. racial–ethnic groups (Franklin, 2000; Tucker & Mitchell-Kernan, 1995). In this chapter, we examine the romantic relationships of the nine mothers who participated in our study, describing the challenges they faced as they sought to establish and maintain relationships with men. There were, of course, individual differences in the mothers' relationship histories. Here, however, we focus on themes that seemed typical and link these commonalities to the socioeconomic conditions in which the mothers and their partners lived.

As other researchers have pointed out, unbalanced sex ratios (i.e., the ratios of males to females in given populations) and high male unemployment and incarceration rates—inextricably linked to poverty—influence African American romantic relationships (Tucker & Mitchell-Kernan, 1995). In the year 2000, only 46.6% of African American 15- to 34-year-olds were male, compared with 50.2% of Whites in the same age range (U.S. Census Bureau, 2000). Unbalanced sex ratios have been associated with reduced male commitment to relationships and high rates of singlehood, nonmarital births, infidelity, and transience in relationships (Guttentag & Secord, 1983). Likewise, male unemployment has been linked to negative consequences for individuals and relationships (e.g., Bowman & Forman, 1997; Gibbs, 1988; Massey & Shibuya, 1995). Even in 1998, during a time of economic prosperity, African American men faced unemployment rates of 7.4%, more than twice the 3.2% rate for White men (U.S. Department of Labor, 1999). Challenges for

African American women seeking stable romantic relationships are further exacerbated by high male imprisonment rates. In the 1990s, on any given day, a third of all Black men in their 20s were incarcerated or on parole (Cherlin, 2002; Mauer & Huling, 1995).

In addition to these forces, societal ideologies about marriage and families are important influences on women's personal relationships. Previous studies have suggested that African American women across socioeconomic levels express a desire for marriage and view the nuclear family (mother, father, and children living together) as ideal (e.g., Tucker, 2000; Tucker & Mitchell-Kernan, 1995). Other research indicates that although low-income African American mothers desire marriage and a nuclear family, many are uncertain that this will come to pass (Jarrett, 1994).

It also is important to consider the ages of the mothers in our sample. Because they were in their teens or early 20s when they became pregnant, it is reasonable to suggest that their youth played a role in the quality of their relationships and in their patterns of breakup. Adolescents tend to have romantic relationships that are less stable than those of adults (Galliher, Rostosky, Welsh, & Kawaguchi, 1999). Moreover, relationship stress was no doubt exacerbated by the demands of pregnancy and child rearing, as well as by the compounding hardships of poverty and racism.

MAJOR THEMES IN MOTHERS' RELATIONSHIPS WITH THEIR CHILDREN'S BIOLOGICAL FATHERS

The influences of all the aforementioned pressures were brought to life in our mothers' stories about their romantic relationships. We have identified six themes that stood out as particularly prominent. First, when they became pregnant for the first time, most of the mothers were committed to their romantic partners and believed that they were in long-term relationships; however, none of the relationships lasted. Constraints related to the men's financial instability seemed to be the dominant influence on the deterioration of relationships. Issues related to money thus make up our second theme. Our third theme involves the infidelity of both partners, but especially the men. Our fourth theme centered on the biological fathers of the women's children: Whether the romances continued or ended, the women wanted the fathers to remain involved in their children's lives and were disappointed and frustrated when that involvement was nonexistent or sporadic. Fifth, at the time of most of our interviews, the women held negative views of men, mistrusting them especially because they viewed the men as unwilling to remain faithful, pay adequate child support, or spend sufficient time with their children. Nevertheless, our sixth theme revolves around the mothers' optimism that they would eventually find satisfying and lasting relationships. Despite their negative experiences and feelings, all of the women remained open to new romances and most were hopeful for marriage, often expressing a belief in the ideal of the nuclear family.

Love, Commitment, and Trust in the Permanence of Relationships

Around the onset of their pregnancies, most of the women had dated their partners for several months, and we came to understand that all except perhaps one were in love at the time. For several women, the biological father of their children was their first serious romantic partner.

Andreya's story in Section II of this book provides a detailed description of her feelings toward William at the time of her pregnancy and thereafter. Recall that she had been seeing William for close to a year and was in love with him. She believed that William would always "be there" for her and her baby. Her account of her relationship with William is similar to several stories we heard. Maria, after dating Marcus for 2½ years, became pregnant unexpectedly. She explained that her decision to keep her baby was rooted in the fact that "I made this baby with someone that I loved very much." Sherryce also indicated that she had felt a close attachment to the father of her baby and had expected their relationship to last. She reflected, "I thought he would be there, because I've been with him [off and on] since I was like 10 or 11 and we were supposed to be married twice."

Shardae and Kyierra also expressed strong attachments to the biological fathers of their babies. Shardae had dated Jerome for 5 months before her pregnancy. She explained her closeness to Jerome by describing how her family had liked him and included him in several family events. "You know," she said, "he went to Texas, he went with us, he was taking trips with us . . . my mom bought him something for Christmas last year, and he came over here and ate Thanksgiving dinner with us and everything." Kyierra lived with Bryan for more than 6 months before becoming pregnant. She indicated her devotion to him by telling us about her mother's initial impression of him. Her mother, she explained, had liked Bryan because "He said, 'Oh, I'm gonna take such good care of Kyierra. I'm gonna make sure that she has this, make sure that she has that.'"

Despite the attachment the mothers felt toward their partners prior to pregnancy, most of the romantic relationships ended before the children were born. Only three mothers, Roneeka, Andreya, and Chandra, remained romantically involved with the fathers after the births of their children, and these relationships also eventually ended during our study. After their romances with the biological fathers of their children were over, all of the mothers formed romantic attachments with other men; all but two of these relationships also ended before our final interviews. The ending of relationships brought heartache to all of the young women. Feelings of hurt, disappointment, anger, betrayal, and sadness often accompanied the breakups, especially ones involving the biological fathers of their children.

The women's thoughts concerning failed relationships reflected the significance they had given to them. Past mistakes were conceptualized as having provided valuable learning experiences. For example, Sherryce shared her resolve never again to become involved with a man who placed high priorities on his friends, drinking, and "clubbing." She said, "I'm not going to go through this again, the way it [her relationship with her second baby's father] was, I refuse to do it." She went on to say, "Like he wanted to go out and hang out, he wanted to do whatever—his thing—and then when he got through doing his thing, then he'd come see me. I just don't have time for that. And I'm like, that's not what I want, and that's why I left." Looking at the bright side, at what she had gained from her failed relationship with her baby's father, Shardae commented that "Even though he was a disadvantage, even though the relationship was negative, it's made me focus. Having that negativity in that part of my life has made me look forward to what's good, look past the negative. I've gotten stronger."

Problems Due to Male Partners' Financial Instability

The financial instability of the males in the women's lives was a powerful influence on their romantic relationships. Male unemployment was a central feature in relationship problems. When the women's partners were out of work, the romantic relationships were likely to suffer.

Effects of Male Unemployment   It is well established that the movement of manufacturing jobs out of city centers has had a devastating effect on the ability of unskilled African American men to secure work paying a living wage. Moreover, structural constraints related to racism help ensure that African American blue collar workers have fragile job prospects (Massey & Shibuya, 1995; Wilson, 1987). Because African American men tend to believe in the ideal of the male breadwinner, employment problems often lead to feelings of unworthiness and discomfort in family roles (Bowman & Forman, 1997; see also Chapter 11). In our study, male unemployment seemed to have far-reaching consequences, both direct and indirect, on the entry into, development of, and dissolution of relationships. Our assertion is consistent with Carol Stack's (1974) conclusion, based on her ethnographic work, that male unemployment was the most influential factor affecting the relationships of the low-income, African American women she studied.

Most of our mothers identified "steady employment" as a critical characteristic of an ideal romantic partner. A typical response to our question about ideal men underscored a desire for "someone who is working and reliable." Nonetheless, almost all of the mothers had involvements with men who, at one time or another, were out of work. Several mothers expressed simultaneously both understanding and frustration relating to their partners' unemployment. On the one hand, they sympathized with their partners because they understood the difficulties African American men face acquiring and keeping jobs in their impoverished neighborhoods. At the same time, however, many grew frustrated, especially when their partners' jobless state was protracted. Reflecting these contradictory feelings, Tanisha explained, "Yes, Dwayne needs a job and sometimes it stresses me out because I know I have a job and I have to pay the bills. Sometimes I feel like, you know, he's not trying to help. He's not trying to get a job or whatever. But he is. One time he took me with him so I could see that he tried."

Similarly, Shardae felt annoyed when her partner was not working even though she understood that he was actively searching for a job, "He was going through temporary agencies to try to find a job. I don't know if he wasn't looking hard enough or what. He'd get like assignments for a few days and that's it. I don't know if he was being choosy about what type of work he would take. I don't know, I don't know, but he was getting real frustrated too."

Kyierra expressed contradictory feelings about issues related to unemployment. Although she realized that her boyfriend Tejon was providing economic support by taking care of her daughter while she worked, she sometimes experienced anger because of the arrangement. "I kinda get mad 'cause I'll be at work and they're [Tejon and her child] just at home chilling." During a later interview, both Kyierra and Tejon were unemployed and their relationship was tense. Unemployment likely fueled their arguments and contributed to her temporary psychological withdrawal from the relationship. She explained, "I was backing away just because we weren't getting along. I felt myself backing away. The fights could be caused because neither one of us was working at the time."

The mothers criticized their partners for not working, nagged them to get a job, and described them as "bothering" or "stressing them out." Complaints tended to diminish when jobs were found. For example,

Chandra told us, "As long as Patrick got a job, I ain't complaining because at first I was complaining that he didn't have a job, and now he got one."

Some women, after having dated men who were unemployed, expressed their determination to avoid future romances with such men. Sherryce, in our last interview with her, told us in a resolved manner, "He [a potential boyfriend] has to bring something to the table. I have a full table. You know, he need to bring something. He just can't bring himself and then go live off me 'cause that ain't right." Andreya, ruing her past experiences, told us that she "would never mess with another man that don't already have a job." She did, however, later date at least one man who was fired or laid off after she met him.

Marriage decisions often hinged on male employment success. Other research similarly suggests that one factor influencing single teenage mothers not to marry is joblessness (Furstenberg, 1976; Jarrett, 1994; Stack, 1974). Recall Andreya's refusal of William's marriage proposal near the beginning of their relationship (see Chapter 5). She did not want to marry before they could afford to live independent of their mothers. Kyierra's boyfriend Tejon did not want to marry her until he had steady employment. He explained, "We got plans on getting married; I'd like to be married and have a little comfortable life, just real comfortable. I want to be married and living comfortable." When asked about barriers to marriage, he responded, "Man, jobs. You know, just finding one; it is hard finding a good job." He proposed 18 months later, after holding the same job for more than a year.

Interestingly, when asked if her fiancé's steady employment was related to the timing of their engagement, Kyierra did not think so. Instead, she told us, "He was just ready." Unlike other women in the study, Kyierra was unwavering in her desire to marry Tejon; she wanted to marry him despite the ups and downs in their relationship and even when he was out of work for an extended time. However, Tejon's comment quoted in the previous paragraph strongly suggests that he would not have proposed to her had he not been confident that he was now steadily employed.

Connection Between Unemployment and Incarceration   Research has indicated that young men who have little likelihood of earning adequate income via legitimate work may respond by turning to lucrative illegal activities such as robbery, pimping, or selling drugs. For African American men living in low-income neighborhoods, jail is an all-too-common consequence (Jankowski, 1991; Wilson, 2003). A strikingly large number of the mothers' fathers, uncles, and brothers had spent time in jail or in prison. At least six boyfriends were incarcerated during the years of our study.

Keeping a job or finding a new one was made much more difficult by a history of incarceration. Young men were likely to be fired when employers found out that an absence, however temporary, was due to incarceration. In at least two cases the women's partners lost their jobs because they had been in prison for a brief period (i.e., a week or less). One partner, jailed for 3 days because of speeding tickets, was fired even though he had worked at the job for close to 2 years and had recently earned a promotion. Another was fired after spending a week in jail because he had not checked in with his parole officer. As Andreya's grandmother explained during one of our conversations with her, the problem was exacerbated by the fact that potential employers were reluctant to hire applicants who had been incarcerated. (Potential employers obtained this information during job interviews and/or from questions on application forms about past arrests.)

Though imprisonment certainly played a role in relationship formation and maintenance, it seemed to us that employment issues played a more prominent role in women's decisions regarding the initiation, continuation, and dissolution of romantic relationships. Mothers did not speak at length about past or current partners' incarcerations. Nonetheless, Tanisha did explicitly link financial issues related to imprisonment to her decision to end her relationship with Dwayne, "Mainly I was depressed because of him calling me, the bills. The collect calls [he was in jail]. He wasn't benefiting me any. Basically he didn't help me any [financially] so I had to let him go."

Dwayne and Tanisha did eventually get back together during the 2 years he was in jail. However, their relationship remained tenuous even after he was out of jail. He told us that his relationship with Tanisha "is not going as I planned or as smoothly as I like because of me being gone, you know." Bowser (1995) pointed out that because having a jail record lowers men's chances of getting a good job, imprisonment and unemployment are closely intertwined and have similar consequences for intimate relationships.

Exchange of Money for Intimacy   Finally, the men's economic instability combined with the women's poverty seemed to have another side effect on romantic involvement patterns. It was our impression that some of the mothers consciously or unconsciously accepted money and gifts in exchange for sexual intimacy. Although this behavior occurs in other income groups as well (Sprecher & McKinney, 1993), the conditions of poverty may make such exchanges more obvious. In our study, boyfriends and potential boyfriends often had little money, which perhaps made the times when they did have cash to spend on gifts for women particularly special. Andreya's recollections (in Chapter 4) about William's gifts to her when he was first courting her are illustrative. William's strategy was reminiscent of the plan described by one of the teenage boys interviewed by Steve Eyre (as reported by Strauss & Corbin, [1998]): Buy things for the girl until she feels she must reciprocate. Chances are that the only way she can match the magnitude of the gifts he has given her is to offer him her body. Note that Patricia, Andreya's mother, was acutely aware of the danger in William's gifts; recall her alarm when Andreya came home with a new dress that William, not she, had paid for. Patricia worried that William was "buying" her daughter. And as Andreya said in Chapter 4, she also came to believe that William used "presents, jewelry, rings, and watches" as lures.

We saw similar patterns in some of the brief romantic relationships of Tanisha and Chandra. Tanisha met a man who gave her a gift of bedroom furniture soon after they met. Although she did not tell us much about this man or the relationship, we were under the impression that she had been physically intimate with him and later regretted it. Chandra, on a number of occasions, told us about men buying food and other things for her and her son. One man had even bought her a car. Just before our last interview, a man (not her boyfriend) had bought her a TV, DVD player, and a sofa set and was paying her rent. Although she never told us outright, it seems reasonable to speculate that she was exchanging sexual intimacy for his monetary gifts.

As this example might suggest, it would be a mistake to conclude that men were the only ones feeling that they were coming out ahead in these exchanges. At least three of the mothers talked about women they knew who had tricked men into fatherhood in hopes of keeping them. Interestingly, Kyierra had woven thoughts about "going after men's pocketbooks" into wishes for her daughters' futures. She hoped they would grow up to have a lot of money so that their lives would be easier than hers. She reasoned that, in addition to taking on professional careers (doctor or lawyer), they would be smart to be "gold diggers." When we asked what that meant, she replied that it meant dating men with money and enjoying the things they could provide. She went on to say that marrying a man with money would also be wise. Surprised, we asked what she thought of marrying for love. She explained that truly loving relationships take a lot of time to find, and that, meanwhile, "while they're single, they can gold dig." Earlier in that same interview, Kyierra had talked about the financial strains she and Tejon were experiencing. First-hand experiences with economic hardship could lend special significance to monetary issues in romantic relationship considerations.

Male Infidelity

In several cases, male unemployment and infidelity were intertwined, and it was the latter that was the more immediate reason for relationship dissolution. Research suggests that male infidelity increases when men experience unemployment, perhaps because unemployment is linked to diminished self-esteem (Broman, 1997; Testa, 1989). One of Shardae's relationships illustrates the complex associations among employment, infidelity, and relationship dissolution. Orlando was employed when he and Shardae started dating. Several months later, he lost his job and became involved with another woman. On learning about his other girlfriend, Shardae terminated her relationship with him. Although we are not certain that the breakup was tied to his unemployed status, it is likely that it contributed to heightened frustration and tension, which, in turn, may have been the underlying cause, as well as the consequence, of Orlando's infidelity.

Discovering that partners were "messing with" other women prompted relationship dissolution for several of the mothers in our study. For example, we know that Maria ended a relationship when she learned her partner was also involved with one of her coworkers. Similarly, Andreya said that she would refuse "to mess" with William while he was involved with another woman. She also ended her relationship with a later boyfriend Steve when she had convincing evidence that he was married. She told us, "Me and Steve are not supposed to be together. . . . I chose not to be with a married man . . . now I feel like a mistress . . . and I mean I can't put up with it, the lying and stuff and being conniving—it's not worth it. 'Cause I have kids that look up to him and I can't keep on letting my kids look up to this man. He's not being right."

Several women learned about their partner's infidelity through the other girlfriend, sometimes through incidents of verbal harassment. Shardae found out about Jerome's other woman when she harassed Shardae on the phone.

"It's just the woman coming to my house. This woman he was messing around with. And that's when I put him out. She was harassing me. She initially called me to tell me that they were together because she found my number in his pager and he told her that we were together. She was calling my old house, harassing me. She's threatened me; she's just acted really ignorant with me. I didn't even know that they were together, you know; he told me that they had been together for almost a year."

Andreya, too, received harassing phone calls from William's other girl-friend Sonya. On numerous occasions, Sonya called Andreya to insult her and tell her that she wished her children would die. (The calls continued even after Andreya had ended her romantic involvement with William.) Andreya also experienced "getting cussed out by Steve's wife."

At times, harassment escalated into physical fights. One night, the wife of the man who fathered two of Roneeka's children went to Roneeka's home and tried to start a fight. Roneeka explained, "That's when all the confusion started. She got in my face. I pushed her out of my face. I was about to fight her but my mama jumped in the way." Similarly, Andreya and Sonya had a fight that became violent when Sonya pulled out a knife.

Another response to partners' infidelity involved retaliation by "messing with" other men. In our last interview with Roneeka, we asked what she would do if her current boyfriend cheated on her. She responded, "I wouldn't care" if he was unfaithful because "I know I can go do the same thing." Andreya told us that she slept with one man, Leonard, to convince William (and probably herself) that their relationship was over. "I messed with Leonard just so William could get away from me. I told him I did it because I wanted a way out of this. Because telling him wasn't working. Asking him wasn't working. I even asked William to stay away." We wondered if this also was a strategy (conscious or unconscious) to make William jealous.

Kyierra surmised that the reason her female friends cheated was to protect themselves. She explained, speaking of her friends, "Well, if I have sex with this one, I won't be attached to this one. That way if one cheats on me, then I go to the other one." This idea of protection may be connected to the women's pride. Stack (1974) wrote that one woman in her study would not let her partner "make an ass out" of her (pp. 110–111); toward this end, she slept with another man to make her partner jealous.

Although desire for retaliation may have been behind some episodes in which mothers were unfaithful to their primary boyfriends, we do not think it was always the dominant reason. Several incidents seemed more closely tied to waning interest in partners than in motivation to get back at them. Chandra, for example, had other boyfriends while dating Patrick. Several months after complaining that she could not altogether trust Patrick, she told us that she no longer thought of him as the man of her dreams. Around this time, observing that two different men were giving Chandra rides to and from the Early Head Start building, the program's director expressed concern to us that Chandra was "playing" two men and that neither one knew about the other. Moreover, Chandra often told us about a number of different men that she was "talking to." At one point, she said, "I can juggle three men and that's about it, but men can juggle about 10!" (Indeed, she used the expression "ten-timing" instead of "two-timing" when referring to men's patterns of infidelity.) Near the end of our study, Chandra was involved with a man twice her age. She gave us the impression that she was not fully committed to him though he thought she was. Tanisha was also involved with more than one man at a time. Her home visitor told us, "Tanisha started seeing this other guy pretty seriously. Then she was kind of in a dilemma because I guess Dwayne is either out of jail now or he's getting out soon. She was really bothered about what to do because she was serious with both of them."

Wesley, the father of two of Roneeka's children, was married while she was involved with him. She told us that sleeping with a married man was not "right" but explained, "I mean it was wrong but yet and still, it takes two to tango. But he came to me. He still trying to come to me. I'm not bothering him and his wife at all. I ain't never called their house." Roneeka's mother tried to discourage the relationship. At one point, she told Wesley to "stay away because he was married to keep the confusion down." Roneeka finally severed her relationship with Wesley when she became involved with Lonnie. Roneeka and Lonnie both cheated on each other during the beginning of their relationship. She told us, "Yeah, we've been, we did one time [cheated], we did each other like that." She went on to explain that she felt it was important to admit to Lonnie that she had been unfaithful.

"Yeah, I would leave him before I do that [lie about being unfaithful], because I wouldn't want no one to hurt my feelings. That's why I said that I would come to him and let him know, you know. If I don't want him no more, I would rather just go my own way. I wouldn't want him just to be in the dark. He know I cheated then to get to him by someone else. Why not let me tell him? It's gonna really make a problem if someone else coming back and tell him his woman is cheating."

In a number of cases, women reported that their boyfriends wanted to continue to sleep with both women even after they found out about each other. This may not be uncommon, as other researchers have found similar patterns (Eyre, Auerswald, Hoffman, & Millstein, 1998). In our study, for example, William told Andreya that he wanted to be with her without leaving Sonya. Andreya refused. Another one of Andreya's boyfriends, Steve, made a similar offer. "He like he wants me to be with him while he over there with her [the mother of his baby] . . . and I'm like I'm not gonna be in between that." Shardae also felt that Jerome wanted to continue to sleep with her while being with the other woman. She told us, "He's been living with this girl then. So I guess he wanted me to continue to see him." She rebuffed his offer.

Perhaps indicative of the pervasiveness of infidelity in the relationships is the fact that all but one of the mothers discussed male infidelity during our interviews. Many mothers experienced several relationships in which their partners cheated on them. Reflecting the intensity of their feelings about infidelity, most women identified being faithful as a high priority characteristic of an ideal partner. Shardae wanted a faithful partner but was pessimistic that she would find such a man. She explained, "You know, I think there is not too many of 'em [faithful men] out there." Describing one of her past partners, she said, "I don't think he knows how to be faithful. I mean he's a good person but if he can't be faithful, I don't wanna be bothered with him." Along similar lines, Chandra explained that she wanted "someone who is faithful that doesn't lie to me, that I can trust. . . . Someone who doesn't lie, you know, they can let me know if they messin' with somebody, that don't always play those kid games. I want someone honest."

Belief that Fathers Should Remain Involved with Their Children

Responsibility for their children was another highly desired characteristic of the ideal partner. The mothers especially wished for this quality in their children's biological fathers. In the mothers' minds, responsibility and father involvement were intertwined; all of the mothers held strong beliefs that the fathers should maintain close contact with their children and provide some financial support. In the vignette at the end of this section, Breanna's efforts to support the involvement of her daughter's biological and social fathers illustrates the mothers' deeply felt belief about the importance of fathers. (*Social fathers* are men who enact the role of father although they are not biologically related to the children.)

At the same time, we saw a complicated connection between romantic attachment and a desire for father involvement. It seemed to us that in many, though not all, cases, the mothers' level of attachment to the fathers was related to their expectations regarding biological fathers' involvement with their children. Although most of the mothers wanted the biological fathers to be consistently involved, those who continued to have romantic feelings for the fathers were especially likely to express frustration and anger when the fathers displayed sporadic involvement. The mothers who were less attached to their children's biological fathers seemed less emotionally reactive to their inconsistent behaviors.

Biological father involvement and financial support seemed strongly connected to the quality of the relationships between the mothers and fathers. This pattern is consistent with previous research suggesting that the mother–father relationship has considerable influence on the nonresidential father's relationship with his children (Doherty, 1997; Doherty, Kouneski, & Erickson, 1998; Furstenberg & Cherlin, 1991). The mothers understood that the fathers were more likely to be involved with their children and to lend financial support if they were romantically involved with them. Some fathers made this connection explicit. Jerome, the father of Shardae's daughter, threatened that he would not be part of their daughter's life if Shardae was not romantically involved with him. "As long as we are not together," Shardae told us, "he's not going to do anything for her [his daughter]. He made it clear that if I didn't want to be with him, he wasn't going to do anything." Despite her feelings about the importance of father involvement, she did not want to get back together with him. True to his word, Jerome saw his daughter only a few times and provided no financial support over the years of our study.

Andreya also considered the connection between William's unwillingness to pay any child support and her refusal to continue sleeping with him. She told us, "I have to pay rent $207 and I only make $6 an hour. I can't even do nothing for the kids. And then William is not helping because he wants me to be with him."

Often, when the fathers had hopes of getting back together with the mothers, they came around more and brought money or gifts. A few of the mothers felt torn when the fathers showed increased interest in their children and pressured the mothers for an intimate relationship. In Andreya's case, William used their children as a route to romantic involvement on a number of occasions. He promised that they would be together as a family. Andreya told us, "Every time he came down here he made me feel like it was going to be us. 'Oh, I'm gonna be here for these babies. We gonna get back together, I promise.' Me and him was gonna get back together for the kids. And it was always for the kids. And it was like every time I let him just really get to me with that. It's like I set up there and I fell for it again. All he want to do is have babies by me. He don't want to be there for these babies."

The fathers' promises of increased commitment to their children and pressures to re-kindling romantic relationships presented the mothers with a dilemma. Often they still had romantic feelings for the fathers but did not want to become involved again because of the fathers' histories of being unreliable. Roneeka was determined to avoid getting back with her children's father, "I mean I don't be with him. I be at school four or five times a week. I'm trying to focus on myself and my kids, you know. 'Cause see, he's married and doing what he's doing, you know, so I could see him if I want to, but I choose not to. He can see his kids all he wants, but, you know, I choose not to see him 'cause I'm trying not to be in that situation. You know, I'll find my own man."

In the vignette below, Breanna illustrates the balancing act that mothers experience when they want their baby's father to be involved in the child's life, but are no longer interested in having a romantic relationship with the father. Breanna's case also shows the commitment that most mothers had to finding ways to keep the fathers involved with their children.

Breanna—Making Father Involvement Happen

During Breanna's pregnancy, her relationship with Corrina's biological father Lance ended, and she worried that her baby would not have a father. As she explained, "He started telling me he didn't want to be a part of my baby's life, that this wasn't his baby. I don't know what was wrong with him. I just kind of started thinking I was going to be by myself and how she was going to be without a father."

As it turned out, her concerns were unfounded. Late in her pregnancy, she started dating Denzel and remained in a relationship with him until Corrina was 3 years old. Denzel assumed the role of a father figure for Corrina.

Shortly after Corrina's birth, however, Lance came back into Breanna's life, saying that he realized the baby was his. Around the time of our first interview, when Corinna was 2 months old, Lance saw her once or twice a week. "When he comes and brings stuff, he just don't come in and leave," Breanna told us. "He comes and speaks to her and kisses her and holds her. When he comes and drops something off, he stays about 20 minutes, but when he just, when he's here to actually visit, he stays 3 to 4 hours."

Lance's involvement turned out to be inconsistent and, as a result, Corrina often cried during his visits. When Corrina was 18 months old, Breanna decided that it would be good for Corrina and Lance's relationship if Corrina saw that she (Breanna) was comfortable at Lance's place. To that end, on days when Corrina was to spend the night at Lance's, instead of just dropping her off and leaving right away, Breanna would go inside for a while and role model positive, happy conversation with Lance. She thought this would make Corrina feel more comfortable about staying with her father.

Despite her efforts, Lance's involvement remained sporadic and Breanna grew frustrated. During one of our interviews, she complained, "I don't call him anymore because I'm just fed up. [I warned him] either you come on your own or wait 'til she gets older and she is either going to reject you or not be as close as she should be to you."

Eventually, Lance began visiting more regularly and, by the time Corrina was 2 1/2 years old, she was staying at Lance's house for several days or even a week at a time. Breanna told us that both Denzel and Lance loved Corrina and they are "gonna have to work together" for Corrina's sake. She explained, "I think it's really good that she does have two people [father figures] around her."

Breanna later broke up with Denzel, and a few months later met Lamont. Breanna was resolved to have Lance, Denzel, and Lamont involved in Corrina's life regardless of the complications this arrangement might bring. Breanna summed up her hopes, "Lamont understands that because of Corrina, Denzel will be here no matter what happens. And Lance knows that Denzel and Lamont will be here. I mean everybody knows that we're all in this together. We all have to love the same people in this so we have to at least be friends. We have to respect each other."

Mothers' Negative Opinion of Men

Largely as a result of male unemployment, infidelity, and sporadic father involvement, most of the mothers complained that men were untrustworthy and unreliable. As other researchers have suggested, many African American women have negative perceptions of African American men (Eyre et al., 1998; Franklin, 2000).

Kyierra described her impressions of men, "All men are dawgs. I'm pessimistic when it comes to men 'cause I really don't like men other than my boyfriend. . . . Most of them just want a piece of butt. I don't have very many nice things to say about men." She continued, "They don't want to work. They don't want to take care of their kids. They can't stay in a stable relationship. They got to float from this one to this one. Others got four kids with four different mothers."

Roneeka told us, "I think some of them [men] are dawgs still. And some of them, there's some good men out there." When asked what made a man a "dawg," she answered, "How they treat women, you know, cheat on them, or, you know, the way they just treat them, you know treat them bad."

Chandra shared similar views with us, "What man can you trust? A man will be a man." Later in the same interview, she said, "A man's gonna do what a man's gonna do. I mean, what man hasn't been a player? I mean, a lot of men are pure *dawgs*. She said that she did not know any man who had been faithful. Because of this, she maintained that men have natural tendencies to cheat.

As a result of these perceptions of men, some women were never certain whether their partners were faithful. When asked if she thought her boyfriend had been faithful, Chandra responded, "I hope he has, but who's to say?"

Andreya, in our last interview with her, described her perspective on turbulent relationships between men and women, "A man is looking for a reason to disrespect you in the first place. You are the opposite of him, he feel that you got a whole lot more than him. All he is looking for is something to bring you down. And that's essentially one of the things that men do is put women down all the time."

Mothers' Optimism Regarding Future Relationships and Marriage

Of course, not all experiences with men were unhappy. At the end of our study, two of the mothers were involved with men who demonstrated a long-term and reliable commitment to both the mothers and their children. One union had lasted more than 4 years and the other more than 2 years. Even for the other women, positive experiences coupled with ideologies of romance and marriage seemed to reinforce a continued desire for an intimate relationship even given broken hearts and a general distrust of men. In fact, as mentioned previously, all of the women had romances with men after their breakups with the biological fathers of their children.

This unflagging optimism is probably best illustrated by comments from Shardae, Breanna, and Sherryce. Although Shardae had experienced two consecutive unfaithful boyfriends, she remained open to a new relationship, "I mean, yeah, as soon as the right man come along, I will date again." Breanna, at one point, described her ideal relationship by saying, "I mean, I just look for somebody that will respect me and be nice to me and accept me for who I am and also know that they have to accept my daughter too. It's just like attention and love and respectfulness, if you have that, and I mean, we'll start off as friends and see how it goes from there." Sherryce similarly described an ideal mate, and when asked if she would find a man to meet her criteria, she confidently told us, "Well, I'm going to find someone."

We understood that Sherryce was looking for a lifelong partner, which was not uncommon for the women in our study, even though marriage tended to be relatively rare among their friends and family members. Other women, as mentioned earlier, felt that they had learned valuable lessons from past mistakes and were hopeful that they would find the partner they wanted. In fact, the likelihood of marriage for the women in our sample is low; the majority of African American women living in poverty do not marry (Jarrett, 1994; Tucker, 2000). This disconnect between our case study women's ideas and reality may stem from their positions straddling two worlds: the mainstream culture and their subculture (Stack, 1974; Thompson & Walker, 1995). The mainstream culture endorses a strong nuclear family ideology; messages about the importance of love and marriage are pervasive (Thornton, 1989). The women in our sample, like those in other samples (Jarrett, 1994), tended to adhere to conventional family values.

As further evidence of adherence to conventional ideas, most of the mothers not only wanted to get married at some point in their lives, but also hoped their children would one day marry (and that they would wait to have children until after they were married). When asked about her expectations of marriage for her daughter, Roneeka responded, "I hope that she will get married. You know, I can't tell her to get married or not but that's the right thing to do. You know, before she has kids. I wouldn't want her to do what I did." Similarly, Sherryce told us, "Yeah, I hope both of us get married. I hope we all get married someday."

However, it must be said that two of the mothers were not particularly eager to marry. Two of the youngest, Chandra and Tanisha, expressed considerable apprehension about marriage. In early interviews, Chandra told us, "I think way down the line—when I'm in my middle 20s—I'll get married. Not like now that I'm still young." A few years later, she said, "We [she and her boyfriend] talk about marriage. But it's like, well, he'd want to be able to buy me a big ring and all this stuff. I'm like, if it happens, it happens; if it don't, it don't. I mean, just to get married, what's going to change? Besides, we dating now. It's still going to be the same things. When you get married, you have some rings and, you know, a paper."

In our most recent interview with Chandra, she described serious reservations about marriage, saying, "I wouldn't really want to marry anybody, not for a long time, I'll be about 50. I want to be by myself." She then told us, "I mean, I think it [getting married] is too much trouble for me. I mean, I would rather not be married. That way, I won't have to fight over what's mine, what's yours. I would have mine, you have your own. It ain't worth it."

Similar tentativeness was expressed by Tanisha, "Yeah, if he [Dwayne, her boyfriend] acts right, we might get married. You know how a relationship goes, and I'm young. I can't predict the future but I hope so and I hope he gets himself together like I'm trying to do so I hope it works out; I'm not sure." A few months later, they were engaged. "And we haven't decided if we're going to get married this year, but we got engaged, so then we start planning, and I was all happy." Near the end of the same interview, Tanisha expressed doubts about marrying Dwayne. "Well, I don't want to stay with Dwayne. I got my whole life ahead of me. [She was 18 at the time.] I'm young. Maybe we can somewhat be friends. And I can just go out and party sometimes. I don't actually think I want to do that but I have thoughts. You can have thoughts." Tanisha later broke up with Dwayne, but got back together with him after experiencing heartache with two other men.

The fact that the mothers were pregnant or already had children did not seem to dampen men's interest in them. Four of the mothers

(Breanna, Kyierra, Tanisha, and Andreya) began dating new partners during their pregnancies. Furthermore, regardless of the number of children they had (one, two, or three), all of the mothers entered into new relationships at some point after their romances with the biological fathers of their children had soured. Maria told us that young men seemed no less interested in her now that she had a son, "Well, I don't think that having had Bryce already has prevented me from meeting any guys. Most guys I've met—they've been open to the fact that I already have a child whether they have one or not. And you know Bryce—he's so charming and, you know, guys like him."

At the same time, mothers told us that now that they had children, they were more cautious about the men they dated. They talked about needing to keep their children's welfare in mind; they did not want to expose them to temporary relationships with unsuitable men. Andreya, for instance, explained why she was not inviting a man with whom she was flirting to her home, "I have to respect my kids just like I want them to respect me, to the point where only way I'll let a man come over is if I trust him to come in my house after my kids are sleeping. It's not that we're gonna have sex, it's not that. It's just because my kids get used to a man and they gone. It's just like they feel hurt. . . . I don't want that to happen no more."

Concern for their children thus became a filter for choices in new partners. Sherryce maintained that "the men I date have to be very active in raising my children. I wouldn't date them if they wouldn't be over here. I need a good role model, an example." Tanisha had similar standards. Explaining that her relationship with her partner was contingent on how he treated her daughter, she told us, "We have our couple of arguments, but I get along with him and like on her birthday, he got her a ring, he tries to show that he cares, so I guess we get along." In at least one case, a relationship with a child's biological father continued past the time when the mother would otherwise have broken it off. Chandra told us that if she had not had a child with Patrick, "I don't think, I just don't think that I would still be dating him. If I was dating him, we wouldn't be serious."

For some of the mothers, optimism was reinforced when new partners demonstrated commitment to both the mothers and their children. Describing the relationship between her new boyfriend and her daughter, Breanna explained, "He thinks she is so pretty, he accepts her, but he don't have no other choice, but to accept it." A year later she told us, "He loves her. I mean he's attached to her and I know he loves her. I mean, and not to mention he's all she knows." Kyierra explained the relationship between her daughter and Tejon, her daughter's social father, "Yeah, ever since I was pregnant. He was there when she was born. He's been there. He loves her. He takes care of her. It's her dad. It's her father. I mean [with the biological father], there's no bond."

At least two social fathers remained involved in the children's lives even many months after breaking up with the mother. It may have been that they were partially motivated by continued interest in the mother. (See Chapter 11 for more on biological and social fathers' relationships with their children.)

Yet, although new partners were accepting of other men's children, all wanted a baby of their own. Tanisha illustrated this theme when she told us, "He would like for me to have his child one day, but I told him if everything is okay, and he has a good job and I have a good job, then I'll have another baby because I know how hard it is just having one baby." In a later interview, she told us that she had made her conditions clear to him, "Dwayne wants another kid but I'm not ready for all of that. I was like, 'You need to get a job and you'll be a help with the kids and so.'" Tejon also wanted Kyierra to have a baby and they eventually did. Breanna told us that "Denzel wants a child 'cause he don't have any. But he says he's willing to wait until I'm ready."

Our vignette describing Kyierra's relationship with Tejon illustrates the theme of optimism regarding relationships and marriage. In particular, Kyierra's story depicts her unflagging openness to romance despite previous bad experiences with men, the role unemployment and employment had on marriage plans, Tejon's devotion to her and her child, and the possibility for a stable romance despite the impressive challenges fostered by poverty.

Kyierra and Tejon

Kyierra and Tejon had dated briefly while they were seniors in high school. After high school, Kyierra went to a local college for a short period and she and Tejon lost touch. She met James on a bus on her way to class, and they began dating. Not long after they met, James moved in with Kyierra and her mother. Several months later, Kyierra discovered that she was pregnant. She and James were already having relationship troubles, which were intensified by the pregnancy. Kyierra told us that James was unemployed and an alcoholic, and that, after the onset of the pregnancy, he became physically abusive. In fact, when she was 6 weeks pregnant, James cracked her jawbone. He was arrested and served time in jail, and Kyierra has not seen him since. She described her relationship with him as "the biggest downfall of my life."

Tejon came back into Kyierra's life when she was in her last trimester. He was there for Kyierra through the end of her pregnancy, offering emotional and physical support. Tejon told us that he "even went to those doggoned Lamaze classes."

When we first met Kyierra, she described Tejon in loving and appreciative terms, "He's my backbone. He's there when I need him. If I need to cry, he's there to listen. He's there to hold me up." She later described him as "helping in every way. He's my emotional support, my everything. Every way possible that he can help me, he does. That's my backbone. As far as grocery shopping or going here and going there, he's there to help." Kyierra thought that Tejon gave up joining the Marines so that he would be there for her and her baby.

Tejon assumed the role of father for Kyierra's baby Jalisa. Kyierra refers to Tejon as the father saying, "She's his. He is the father. He's been there." Soon after Jalisa's birth, however, Kyierra wondered if she should try to encourage a relationship between Jalisa and James. She told us, "Well, she needs to see James, but then again, she doesn't; she has a father." Through letters sent from prison, James promised Kyierra that he would be there for her and Jalisa. However, at the time of our last interview, he had not seen his daughter nor had he provided any monetary support.

Over time, Kyierra and Tejon's relationship remained stable. During our interviews, they often expressed fond feelings for each other. At our second interview, she told us that she and Tejon were "getting along real good." About 2 years after that, Tejon told us, "I don't know what I would do without Kyierra. She's in my heart. I wouldn't know what to do without her. There ain't nothing I wouldn't do for her." He then went on to express his feelings for Jalisa, "She is part of me and I want to be involved in everything she do."

During our third interview, however, Kyierra indicated that although she wanted to marry Tejon, "He doesn't want to." Over the course of the next 2 years, Kyierra expressed frustration with Tejon several times because he did not have a job (other than providing child care for her daughter) while she worked. Her mother's criticisms of Tejon's prolonged unemployment didn't help the situation. Kyierra regularly found herself defending Tejon to her mother and her mother's partner, "I'm like, 'He's good for more things than just money, you know. Just because he doesn't have a job doesn't mean he's not a good father. I haven't once heard you say what a good father he is. I get tired of hearing, "When Tejon has a job" 'cause that's not what it all boils down to. I'm wanting you to look at the big picture. . . . And I don't feel like I should have to defend my love for Tejon.'"

Four months later, Tejon explained that he wanted to marry Kyierra, but that his unemployment was a barrier. He planned to marry her someday but wanted to wait until he had a steady job. Kyierra told us that despite the fact that he was unemployed, "Tejon's been good to me and I love him to death."

When we last saw them, Kyierra and Tejon were engaged. Kyierra was delighted, although she admitted to concerns about Tejon's level of involvement in household work. She complained that in the beginning of their relationship, he had done a lot more cooking and cleaning. Tejon, for his part, worried that sometimes Kyierra did not treat him as well as she expected him to treat her. For example, he grumbled that Kyierra often called him on his cell phone when he was away from home, asking where he was and when he would return, yet when she was out with a girlfriend, she would never let him know where she was or at what time she would come home.

Nonetheless, their commitment to each other was clearly greater than their apprehensions. Kyierra's excitement was openly conveyed in her lengthy descriptions of wedding plans, including decisions about bridesmaids, the location of the reception, and her dress.

CONCLUSIONS

Our close examination of nine women's thoughts and feelings regarding their experiences with men underscores the interplay between macro and micro influences. Their stories help illustrate the complexity of their personal lives and the ways in which their relationships are embedded in larger political and ideological contexts (Dickerson, 1995; Thompson & Walker, 1995).

The Negative Role Played by Unemployment

We have concluded that the paramount negative influence on the mothers' romantic lives was male unemployment. Through painful accounts of male joblessness and its apparent consequences—jail, infidelity, sporadic involvement—we witnessed the manifestation of macro-level forces on individual lives. Relationships seemed to have had considerably better chances of survival when the men were employed. This connection has been made before (e.g., Liebow, 1967; Wilson, 2003).

The Power of Conventional Ideologies

Conventional ideologies of marriage and the nuclear family also seemed powerful. Adherence to traditional notions of families fostered both frustration and optimism regarding potential future relationships.

Challenging distorted images of women is central to feminist theory (Thompson & Walker, 1995). Stereotypes of African American, low-income, single mothers tend to be especially negative and pervasive (Dickerson, 1995). In this chapter, consistent with both feminist and Afrocentric tenants (Collins, 1990), we question such assumptions. As a case in point, although popular opinion might hold that births to young, low-income African American mothers are the result of frivolous sexual encounters, we found that this was not the experience of the mothers we studied. On the contrary, at the onset of pregnancy all but two of the mothers believed that they were in lasting relationships with the fathers of their babies.

Finally, we remind the reader that most of this chapter was based on conversations with the *women* in our study. Although there were occasions when we discussed romantic relationships with the men and some of their comments are included, the great majority of interviews were with the mothers. The chapter, accordingly, largely reflects impressions from a female point of view. In Chapter 11, we offer impressions about relationships and fathering from the male perspective.

REFERENCES

Bowman, P.J., & Forman, T.A. (1997). Instrumental and expressive family roles among African American fathers. In R.J. Taylor, J.S. Jackson, & L.M. Chatters (Eds.), *Family life in Black America* (pp. 216–247). Thousand Oaks, CA: Sage.

Bowser, B. (1995). *Racism and anti-racism in world perspective.* Thousand Oaks, CA: Sage.

Broman, C.L. (1997). Families, unemployment, and well-being. In R.J. Taylor, J.S. Jackson, & L.M. Chatters (Eds.), *Family life in Black America* (pp. 157–166). Thousand Oaks, CA: Sage.

Cherlin, A.J. (2002). *Public and private families: An introduction* (3rd ed.). Boston: McGraw-Hill.

Clayton, O., & Moore, J. (2003). The effects of crime and imprisonment on family formation. In O. Clayton, R.B. Mincy, & D. Blankenhorn (Eds.). *Black fathers in contemporary American society: Strengths, weaknesses, and strategies for change.* New York: Russell Sage Foundation.

Collins, P.H. (1990). *Black feminist thought.* Boston: Unwin Hyman.

Dickerson, B.J. (Ed.). (1995). *African American single mothers: Understanding their lives and families.* Thousand Oaks, CA: Sage.

Doherty, W.J. (1997). The best of times and the worst of times: Fathering as contested area of academic discourse. In A. Hawkins & D. Dollahite (Eds.), *Generative fathering: Beyond deficit perspectives* (pp. 217–227). Thousand Oaks, CA: Sage.

Doherty, W.J., Kouneski, E.F., & Erickson, M.F. (1998). Responsible fathering: An overview and conceptual framework. *Journal of Marriage and the Family, 60,* 277–292.

Eyre, S.L., Auerswald, C., Hoffman, V., & Millstein, S.G. (1998). Fidelity management: African-American adolescents' attempts to control the sexual behavior of their partners. *Journal of Health Psychology, 3,* 393–406.

Franklin, D. (2000). *What's love got to do with it?: Understanding and healing the rift between Black men and women.* New York: Touchstone.

Furstenberg, F.F. (1976). *Unplanned parenthood: The social consequences of teenage childbearing.* New York: Free Press.

Furstenberg, F.F., & Cherlin, A. (1991). *Divided families: What happens to children when parents part.* Cambridge, MA: Harvard University Press.

Galliher, R.V., Rostosky, S.S., Welsh, D.P., & Kawaguchi, M.C. (1999). Power and psychological well-being in late adolescent romantic relationships. *Sex Roles, 40,* 689–710.

Gibbs, J. (1988). *Young, black, and male in American: An endangered species.* Dover, MA: Auburn Publishing.

Guttentag, M., & Secord, P. (1983). *Too many women: The sex ratio question.* Beverly Hills, CA: Sage.

Jankowski, M.S. (1991). *Islands in the streets: Gangs and American urban society.* Berkley: The University of California Press.

Jarrett, R.L. (1994). Living poor: Family life among single parent, African-American women. *Social Problems, 41,* 30–49.

Liebow, E. (1967). *Tally's corner: A study of negro streetcorner men.* Boston: Little, Brown, & Co.

Massey, D.S., & Shibuya, K. (1995). Unraveling the tangle of pathology: The effect of spatially concentrated joblessness on the well-being of African Americans. *Social Science Research, 24,* 352–366.

Mauer, M., & Huling, T. (1995). *Young Black Americans and the criminal justice system.* Washington, DC: Sentencing Project.

Sprecher, S., & McKinney, K. (1993). *Sexuality.* Newbury Park, CA: Sage.

Stack, C. (1974). *All our kin.* New York: Harper & Row.

Strauss, A., & Corbin, J. (1998). *Basics of qualitative research: Techniques and procedures for developing grounded theory* (2nd ed.). Thousand Oaks, CA: Sage.

Testa, M. (1989). Employment and marriage among inner-city fathers. *The Annuals, 501,* 79–91.

Thompson, L., & Walker, A. (1995). The place of feminism in family studies. *Journal of Marriage and the Family, 57,* 847–865.

Thornton, A. (1989). Changing attitudes toward family issues in the United States. *Journal of Marriage and the Family, 51,* 873–893.

Tucker, M.B. (2000). Marital values and expectations in context: Results from a 21-city study. In L.J. Waite (Ed.), *The ties that bind: Perspectives on marriage and cohabitation* (pp. 166–187). New York: Aldine de Gruyter.

Tucker, M.B., & Mitchell-Kernan, C. (Eds.). (1995). *The decline in marriage among African Americans: Causes, consequences, and policy implications.* New York: Russell Sage Foundation.

U.S. Census Bureau, Racial Statistics Branch, Population Division. (2000, March). Current Population Survey. Retrieved September 25, 2002, from http://www.census.gov/population/socdemo/race/black/ppl-142/tab01.txt

U.S. Department of Labor, Bureau of Labor Statistics. (1999). *Unemployment rate by race, age, and sex, 1998–1999.*

Wilson, W.J. (1987). *The truly disadvantaged: The inner city, the underclass, and public policy.* Chicago: The University of Chicago Press.

Wilson, W.J. (2003). The woes of the inner-city African American father. In O. Clayton, R.B. Mincy, & D. Blankenhorn (Eds.). *Black fathers in contemporary American society: Strengths, weaknesses, and strategies for change* (pp. 9–29). New York: Russell Sage Foundation.

10

Raising Children

Jean M. Ispa and Linda C. Halgunseth

ecent research on parent–child relationships has indicated that parenting practices that have positive or negative outcomes in one cultural or socioeconomic group do not necessarily have the same outcomes in other cultural or socioeconomic groups. For example, maternal firm control, although potentially damaging to European American children in middle-income families, appears to have either a neutral or a beneficial impact on African American children living in poverty (Brody & Flor, 1998; Deater-Deckard & Dodge, 1997; Ispa et al., 2004). The context in which particular parenting behaviors are embedded plays a critical role in determining the meanings that children give to these behaviors and how they react to them.

There is therefore a need for a culture-specific study of the feelings, intentions, and meanings that individuals attach to given child-rearing practices. This chapter describes the parenting feelings, ideas, and behaviors that characterized the nine mothers in our study. Our data come from interviews with the mothers, from observations of the mothers and their children during separate 2-hour visits, and from three questionnaires we asked the mothers to complete. As we analyzed our data, we focused especially on themes concerning the mothers' feelings about motherhood, their goals for their children, and their hoped-for and actual strategies for reaching those goals.

FEELINGS ABOUT MOTHERHOOD

We begin by sharing our simple observation that all nine mothers loved their children and cared very much about their futures. Our transcripts are filled with statements demonstrating the mothers' enjoyment of their children and their determination to be good mothers. When her daughter was 14 months old, Breanna told us, "I'm the mother, 16. And I dedicate my whole life to Corrina." During another interview, Andreya compared a troubled boy in the child care center where she worked with her own sons, "He ain't like my kids that's at home getting love from the sky, the moon, and the stars." When Shardae and Roneeka were asked what they liked most about their lives, without hesitation they pointed to their children. "I'm happy; I got a beautiful baby," Roneeka said. Shardae's answer was similar, "Having her. That's probably the best thing in my life."

Conversations about the mothers' schooling or work sometimes came back to how much they missed their children when they were away from home. Maria told us that while at work, she found herself staring at her son's photograph and wishing she could call home to see how he was doing. Andreya called her son's child care center during breaks between classes—just to assure herself that he was all right. Breanna said that while at school, she wondered what her daughter was doing and how she was feeling. "I be worried. I don't have to be, but I just be worried anyway," she said. Kyierra liked working and the money she earned but she missed Jalisa. It bothered her that she wasn't home the first time Jalisa held her bottle by herself.

Only Chandra and Sherryce never talked outright about loving their children. Yet Chandra's love was clear from the way she looked at Patrick, the spontaneous kisses she gave him, and the personal sacrifices she made for him, especially when he was an infant. Sherryce was unique among the mothers in that during our visits, she rarely expressed physical or verbal affection for Michael. Yet, she told us that she had always wanted to be a mother, and she clearly demonstrated a determination to do whatever she thought was necessary for her son's well-being. She also let us know that she agreed with her home visitor's assessment that Michael was gifted.

Positive Aspects of Motherhood

When we asked the mothers what they liked about motherhood, Shardae and Tanisha said that their daughters kept them company and were fun to talk to. Breanna, Kyierra, and Maria liked caring for someone and feeling needed. "You have this sense of importance; you know you're the main thing in this person's life and this person looks up to you," Maria explained. Kyierra, Tanisha, and Andreya added that they found their children entertaining and funny; they enjoyed watching them and listening to them.

Interestingly, six of the nine mothers spontaneously remarked that motherhood had made them better people. Most of these comments revolved around their becoming more responsible, as well as an awareness that they were role models for their children. Kyierra commented that she was "stronger now than I've ever been in my whole entire life," and Maria said that she saw things "totally differently and, you know, things that I thought were okay, I don't think that they are okay anymore." Tanisha believed that she had "a purpose" now and was more attentive in class than she used to be. Similarly, Andreya thought about her children and "where we was gonna be at in the future if I didn't do nothing, if I just sat at home." Illustrating the mothers' desire to be good role models, Breanna talked about making herself get out of bed even when she was still tired "because I want the best for Corinna. If I don't get up this morning, what kind of example does that set? She's helping me; she's who's restricting me and making me a better person." Roneeka had similar thoughts, "I want to be her role model right now. Kids, they'll look at what you're doing, you know. If I ain't doing right, she'll think she can do it. I'd rather do right than do wrong, especially now that I have a baby."

We also heard very strong messages that the welfare of their children was the mothers' first priority. All of them talked about putting their children's material needs above their own. We saw that Sherryce, having moved into a little house obtained through Section 8 (a federally supported housing subsidy program), had furnished and stocked Michael's room while the rest of the house remained bare. At Christmas time, the mothers used layaway plans and tried to get "adopted" by charities and churches. These efforts were for their children, not for themselves. Chandra provided an example that was touching because we knew how much she loved to dress attractively. One day we asked her how she managed to get clothes for herself. "Well, see, really my first priority is my son," she answered. "I put myself on wait and I get his stuff. I like get me an outfit every now and then, hopefully buy me some tennis shoes, but it always seems like I see something for him and I'll buy it for him. So I'm really just trying to get him out the way, and then I'll do for myself." Other mothers made statements similar to Roneeka's, "Before I dress myself I would dress my kids any day. I'd rather be left out than my daughter." We saw, in fact, that the children were almost always nicely dressed, often better than their mothers. Seccombe, James, and Walters (1998) wrote about the importance mothers living in poverty give to dressing their children well. Mothers reason that their children will feel better about themselves and be treated better by others if they look well cared for. Relatedly, we saw that the mothers in our study sometimes put off paying essential bills such as those for rent and utilities because of the pressing needs of their children. If they had to make a choice between paying bills and buying a necessity for their children, unless utilities were about to be cut off, the children's direct needs came first. As Andreya put it, "It's like the kids come first, then the bills."

Besides money, time was in short supply as the mothers juggled school, work, social events with friends, and child rearing. Giving time to children was therefore another indicator of the mothers' decision making regarding priorities. Andreya and Breanna talked about sacrificing study time (and, hence, good grades) to be with their children. All talked about giving up time they used to spend with friends. Andreya told us she would not answer the phone if it rang soon after she came home from work—she wanted to devote the first hour or so of the evening entirely to getting dinner ready and the children settled.

Stress-Inducing Aspects of Motherhood

Having pointed out that the mothers loved their children, enjoyed them, and were dedicated to them, we would be remiss if we did not also write about the stresses and frustrations motherhood brought. All nine mothers at one time or another talked about feeling trapped, over-burdened, and exhausted. Words like, "My life stopped. I'm stretched and stressed," and "I feel like I'm on lock-down," expressed these sentiments. Juggling work or school and the needs of children was not easy, and some acknowledged that it would have been better for them as well as their children if they had waited until they were married and/or had steady, decently paying jobs. A large body of research now documents the stresses associated with parenting when financial resources and other forms of support are wanting (Brookes-Gunn, 1997; Magnuson & Duncan, 2002; McLoyd, 1998). For African American single-mother families, minority racial status and gender bring heightened problems accessing resources and therefore additional strains (Collins, 2000). The ecological context in which the mothers in our study lived must be kept in mind as the backdrop for many of their frustrations.

Fatigue and Loneliness   Most of the mothers complained that they rarely had time to relax or take care of themselves. Some worried that their harried lifestyles hurt their children. Shardae, for example, commented that because she was so tired in the evenings, she was often on the verge of losing patience with her daughter. She reminded herself that "Alexis has had a long day just like me" and resolved not to spank her for her "silly" behavior. Tanisha's reflections on this issue were poignant. She was not close to any member of her family, and Tierra's father had died in an automobile accident before she was born. Tanisha talked about feeling alone and bitter because none of the people who should be helping her were doing so. When asked if she had good sources for learning about child development, she admitted that such issues took a backseat in her life because she was lonely and preoccupied with earning enough money to meet her own and her daughter's basic needs. She said that she felt depressed and slept a lot. Showing insight into the ways depression and stress can spill over into child rearing, she worried that she was not giving Tierra as much attention as she needed, and, worse yet, that she sometimes found herself "taking it out on her, and I understand why because I am frustrated with myself."

Stuck in Low-Paying Jobs   When we asked the mothers what they thought life would be like if they hadn't had children or had waited until they were older, all but Chandra said that they would have finished school or gotten more post-high-school training for desired careers. Six of the mothers also thought that their current employment problems were exacerbated by the fact that they had children. They complained that it was difficult to secure an adequate income when the requirements of child care precluded work during evenings or weekends, or when their beliefs in the importance of spending time with their children led them to limit themselves to part-time work. As some explained, they knew that to be good mothers, they had to provide financially for their children and also "be there" for them. The two goals were to some extent incompatible. Andreya often pointed out the problems she had keeping jobs because of the frequency with which she was tardy or absent. When she was tardy, it was almost always because it was difficult to get her children ready to leave on time in the mornings. When she was absent, it was almost always because of the children's bouts with asthma, requiring frequent trips to the emergency room. The tensions the mothers experienced between work and family responsibilities reminded us of the degree to which U.S. policies are lacking when it comes to family leave and the provision of affordable, accessible, and high-quality child care for the children of working parents (Gornick & Meyers, 2003).

No Time for Fun   Of course it wasn't only school and work that were compromised by the births of their children. At one time or another, all of the mothers talked longingly about "the fun things" and the social life they were missing because they had to be home with their children. Tanisha described a common sentiment when she compared the days "before I had her when I could do whatever, whatever," with her current situation, when "I don't have much friends anymore. It's just me and my daughter." Andreya was wistful about having missed high school pep rallies, her prom, and other normative adolescent experiences because she was pregnant or caring for Lavell. Sherryce talked about getting bored staying home with her son all the time; she, Andreya, and Roneeka wished they had friends or relatives who would agree to watch their children some evenings so they could "have a life," or at least go to the movies. Maria was the most fortunate in this regard. Her parents willingly took care of Bryce some evenings so that she could meet with friends.

Of the nine mothers, Chandra seemed the most concerned with what she was missing. When Patrick was a little over a year old, she told us it was "fun when I don't have him," and that if she didn't have a child, she would "just be kicking it. I'd just be having fun. Kicking it and partying." During one of our last interviews, when Patrick was 4, Chandra earnestly told us that "I just really want to kick it. I want to have so much fun." These words haunted us a few months later when she asked her ex-stepmother to take Patrick from her until she was more ready to be a responsible mother. That arrangement was to last a year.

It must be said that more advantaged parents (i.e., those who are married and have higher household incomes), like their less advantaged counterparts, also are likely to find that the demands of caring for infants and young children, including the limitations placed on leisure activities and socializing, require significant emotional adjustments (Belsky, Spanier, & Rovine, 1983; Cowan & Cowan, 1995; Demo & Cox, 2000). Clearly, this challenge is not limited to single mothers in poverty. However, the intensity of the feelings may be greater for mothers who have limited financial resources and who are at an age when considerable autonomy in how time is spent is expected and normative in U.S. culture. (Recall that seven of the nine mothers were 20 or younger when their first children were born.)

Several of the mothers in our study echoed low-income mothers in other studies when they commented that their dedication to their children's welfare was greater than that of other young mothers in their neighborhoods. They reported that many of the young mothers they knew continued to be "in the streets" and "partying" a lot even though they had children, while they thought of themselves as "homebodies." Seccombe (1999) reasoned that individuals with low incomes know that mainstream America holds them responsible for their circumstances. To some extent they also have internalized the negative notion that the struggles of people in poverty are the deserved consequences of their own faults. They do not, however, accept that explanation for their own situations; instead they believe that they have done the best they can in the face of challenging circumstances.

Dealing with Typical Toddler Curiosity and Negativism   In addition to feeling stressed by the restricted opportunities for education, employment, leisure, and socializing brought on by parenthood, the mothers were sometimes frustrated by their children's behavior, especially as the children became toddlers. Our strong impression was that almost all of the mothers interacted warmly with their *infants*. Even though caring for an infant was harder than they'd expected and they acknowledged disliking certain aspects of infant care such as interrupted sleep at night, bouts of crying, diapers, and illnesses, the demeanor and comments of all of the mothers were warm and affectionate when interacting with their infants.

It was when the children became toddlers that the mothers' annoyance became noticeable. Roneeka was convinced that the onset of walking signaled a transition to more negative behavior and the need for discipline, "That's when all the discipline came in; that's when you're going from baby needs to toddler needs, you know, and it's just been a lot." It was clear that Roneeka enjoyed her child before he began to walk. Andreya echoed this thought when she confided that she wished Lavell was still a baby. Earlier observational studies of low-income African American families likewise showed great nurturance toward infants followed by a drop in warmth and the development of a more "contest-like" relationship beginning in toddlerhood (see review by Ogbu, 1985). However, as shown in a study by O'Brien (1996), parental stress over developmentally typical difficult toddler behaviors cuts across racial and social class lines; again, these feelings are not exclusive to young African American mothers living in poverty.

There were two areas of major concern for the mothers regarding their toddlers. The first was the children's desire to "get into everything," which too often resulted in breakages, messes, and occasionally dangerous situations, such as when Kevon drank Pine Sol and had to be rushed to the hospital. The exploratory behavior of Roneeka's and Andreya's toddlers caused friction between the mothers and the grandmothers, because the grandmothers did not want to babyproof their homes and blamed the damage their grandchildren caused on their daughters' inability to discipline correctly. (See Chapter 5 for an example involving Lavell, Andreya, and Patricia.)

The second area of concern was typical toddler negativism. One mother complained that "it can really drive your nerves" when children ignore commands, say no to the simplest requests, throw tantrums when denied what they want, and refuse to share toys with peers. Kyierra, Tanisha, and Chandra were bothered by their observation that their children were better behaved when they were with other adults. Maria had learned from Early Head Start and other sources that toddlers like to make some of their own decisions about foods they will eat, but she complained that "his independence is interfering with choices I want to make for him." Sherryce and Roneeka worried that their children were selfish because they claimed toys and other objects, calling them "mine."

A deeper knowledge of child development would probably have been comforting. Research has shown that exploratory behavior benefits toddlers' cognitive development (Bradley et al., 1989) and the exercise of their newfound ability to say "no" and "mine" supports the development of autonomy and even the eventual development of prosocial behavior (including sharing). These behaviors are typical of 1- and 2-year-olds and they eventually subside naturally; they are not a predictor of later self-centeredness (Laible & Thompson, 2002; Levine, 1983). Moreover, as Brazelton (1974) pointed out, it is typical for young children to reserve their misbehavior for those whom they know best and trust the most.

At the same time, it should be said that providing mothers with more information about typical stages in child development and more suggestions for successful coping with the toddler period may not be sufficient to relieve the irritation often aroused by the curiosity- and autonomy-driven behaviors of this age group. Early Head Start home visitors did tell the mothers that the behaviors they were seeing were typical and normal and urged them to prevent problems by using strategies such as babyproofing and redirection (substituting an acceptable object for a forbidden one). As illustrated by the case study of Andreya, however, other family members and the predominant practices used in one's community greatly impact mothers' options. Efforts should be made to extend the educational efforts of parenting programs to include significant figures in young mothers' social networks. We must also consider macrosystem influences: The stresses associated with poverty and single parenthood may make it especially difficult for mothers to view even mildly difficult child behavior with equanimity (Magnuson & Duncan, 2002).

PARENTS' CHILD-REARING GOALS

A considerable body of research shows that parents' child-rearing goals differ according to cultural background and socioeconomic status, and that the goals parents hold most dear guide their child-rearing practices (Hastings & Grusec, 1998; Kohn, 1977; LeVine, 1988). We therefore thought it important to learn about the characteristics the mothers hoped to see in their children. We analyzed the mothers' statements about what they wanted their children to be like when they were older and statements in which goals for their children were implicit (as in complaints about children who refused to share). Some of these statements were made in response to our direct questions about desired characteristics in children, some were in reaction to problematic child behaviors featured in several hypothetical vignettes we presented during two different interviews, and some were elicited by an instrument we presented twice that required the mothers to rank 18 child-rearing goals from most to least important.

Fifteen of these eighteen items were drawn from the Maternal Child-Rearing Values and Behaviors Inventory (MCR-VBI; see Lausell-Bryant, Gonzalez-Ramos, Zayas, & Cohen, 1998); another three were added based on the literature on African American child rearing and themes from our prior interviews. Each goal was printed on a card, with the definition and an example on the back. The goals identified hopes that the children would grow up to be assertive, community-minded, creative, educated, emotionally expressive, honest, independent, leader-like, loving, persevering, proud of their African American heritage, respectable, respectful, responsible, self-sufficient, streetwise, family-minded, and placing a value on their own self-worth. All nine mothers participated in this activity approximately a year and a half after we met them. A year later, all but Tanisha repeated the exercise. (We could not locate her for the interview that included the second administration of the MCR-VBI.) Among the eight mothers who ranked the goals twice, seven gave the same items highest priority both times. Stability over a year is noteworthy because it suggests that these values are deeply held.

African American scholars (e.g., Hill, 1999) have cautioned that researchers should expect diversity even within narrowly defined groups such as "low-income African American single mothers." We did, in fact, find heterogeneity even in our small sample. When ranking goals on the MCR-VBI, all of the mothers included items related to both accomplishment and socioemotional functioning among their top five. Nevertheless, Q-technique of factor analysis (Sexton, 1998), a statistical method that groups individuals based on the ways in which they respond to multiple items, indicated that the mothers could be divided into two groups: those whose foremost goals focused especially on their children's accomplishment, and those whose foremost goals were relationship-oriented, focusing on the development of their children's respect for self and others. This division fits closely with Baumrind's (1996) classification of parenting goals into those concerned with agency or competence and those concerned with fostering morality and connectedness with others. In theory and in reality the two sets of goals are intertwined; the qualities that support one also support the other. Nonetheless, as we found, mothers may emphasize one set more than the other.

Highest-Priority Goals

In our study, three of the mothers were in the first group; they ranked education, responsibility, and independence as their top child-rearing goals. Conversations with these mothers suggested that the unifying theme across their goals was the hope that their children would grow up to be responsible, efficacious, working adults who would contribute to, not burden, their families. The six mothers in the second group also valued these accomplishment-related goals (all but Maria and Tanisha placed education in their top four goals), but they ranked those concerned with respect for self and others even higher. Their highest-ranking goals were valuing family, valuing self, being loving, and being respectful. In the following paragraphs, we elaborate on the mothers' thoughts regarding the two sets of goals and note distinctions that appeared to be related to sex-role concerns.

Education and Accomplishment   As just mentioned, all but two of the mothers included education in their four top goals on the MCR-VBI and at various points during our interviews, and even those two mothers shared hopes that their children would obtain good educations. For all of the mothers, these hopes were mixed with well-founded concerns regarding the quality of the schools in their neighborhoods. Showing energy and determination, Andreya and Shardae later succeeded in getting their children admitted to charter schools, and Sherryce moved to a section of town in which the schools were better. Other researchers similarly have found a high value placed on education among low-income African American parents, explaining that it is viewed as a route to better jobs and economic improvement (Billingsley, 1992; Hill & Sprague, 1999).

Gender Issues   We detected no sex-of-child differences in the mothers' hopes for their children's educational success. However, many comments about the other accomplishment-related goals, responsibility and independence, contained clear messages about gender. Conversations about child-rearing goals sometimes flowed from complaints that women shoulder too much of the household labor and that men can't be depended on, lie, are disrespectful, and "come and go." These negative perceptions about the men in the mothers' lives (see Chapter 9) seemed to shape some of their child-rearing goals for both boys and girls.

The mothers of sons tended to couch their child-rearing aspirations in terms of counter-examples—they wanted their sons to be different from most of the men they knew. Desired qualities reflected some of the elements described in Chapter 9 as characteristics of ideal romantic partners. Goals for sons to grow up to be "good men" in part revolved around hopes that they would hold stable jobs that would allow them to provide financially for their families, and that they would, in general, be responsible and dependable. Sherryce reflected these themes when she exclaimed, "These guys, they don't want to work, they don't want to do nothing. I don't want Michael to be like these men that don't want to take care of their responsibilities. You have to be responsible enough to get up and go every day and do what you gotta do."

Most of the mothers of boys expressed grave concern that in adolescence their sons' futures would be compromised by temptations to join delinquent peer groups. "It takes a lot more when you raising boys because you have to watch out for kids who will try to encourage them to do bad things, such as selling drugs, stealing, fighting," Andreya told us. Such thinking may have been one of the reasons most of the mothers ranked independence among their top five goals. Chandra explained that if Patrick could "be his own person," he would have the strength to rebuff negative peer pressures. The mothers' belief that it was vital for their children to develop goals, independence of mind, and confidence in their ability to resist negative group influences was in keeping with the important role played by perceived self-efficacy in adolescent avoidance of antisocial peer pressure (Bandura, Caprara, Barbaranelli, Gerbino, & Pastorelli, 2003).

The mothers' accomplishment-related child-rearing goals for daughters likewise seemed partially based on their negative perceptions of men. It was striking that all seven mothers with daughters said that they wanted to raise them to be independent, self-sufficient, and strong. Four also spontaneously mentioned wanting their daughters to grow up to "be somebody," to be assertive, to feel free to speak their minds, and to be leaders rather than followers. In addition, the mothers spoke about conveying to their girls the importance of "staying away from those boys" so that they could get good grades and finish school. They explained that girls should understand that they are likely to have to take care of themselves—they should not expect that they will have a man on whom they can depend. Although the mothers worried about their boys' potential for future association with delinquent groups, the mothers of girls were especially concerned about the possibility that their daughters' schooling would be derailed by early pregnancies (as their own had been). Kyierra reflected a common theme when she noted that she didn't want her daughter to value "love more than education."

Strong, self-confident, and *self-reliant* are adjectives frequently used to describe African American women and the characteristics they wish to foster in their school-age and adolescent daughters (Collins, 2000; Wade-Gayles, 1984). It was interesting to see that these child-rearing goals were already evident in the discourse of the very young mothers whose daughters were still infants and toddlers. It was also noteworthy that the mothers reflected previous research on egalitarian sex-role beliefs in African American families (Billingsley, 1992; Peters, 1997) when they indicated that they wanted their children to grow up viewing household tasks as gender-neutral.

Yet, none had actually experienced equal participation by men in domestic chores. Recall, for example, from Chapter 5 Andreya's surprise when Rickie, her male Early Head Start home visitor, helped her cook a meal. As pointed out by students of gender in European American as well as African American relationships, ideologies concerning equal division of household labor are often not realized in actual practice (Billingsley, 1992; Dempsey, 2002). Recall that Kyierra had some reservations about marrying Tejon because she was dissatisfied with his level of participation in domestic chores. We also noticed that when we asked the mothers general questions about gender roles in household labor, their answers were overwhelmingly in favor of equality, but when we asked for opinions about responsibility for specific tasks, stereotyped notions surfaced. For example, the mothers said that boys should learn how to cook and clean and should participate in these chores as much as girls. However, two added that the reason these skills were important for boys was that they might not get married. In a similar vein, although Roneeka thought that children of both sexes should be required to learn how to clean, she offered that girls should learn how to change automobile oil only if they wanted to; then, on second thought, she added that they should indeed learn because as adults they might not be able to find a man to do it for them when necessary.

Respect for Self and Others   Although accomplishment-related goals were salient for all mothers, most of them felt that goals related to valuing self and others were of even greater importance. We saw in our small sample the orientation toward family and interpersonal skills that many have pointed to as central to African American socialization emphases (Billingsley, 1992; McAdoo, 1997; Nobles, 1997; Sudarkasa, 1997). Gender role issues did not emerge as strongly in the themes regarding these family and relationship goals as in the accomplishment-related goals.

We learned that valuing self and family, respectfulness, and lovingness were tightly intertwined in the mothers' minds. Valuing self seemed important for some mothers largely as a necessary prerequisite for valuing others. Shardae, for example, told us, "I want her to value herself. I guess you gotta place value on yourself before you can on others—that's rule number one." Maria put it this way, "I'm not good to anybody if I don't love myself. If you don't love yourself, you're not gonna love anybody else."

When asked why they had given a high ranking to valuing self, Breanna and Maria added reasons that reminded us of the overlap between this goal and the accomplishment-related goals. Breanna explained that she would instill self-valuing in her daughter by telling her to stay away from boys, to "keep your mind on you and your goals. And set you some. And always have respect for yourself. And never let anyone put you down. Never let anyone tell you that you can't." Similarly, Maria demonstrated a tight connection between understanding of the goals "value oneself" and "independence" when she remarked that she hoped Bryce would have "love for his own self" so he wouldn't always be "giving in to all the others." She wanted him to care for others, but not to be so other-oriented as to be ready to conform when it was ill-advised. Respect for himself, she thought, would support him in "doing right by hisself and by everyone else's life he touches."

The word *respect* came up often relative to how children should treat others and how they should expect to be treated themselves. Andreya and Roneeka explained in nearly identical words that respect meant "treating other people like you want to be treated." Components to be encouraged in children included politeness, controlling the expression of negative affect to spare the feelings of others, tidying up after oneself so that living spaces would be pleasant for others, sharing, and apologizing after slipping into disrespectfulness. Several mothers and one of the fathers mentioned the particular importance of respect toward one's elders.

The mothers who especially prized respectfulness in children also tended to put a high priority on becoming a loving person, valuing family, and valuing oneself. Breanna, Kyierra, Chandra, and Andreya echoed one another in explaining that being a loving person meant being someone who cares about others and who is gentle and empathetic when others are hurt or in need. Breanna proudly told the story of Corrina rubbing Breanna's stubbed toe as an illustration of her daughter "becoming a loving person." Shardae thought the capacity for love was essential for life itself. "If you don't have love for yourself, love for family, love for anybody else," she said, "then you can't survive." Similarly, Maria said she wanted Bryce to develop lovingness because "as long as you're loving others you shouldn't be hurting them and doing wrong by them." As we pointed out earlier, Sherryce and Roneeka worried when their toddlers did not readily share toys with other children. Although such worry suggested a lack of knowledge about this typical developmental phase, on the positive side it must be recognized that their concern stemmed from a strong desire to see their children become generous, giving people. Sharing was deemed of great importance by all of the mothers; all responded with disapproval to a hypothetical vignette about a 3-year-old who refused to share toys.

As demonstrated by Shardae, most of the mothers whose highest-priority goals for their children were focused on valuing self and others

saw valuing family as central, placing it first, second, or third among
the 18 child-rearing goals we asked them to rank. Conversations about
the importance of valuing family tended to highlight two issues: family
as a location for fostering (and receiving) empathy and kindness, and
family as the one source of support one can always count on. When we
asked Andreya to explain why valuing family was a top priority for her,
she told us how empathy and kindness develop through family interactions and undergird all other aspects of life.

*"And family value is like Lavell might see me crying and he'll say, 'Mama
what's the matter?' And I'll be like, 'I'm mad,' and he'll say, 'Mama don't cry
no more; don't cry no more.' So what I do is, I'll get him to feel better so he'll
know I feel better. And that's how I can teach family values and importance of
them. If you don't value family how can you value anything else? How can you
value a job? How can you value a car or a house or anything if you can't value
family? I mean family, I feel the value of family is the most important part of
your life."*

Several mothers talked about the second reason for valuing family—
that family is "always there for you." Andreya told us that even during
those times when her relationships with her brothers and mother were
strained, deep down she knew that "family is still there. If something
happens, they are going to be there and when you ain't got nobody
else, you can always go back to it." Maria's sentiments were similar, "I
want Bryce to know that his family will always be there for him. And
that it's a real good backbone, a skeleton, a foundation."

Lowest-Priority Goals

We also were interested in learning which of the 18 goals on our list
were accorded the *lowest* priority. Four were given rankings of 16, 17,
or 18 by the majority (five or more) of the mothers one or both times
we asked them to do the rankings. These low-ranked goals were "creativity," "being streetwise," "feeling proud of one's African American
heritage," and "community-mindedness."

    Six mothers gave creativity a low ranking. This has been a consis-
tent finding in many studies of the child-rearing goals and practices of
families with low socioeconomic status (Ispa, 1994; Kohn, 1977; Okagaki & Sternberg, 1993). The pattern has been explained with reference
to the types of jobs that low-income parents hold and expect that their
children will obtain. These jobs are likely to require obedience and conformity rather than openness of thought (Kohn, 1977). It should be
noted, however, that four of the six mothers who gave low priority to

creativity did so only the first time we asked them to rank the 18 goals. Perhaps exposure to Early Head Start and the music, art, and language activities they saw their children enjoying and profiting from in their child care settings had an impact on their later assessments of what is important.

Six mothers (two both times and four once) also gave a low ranking to being streetwise. We believe the mothers interpreted this item as reflecting familiarity with the criminal activity that too often takes place in their neighborhoods. They did not want to see their children become "wise" about that scene for fear that they would become part of it. Low ranking of the goal of becoming community-minded (five mothers both times and one mother once) may have been related to the isolation that currently exists in low-income neighborhoods characterized by high mobility and high crime. The mothers appeared to see little payoff from caring about or working toward the welfare of the community as a whole, and did not plan to inculcate this value in their children. We discuss this further in Chapter 12.

Lastly, five mothers gave a low ranking to the goal of feeling pride in one's African American heritage. Recent research on the positive role played by racial socialization and identity in the psychological adjustment and cognitive competence of minority children and adolescents (Caldwell, Zimmerman, Bernat, Sellers, & Notaro, 2002; Caughy, O'Campo, Randolph, & Nickerson, 2002) suggested that it is unfortunate that the mothers did not appear to put a high priority on fostering racial pride. Though surprised at first, we later understood that we were seeing examples fitting Hill's (1999) observation that low-income African American parents are less likely than their middle-income counterparts to believe that their children have experienced racism or to view race as a barrier to their children's eventual success. In fact, Hill reported that low-income African American parents in her study were likely to attribute their own low status solely to a lack of education and to think that their children could get ahead if they would only apply themselves in school. Her findings help explain both the mothers' high ranking of education and their low ranking of African American pride.

CHILD-REARING PRACTICES

At the end of the second year of our study, we asked the mothers if we could observe them and their children for a couple of hours doing the things they ordinarily do at home. We made it clear that there would be no interview that day—that we would just sit quietly and write notes on the things that they and their children did. After the notes were typed up, we divided them into two sets. One set described relatively long, playful, and warm interactions between the mothers and their children. The other set described mothering that was more distant and/or that reflected irritation with children. Interestingly, the mothers in the "warm and interactive" set were the same mothers who had especially endorsed the relationship-centered child-rearing goals, whereas those who were in the "distant or irritated" set were those who had given the accomplishment-related goals their top rankings.

When their children were between 6 months and 1½ years in age, the mothers completed the spoiling and the control subscales of the Parental Opinion Survey (Luster, Rhoades, & Hass, 1989). These subscales measure a maternal belief that responsive caretaking will result in spoiling and that therefore firm control is necessary in dealing with infants and young children. Using a statistical procedure called t-tests, we were able to show with a high degree of certainty that, compared with the mothers who ranked respect highest, those who ranked accomplishment highest were more concerned that responsiveness would result in spoiling, but less likely to believe that firm control is necessary during early childhood. We wondered if the mothers who valued accomplishment most of all believed that this is a goal they would wait to work on when their children were older. The mothers also may have seen it as a goal to be facilitated by *other* people (e.g., teachers) rather than by themselves. Moreover, they may have viewed the constellation of education/responsibility/independence as either requiring or promoting distance from themselves. The mothers who valued connectedness above all may have recognized that the early years were the time to instill the good manners, the sensitivity, and the sense of belonging that they hoped to see in their children. Their observed behavior, their lesser worry about spoiling, and their greater belief in the necessity of firm control suggested more commitment to active engagement with their children.

Practices Promoting Accomplishment-Related Goals

All but one of the mothers at one time or another proudly told us that their children were "smart." Moreover, all let us know that they wanted to provide their infants and toddlers with toys, books, and/or other experiences that would facilitate their language and cognitive development. Holloway, Fuller, Rambaud, and Eggers-Piérola (1997) similarly reported that the mothers in their ethnically diverse poverty sample believed their preschoolers to be very intelligent. All wanted their children to be provided with stimulating educational experiences, although some thought this was the preschool's responsibility more than theirs. Because language and literacy experiences during early childhood predict later academic success (for a review, see Whitehurst & Lonigan, 1998), we were especially interested in the mothers' beliefs and behaviors regarding talking and reading to young children.

Reading to Young Children The Parent Opinion Survey (Luster, Rhoades, & Haas, 1989), used in the national evaluation of Early Head Start when children were about 24 months old, contains a subscale that asks for parents' agreement with three statements about the usefulness or futility of reading and talking to infants and toddlers. Six of the seven mothers who responded to this questionnaire strongly disagreed with the statement that there is no use in reading to children under the age of 2, and all seven agreed that it is important for adults to talk to infants even before the infants can understand what is being said to them. Support for talking and reading to infants characterized our larger African American sample as well (whether or not they were receiving Early Head Start services).

We know that the Early Head Start home visitors emphasized the importance of reading to children, and most of the mothers accepted this wisdom even though not all understood *why* it was important. For example, Breanna told us that she read to baby Corrina often, and not just from books for infants, "It could be anything, like stuff on the cereal boxes, instructions. I just read it all to her. It's got to be helpful for something." Similarly, when we asked Tanisha what she thought about reading to small children, she answered, "I feel that it's very important. I don't know why, but it probably stimulates their mind as far as development. I hear about reading books on commercials, and I hear about it all the time, so I got it in my head. I'm not sure in what ways, but I know it helps her out." Her statement also reflected the positive effects that can come from televised advice to parents (even from infomercials).

Frequency of Reading to Children Not all of the mothers who said they thought reading was important actually read to their children with any degree of frequency. Sherryce, for example, stocked Michael's room with many good children's books, but the ones we picked up seemed stiff, as if they hadn't been read. She told us she was too busy and too tired to read to Michael. Kyierra and her boyfriend Tejon also provided books for their daughters, but, similarly, little reading seemed to be taking place. Chandra was glad that Patrick's child care teachers read to him, but there were few books (adults' or children's) in the homes in which they stayed. Perhaps the fact that Chandra and Patrick moved every few months was a factor. It is difficult to accumulate possessions when one has no stable home of one's own.

Given that a belief in the importance of reading to infants and toddlers did not always match up with actual behavior, we searched for reasons why some mothers engaged in these activities with children more than others. Two associations were striking: the extent to which mothers talked to and read to their children, and the influence the children had on the mothers.

We divided the mothers into two groups based on how much they said they read to their children; later we divided them into two groups according to the amount of dialogue we witnessed between them and their children. Interestingly, we discovered a perfect match: The six mothers who talked to their infants and toddlers more were also the ones who read to them more. It followed, then, that the other three mothers talked to their children relatively little and read to them seldom. Perhaps an underlying common characteristic of the mothers in the high reading/dialogue group is enjoyment of verbal activity. Andreya was probably the most talkative of our nine mothers; as interviewers we benefited from her love of conversation and saw that she also talked to her children a great deal. When they were very young, she read at least one book a day to her children. Recall from Chapter 5 her determination to talk, sing, and read to Lavell even before he was born and later when he was a baby, even when ridiculed by others. Sherryce, on the other hand, did not talk to her children very much and did not read to them. Talking and reading may go hand-in-hand.

Children's Role in Determining Reading Frequency   Another theme that emerged from the transcripts concerned the pivotal role played *by the children* in either encouraging or discouraging their mothers from reading to them. Breanna, for example, told us that her daughter often came up to her saying, "Read to me, Mama." Tanisha similarly explained, "She brings her own book in here and wants you to read to her, so she basically reminds you that she wants to read." We always read to Lavell during our visits and were invariably impressed that, despite his generally high activity level, he always sat still and listened with great interest to children's books. It was clear that he loved to be read to just as much as Andreya loved to read to him. Chandra's child Patrick, on the other hand, typically wandered off after a few pages; this may partially explain why Chandra seldom read to him. Kyierra, Roneeka, and Tanisha put into words the connection between their children's disinterest and their own reluctance to read to them. Kyierra said that she seldom read because her daughter wasn't very interested in books. Roneeka said that Regina liked to look at books but preferred doing so alone. We wondered if the way in which Roneeka read to her daughter was somehow aversive; we knew she had a tendency to be impatient. A large body of child development theory and research speaks to the reciprocal nature of parent–child influences (Bornstein, Tamis-LeMonda, & Haynes, 1999; Bronfenbrenner, 1979).

By the time their children turned 2, seven of the mothers thought it was time for them to begin learning the alphabet and some numbers. The strategies of choice for teaching the alphabet included exposing the children to *Sesame Street* and singing the "ABC song" with them. Andreya and Shardae made a point of also dancing to the ABC song because they wanted the experience to be enjoyable. Some mothers used flash cards, although these were more likely to be used to teach color words than to teach the alphabet or counting. All of the mothers also wanted their child care providers to teach these skills (see Chapter 14). It is important to keep in mind that the mothers favored such teaching only if it could be made fun for the children. In a multiracial sample of low-income women, Holloway, Rambaud, Fuller, and Eggers-Piérola (1995) likewise found endorsement of an intermingling of didactic and play-based teaching methods.

Several mothers saw their toddlers' proclivity to imitate as a mixed blessing. Although all understood the benefits of imitation for vocabulary development and alphabet and number recitation, at least three (Andreya, Chandra, and Shardae) also pointed out negative implications. Specifically, they worried about their children repeating swear words they'd heard. During one of our visits to Chandra, she went out of the room twice to tell her child's father and his friends to stop cussing. She told us she didn't want Patrick to hear this kind of talk. Recall also Andreya's great concern about the words Lavell was learning from her younger brother.

We end this section with a concern—the omnipresence of television. All of the mothers had the television set on for many hours a day. Often, when we arrived for visits, we had to ask that it be turned off so that it would not interfere with our tape recording. Sometimes children's shows were on, but more often the programs were not for children. The mothers told us that their children were not interested in these shows and did not watch them, but we were concerned for two reasons. First, some of the shows the mothers watched had violent and/or sexual content that was clearly inappropriate for children (e.g., *Jerry Springer*); most of the mothers did not seem to worry that their children would be affected by such shows. However, we know from research that young children are quite prone to imitate televised behavior (Comstock & Paik, 1994). Second, there is research evidence that television is not conducive to children's language development, partially because it takes time away from play and active conversation between adults and children (Singer & Singer, 1990).

Practices Promoting Discipline and Respect

As described previously, six of the nine mothers wanted above all for their children to grow up to be self-disciplined, to value themselves, and to be loving and respectful toward others. We asked the mothers to describe the child-rearing strategies they believed in and used to produce these qualities in their children, and during every visit we also observed actual interactions with children. It seemed that the mothers' thoughts and practices related to fostering respect for self and others fell into two broad areas: methods for preventing problems from occurring in the first place, and strategies to use when children nevertheless misbehaved. We report only on strategies that were used and/or endorsed by at least three of the mothers.

Strategies for Preventing Problems   The mothers thought that many future problems could be prevented if they adopted child-rearing practices that fostered children's security and knowledge of right and wrong. We heard emphasis on several specific practices as well as reasons why some were difficult to maintain.

Providing Love, Availability, and Approval   Many times the mothers told us that parents must show their children love, must *be there* for them, and must show approval for good behavior. A large body of research supports their view that parental love, availability, and approval serve to prevent psychosocial problems in children and adolescents (see reviews in Cassidy & Shaver, 1999).

Showing love meant hugging, kissing, patting, and saying "I love you." *Being there* meant being available—spending time with the children on a frequent and consistent basis, being ever-ready to provide material and emotional support, and generally taking care of them. All of the parents we talked to (fathers as well as mothers) strongly believed that children whose parents are loving and *there* for them will be secure, self-confident, and much less likely to get into trouble than children whose parents are more distant. (See Chapter 11 for a discussion of fathers' perspectives on child rearing.)

Praising and thanking children for good behavior were ways of supporting desired behavior. In keeping with their interest in teaching their children to be polite, and in their awareness of the power of modeling (see below), almost all of the mothers talked about saying "thank you" when their children gave them something or complied with a request. Though we sometimes wished we saw this happen more often, we did indeed hear mothers praise and thank their children for nice artwork, for being helpful, and for obeying. One instance we especially enjoyed involved Andreya's praise when her boys brought her a broom and dustpan she had asked for. "Thank you. I got some true working men here!" she exclaimed. Maria made it clear to Bryce that his behavior pleased her when she told him, "Thanks, Bryce, I'm really happy you did that."

Taking Care Not to Spoil Children   At the same time, the mothers' desire to show love and be responsive was complicated by their belief that harm could ensue if certain limits were exceeded. Seven mothers were concerned about spoiling even in infancy. Kyierra, for example, told us that she worried that "I'm spoiling her and I don't know how to stop." When we asked what she meant, she replied, "'Cause I always feel like I have to hold her and kiss her and stroke her back, and I feel like I have to be touching her." Asked if there is something wrong with showing so much love to an 8-month-old, she answered, "Yeah, to a certain extent, 'cause I do it too much, I know I do." Similarly, when Bryce was 5 months old, Maria was already trying to control her impulse to respond right away, "When he cries I try not to pick him up right away anymore 'cause I know that he's getting to that critical stage where, you know, he might start getting used to whenever he cries, 'I want to be picked up,' and I don't want him to get spoiled."

Once the children entered toddlerhood, the definition of spoiling broadened to include giving children all the material things they wanted. As Andreya told us, "I think spoiling is when kids get everything they ask for and when they can't have it they get a tantrum."

We asked about the long-term dangers of spoiling. Mothers described two categories of spoiled children. The first included children who would "get into things" they weren't supposed to touch, who would refuse to share with other children, and who would "run over you" if they didn't get their way, crying and throwing tantrums. A particular concern was that such children create disturbances in stores with their persistent demands for items the mothers didn't want to buy or couldn't afford. Tanisha, for example, regretted giving in to Tierra too often, "I mean what I do is wrong—every time we're going to the store, it's a habit, everything she sees. Like I get her candy out of the machine. It will be bad in the end when she gets older."

The second type of spoiled child was one who refused to be touched or cared for by anyone but a select few family members. Andreya distinguished between the two types of spoiled children when describing Lavell, "He's not spoiled like most kids are—won't let anybody touch them, won't go to anybody, won't be friendly. I say spoiled—I mean to get his way." Maria worried that her son was in fact demonstrating this second type, "I don't know if Bryce is spoiled or what he is. When a lot of people are around he does not want to be handled by anyone but my mom or me, or his grandfather and that—it kind of worries me, you know." The mothers thus wanted to avoid spoiling because they viewed spoiled children as rude and inconsiderate.

Besides refraining from responding when the children's demands seemed unreasonable, the mothers thought participation in group care would be an effective antidote to spoiling. They believed that their children could learn appropriate behavior by watching and being exposed to other children. For example, Maria said, "Right now like he's real spoiled to me and I really need help trying to figure how to get him out of that. Maybe getting him around other kids or something." When read a hypothetical scenario about a 4-year-old who still wanted a pacifier, Kyierra's boyfriend Tejon exclaimed, "His mama's spoiled the heck out of that child," and Kyierra advised that this level of spoiling would have been prevented had the child been in child care.

It was obvious that dealing with spoiling issues was emotionally trying for the mothers. Conflicts with boyfriends and their own mothers around spoiling exacerbated these tensions. In keeping with previous research on differences between mothers and fathers in orientation toward discipline (e.g., Coe, Thornburg, & Ispa, 1996), boyfriends seemed in favor of stricter anti-spoiling stances than mothers. Several mothers also mentioned that their own mothers had counseled them against showing too much affection and against giving in to demands perceived as unreasonable, yet they did this themselves, leading to mixed messages for the children. (See Chapter 8 for more on grandmother–mother conflict over spoiling.) A comment from Roneeka reflects the strains these mothers faced, "Regina's very spoiled. I can't stop her being spoiled. I mean, everybody spoils her. . . .They tell me not to hold her when she's asleep. You know, 'You can't keep picking her up every time she makes a little sound; that's just going to make her even worse.' But I know my mother ain't going to let her cry. She's very spoiled. Rotten."

Keeping a Close Eye on Children and Keeping Them Occupied   A frequently mentioned strategy for preventing problems involved keeping a close eye on children. Tanisha, for example, said that she thought it wise to "pay attention to her, focus on her and she won't be doing nothing else 'cause she knows that you're watching her."

Keeping children occupied also was deemed useful. Breanna believed that "As long as I have something she can play with so she don't have to wander off and find something to play with that she's not supposed to," everything would be fine. Andreya partially blamed Lavell's aggressive behavior in his child care center on an insufficient variety of interesting activities there. The mothers understood that keeping their children occupied entailed permitting them to choose activities that were interesting to them. Much scholarly writing has focused on the greater degree to which low-income parents, compared with middle- and upper-income parents, emphasize obedience in their children (Ispa, 1994; Kohn, 1977). This relative difference should not be taken to mean that low-income children are allowed no choices at all. Many times we saw mothers and grandmothers respect children's preferences, especially in matters related to play.

Teaching and Modeling the Golden Rule   Earlier in this chapter, we quoted some of the mothers expressing their awareness that children look to adults as role models. Here we only briefly remind readers of those ideas; that is, that the mothers understood that their modeling of appropriate behavior was a powerful method for supporting positive behavior and preventing negative behavior.

Related to modeling was the notion of reciprocity. As Sherryce put it, "Basically it's one of those 'treat them how *you* wanna be treated' things." Breanna figured that because she was good to Corrina, Corrina in turn "doesn't want my feelings hurt, so she'll say, 'Okay, okay, Mama.'" Recall Andreya's assertion that "I'm the type of person if you don't show me no respect, I'm not going to show you none." She firmly believed that the same holds true for children: They reflect back the respect with which they are treated. "Little kids coming up—they see other people mouthing off, they gonna copy," she said. "As far as respect, it goes both ways. You don't give it, you don't get it." Describing a time when Lavell told her she was talking too loudly, she explained, "It's like sometimes he correct me; sometimes I correct him. I mean, they teaching me just as well as I'm teaching them. And it's fun."

Providing Peer Interaction   A final piece of advice the mothers gave frequently when asked how to prevent the development of a variety of objectionable behaviors involved making sure that children participate in peer groups. All nine mothers thought exposing young children to other children their age would prevent difficulties. In fact, this belief was a major reason for their unanimous agreement that good-quality group child care benefits children. (Recall that participation in child care also was considered an antidote to spoiling.) When read a hypothetical vignette about a child who was still sucking on a pacifier at age 4, Sherryce exclaimed, "She needs to go around other kids her age. She's gonna feel embarrassed." Four mothers thought participating in child care helps prevent over-dependence, and four thought it teaches children to share and in general to get along with others. Three mothers mentioned that interaction with peers is so important that mothers who are home with their children all day should arrange play groups with other families.

Encouraging Religious Involvement   When our project began, only Sherryce attended church regularly. Most of the mothers told us that organized religion played little role in their lives, although they all said that they believed in God. We therefore did not list spirituality as one of the child-rearing goals on the MCR-VBI. (In Chapter 12 we explore the mothers' reasons for initially avoiding church.) By our last interviews, however, all but Chandra, Maria, and Tanisha were going to church at least occasionally, and even these three wanted some religious influence in their children's lives. Maria, for example, said that although she rarely went to church, she had seen to it that Bryce was baptized. She said she was "teary-eyed" during the ceremony. Tanisha and Chandra also thought that church attendance would benefit their children. Indeed, one of the reasons Chandra sent Patrick to live with Cecelia, her ex-stepmother, after his fourth birthday was that she knew he would be taken to church every Sunday. When we visited Chandra that year, she told us that her decision had been a good one because now Patrick was going to church regularly and was being taught to say grace before meals. She was also pleased that Cecelia had bought him a Bible.

As we explored the mothers' reasons for wanting their children to be affiliated with organized religion (even if they themselves were not), we realized that they saw religious teachings as facilitating the attainment of their overarching goals regarding accomplishment and the development of respect and caring for self and others. After Chandra told us that she wanted Patrick to grow up to "be his own person, not a follower" and to go to college, we asked her what she could do to ensure those outcomes. Having a positive environment such as "a church-wise" environment would be key, she said. She also thought that connection to a church might be protection against "drugs, drinking, and partying on the streets." In fact, at one time or another, all of the mothers except Maria said that church affiliation would benefit their children by teaching them to "follow God's rules" and learn "morals" and "right from wrong." Research suggests that they were correct; several studies have indicated that religion and church affiliation play a positive role in teaching African American children and youth the ideals of responsibility, concern for others, and avoidance of risky or delinquent behaviors (Haight, 2002; Smith & Faris, 2002). Prayer as an avenue for expressing kind thoughts about others (as well as hopes for one's own well-being) was demonstrated in the bedtime prayer Breanna taught Corinna to say every night: "Now I lay me down to sleep. If I should die before I wake, I pray the Lord my soul to keep. Bless my mother, my father, all my enemies, and all my family."

Other benefits of religious belief or spirituality mentioned by all but two of the mothers concerned resiliency and coping. Our transcripts include many statements about prayer and church attendance serving as a "stress reliever," helping mothers "relax" and regain perspective. Breanna, for example, told us that going to church "fills an emptiness inside" and makes "you feel cleansed and relieved and a lot off your shoulders." Sherryce explained that "They teach you how to cope with stuff, like when you get depressed." Although none of the mothers explicitly mentioned the development of coping skills as a reason for wanting their children to be affiliated with a church, one can assume that they would want this benefit for their children as well as for themselves. Sherryce came closest when she talked about being glad that her son was learning spirituality in his Sunday School class. She was clear that this was a vital function of church membership, over and above the social support it provided. As indicated by studies of the role of religion in African American life during slavery and afterward, spirituality has served as a powerful protective factor reminding people of their worth and maintaining their belief in ultimate justice and equality while helping them cope with the realities of an unfair world (Coles, 1990; Haight, 2002; Rucker, 2001).

Babyproofing   As mentioned earlier, some aspects of typical toddler behavior irritated the mothers. And although they understood that "kids are gonna be kids," their toddlers' propensity to "get into everything" created problems, especially when the children started walking. Babyproofing was advocated by the home visitors as a way to reduce the messes and dangers associated with the children's exploration. The mothers were encouraged, for example, to cover electrical outlets, put away small items on which infants and toddlers could choke, and keep sharp things, breakable objects, and poisons well out of reach of small hands. Such practices, they were told, would not only sharply decrease the likelihood of harm to their children, but also the number of times they would have to say no to them.

We discovered that, although all the mothers followed some of this advice, the application of babyproofing methods was uneven. Several of the children had to be taken to the hospital because they had burned themselves on irons or swallowed pills or cleaning liquids. Three reasons the mothers were not more careful seemed to involve 1) underestimating the toddlers' ability to unscrew caps, 2) being unaware that the smell of cleaning supplies does not always deter this age-group from tasting them, and 3) not having full control of their living envi-

ronments when they were living with their own mothers or with other
kin or friends. Recall from Chapter 5 how Patricia, Andreya's mother,
refused to put away treasured but fragile knick-knacks. She felt that by
her age, she had earned the right to enjoy having items with sentimen-
tal value in full view, and that when Lavell handled and, worse yet,
broke them, it was testimony to Andreya's poor parenting skills rather
than to the inappropriate arrangement of the objects in their home. Roneeka, Shardae, and Tanisha complained about similar circumstances
vis-à-vis their mothers or, as in Tanisha's case, her daughter's paternal
grandmother.

The Mothers' Strategies for Managing Child Misbehavior   Below,
we discuss the mothers' strategies for stopping unwanted behavior.
First, we want to note that most of the prevention strategies described
above could also be used for this purpose. Putting a child in a group-
care situation, for example, was viewed as an effective *preventative*
strategy and as a *corrective* approach for immature or selfish behavior.
We have grouped the techniques described below into a separate section because all were applied *only after* children had misbehaved.

    Correcting Misbehavior Immediately and Consistently   A clear theme
in the mothers' thoughts about discipline was that the wrongdoing of
even very young children must not be ignored. Every infraction must
be immediately addressed or the misbehavior will continue and escalate. The mothers believed that their children "know better" and are
simply testing limits. For example, Shardae, told us, "She [2-year-old
Alexis] knows. A lot of times she looks back at me, 'I know what I'm
doing wrong; let me see if she's looking at me.' You've got to be consistent or otherwise they can get away with stuff. You let them know,
'I love you but I'm not gonna take that.' You know, they can learn already at 2 that they can run over you."

    After telling us about a child whose mother often threatened pun-
ishment but did not actually mete it out, Shardae continued, "If you
keep doing that, she is going to think you don't mean what you said.
You have to stay consistent with it. If you are going to threaten her, you
might as well do it." Similarly, Breanna's reaction to a hypothetical
vignette about a toddler who threw tantrums when asked to share was
to admonish the mother for not having firmly "put her foot down"
every time this happened.

    In the mothers' minds, the long-term consequences of "letting
things go" were serious. Andreya described children who are not consistently disciplined from an early age, "And they have they own mind-
set to where, 'Hey, I'm going to do this whether my mama tells me to
or not. I know it ain't right but I'm gonna do it.' You do get tired when

your kids being conniving but you have to teach them when they get 4 and 5, not when they get 10, 11, 12, 13. I mean, you don't just start disciplining a kid when they get 10 and 11. If I don't correct him now and get his attention and I wait till he gets 10, then it's gonna be a little too late for all that."

Roneeka's thoughts on this score alluded to the violence in her community. She worried that if she didn't teach Regina not to hit now, she would later antagonize others and might get hurt, "Sometimes she hits other people. I'm like 'No!' I know she's a child but some grownups won't see her as a child. They'll see her as a grown person, you know, and just hit her. Nowadays you can't do that. Bigger kids are knocking these little babies down, you know, to where they're crying and out of breath and all that. So I'm trying to teach her not to do them kind of things."

Readers should keep in mind that when the mothers talked about the importance of consistency in discipline, they were talking about a *goal* for themselves. No parent catches every misbehavior, and we observed times when the mothers did not respond to their children's mischief. Some mothers commented thoughtfully that they wanted to do better in this regard. Tanisha, for example, blamed herself for letting Tierra "get away with stuff," figuring "that's probably why she doesn't listen."

Redirecting and Enticing Home visitors recommended to the mothers that they use redirection when their children wanted a forbidden object or activity. The mothers agreed that when infants and toddlers obtained objects they shouldn't handle or grabbed something from another child, distracting them with another object or activity was a good idea. Breanna, for example, told us that when her daughter started playing with something she shouldn't have, Breanna would "move her away and give her something else to do." Andreya called the technique "conning."

The word "conning" had a twofold meaning for Andreya. She used it to refer to instances when she distracted Lavell from doing something forbidden, and also when she enticed him with promises of rewards for better behavior. A promise of a reward was implicit, for example, in her assertion to Lavell that Santa Claus likes it when children sleep in their own beds. Sometimes she, like other mothers, offered candy, popsicles, or a favorite video or TV cartoon if her children would stop misbehaving.

Using Time-Out As the children left babyhood, became mobile, and moved into the typical "No!" stage, the mothers struggled with discipline issues. A time-out was an option recommended by Early Head Start. It also was a practice some mothers remembered from their own childhoods or from the families they had babysat for before they had children of their own. Our transcripts and field notes show considerable diversity in the mothers' opinions about time-out and in their methods of applying it.

At one time or another, all of the mothers except Maria talked about the use of time-out when children touched something they shouldn't touch, hit someone, used cusswords, had tantrums, or refused to obey their mothers' instructions. Almost all of the mothers used two or more time-out methods, with the one chosen for a particular instance depending on the perceived seriousness of the infraction and on the circumstances of the moment (e.g., the mothers' moods, the presence of company). These methods included ordering the children to stand or sit in a corner, confining toddlers to their highchairs, making them sit near them or stay in their bedrooms, or requiring them to take a nap. (Shardae explained that often misbehavior is the result of fatigue, so it makes sense to require a nap. We might also note that most of our infants and toddlers had no regular sleeping schedule.) Four mothers thought that time-out was most effective if the children had "no toys, no TV, no nothin'" during the time-out period. We began to hear about time-out shortly after the children turned 1, but not all of the mothers thought it appropriate to start so young. Andreya complained about the use of time-out in Lavell's child care center when he was 14 months old, calling it "kind of like torture." Shardae thought that parents should wait until their children were 2 because until then they couldn't understand why they were in time-out. All of the mothers said time-out usually lasted 3 minutes or less. Three of them said that if their children cried, they would keep them in time-out until they stopped.

Time-out was often used in combination with demands for apologies and/or with reasoning about the inappropriateness and consequences of misbehavior. Shardae and Andreya both acted on the value they put on politeness when they required their children to "say you're sorry" before they could leave time-out. After hearing the vignette about the child who hit and threw things, Breanna said, "He needs a time-out and a talking to, a real good talking to eye-to-eye." A "talking to" typically involved demands for acceptable behavior and explanations concerning the likely costs of continued wrongdoing. After hearing the vignette about a 3-year-old who refused to share toys with her cousins, Shardae said that she would "Make her sit down. She's 3. Let her know why she's sitting out. Sit her down and tell her she's old enough to share with her friends, family, and let her know she needs to share with them and if you can't share, then sit down until you understand that you can." We were present one day when Lavell hit a playmate. Making him sit in a time-out on the sofa, Andreya told him that he had hurt the girl, that if he behaved like this, eventually she wouldn't want to play with him anymore, and that, in fact, the girl's mother might not *let* her play with him. "I thought she was your friend. Why did you do that to her? You will sit there until you are ready to play without hurting anybody. You have to think about it." Kyierra took a different approach, believing it best to ignore Jalisa while she was in time-out so as not to reward her tears with any sort of attention.

The four mothers who made explicit statements in favor of time-out thought that it worked because children don't like to be "locked up" in their highchairs or bedrooms, because they "suffer" while in time-out, and/or because they hate to be deprived of parental attention. Two added that time-out presents an opportunity for children to think about their behavior.

It was clear, however, that even though most of the mothers used time-out, some had reservations about its effectiveness or thought it was not the whole answer to disciplinary problems. Kyierra said that her mother had used time-out with her but "It never worked. I didn't like to sit still but it didn't teach me anything." Roneeka thought that time-out was too "nice"—it didn't make enough of an impression on her "hard-headed" daughter. Recall from the case study how Andreya vacillated between liking the concept of time-out and her belief that "Time-out—it don't work." She worried that if she used it a lot, it would become meaningless to Lavell, "He will get used to it and it's like it don't mean nothing."

The Early Head Start home visitors hoped that they could influence the mothers to use time-out instead of corporal punishment. The mothers, however, tended to use it in conjunction with corporal punishment, or as a first attempt to discipline their children before giving up and resorting to spanking. When Tierra was 34 months old, Tanisha told us she thought "the corner" was much more effective than spankings; yet later in the same interview, she told us that although time-out was appropriate for "petty" misbehaviors like touching forbidden objects, when Tierra did something "really bad," she needed a whupping. (The various words the mothers used to describe corporal punishment are defined below in the section devoted to this topic.) Illustrating the point that the two strategies might be used together, she responded to the vignette about a child who hit and threw things at his grandmother with a recommendation that the mother should "Look her in her face and be very serious and say, 'Don't do that,' and I would whup her really, really good and put her in the corner. And next time I feel that once you do that, they'll understand, 'Oh, no, that's bad,' and so she probably wouldn't do it as much."

The mothers' mixed feelings about time-out seemed to be rooted in several issues. First, although early childhood professionals recommend that time-out should be used infrequently, and when it is used, it should be accompanied by teaching desirable behavior (Marion, 2002), our observations suggested that some mothers used it often and without accompanying words about appropriate behavior. As Andreya insightfully noted, the result was that it appeared to have become meaningless for children. Second, and perhaps most important, time-out was not consistently applied or enforced. We saw, for example, that Lavell might or might not be put in time-out for the same misbehavior, and that Andreya often let it go when he snuck out of time-out before she told him he could get up. (To be fair, we should mention that she may have been especially distracted because of our presence; perhaps she was more consistent when she was alone with her children.) Moreover, consistency was often lacking among family members. As shown in the case study of Andreya and as we saw in other families, even when the mothers tried to replace corporal punishment with time-out, grandmothers, aunts, and uncles were not always on the same page. Finally, we heard some mothers rather frequently threaten children with time-out but not carry through. Over time, empty threats, of course, lose their power as children learn that "this time" they may be able to escape punishment.

Yelling and Threatening   Regardless of socioeconomic status or race, it is a near-universal experience of American children to be yelled at or threatened with unpleasant consequences for noncompliance with parental demands. Analyzing telephone survey data gathered from a nationally representative sample, Straus and Field (2003) found that 90% of American parents admitted to having yelled at their 2- through 4-year-olds in the past year; 67% said that they had threatened to spank. Younger mothers (ages 18–29) reported more frequent use of these practices than older parents. Other studies (e.g., Brody, Murry, Kim, & Brown, 2002) have documented a link between family financial hardship and parental harshness with children. It should therefore come as no surprise that the women in our sample of young and economically stressed mothers found themselves yelling at their children on quite a number of occasions. Often, as might be expected, yelling was accompanied by threats.

The most frequently shouted word was "stop," but, of course, there also were many others. Of the three mothers who most often yelled at their children during our visits, only Tanisha spoke in favor of it. "I yell at her and she'll stop. She'll know I'm serious." Roneeka and Andreya, on the other hand, struggled because they thought it would be better to yell less. In Chapter 13 we quote Roneeka's appreciation for her

Early Head Start home visitors' efforts to help her find better ways to discipline than through yelling. Andreya was similarly grateful for talks she'd had with Rickie (her home visitor). She had become aware that when she yelled, she was modeling a communication style she disliked. "You know how people just, 'You getting on my nerves.' 'You better sit down.' Or 'Shut up.' They hollering and all that. They [Early Head Start] give you a better way to talk to your kids. If you tell a kid to shut up, they'll tell you to shut up." She had concluded that it would be better to calmly tell her children to "be quiet" because that was "another way of [showing kids] respect really." During subsequent visits, we observed that she did not always follow her own advice.

The threats delivered to misbehaving children tended to fall into four categories. The first was in keeping with the mothers' beliefs about time-out: We heard four mothers threaten misbehaving children with the corner or with having to lie down, take a nap, or simply leave the room. Roneeka and Andreya were likely to show how peeved they were by exclaiming "Bye!" (meaning that children should leave the room) after these time-out-related threats. A second category included threats of corporal punishment (e.g., "I'm going to spank you." "You gonna get a whuppin'," "I'm not playin', I'm gonna get you."). The third category involved threatened loss of something enjoyable—having to forgo a trip to a park or a fast food restaurant (or having to leave if they were already there), not getting pizza or a dessert, or removal of a favorite toy or video. Threats that *someone else* besides the mother would find out about the misbehavior and be displeased comprised our final (and most colorful) category of threats. For example, we heard three mothers threaten children that they would inform grandmothers or other relatives about their misbehavior, and that these individuals would be angry and would not want to come get them for a promised outing. During one visit, Andreya told us that this was the only strategy that worked to control Lavell's naughtiness. Another time, she threatened that she would call William, his father. She and Shardae also threatened to tell their children's child care providers. Andreya went so far as to predict that Lavell might not be admitted to Head Start if he continued "not knowing how to act." On other occasions, she announced that she was going to "tell Santa Claus to take you off his list; you not getting a Christmas," or that she was going to "call the cops."

At least two problems were evident regarding the mothers' use of threats. First was a concern that applied to some mothers more than others: a lack of follow-through. Too often, we heard mothers threaten some consequence that never materialized. When threats are empty, children learn to disregard them (Comer & Poussaint, 1992). We think that some mothers understood this principle, but it was knowledge that was not always put into practice. A second concern stemmed from the rejection or negative appraisal of the child implied in some of the language used in the threats. In fact, some researchers subsume yelling and threats in a construct called "psychological aggression"; they see its use by parents as motivated by the intention to cause the child psychological pain (for a review, see Straus & Field, 2003). Although acknowledging that psychological aggression is normative in American families, researchers worry because studies have linked this type of aggression to problems in children's social and emotional development. Care, of course, must be taken when interpreting such results because it is not altogether clear to what extent parents are reacting to their children's misbehavior as opposed to causing it. In any event, it was our impression that some of the mothers and children in our study would indeed have benefited from a reduction in the frequency of threats that were empty (not acted on) and that carried messages of rejection or disapproval of the child (not just disapproval of a specific behavior).

At the same time, we also want to point out a very important sociocultural feature of some of the disciplinary statements we heard: What might seem jarring to European American, middle-class ears may actually convey humor and affection. Haight (2002), for example, quoted African American Sunday school teachers as scolding-yet-joshing students with pronouncements like "You need your little butt whipped!" (p. 139). The ensuing laughter on both sides demonstrated that these exclamations were funny and not to be taken literally. Garvey and Shantz's (1992) research on "nonserious oppositional speech" showed how the speaker's nonverbal cues (such as laughter) and the outlandishness of obviously false threats and insults tell the listener that the speaker is being playful and even affectionate. Along these lines, we recorded Andreya mock-complaining to 15-month-old Lavell that she had a mind to "throw you in the trash can," or "trade you in." A little later, when Lavell babbled "Ba, ba," Andreya responded, "Yep, you be bad! You be bad!" In both instances it was clear from the context and from the little smile in her voice that she was having fun and didn't mean a word of it. She also liked to tell us about times when she and her mother had teased each other. We used the mothers' and children's demeanor to help us distinguish between threats that were delivered jokingly and lovingly, and threats that were rooted in anger and could be read verbatim. We want to emphasize, however, that caution is called for when interpreting the meaning of talk by parents in cultures other than one's own.

Using Corporal Punishment   The use of corporal punishment (see Ispa and Halgunseth [2004] for a lengthier treatment of the mothers' use of corporal punishment) is common in the United States. Surveys indicate that more than 90% of American parents spank, with frequencies highest for children between the ages of 2 and 5, and when parents are young, unmarried, African American (as opposed to European American), and/or have little income (Giles-Sims, Straus, & Sugarman, 1995; Pinderhughes, Dodge, Bates, Pettit, & Zelli, 2000; Straus & Stewart, 1999). That African Americans use corporal punishment more than European Americans must be considered in tandem with findings from some studies indicating that it has fewer adverse consequences for African American children than for European American children, especially when it is combined with warmth. Corporal punishment may have different meanings for African American parents and children than for European American parents and children (Deater-Deckard & Dodge, 1997).

As mentioned earlier, Early Head Start home visitors tried to encourage the use of "positive guidance" strategies such as redirection, reasoning, and time-out instead of corporal punishment. Most of the mothers were receptive to this message, and some tried to replace corporal punishment with these strategies. At the time of our last interviews, however, all were physically punishing their children at least occasionally. One of our goals as we analyzed our data on corporal punishment was to try to understand why the use of corporal punishment persisted.

Before proceeding to that discussion, however, we will review the language of corporal punishment as used by the mothers in our study. To our knowledge, the meanings of the words they used to denote various types of corporal punishment were typical for the African American community and somewhat different from the language used by Americans of European descent. We learned that some words clearly denote the severity of the corporal punishment administered, whereas the exact meaning of other words is more variable. Mutual understanding between European American and African American parents and professionals cannot take place without an understanding of this vocabulary.

The mothers in our study used the words *popping* and *tapping* interchangeably. *Popping* was the more frequently used of the two; both referred to light hits on a hand, arm, leg, buttocks, or head. The children tended to be popped for repeated but minor transgressions or when they were judged to be too young to really "know better." Chandra popped 10-month old Patrick's hand when he "messed with plugs and things like that." When Alexis was 13 months old, Shardae told us, "Well, she knows the concept of 'no, no' but it doesn't always sink in sometimes. Right now, she's a little too young for a spanking. I mean, sometimes if she messes with something, like glass or something, then

I'll pop her hand. But I never actually hit her or, you know, spank her." She thought poppings hurt Alexis's feelings more than they hurt her physically.

Most of the mothers thought *whuppings* were in order when transgressions were more serious, when children "knew better," and/or when children didn't respond to milder forms of discipline, especially after they turned 2. Whuppings involved repeated and/or hard strikes, usually to the buttocks, with an open hand, brush, or belt. In the mothers' eyes the transgressions warranting whuppings tended to involve the breakage of valued objects, potential danger to self (e.g., running into the street) or threatened or actual physical harm to others, and/or disrespect. Two-year-old Lavell got a whupping for holding his baby brother halfway in the toilet, and both Chandra and Kyierra thought a child who threw things at a grandmother needed a whupping. Kyierra whupped her daughter for jumping on the sofa despite repeated warnings. Talking back, using swear words, and in general "not listening" might elicit whuppings in part because the mothers interpreted such behaviors as disrespectful.

The word *spanking* seemed to have a less definite meaning. Five of the mothers sometimes used it to refer to hits to the hand, suggesting that spankings were the same as poppings, but these same mothers, like others, also used *spanking* to refer to repeated or harder hits to the legs or buttocks. Overall, in terms of severity, a spanking seemed to be between a popping and a whupping. Roneeka, for example, told us that she wouldn't want her daughter's teacher to think she'd been whupped when she'd only been spanked, and Maria said that she sometimes spanked but would never whup ("I don't spank Bryce to where you'd call it a whupping"). Spankings tended to be administered when children persisted in a behavior despite repeated admonitions. When Alexis was 33 months old, Shardae told us, "A spanking's just to me, if you're not doing what I say after I told you over and over and I wanna scare you a little bit, I may spank your legs to where you're just shocked. Alexis gets so shocked; it hurts her feelings so I don't even have to really put any force or hit her hard. It's just when she's just totally just being really disobedient."

Similarly, Maria said that she spanked 19-month-old Bryce "on the bottom" to "startle him, to scare him to not do it again" when he repeatedly refused to listen. When Tierra was 17 months old, Tanisha thought she was too young for the corner, so a spanking was the only way to teach her that she couldn't get away with misbehavior.

Another word we heard fairly regularly was *hit*. For Shardae, the term implied more forceful corporal punishment than a popping, but five other mothers used the term to refer to any degree of force, from a tap on the hand to a strike on the buttocks. Finally, at one time or another, three of the mothers said they had *smacked* their children. A smack involved a single hard hit.

Hoping to understand why all nine mothers continued to use corporal punishment despite the efforts of Early Head Start staff to teach them to replace it with "positive guidance" strategies, we searched our transcripts for the mothers' explanations. It became clear that all of the mothers had given this issue some thought. Some had heeded the Early Head Start message by reducing the frequency of corporal punishment and/or trying for a while to refrain from it altogether. Nonetheless, although the extent to which the children were popped, spanked, and/or whupped varied from family to family, at the end of our 5-year study, none of the mothers had entirely given up the practice. Our impression was that they had added positive guidance techniques to their child-rearing repertoires; they viewed them as an option but not as a replacement for corporal punishment. We suggest six explanations for the persistence of corporal punishment.

First, several of the mothers thought that positive guidance techniques were too mild, especially for serious or repeated offenses and when the child was judged to already know right from wrong. When misbehavior continued despite redirection, reasoning, or time-out, the mothers concluded that the children viewed these techniques as playing games. Recall that Tanisha continued to resort to corporal punishment even while asserting that the corner worked better. Clearly, she thought she should reserve that option for situations she saw as too troubling for time-out.

Our second explanation for the persistence of corporal punishment involves the other adults in the mothers' lives. Even when the mothers wanted to refrain from physical punishment, and even when they explained their reasoning to their mothers, siblings, aunts, and uncles, these individuals were unlikely to follow suit. The mothers then found themselves in the uncomfortable position of being the only ones not using corporal punishment. The result, they feared, would be that their children would start disobeying them while continuing to obey those relatives who spanked them.

Third, the mothers looked at their siblings and friends and at themselves and came to conclusions regarding the long-term effectiveness of corporal punishment. Andreya and her mother regretfully recalled that her brothers had not received much physical punishment when they were children; they thought this might be the reason they were now "in the streets" and in so much trouble. Maria accepted her friends' comments that she herself would not have been such a wild teenager had her parents spanked her when she was little. (Maria was the only mother who had not been spanked as a child.) Mothers who had been spanked thought this had contributed to their current ability to be responsible young adults.

Fourth, three beliefs concerning the nature of small children seemed central to the mothers' valuing of corporal punishment: The mothers thought that it was natural for small children to test limits, that such behavior would escalate if not punished early, and that toddlers were already capable of "knowing better" after they have been admonished once for a given transgression.

The mothers' acceptance of the notion that it is natural for toddlers to test limits was not accompanied by tolerance of disobedience. We are reminded here of Willis's (1992) observation that "The permissive child-rearing practices common in many European American, middle-class households in which discipline is seen as stifling creative expression would not be tolerated in most African American families" (p. 138). Mothers did not think that toddler-style noncompliance or defiance would diminish over time simply as children matured. "They gonna try you, you know, to see how far they can get," Roneeka explained. She, like other mothers, thought that parents must actively and firmly "stay on" their children lest disobedience continue and become even more serious in later years. "A hard head makes a soft butt," Breanna noted when asked for sayings familiar to her community. It stands to reason that all of these thoughts followed from the mothers' beliefs that toddlers were cognitively capable of understanding, after just one or two verbal prohibitions, what behaviors were or were not acceptable, what was right and what was wrong. "She knows" was a justification we heard a number of times. Along these lines, other researchers have reported that young mothers are more likely than older mothers to expect unrealistically early cognitive and skill achievement and that these expectations are linked to punitive disciplinary practices (O'Callaghan, Borkowski, Whitman, Maxwell, & Keogh, 1999; Tamis-Lemonda, Shannon, & Spellmann, 2002).

Fifth, the risk-filled neighborhoods in which the mothers were raising their children must be taken into account. As mentioned earlier, the mothers knew that, come adolescence, their children would be faced with difficult choices that could well result in delinquency, early pregnancy, and even death. Corporal punishment, they thought, would keep them in line, help them learn self-restraint so that they could resist the temptation to join gangs and engage in premature sexual activity. The stakes for families living in such circumstances are high; it is perhaps no wonder that the punishment of choice is one of high intensity.

The sixth and final reason we could detect for the persistence of corporal punishment was also related to the violence prevalent in the families' neighborhoods: The mothers wanted their children to be ready to defend themselves against aggression by others. They didn't want them to be passive victims. The home visitors' message that corporal punishment teaches children that hitting is an acceptable strategy to use when interpersonal problems surface was therefore met with some ambivalence. Kyierra, for example, told us that her mother had told her to "walk away" from peers who wanted to hit her, and that as a result, she'd gotten her "butt kicked a lot 'cause I did walk away." She did not plan to counsel her daughters to do the same.

Corporal punishment was thus an issue that sharply illustrated the tensions that can arise when minority-group parents are asked to consider the child-rearing wisdom of mainstream child development professionals. Mothers seemed to understand the rationales against corporal punishment presented by their Early Head Start home visitors, but by the end of our study none had chosen to abandon it. It is important that individuals outside of this community understand the factors that mothers such as those in our study must balance as they weigh the alternatives to the disciplinary strategies familiar to them from their own childhoods and that are still used by those close to them. We must appreciate the impacts of their histories and the circumstances in which they presently live, and we must remember that corporal punishment is usually administered not out of rejection, but because parents think it is an effective option. For effective communication, it is also essential that we know the meanings of the corporal punishment vocabulary used by African Americans in low-income communities. Imagine, for example, the misunderstandings that can occur when mothers are advised to refrain from spanking but interpret this to mean that the person giving the advice is comfortable with popping.

Involving Fathers   Earlier we mentioned the mothers' belief that fathers must *be there* for their children. In a related theme, the mothers ruefully noted that their children obeyed their fathers better than they obeyed them. Tanisha, for example, complained that "Dwayne [her live-in boyfriend] is like, 'No!' and he'll look at her like this and she'll just stop everything, but I have to actually ignore her or scream at her at the top of my lungs." Andreya was likewise frustrated by her children's greater compliance with their father than with her.

"You know, it's different between a female and a male parent because that male parent can say, 'Son, sit down,' or 'Go sit in time-out' and that kid do it like then and there, but a mother have to say, 'I told you, didn't I tell you to do this?' and 'Didn't I tell you to do that?' and 'Don't do that.' You have to say it over and over again. It seem like the father role, it's got the upper hand over the mother.

It's like a mother's there for the love, the comfort, the nurturing and all that, but the father's there for like you know, the rough times, the discipline, the respect."

Kyierra thought that Tejon's low voice led Jalisa to more readily "mind" him than her, although she also wondered if it was because "little girls side with their daddies more anyway." Besides, she noted, Tejon had built a strong relationship with Jalisa because he was home with her all day while she was at work. Tanisha, on the other hand, thought that because she played with Tierra more than Dwayne did, Tierra viewed him as "eviler" and complied with him out of fear. Maria went so far as to worry that in the long run, it might be better for Bryce to live with his father than with her because he might then be better behaved.

Mothers did not think it had to be the biological father who played the fathering role (in fact, Tejon and Dwayne were not Jalisa's and Tierra's biological fathers). Andreya thought that a man who didn't have children would be honored if the woman he was with allowed him to be their father figure, "It's like when you a male and you with a female that already got kids and you don't have none, a male will look like, 'Dang, she give me an opportunity to be with her kids, you know, to play that role in their life.'"

BELIEFS AND DOUBTS
CONCERNING PARENTING EFFICACY

The mothers' perceptions that fathers had an easier time eliciting compliance than they did raises the issue of parenting efficacy, or a belief in one's own child-rearing effectiveness. Researchers have shown that mothers' sense of competence as parents predicts good child outcomes (Murry & Brody, 1999). Careful analysis of our transcripts suggests that the mothers varied amongst themselves in this regard. Moreover, their confidence in their mothering skills differed depending on the ages of their children and the support they were getting from relatives and friends.

The mothers told us that although some aspects of infant behavior such as persistent crying were puzzling, in general they were well-prepared for infant care because they had had considerable experience caring for their little cousins and the children of friends. Also, most said that although their own mothers had been upset when they found out that their daughters were pregnant, they were generous with support and advice once their grandchildren were born.

In spite of this, however, for some mothers raising toddlers presented clear challenges to feelings of efficacy. Kyierra told us that she felt hurt when Jalisa told her to "shut up." Others reflected anger, as when after yelling "stop!" to 17-month-old Patrick, Chandra blurted,

"He pisses me off. I can't handle him. He listens to everybody else but me." Wondering if 18-month-old Corinna was "going on her terrible twos or something," Breanna described a typical instance, "'Corinna, get down.' 'No! No! No! No!' to *everything*. I'm pretty sure she's understanding me and she knows what she's doing is wrong, but I don't know what to do. I honestly do not know what to do. She won't listen." Along the same lines, Tanisha wished she had more knowledge about child rearing because "I just don't understand the tantrums," while Roneeka felt that she knew enough but wasn't always good about doing what she knew she should do. Maria wondered if Bryce's noncompliance was her fault; perhaps she'd done something wrong. We noticed that the two oldest mothers (Shardae and Sherryce) were the least likely to question their parenting competence. The greater maturity of these women, combined with the fact that their children seemed temperamentally easy, may have worked in their favor.

What struck us the most regarding efficacy, however, was the juxtaposition of the mothers' twin convictions that 1) they must try as hard as possible to raise their children well, but that 2) what happened later in adolescence and adulthood was ultimately out of their control. We have already described the mothers' painful awareness of the violence, drugs, and early sexual activity that might tempt their children when they got older. Hoping that they would instill the strength of character that would be necessary to keep these influences at bay, they nevertheless made remarks such as Roneeka's, "I have a lot of goals for her but that don't mean she will follow them, so that will have to be up to her," and "Boys are gonna be boys. They gonna do what they wanna do regardless of what their mother says. I'll bring him up the best way I can not to, you know, try to get out there and live that fast lane drug life or, you know, jail life. But like they say, You can raise kids one way and they go another way." Determination to "try my best to teach them" was thus mixed with a degree of fatalism that was realistic given the restricted options of their socioeconomic contexts.

CONCLUSIONS

Awareness of the multiple levels of context in which the mothers in our study lived is critical if we are to understand the emotions, goals, beliefs, and practices they brought to the work of raising their children. The power of distal, or macrosystem, influences was apparent in that mothers' goals for their children, their feelings about motherhood, and their child-rearing strategies, which were marked by a blend of mainstream American and African American values (e.g., independence, education, family, respect) playing out against the backdrop of policies that made it difficult for their families to escape economic hardship and the stresses it engenders. At the more proximal, or microsystem, level we saw that the mothers' child-rearing decisions took into account the opinions and actions of other family members as well as the nature of the children themselves. We also saw that child-rearing-related joys, frustrations, goals, and practices were complexly interwoven. We are reminded of Jonathan Kozol's observation that many of the people he has known who live in poverty experience "contradictory emotions, and at times a roller-coaster of emotions" (Kozol, 2000, p. 98) depending on the current and anticipated conditions of their lives. There was nothing simple in the mothers' child-rearing accounts, combining as they did expressions of joy, pride, and dedication alongside admissions of fatalism, worry, self-questioning, and aggravation. Knowing that there was little room for error in the neighborhoods in which they lived, it is not surprising that they had adopted a vigilant, controlling approach to misbehavior even as they wondered if, in the end, their efforts will have even mattered.

Throughout the chapter, we have emphasized the importance of knowing and understanding the child-rearing beliefs and practices of mothers such as those in our study; we also have suggested some implications for practice. First, and perhaps of greatest importance, is our conclusion that it is essential that individuals do not interpret occasions when mothers complain about their children, or discipline them in a manner that, although not abusive, seems harsh by European American, middle-class standards, as meaning that they do not love their children or do not derive purpose and happiness from having them. Second, it is clear that parenting feelings, beliefs, and practices are rooted in intricate relations among the standards, opportunities, and constraints of the larger society, the proximal culture, community conditions, and family involvements. If they are to be successful, parenting programs must link with family and other community members, adapting their strategies to the local context and bringing these partners on board through respectful give and take. A third major set of points flows from the reality that African Americans live in a bicultural world in which they must learn to apply European American as well as African American standards and perspectives. As explained in Chapter 3, feminist theory posits that those in low-status positions must learn the ways of those with more power as well as the ways of their own group. This *double-consciousness* (Du Bois, 1899, as cited in McAdoo, 2002) may have figured in the mothers' willingness to consider the Early Head Start messages supporting positive guidance without abandoning disciplinary methods, such as corporal punishment, with which they were the most familiar. Understanding the various worlds that African American mothers living in poverty must negotiate should help professionals become sensitive listeners and careful interventionists. In Chapter 13, we discuss this issue further as we delve into the balancing acts that were involved in the work of Early Head Start home visitors.

At a more distal level, the mothers' stories also suggest needed policy modifications and changes. One of the simplest came to mind as we learned that the television set was almost always on in the homes we visited and that at least two of the mothers had taken to heart some advice they had heard in public service announcements. It would thus seem that the funding of television spots on child-rearing issues may be worthwhile. On a larger scale, the provision of accessible, high-quality child care with flexible hours for all families who need it would greatly reduce some of the frustrations experienced by parents who work or go to school. The mothers' desire for additional knowledge about child development and child-rearing methods also supports the critical role that parent education can play, whether through home visiting, involvement in children's child care settings, or exposure to public service announcements in the popular media.

REFERENCES

Bandura, A., Caprara, G.V., Barbaranelli, C., Gerbino, M., & Pastorelli, C. (2003). Role of affective self-regulatory efficacy in diverse spheres of psychosocial functioning. *Child Development, 74,* 769–782.

Baumrind, D. (1996). The discipline controversy revisited. *Family Relations, 45,* 405–414.

Belsky, J., Spanier, G., & Rovine, M. (1983). Stability and change in marriage across the transition to parenthood. *Journal of Marriage and the Family, 45,* 567–577.

Billingsley, A. (1992). *Climbing Jacob's ladder: The enduring legacy of African American families.* New York: Simon & Schuster.

Bornstein, M., Tamis-LeMonda, C., & Haynes, O.M. (1999). First words in the second year: Continuity, stability, and models of concurrent and predictive correspondence in vocabulary and verbal responsiveness across age and context. *Infant Behavior and Development, 22,* 65–85.

Bradley, R.H., Caldwell, B.M., Rock, S. II, Ramey, C.T., Barnard, D.E., Gray, C., Hammond, M.A., Mitchell, S., Gottfried, A., Siegel, I., & Johnson, D.L. (1989). Home environment and cognitive development in the first 3 years of life: A collaborative study involving six sites and three ethnic groups in North America. *Developmental Psychology, 25,* 217–235.

Brazelton, T.B. (1974). *Toddlers and parents: A declaration of independence.* Riverdale, MD: Bantam Doubleday Dell Publishing Group Inc.

Brody, G.H., & Flor, D.L. (1998). Maternal resources, parenting practices, and child competence in rural, single-parent African American families. *Child Development, 69,* 803–816.

Brody, G.H., Murry, V.M., Kim, S., & Brown, A.C. (2002). Longitudinal pathways to competence and psychological adjustment among African American children living in rural single-parent households. *Child Development, 73*(5), 1505–1516.

Bronfenbrenner, U. (1979). *The ecology of human development: Experiments by nature and design.* Cambridge, MA: Harvard University Press.

Brookes-Gunn, J. (1997). The effects of poverty on children. *Future of Children, 7*(2), 55–71.

Caldwell, C., Zimmerman, M.A., Bernat, D.H., Sellers, R.M., & Notaro, P.C. (2002). Racial identity, maternal support, and psychological distress among African American adolescents. *Child Development, 2002,* 1322–1336.

Cassidy, J., & Shaver, P. (Eds.). (1999). *Handbook of attachment.* New York: Guilford.

Caughy, M.O., O'Campo, P.J., Randolph, S.M., & Nickerson, K. (2002). The influence of racial socialization practices on the cognitive and behavioral competence of African American preschoolers. *Child Development, 73,* 1611–1625.

Coe, G., Thornburg, K.R., & Ispa, J. (1996). Infant child-rearing: Beliefs of parents and child care providers. *The Child Study Journal, 26,* 109–124.

Coles, R. (1990). *The spiritual life of children.* Boston: Houghton Mifflin.

Collins, P.H. (2000). *Black feminist thought: Knowledge, consciousness, and the politics of empowerment* (2nd ed.). New York: Routledge.

Comer, J.P., & Poussaint, A.F. (1992). *Raising Black children.* New York: Plume.

Comstock, G.A., & Paik, H. (1994). The effects of television violence on antisocial behavior: A meta-analysis. *Communication Research, 21,* 269–277.

Cowan, C.P., & Cowan, P.A. (1995). Interventions to ease the transition to parenthood: Why they are needed and what they can do. *Family Relations, 44,* 412–423.

Deater-Deckard, K., & Dodge, K.A. (1997). Externalizing behavior problems and discipline revisited: Nonlinear effects and variation by culture, context, and gender. *Psychological Inquiry, 8*(3), 161–175.

Demo, D.H., & Cox, M.J. (2000). Families with young children: A review of research in the 1990s. *Journal of Marriage and the Family, 62*(4), 876–895.

Dempsey, K. (2002). Who gets the best deal from marriage: Women or men? *Journal of Sociology, 38*(2), 91–110.

Garvey, C., & Shantz, C. (1992). Conflict talk: Approaches to adversative discourse. In C.U. Shantz & W.W. Hartup (Eds.), *Conflict in child and adolescent development* (pp. 91–121). New York: Cambridge University Press.

Giles-Sims, J., Straus, M.A., & Sugarman, D.B. (1995). Child, maternal, and family characteristics associated with spanking. *Family Relations, 44,* 170–176.

Gornick, J.C., & Meyers, M.K. (2003). *Families that work: Policies for reconciling parenthood and employment.* New York: Russell Sage Foundation.

Haight, W.L. (2002). *African American children at church: A sociocultural perspective.* New York: Cambridge University Press.

Hastings, P.D., & Grusec, J.E. (1998). Parenting goals as organizers of responses to parent–child disagreement. *Developmental Psychology, 34,* 465–479.

Hill, S.A. (1999). *African American children: Socialization and development in families.* Thousand Oaks, CA: Sage.

Hill, S.A., & Sprague, J. (1999). Parenting in Black and White families: The interaction of gender with race and class. *Gender & Society, 13,* 480–502.

Holloway, S.D., Fuller, B., Rambaud, M.F., & Eggers-Piérola, C. (1997). *Through my own eyes: Single mothers and the cultures of poverty.* Cambridge, MA: Harvard University Press.

Holloway, S.D., Rambaud, M.F., Fuller, B., & Eggers-Piérola, E. (1995). What is "appropriate practice" at home and in child care? Low-income mothers' views on preparing their children for school. *Early Childhood Research Quarterly, 10,* 451–473.

Ispa, J.M. (1994). Child rearing ideas and feelings of Russian and American mothers and early childhood teachers: Some comparisons. In S. Reifel (Ed.), *Advances in early education and day care: Vol. 6. Topics in early literacy, teacher preparation, and international perspectives on early care* (pp. 235–257). Greenwich, CT: JAI Press, Inc.

Ispa, J.M., Fine, M.A., Halgunseth, L., Harper, S., Robinson, J., Boyce, L., Brookes-Gunn, J., & Brady-Smith, C. (2004). Maternal intrusiveness, maternal warmth, and mother–toddler relationship outcomes: Variations across low-income ethnic and acculturation groups. *Child Development, 75,* 1613–1631.

Ispa, J.M., & Halgunseth, L.C. (2004). Talking about corporal punishment: Nine low-income African American mothers' perspectives. *Early Childhood Research Quarterly, 19,* 463–484.

Kohn, M. (1977). *Class and conformity: A study in values, with a reassessment.* Chicago: University of Chicago Press.

Kozol, J. (2000). *Ordinary resurrections: Children in the years of hope.* New York: Crown Publishers.

Laible, D.J., & Thompson, R.A. (2002). Mother–child conflict in the toddler years: Lessons in emotion, morality, and relationships. *Child Development, 73,* 1187–1203.

Lausell-Bryant, L., Gonzalez-Ramos, G., Zayas, L., & Cohen, E. (1998). *Maternal child-rearing values and behaviors inventory.* Unpublished manuscript, New York University.

Levine, L.E. (1983). Mine: Self-definition in 2-year-old boys. *Developmental Psychology, 19,* 544–549.

LeVine, R.A. (1988). Human parental care: Universal goals, cultural strategies, individual behavior. In R.A. LeVine, P.M. Miller, & M. Maxwell (Eds.), *Parental behavior in diverse societies* (pp. 3–12). San Francisco: Jossey-Bass.

Luster, T., Rhoades, K., & Haas, B. (1989). The relation between parental values and parenting behavior: A test of the Kohn hypothesis. *Journal of Marriage and the Family, 51,* 139–147.

Magnuson, K.A., & Duncan, G.J. (2002). Parents in poverty. In M.H. Bornstein (Ed.), *Handbook of parenting, Vol. 4: Social conditions and applied parenting* (2nd ed., pp. 95–121). Mahwah, NJ: Erlbaum.

Marion, M. (2002). *Guidance of young children* (6th ed.) Upper Saddle River, NJ: Prentice Hall.

McAdoo, H.P. (1997). Upward mobility across generations in African American families. In H.P. McAdoo (Ed.), *Black families* (3rd ed., pp. 139–162). Thousand Oaks, CA: Sage.

McAdoo, H.P. (2002). African American parenting. In M.H. Bornstein (Ed.), *Handbook of parenting, Vol. 4: Social conditions and applied parenting.* Mahwah, NJ: Lawrence Erlbaum Associates, Inc.

McLoyd, V.C. (1998). Socioeconomic disadvantage and child development. *American Psychologist, 53,* 185–204.

Murry, V.M., & Brody, G.H. (1999). Self-regulation and self-worth of Black children reared in economically stressed, rural, single mother-headed families: The contribution of risk and protective factors. *Journal of Family Issues, 20,* 458–484.

Nobles, W.W. (1997). African American family life. In H.P. McAdoo (Ed.), *Black families* (3rd ed., pp. 83–93). Thousand Oaks, CA: Sage.

O'Brien, M. (1996). Child-rearing difficulties reported by parents of infants and toddlers. *Journal of Pediatric Psychology, 21*(3) 433–446.

O'Callaghan, M.F., Borkowski, J.G., Whitman, T.L., Maxwell, S., & Keogh, D. (1999). A model of adolescent parenting: The role of cognitive readiness to parent. *Journal of Research on Adolescence, 9,* 203–225.

Ogbu, J.U. (1985). A cultural ecology of competence among inner-city Blacks. In M.B. Spencer, G.K. Brookins, & W.R. Allen (Eds.), *Beginnings: The social and affective development of Black children* (pp. 45–66). Hillsdale, NJ: Erlbaum.

Okagaki, L., & Sternberg, R.J. (1993). Parental beliefs and children's school performance. *Child Development, 64,* 36–56.

Peters, F.M. (1997). Historical note: Parenting of young children in black families. In H.P. McAdoo (Ed.), *Black families* (3rd ed., pp. 167–182). Thousand Oaks: Sage.

Pinderhughes, E.E., Dodge, K.A., Bates, J.E., Pettit, G.S., & Zelli, A. (2000). Discipline responses: Influences of parents' socioeconomic status, ethnicity, beliefs about parenting, stress, and cognitive-emotional processes. *Journal of Family Psychology, 14,* 380–400.

Rucker, W. (2001). Conjure, magic, and power: The influence of Afro-Atlantic religious practices on slave resistance and rebellion. *Journal of Black Studies, 32,* 84–103.

Seccombe, K. (1999). *"So you think I drive a Cadillac?" Welfare recipients' perspectives on the system and its reform.* Boston: Allyn & Bacon.

Seccombe, K., James, D., & Walters, K.B. (1998). "They think you ain't much of nothing": The social construction of the welfare mother. *Journal of Marriage and the Family, 60,* 849–865.

Sexton, D. (1998). Applying Q methodology to investigations of subjective judgments of early intervention effectiveness. *Topics in Early Childhood Special Education, 18,* 95–107.

Singer, D.G., & Singer, J.L. (1990). *The house of make-believe.* Cambridge, MA: Harvard University Press.

Smith, C., & Faris, R. (2002). Religion and American adolescent delinquency, risk behaviors and constructive social activities. National Study of Youth and

Religion. Chapel Hill, NC. Retrieved Nov. 26, 2003, from http://www.youth andreligion.org/publications/docs/RiskReport1.pdf

Straus, M.A., & Field, C.J. (2003). Psychological aggression by American parents: National data on prevalence, chronicity, and severity. *Journal of Marriage and the Family, 65*, 795–808.

Straus, M.A., & Stewart, J.H. (1999). Corporal punishment by American parents. National data on prevalence, chronicity, severity, and duration in relation to child and family characteristics. *Clinical Child and Family Psychology Review, 2*, 55–70.

Sudarkasa, N. (1997). African American families and family values. In H.P. McAdoo (Ed.), *Black families* (3rd ed., pp. 9–40). Thousand Oaks, CA: Sage.

Tamis-Lemonda, C.S., Shannon, J., & Spellmann, M. (2002). Low-income adolescent mothers' knowledge about domains of child development. *Infant Mental Health Journal, 23*, 88–103.

Wade-Gayles, G. (1984). The truths of our mothers' lives: Mother–daughter relationships in Black women's fiction. *Sage: A Scholarly Journal on Black Women, 1*, 8–12.

Whitehurst, G.J., & Lonigan, C.J. (1998). Child development and emergent literacy. *Child Development, 69*, 848–872.

Willis, W. (1992). Families with African American roots. In E.W. Lynch & M.J. Hanson (Eds.), *Developing cross-cultural competence: A guide for working with young children and their families* (pp. 121–150). Baltimore: Paul H. Brookes Publishing Co.

11

The Children's Fathers

Elizabeth A. Sharp and Jean M. Ispa

"My son slowed me down 'cause usually I be out
on the street with my friends and stuff. Now I'm slowed
down 'cause I got a life to live and I want to see him grow up."
—Patrick

Expanding on themes introduced in Chapters 9 and 10 on romantic relationships and child rearing, this chapter explores the role of fathers in the lives of their children. Although the presence—or absence—of fathers has important consequences for children and their mothers, until recently men's perspective on fatherhood was largely overlooked (Coley, 2001; Marsiglio & Cohan, 1997; Thornberry, Smith, & Howard, 1997). Instead, mothers' impressions of fathers tended to dominate the discourse on fatherhood (Coley & Morris, 2002; Marsiglio, 1995). Moreover, data often have been collected only on *biological* fathers' perspectives and behaviors, thereby largely neglecting the role of other men in children's lives (Jayakody & Kalil, 2002).

Recognizing the importance of fathers and the paucity of research focused on men's impressions and experiences of fatherhood, we devote the first part of this chapter to the perspectives of both biological and social fathers. Recall that *social fathers* play the role of fathers but they are not the biological fathers. Although social fathers can include male relatives and friends, the social fathers in this chapter were all romantic partners of the mothers.

In the second part of the chapter, we discuss mothers' views and experiences concerning fathers' responsibilities. Throughout the chapter, we explain why some fathers, despite well-meaning intentions, did not always live up to their own and the mothers' expectations of fatherhood. Finally, we suggest ideas for future research and for policy concerning fathers.

Unlike Chapter 9, the focus of this chapter is on fathers' and mothers' perspectives on fathering rather than on romantic relationships, and, unlike Chapter 10, the chapter contains themes related to fathers' (not just mothers') ideas about child rearing. It is important to understand the similarities and differences between the different perspectives and the ways in which themes may cut across domains (as when financial issues affect both the father role and the romantic partner role).

OVERVIEW OF THE FATHERS

It can be difficult to obtain the consent of low-income, African American fathers to participate in research, and our experience was no exception. In our case, because the primary focus of our project was on the mothers enrolled in Early Head Start, we spent considerably more time and effort contacting and interviewing the mothers than the fathers. In addition, over the years, the mothers were easier to reach than the fathers because the Early Head Start home visitors shared the mothers' contact information with us. Some scholars have attributed difficulty in getting low-income fathers to participate in research partly to a widespread perception that researchers might be part of the "system" that is often hostile to young Black men (Kaplan, 1997; Waller, 2002). Although this problem did not seem to pertain to most of the men we spoke to, we know that it was an issue for one father who spoke with us but did not give us permission to use his interview in our analyses. After we interviewed him, the mother of his baby told us, "He thought you were social service people about child support. Yeah, he thinks everybody's against him, so he didn't understand."

Out of a total of 17 fathers (eight biological and nine social), we interviewed six. Three were biological fathers and three were social fathers. One biological father and all three social fathers were romantically involved with the mothers at the time of the interviews. One biological father was not interviewed because the mother did not want to provide contact information. We could not locate a second father from the information provided by the mother. Two mothers did not have contact information, and, as previously mentioned, one father we interviewed refused to allow us to use his data. (Table 11.1 illustrates the demographic characteristics of the fathers we interviewed as well as information about the fathers we were unable to interview.)

All six of the men we interviewed, whether at the time involved romantically with the mothers or not, had amiable relationships with them. The mothers reported that the fathers we interviewed tended to

Table 11.1. Demographic description of the fathers at the onset of the study (Fall 1996)

Father's name	Mother's name	Father status	Number of interviews	Number of biological children at onset of study	Employment status at time of interview	Residence	Education level
				Fathers we interviewed			
Lance	Breanna	Biological	1	2	Painter	By himself	11th grade
Marcus	Maria	Biological	1	1	Part-time student; job training	By himself	Some college
Patrick	Chandra	Biological	3	2	Machinist	With his mother	11th grade
Tejon	Kyierra	Social	3	0	Not working; full-time child care	With Kyierra	Completed high school
Dwayne	Tanisha	Social	1	0	Not working	With Tanisha	11th grade
Denzel	Breanna	Social	3	0	Not working	With his mother	12th grade
				Fathers we did not interview			
William	Andreya	Biological	0	3	Laborer	With new girlfriend	11th grade
Wesley	Roneeka	Biological	0	3	Machinist	With wife	Not known
Jerome	Shardae	Biological	0	2	Jail	In jail	Not known
Frank	Sherryce	Biological	0	2	Salesperson	With new wife	Completed high school
Bryan	Kyierra	Biological	0	2	Jail	In jail	Some college
Davian (deceased)	Tanisha	Biological	0	Unknown	N/A	N/A	High school

be more involved with their children than the fathers we were not able to interview. Because of this pattern, we are aware that the perspectives we identify in the first part of the chapter may not reflect the views and experiences of the fathers who had sporadic or no involvement with their children and/or had hostile relationships with the mothers.

Half of the fathers we spoke to had themselves lacked a steady father or father figure during childhood, yet all seemed committed to playing a significant role in their children's lives. One young man said that he had learned to be a father by counter-example; he wanted to do the opposite of what his father had done. In several cases in which there had been no personal father role model, the men indicated that their mothers had taught them about fatherhood. Patrick, for example, said, "Mostly my mother [taught me about fatherhood] 'cause she was there the most of the time." The men also mentioned learning about children from interacting with their nieces and nephews. Like the mothers in our study, Patrick said that he thought he knew a lot about child rearing because, as he explained, "I got so many nieces and nephews. I think I pretty much know a lot about it, about taking care of kids, as far as knowing them—attitudes and everything else about it [parenting]." Marcus, too, indicated that he knew how to parent because he had been an uncle since he was 5 years old.

FATHERS' THOUGHTS ON FATHERHOOD

The fathers' interview data fell into two broad categories: *the benefits of fatherhood* and *responsibilities toward children.* Because the comments of the biological fathers and the social fathers were frequently indistinguishable, unless noted, we grouped them together. An important exception, as discussed in Chapter 9, concerned some of the social fathers' strong desire to father children of their own. This was especially true of the social fathers who did not yet have biological children. One couple, Kyierra and Tejon, had a child together during the time of our study.

The Benefits of Fatherhood

The overriding sentiment expressed by the men we spoke with was that fatherhood was a positive experience. Fathers spoke about enjoying their children and feeling that fatherhood was making them become better men.

Feeling Love and Pride   The fathers indicated pride when talking about their children and seemed to especially enjoy sons who looked like or imitated them. As was discovered in other research on the experiences of African American young fathers, being a father was an important part of the identities of the men in our project (Allen & Doherty, 1995; Mincy & Pouncy, 2002). Expressing this, Tejon, devoted social father of Kyierra's daughter Jalisa, described the centrality of fatherhood in his life, "I always wanted to be a father. That's what I wanted to be most of all, a father." He added, "That's my heart. That's my firstborn even though she's not really my [biological] first . . . I'm going to love her like that." In a similar vein, Patrick, biological father of Chandra's son Patrick Jr., said, "I feel I'm proud to be a father to him." Lance described being a father as "cool to me. . . . I love her, she's my daughter." And Dwayne, social father of Tanisha's daughter Tierra, said of Tierra, "I just love her all the way around. . . . She gives me something to look forward to."

Not all of the men initially had a strong desire to be a father. Dwayne told us, "At first, I didn't want no child, but as Tanisha grew bigger, I started anticipating for the baby to come out." Marcus explained that when his girlfriend Maria became pregnant unexpectedly, he was hesitant about being a father mostly because of financial constraints. He told us how his feelings about fatherhood have changed since then. "As far as now," he said, "I mean I love it [being a father]. He [Bryce, his son] starting to grow and emotional attachment grows along with that." As is true of other young, low-income fathers (Mincy & Pouncy, 2002), some of Marcus's growing feelings for his son may have been connected to his emerging perception that they were similar in some ways. Marcus told us, "I like the fact that he's a little sponge, he's just like a little reflection of me. I see him getting into stuff. They tell me it was the same way I was, getting into stuff, or just being mischievous around the house."

Having a Reason to Become "Better"   An important feature of fatherhood for the young men we interviewed as well as for men described in other research (Coley, 2001; Mincy & Pouncy, 2002) was that it was perceived as having helped them become better people. (Recall from Chapter 10 that the mothers believed motherhood had affected them in the same way.) The men said that having a child helped them become more focused and responsible. They talked particularly about their newfound desire to avoid illegal activities. All in all, becoming a father seemed to have had a significant impact on their lives. Marcus explained how being a father encouraged him to be more proactive, "I mean he gave me some drive, some motivation. Before I was just kind of going through and just ideas that I'd be okay and everything's gonna be okay. But now I know that I *have* to make it okay and make things right so that it'll be right for him."

Becoming fathers also "slowed" the men down. ("Slowing down" means avoiding illegal activities and not hanging out on the streets.) Dwayne described it this way, "I'm just now slowing down a bit. When

I was younger I was stealing. Couldn't keep me out of trouble for real. Now, I still be moving but I can sit still a little." When asked if his girlfriend and her child were helping him avoid the fast life, he responded, "Yeah, definitely, 'cause if I ain't doing something, I steal. She slowed me down a little bit. Obviously not enough, but I am slowed down. I had tunnel vision before she was born." Tejon explained, "My daughter made my life better, 'cause if I didn't have my daughter I'd be out more, I wouldn't be home as much as I am now. I'd probably be doing something I ain't supposed to be doing. Just having a daughter brought me down to earth."

Friends of the fathers were a potent influence on their "fast life." After becoming fathers, some of the men severed relationships with those who would encourage them (or had encouraged them in the past) to be part of illegal activities. Patrick explained, "I used to be running with the fellows. . . . You know, now I am not out there doing this and that. I try to stay away from people who do bad now that I've gotten a little older. 'Cause I'm getting older and I've got a son to take care of, so I try to stay away from the negative things out there."

Marcus restricted his friends' exposure to his son, saying, "You know, he gets to hang out with the fellas every once in a while, but not all the time. I try to limit that somewhat because, you know, men will be men and cursing and talking, and at this point he doesn't need to be around that."

The Responsibilities of Fathers

The fathers' thoughts about their responsibilities toward their children included the need to steer them in the right direction, be there for them, and provide financial support for them. For the most part, the mothers and fathers were in agreement regarding these responsibilities.

Steering Children in the Right Direction   A clear responsibility of fathers, according to the men in our sample, was to steer their children in the right direction. Expressing this sentiment, Dwayne told us that a father should "keep the child on the right track and try to keep the child out of trouble." Patrick's answer to our question asking what he hoped his son would remember about him after he grew up showed that in his mind, valuing family and developing kindness were interconnected. He hoped that Patrick Jr. would remember that "I raised him being a caring person and just being really family-oriented and just being a good person."

Marcus reminisced about how his father and brothers had been role models for him, "My father—he gave me guidance. I mean besides feeding me and clothing me and giving me shelter, he gave me guidance. When presented with a situation, he would give me bits of information and he would allow me to make my own decision. But at the same time keeping me within some type of perimeters so, if I fall and bump my butt, I don't bump it too hard. You know, I don't break it."

There were times when Marcus had not liked his father's advice, but, looking back, he saw that it had usually been sound, and that he should have listened better, "But you know for the most part in my life every time I've ever—and I can truly say this— every time I've thought that he may have been wrong on an issue he might of said, 'Go left' and I just knew that right was the way to go, so I went right. And right was the wrong way to go. Every time he said something in life . . . he's always ended up being right, you know, so until he proves me wrong, you know, or as far as him being right all the time, I'm gonna have to stick with what he's saying."

Marcus's older brothers also helped him. They "just made sure I stayed on the right path," he said. Patrick, too, discussed how his father and older brothers had directed him, "My father—he just showed me the right way. And my brothers, they told me stuff, and I just took heed to what they were saying. And now I see what, you know, what they were saying. Now that I'm older, I see what they meant by it."

The fathers hoped that their children would seek advice from them. For this to happen, they believed that they needed to have a close relationship with the children. Describing the connection he saw between closeness and guidance, Dwayne explained, "I'd like for her to come to me with any problems that she has or talk to me to let me know what is going on with her life. I want to be part of that. Let me know what's going on. . . . I'm trying to . . . hopefully I can help guide her to the right decisions."

Patrick, who also wanted a "real tight father–son relationship," put it this way, "Showing my son the right way to do things and maybe taking care of him and showing him how to be a man. I want him to be close to me. I want him to be like, you know, my friend. I don't want him to be scared to tell me something. I want him to be able to come to me and talk to me about anything."

Marcus, too, expressed his desire to appropriately direct his son in life. "I mean there's a lot of things I'd like to show him along the way . . . just making sure we're [he and Maria] keeping him on the right path."

Being a Loving and Available Father   The fathers echoed the mothers (see Chapter 10) in believing that it was important for children to know that their fathers cared for them and were available to them.

Tejon, for example, explained that a primary responsibility of fathers was "just being there. Taking care of them as much, as best as they possibly could." Later in the same interview, he added, "I'm new to this so I don't really know what a father's supposed to do. I have a little idea . . . the most important thing to give Jalisa is a lot of love and attention." When asked about the most important thing he could give his stepdaughter, Dwayne's response was similar, "Conversation—interact with her a lot." He later added that it was especially important to give children "quality time and attention." Denzel described his central role in his stepdaughter's life as, "Just being there. I'd like to be her backbone." (The men called their girlfriends' children *stepdaughter* or *stepson* even though they were not married to the children's mothers.)

For some, the genuine desire to be there for their children seemed to be rooted in their keen awareness of what they had missed during their own childhood years. Two of the three men who said that they had had supportive and reliable fathers during most of their childhood years, Marcus and Patrick, wished that they had had even more time and attention from their fathers. Patrick, for example, regretted that his father had missed his teenage years, "I just wanted my father to be there. Just wanted him to be there, you know, through my whole adolescent years and all that." When we asked Marcus what he had wanted most from his father, he said, "Time, I'd have to say. I mean 'cause he provided me with everything else. It was just that he worked, just like a lot of other kids' fathers. He didn't always get to catch all the baseball games, all the football games, or go play catch. . . . But, you know, I mean he still, you know he still found ways to make up time, like in the summers, I'd go work with him or whatever it may be."

When asked if they were satisfied with the amount of time they now spent with their children, most of the fathers said they were content, but Lance and Patrick said that they wished they had more time. Still, Lance admitted that he would probably enjoy his daughter more and become more involved when she became a toddler. "I'll spend more time with her [then]. I like it now, but I think I will spend more time with her when she's older and can walk. Then she'll be with me more." Similarly, as previously mentioned, Marcus enjoyed fatherhood more as his son grew older.

Tejon was the most involved of all the fathers in our sample, staying home full time for approximately a year to take care of little Jalisa and Ciera while Kyierra was at work. By mainstream standards, he would be considered particularly committed to his girlfriend and his daughters. (A stay-at-home father is a rare occurrence among men of all races and socioeconomic status levels [Sanderson & Thompson, 2002].) Recognizing this and other positive qualities Tejon had, at times Kyierra commented on how different he was from other men she knew.

When we asked the fathers about their impressions of other fathers living in their neighborhoods, most indicated that they thought those men weren't as involved as they were. Indeed, Denzel believed that a lot of the fathers in the neighborhood were completely uninvolved. He explained, "Because I see a lot daddies that got kids and they ain't there for their kids and don't even know their kids' birthdays." And Dwayne added, "I know a lot of people who have kids and they don't interact with them and don't give them the attention that I feel that a child needs." The tendency for fathers to look down on other fathers in similar economic circumstances had been noted by Allen and Doherty (1995) as well.

Patrick and Denzel thought that among the fathers who were not involved, the relationship with the mother was a critical barrier. Patrick told us, "I think most of them [fathers in his neighborhood] are not involved because of the female status . . . whoever they have the kid by. Maybe something they've done in the past or maybe they can't get along or something." Denzel said, "I think some of 'em is like that 'cause they really didn't want a baby by that person or something." The fathers offered other reasons as well. Patrick suggested, "Or maybe some of them be locked up in jails. Maybe some of them just don't have money." Denzel speculated that "Some of 'em probably just heartless." Dwayne reasoned that the fathers were "too busy." Although Marcus said that the men he was around took care of their children, he was aware that other men in the community might not do so. He, like Patrick, indicated that circumstances could prevent men from seeing their children. "You know as far as the amount of Black males in jail and on the streets and things of that nature . . . but you know as far as my personal experience all the men that I've seen, most of the men that I've seen, not all, nowhere near all [are uninvolved]."

As indicated in Chapter 9, research supports the understanding of these fathers that relationships with the mothers of their children and incarceration patterns are critical determinants of paternal involvement.

Providing Financially   The fathers we spoke to felt obligated to provide financially for their children. Often their contributions involved informal "in-kind" support. In-kind support is not legally mandated and often includes but is not limited to cash, utility or rent payments, food, toys, and supplies such as diapers, shoes, and baby clothing. In-kind support tends to be sporadic, so mothers are often not certain when and how much they will receive (Wilson, 2003). In contrast, formal support is required by law, as in the case of child support stipulated by the courts or child-support enforcement agencies. Investigations have shown that fathers living in poverty tend to give in-kind support more than formal support (Kaplan, 1997; Waller, 2002).

Only one of the fathers we interviewed, Marcus, paid formal child support. Of the other five, three were social fathers and therefore not required to pay child support. The remaining two were biological fathers, but in one case, the mother (Chandra) had not filed for child support because Patrick was providing informal support for their son, and in the other case, the mother (Breanna) had filed for but had not received formal support by the end of the study. Marcus, discussing his financial contribution, told us, "I try to provide him with whatever he [his son] needs. But I mean, I pay child support and then if she [Maria] needs anything additional, I mean she can always ask and I get her, you know, whatever he needs . . . my set amount is for $566 a month. . . . Now I mean we have an agreement right now to pay a lesser amount, you know, but that's my set support of her."

According to Maria, Marcus had initially resisted paying formal child support, wanting her to let him pay less and outside of "the system." She said that he had left messages on her phone asking her to "get the man off his back." He had even suggested that she turn custody of Bryce over to him because he could not imagine that a child could cost as much as the child support enforcement agency was requiring him to pay.

Other fathers (e.g., Patrick, Denzel, Dwayne) described paying in-kind support. Patrick told us how he contributed financially, "As far as Pull-Ups and clothes and shoes, I handle all that." Patrick did not pay formal child support and when asked why not told us, "'Cause I take care of him most of the time." When asked how often, Patrick replied, "As needed." Denzel described giving in-kind support such as clothing and food. As noted in the vignette in Chapter 9 entitled "Breanna— Making Father Involvement Happen," support continued even after he and Breanna terminated their romantic relationship. When another social father, Dwayne, was asked how often he contributed to his stepdaughter's upkeep, he replied, "Probably all the time. If she needs to eat, we eat. We're a family, I feel like we are a unit. If we need our clothes washed, we wash our clothes."

When asked if there was anything they could *not* give their children, some of the fathers commented that at times their financial "situations" interfered with their ability to provide for material needs. Marcus told us that there were "just little material things that I probably couldn't give him . . . I would want to—but I couldn't because of my financial problems." Similarly, Tejon said, "I just wish I could possibly give to her more, but the money is running a little low." Denzel wished that he had money to give for his stepdaughter every time he saw her. Dwayne told us that he wanted Tierra, his stepdaughter, to have "the best education she can" and that for that to happen, they would have to move out of the inner city to another county. Sadly, he worried because they could not really afford to move "because money ain't coming in."

Barriers to Providing Financial Support

As discussed in Chapter 9, one of the reasons there was little money was that the men were frequently out of work, and often the jobs they did have were short-lived. Some job losses were due to brief incarcerations, and, as is too often the case (Clayton & Moore, 2003), even short sentences left men with jail records that limited their employability. In other cases, jobs were treated as dispensable because they did not contribute to the men's self-esteem. Denzel provided an example of this when he quit his job after 2 weeks at a hotel doing housekeeping. He described his work as menial—"dumping liners in the trash"—and left after being told to cut his hair. In Denzel's mind, his hair length was irrelevant to the job he was doing. Tejon was fired from a job in a liquor store and thought the manager's racism was to blame, "'Cause one of the managers [manager A] told me that the manager [manager B] that fired me was kind of racist. He [manager B] tried to say that I stole something out of the back room, but when I had my shift, the back room was always locked. And then when she [manager A] found that out, she asked him [manager B] about it and he tried to say, 'Since I fired him wrong, I'm not going to hire him back 'cause he still might take something.'"

Low-Paying Jobs and Unemployment   During times of unemployment, the men indicated that they wanted to be employed and would be willing to work at almost any job. After job-hunting for a lengthy period, Tejon told us, "I'm not picky on a job. I mean as long as I get a chance, I can learn. I am a fast learner." He considered going into the Air Force and went to job fairs. He eventually got a job as a machinist. Denzel was out of work when we first met him. When we asked him if he wanted to get a job, he told us, "I've been putting in applications. I've been trying. I'll do maintenance work, cleaning up or something. I'll work at a grocery store."

Because both the fathers and the mothers saw providing money as an important responsibility of fathers, it followed that the men's employment was accompanied by feelings of enhanced self-worth and being "real" men, while unemployment tended to have the opposite effect. Patrick articulated this when he told us, "I think my job just made me more of a man. . . . Working just made me a stronger man." We also could extrapolate the meaning that Jerome connected to having a job when he told Shardae that she was insignificant because she didn't have a job and, in contrast, he had worth because he did have one. "He [Jerome] was calling me, cussing me out, telling me that I wasn't anything," said Shardae. "That I was trash. I should be with him . . . telling me that I am worthless because I'm not working. And he's like, 'I'm working.'" This way of thinking has been found in other research (see Chapter 9) and demonstrates that cultural scripts of manhood are tightly connected to employment (Erickson & Gecas, 1991; Lazur & Majors, 1995).

Given these feelings about work and money, it is not surprising that employment seemed to have a profound influence on the extent of the men's involvement with their children. Our interviews with the fathers suggested that painful feelings stemming from their inability to provide financially may have led the men (consciously or not) to distance themselves from their children. Although neither the mothers nor the fathers explicitly said so, the impression left is that the men could not face their children empty-handed. (This pattern also was observed by Liebow [1967].) Unemployment indirectly affected fatherhood in that it appeared to influence the fathers' relationships with the mothers and, therefore, their access to and willingness to see and support their children. Romantic relationships and relationships with children were often highly connected. (See the section, "Beliefs that Fathers Should Remain Involved with Their Children" in Chapter 9.) Other researchers have seen similar connections among employment, monetary support, and the amount of contact fathers had with their children (Liebow, 1967; Thomson, Hanson, & McLanahan, 1994). It has been found that unemployed men are less likely than employed men to feel that they have taken care of their families (Bowman & Forman, 1997).

Self-Blame for Not Meeting Financial Goals   The fathers tended to blame themselves for their lack of progress in establishing financial security. Even those who had jobs seemed to worry that they might "mess up." For example, when asked what might hold him back, Patrick replied, "Things that might hold me back is if I just go down the wrong path. If I slip as far as I lose my job for some type of reason. Or I just start hanging out with the wrong people, but I doubt that, 'cause I got on my head pretty much straight."

Marcus explained his belief in self-determination when we asked him what might prevent him from achieving his goals, "Just myself. Nothing else could hold me back, only myself, you know. If my motivation or desire decreases somehow that would be the only thing that would, that I could foresee as a problem. Other than that, you know,

I'd hate to try to bring any other factors into it because I think you've got your mind set to it, I think for the most part you can do it."

When we asked Denzel what was keeping him from getting a job, he surmised, "My fast life. I'm just now slowing down a little bit." This is an interesting response—he had submitted multiple applications for jobs but attributed not having a job solely to his own behavior. Consistent with this thinking, in a later interview Denzel told us that the only thing that would stand in the way of his achieving his future goals was "Nothing, unless I stop concentrating on that [my goals] and get off to what's out here [street life.]" He believed that "studying real hard and talking to somebody who really knows how to get . . . your business started" would help him achieve his financial goals.

There was one exception to this pattern of blaming themselves. In addition to attributing the loss of one of his jobs to his employer's racism, Tejon also indicated at another time that he was out of work because "It's hard finding a good job . . . I mean if I had a car . . . a reliable car, I would be looking for jobs . . . I be looking in the paper, but most of the jobs are far away."

Much research shows that individuals who take responsibility for their own successes and failures tend to accomplish more than individuals who feel that their fate is out of their own control (Heyman & Dweck, 1992; Seligman, 1990). The United States is often said to be dominated by an individualistic culture that supports a belief in the centrality and power of each person (Oyserman, Coon, & Kemmelmeier, 2002). However, as has been emphasized by researchers who have studied the life experiences of people in poverty, the restricted opportunities available in impoverished neighborhoods are formidable barriers to "making it" (Schiller, 2004; Wilson, 2003). We noted that the young men we spoke to seemed to have wholeheartedly adopted the idea that one can "pull oneself up by one's bootstraps." Although there are positive aspects to this notion inasmuch as it supports initiative, hard work, and persistence, we worried that it could also lead to self-blame and depression if applied without a realistic awareness of the challenges posed by societal structural constraints such as inadequate schooling, few meaningful and well-paying job prospects in or close to their neighborhoods, and inadequate public transportation.

THE MOTHERS' THOUGHTS ON FATHERS' RESPONSIBILITIES

All of the mothers in our study believed that the biological fathers should provide consistent physical and financial support for their children. They, like the fathers, voiced their opinion that the fathers should be there for their children. Tanisha summed up this belief, "To love us. To show that to my daughter. To provide as far as a father could to your household. . . . Like financially. Mentally. You know, to play a role as far as, you know, to teach her. Let her know that you have to get up and work all the time. Provide that first so she can have it in her head when she gets older."

In the sections below, the reader may notice that the mothers paint a more negative picture of the fathers' commitment to their children than was suggested by our interviews with the fathers. This is not atypical. Comparing 228 young, low-income, unmarried parents' reports about fathers' physical involvement, Coley and Morris (2002) found that mothers consistently reported lower levels of paternal involvement than did fathers. A reason for the discrepancy among the pairs in our study may be that, although the fathers felt that they were doing the best they could, the mothers saw the fathers' limited help as insufficient. We also remind the reader that the mothers talked to us about the fathers we did *not* interview as well as about the fathers we did interview. As mentioned previously, the fathers we did not interview were generally less involved with their children than the fathers we did interview.

Fathers Should Spend Time with Their Children

According to the patterns described by the mothers, the time of greatest biological father involvement was around the birth of the baby. Even the fathers who later ceased contact altogether with the mothers were at least in touch with them for a few months following the births of their babies. Kyierra's and Shardae's partners illustrated this behavior. As they described the situation, the fathers' hope of continued romance with the mothers was part of the reason for the continued contact.

Most of the mothers expressed a strong desire for the biological fathers' increased involvement with their children. Sherryce said, "I wish he [Frank] would spend time with Michael." And Andreya frequently discussed with William her wish that he would see his children more often, "Like I told him, if he would just spend time with them and get to know them, who they are." Chandra told us on several occasions that she wanted "Big Patrick [biological father] to mainly spend more time with Little Patrick because I want him to have, like, a father figure." A similar sentiment was expressed by Breanna when she said, "I wish for Lance to come around more and be closer to Corrina." (We remind the reader that both Patrick and Lance, at the time we interviewed them, said that they wanted more time with their children.) As indicated in Chapter 10, part of the reason the mothers wanted the fathers to be more involved was that they thought the fathers were more effective disciplinarians. As the above quotations suggest, however, the mothers also thought that their children would benefit in general from deeper relationships with their fathers.

Kyierra grappled with how much effort she should put into getting the biological father of her daughter involved. She told us, "My daughter needs to see him, but then again she doesn't. She has a father [Tejon] . . . well, I'm confused because I don't know what is right or what's best. People are saying this is Bryan's baby and I don't know how to feel because Tejon, he's been there." Kyierra sometimes referred to Bryan as the "sperm donor," underscoring her contention that he did nothing more than get her pregnant.

Father–Child Contact Should Be Consistent

Most of the mothers wanted contact between biological fathers and their children to be *consistent*. Inconsistent contact, they thought, was more harmful to the children than no contact. Complaints about low and unstable father involvement were most pronounced among the women who were no longer romantically involved with their children's biological fathers. Andreya expressed thoughts common among a few mothers when she told us, "I thought it would be better for him to stay away completely, instead of coming around one week and don't come around the next." She told William, "I don't want you to think you can just keep walking in and out of our lives." Shardae also told us, "If he [the father] is not going to be really active in our lives, I don't want him there at all. If he is going to peep in and peep back out, I don't want him there at all. But if he's going to actually do something for her and want to spend more time with her, then yes, I want him involved." Similarly, Breanna often grew upset at Lance's wavering devotion to Corrina. She told us, "Corrina don't see him. He's never around. I don't try to look for him or see where he's at. If he don't want to come see her then she really probably don't need him in her life anyway." (During our interview with Lance, he indicated higher involvement with his daughter than Breanna had suggested was typical of him.) As other studies have found, a pattern of sporadic or decreasing involvement is not uncommon for low-income, young, African American men, as well as for middle class and White men, who are not romantically involved (or have conflict) with the mothers of their children (Demo & Cox, 2000; Mincy & Pouncy, 2002; Sanderson & Thompson, 2002).

One strategy the mothers used to encourage father involvement was to give the baby the father's last name, even if the romantic relationship had ended by the time of the birth. Using the paternal last name also connected the baby to the father's family, and we know that the mothers wanted paternal kin involved, especially paternal grandmothers (see Chapters 5 and 7). According to other research, giving children the father's last name is interpreted as a sign of respect for the father. Further, mothers believed that if they refused to give the child the father's last name, they might weaken the attachment between the father (and his kin) and the child. In addition, the last name of a child represents a clear mark of immortality for the fathers (a real issue given that African American men living in poverty have the highest death rates among all racial groups in the United States) and perhaps the only chance of upward mobility (vicariously through their children; Nelson, Clampet-Lundquist, & Edin, 2002).

Fathers Should Provide
Financial Support for Their Children

With important exceptions, the mothers reported that the father's financial support was occasional, with the mothers receiving money or gifts (in-kind support) at varying times. The same pattern was described by some of the fathers themselves (see previous discussion in this chapter). Typically, the mothers asked the fathers for money only when they badly needed something for their children. For example, Chandra told us, "He gives me money for Patrick. I haven't asked him for anything 'cause I'm working. When I'm going to need it, I'll say, 'Patrick I need this or something.'" The mothers said that the fathers sometimes rebuffed these requests with complaints that the mothers were being too demanding. Chandra explained, "He thinks I try to boss him around. I just be like, 'Give me this and give me that . . . I need some money.' He be like I don't ever *ask* and am always *telling* him what to do and never asking what he feels about this. So I try to come at him different now." Similarly, Andreya told us that William was upset when he perceived that she was being disrespectful in her demands for money from him. He said to her, "That's the way you talk to me? I'm your baby's daddy."

Some mothers did not believe the fathers' protestations that they could not afford to give the requested money or other resources. Sherryce, for example, told us, "It is frustrating because I can call him and ask him for something, like if I'm completely out of money and paid all [the] bills and don't have money to get diapers. I can call him and he'll say, 'I don't have it,' or, there are a lot of times, even if he didn't have it, he could go get it. Or know where he could get it but he won't even try."

Shardae had similar experiences. She complained, "I asked him to buy her [daughter Alexis] some Pampers. He told me that he couldn't do it." After his refusal and Shardae's realization that he was not likely to help voluntarily, she filed for child support. Alexis was a month and a half old at the time. During our fourth interview with Shardae, she continued to tell us how important a father figure would be in her daughter's life, but she remained skeptical that Jerome would ever fulfill this role. She said, "I don't think he is ever going to turn around. He's stuck on himself. He's out there having other kids and it's not bothering him at all, so I know that he is not going to turn around anytime soon." (The tension between Shardae and Jerome was discussed in Chapter 9 in connection with Jerome's refusal to help support their child if Shardae chose not to be in a romantic relationship with him.)

Some mothers saw a link between the fathers' physical involvement with their children and their financial support of them. Maria explicitly drew this connection when she told us, "Marcus say something to me like, 'I wanna see my son,' and I'll say, 'Yeah, I know you do. I wanna see my child support, too.'" Talking about Frank, Michael's father, Sherryce told us, "He always used the same excuse—he didn't want to come around because he didn't have money and stuff." Although Sherryce was weary of his excuses, she did agree that he seemed more comfortable around Michael and came by more frequently when he was able to give financially. We also noticed that Frank's involvement with Michael appeared to be connected to his employment patterns, with increased involvement when he was employed. We are uncertain if involvement with children increases the likelihood that fathers will provide financially or if providing financially leads to more involvement with children.

Child Support Filing for child support was a decision the women did not take lightly. An implicit rule we learned was that one should not file for child support if the father was giving *any* financial help and/or if he was *trying* to help. This rule applied despite the arbitrariness of payments, and even if this meant that the mother would not know from month to month whether she would receive any financial help at all from the father. For example, Roneeka explained Wesley's very limited financial contribution by saying, "He gives us money or buys them clothes or like, bikes and stuff. I mean, you know he tries to do what he can do." *Putting* a father on child support could even be perceived as a hostile act. Roneeka explained,

"I wouldn't want to get him for child support because he takes care of them [the children]. So why would I? He already paying child support for his other two kids. I wouldn't want to do him like that, no way. The way I feel, if a man take care of their child . . . I wouldn't even go for child support. Because I think that's

wrong. And some people still do that. Even though the father of their kids is taking care of their child, they'll still try to get them for child support. I think that's wrong. I feel if they gonna take care of their child. I mean let them take care of it instead of taking their money and then their money they making."

Other research has indicated that women do not *put* the fathers on child support for several reasons, including fears of hurting the prospect of marriage and protection of fathers from financial consequences and prison (Wattenberg, 1987). In addition, filing for formal support often jeopardizes the chances of receiving any in-kind support, and mothers discussed the slow (and at times unreliable) process of actually receiving money from the formal child support system. Therefore, in one sense, it might be a better strategy to wait to file when one is certain that the father will not contribute at all (Laakso, 2002).

Nonetheless, the majority of the women did resort to filing for child support during the course of our study. This was especially likely to happen when romantic ties were severed for good. Roneeka, approximately 2 years after telling us that she would not file, informed us that she "got him on child support but he ain't working." In this same interview, she told us, "I don't look to him for nothing. If he took care of his responsibilities, I would, but he don't." Later, she said that because he had not been paying child support, "He just going to be sitting behind bars with his orange suit on because the child support amount is going to be too much." She clearly had grown angry with Wesley by this point.

A few mothers believed that the fathers switched jobs to avoid having their wages garnished for child support. Shardae, for example, told us that that Jerome had "just been jumping jobs" to avoid child support. (Mothers who suggested this was occurring were no longer romantically involved with their children's fathers.)

Some of the mothers were not only angry with the fathers who they felt intentionally sidestepped their financial obligations to their children, they also blamed the government for not doing its job regarding child support enforcement. Sherryce provided a poignant example.

"Like I explained to him [Frank], I have to get a second job because he's not helping me. 'Well, I'm struggling too' [he says]. He don't care. I told him, 'You're by yourself and you don't have all these bills I have and that's still your child.' 'I'm struggling' [he says]. So I say, 'But so why can't you struggle and take care of him?' All you hear is, 'Oh! I'm trying.' Basically I think also that the government is made just for men, the reason being because they are letting them get off scott-free. They too busy enforcing stuff like seat belt laws, and I mean there should be seat belt laws, but I'm saying they are too busy into stuff like that in-

stead of making these fathers pay for their kids. You shouldn't have to make them but they are basically letting them get off. They don't have to do anything. We're struggling, and y'all don't want us on welfare, y'all need to get on these men to take care of their children. So that way there'll be two incomes. It's too hard."

Fathers' New Romances Should Not Keep Them from Seeing Their Children

The mothers complained that the fathers' new romantic relationships tended to decrease their involvement with their children. For example, Shardae told us, "His situation, or the woman that he's staying with now, he has a son by her, and she doesn't want him to be any part of her [Shardae's daughter Alexis], and so, I mean, that's his choice. His girlfriend told him that if Alexis has to be in his life, then he has to be out of his son's life, so he's choosing his son over Alexis."

Similarly, Sherryce told us that Frank's new partner was a barrier against his involvement in Michael's life. In our first interview, she told us, "He just moved into an apartment downtown. He takes care of his new girlfriend and her child." At this point, Frank was not spending any time with Michael and was not providing any financial support. This lack of involvement surprised Sherryce because their past together had led her to expect more of him. Later on when he separated from his wife, Frank became more active in Michael's life. At this point, Sherryce told us, "Yeah, they're not divorced yet. He's living with a cousin and so he stayed here with Michael the whole weekend." Andreya also struggled with this issue. William's new girlfriend Sonya discouraged him from seeing his children [with Andreya]. During those months when William and Sonya were not getting along and during their several breakups, he tended to see the children he had with Andreya more often.

Interestingly, paternal kin support also seemed to wane when the father was invested in a new romantic relationship. Andreya thought that Ms. Russell's [William's mother] declining involvement with her grandchildren was based on loyalty to Sonya. (See Chapter 7 for Andreya's ideas about the importance of grandparent–grandchild relations.) Shardae indicated a similar pattern after Jerome's new girlfriend moved in with him and his mother. She told us, "Well, she [paternal grandmother] helped me out when I was pregnant. She got things for the baby. Now she's weird. I don't know, just maybe 'cause he has a relationship with this other girl." These declines in paternal grandparent involvement may have been temporary. We know that Michael's paternal grandparents renewed their presence in Michael's life when he was 4 years old. During one of our visits that year, Michael was out with his grandparents, and Sherryce happily told us that they had offered to take him shopping for new clothes.

CONCLUSIONS

Our study offers a unique vantage point in that we juxtaposed the six fathers' comments with the mothers' impressions of the fathers' commitment to their children. From the understanding we gained about the roles of the fathers in their children's lives, we developed several important recommendations for further research and practice. Some have already been put forth in extant research, but we believe they merit repeating.

Fathers in Poverty Are a Diverse Group

One very basic implication stems from our observation that there are both similarities and considerable diversity among the fatherhood stories in even a small sample of low-income African American young men. It is important that we not assume that all are alike, or generalize from the stories of a selected few to all. The young fathers we interviewed, and those we did not speak to, reflected a wide range in levels of involvement with their children. Explanations for being involved or not involved also varied.

Interventions Should Begin Right after Children's Birth

We reiterate other researchers' call for policy makers and practitioners to intervene with young fathers very early in their children's lives. It seems that the chances for involvement and financial support are highest soon after birth (Mincy & Pouncy, 2002). After the child is a year old, it might be too late, especially because by then hopes of continued romantic involvement with the mothers are likely to have soured. Other studies have found that a common pattern is for unmarried couples in low-income communities to terminate their relationships within a year of their children's births (Kaplan, 1997; Waller, 2002).

Relationships Continue to Be
Influential with Mothers, Friends, and Family

As Kyierra, Denzel, and Patrick indicated, and as we delineated in Chapter 9, a romantic relationship with the mother appears to be one of the strongest influences on father involvement. Like other researchers (Allen & Doherty, 1995; Waller, 2002), we heard maternal reports of greater father involvement when romantic relationships were going well. Toward this end, it seems instructive to explore in-depth the interpersonal strategies used by couples living in poverty that are able to maintain their romantic relationships over time. Which couple patterns or individual father behaviors serve as buffers to the strong influences that so frequently lead to relationship dissolution?

From the present analysis, we can surmise that the most committed fathers tended to avoid the street life after the births of their children. Some devoted fathers seemed to isolate themselves from former friends, only staying in contact with their girlfriends, their children, and their kin. The price they paid for their commitment to family should be acknowledged. It is also important to understand their challenges as they struggled to avoid the "fast life" in favor of the new purpose they were seeing in fatherhood. It seemed that avoiding the streets took considerable will power, and romantic relationships were supportive in this endeavor. In fact, although Patrick believed that he had his head on "pretty straight," he conveyed to us that his girlfriend and his family were important supports for him not to "mess up." "Probably Chandra and my mother and, you know, just my family really keeping me, keeping my head up, keeping me on the track," he said.

Child Support Presents Multiple Quandaries

As suggested in this chapter as well as in Chapter 9, when romantic relationships were over and the biological fathers, as perceived by the mothers, were not financially contributing to their children, the mothers tended to file for child support. The mothers were more likely to receive in-kind support than formal child support, even when they filed for the latter. A few mothers (such as Sherryce, Roneeka, and Andreya) expressed considerable frustration with the current child support policies and operation. Echoing Waller's (2002) recommendations, we encourage policy makers to reconsider the dilemma women are put in when they are forced to file for child support—it tends to be viewed by both men and women as "hostile." One reason is that, as Marcus expressed, it puts men "in the system" for life, thereby increasing their chances of going to jail.

As in other research examining the subjective experiences of fathers, we found that the fathers highly valued the role of physical involvement in their children's lives (*being there*). It seemed as if the financial obligation was important but not as critical as physical involvement to them. This might be a reflection of the realities of the poverty in which the fathers lived. They were certainly well aware of their dismal job opportunities and most, if not all, had experienced unemployment. As such, meeting the traditional primary breadwinner function of fathers is often not a realistic option. As other researchers have suggested, fathers' commitment must be studied not only in terms of their financial contributions (especially formal child support), as it has been for a while, but also in terms of their physical involvement. Otherwise, much of the support for their children will be overlooked and unacknowledged (Jarrett, Roy, & Burton, 2002).

Biological and Social Fathers Are Held to Different Standards

Finally, we recommend that future investigations explore the different expectations both sexes hold for biological fathers as compared with social fathers. It seems that the social father is held to lower standards, with fewer explicit demands. Fathers may, therefore, avoid their biological children (for whom demands are greater) while supporting their social children (for whom even small contributions are appreciated because they are viewed as voluntary).

REFERENCES

Allen, W.D., & Doherty, W.J. (1995). Being there: The perception of fatherhood among a group of African-American adolescent fathers. In H.I. McCubbin, E.A. Thompson, A.E. Thompson, & J.A. Futrell (Eds.), *Resiliency in ethnic minority families: African-American families, Vol. 2,* (pp. 207–244). Madison: University of Wisconsin Press.

Bowman, P.J., & Forman, T.A. (1997). Instrumental and expressive family roles among African American fathers. In R.J. Taylor, J.S. Jackson, & L.M. Chatters (Eds.), *Family life in Black America* (pp. 216–247). Thousand Oaks, CA: Sage.

Clayton, O., & Moore, J. (2003). The effects of crime and imprisonment on family formation. In O. Clayton, R.B. Mincy, & D. Blankenhorn (Eds.), *Black fathers in contemporary American society: Strengths, weaknesses, and strategies for change* (pp. 84–102). New York: Russell Sage Foundation.

Coley, R.L. (2001). (In)visible men: Emerging research on low-income, unmarried, and minority fathers. *American Psychologist, 56,* 743–753.

Coley, R.L., & Morris, J.E. (2002). Comparing father and mother reports of father involvement among low-income minority families. *Journal of Marriage and Family, 64,* 982–997.

Demo, D.H., & Cox, M.J. (2000). Families with young children: A review of research in the 1990s. *Journal of Marriage and the Family, 62,* 876–895.

Erickson, R.J., & Gecas, V. (1991). Social class and fatherhood. In F.W. Bozzett & S.M.H. Hanson (Eds.), *Fatherhood and families in cultural context* (pp. 114–137). New York: Springer.

Heyman, G.D., & Dweck, C.S. (1992). Achievement goals and intrinsic motivation: Their relation and their role in adaptive motivation. *Motivation and Emotion, 16,* 231–247.

Jarrett, R.L., Roy, K.M., & Burton, L.M. (2002). Fathers in the "hood": Insights from qualitative research on low-income African American men. In C.S. Tamis-LeMonda & N. Cabrera (Eds.), *Handbook of father involvement* (pp. 211–248). Mahwah, NJ: Erlbaum.

Jayakody, R., & Kalil, A. (2002). Social fathering in low-income, African American families with preschool children. *Journal of Marriage and Family, 64,* 504–516.

Kaplan, E.B. (1997). *Not our kind of girl: Unraveling the myths of Black teenage motherhood.* Berkeley: University of California Press.

Laakso, J.H. (2002). Key determinants of a mother's decision to file for child support. *Families in Society: The Journal of Contemporary Human Services, 83,* 153–162.

Lazur, R.F., & Majors, R. (1995). Men of color: Ethnocultural variations of male gender role strain. In R.F. Levant & W.S. Pollack (Eds.), *A new psychology of men* (pp. 337–358). New York: Basic Books.

Liebow, E. (1967). *Tally's corner: A study of Negro streetcorner men.* Boston: Little, Brown, & Company.

Marsiglio, W. (Ed.). (1995). *Fatherhood: Contemporary theory, research, and social policy.* Thousand Oaks, CA: Sage.

Marsiglio W., & Cohan, M. (1997) Young fathers and child development. In M.E. Lamb (Ed.), *The role of the father in child development* (pp. 227–244). New York: Wiley.

Mincy, R.B., & Pouncy, H.W. (2002). The responsible fatherhood field: Evolution and goals. In C.S. Tamis-LeMonda & N. Cabrera (Eds.), *Handbook of father involvement* (pp. 555–589). Mahwah, NJ: Lawrence Erlbaum Associates.

Nelson, T.J., Clampet-Lundquist, S., & Edin, K. (2002). Sustaining fragile fatherhood: Father involvement among low-income, noncustodial African American fathers in Philadelphia. In C.S. Tamis-LeMonda & N. Cabrera (Eds.), *Handbook of father involvement* (pp. 525–553). Mahwah, NJ: Lawrence Erlbaum Associates.

Oyserman, D., Coon, H.M., & Kemmelmeier, M. (2002). Rethinking individualism and collectivism: Evaluation of theoretical assumptions and meta-analyses. *Psychological Bulletin, 128,* 3–72.

Sanderson, S., & Thompson, V.L.S. (2002). Factors associated with perceived parental involvement in childrearing. *Sex Roles, 46,* 99–111.

Schiller, B.R. (2004). *The economics of poverty and discrimination* (9th ed.). Upper Saddle River, NJ: Prentice-Hall, Inc.

Seligman, M. (1990). *Learned optimism.* New York: Knopf.

Thomson, E., Hanson, L., & McLanahan, S.S. (1994). Family structure and child well-being: Economic resources vs. parental behaviors. *Social Forces, 73,* 221–242.

Thornberry T.P., Smith, C.A., & Howard, G.J. (1997). Risk factors for teenage fatherhood. *Journal of Marriage and the Family, 59,* 505–522.

Waller, M.R. (2002). *My baby's father: Unmarried parents and parental responsibility.* Ithaca, NY: Cornell University Press.

Wattenberg, E. (1987). Nonmarital children: Do policy and practice discourage adjudication? *Public Welfare, 48,* 8–13.

Wilson, W.J. (2003). The woes of the inner-city African American father. In O. Clayton, R.B. Mincy, & D. Blankenhorn (Eds.), *Black fathers in contemporary American society: Strengths, weaknesses, and strategies for change* (pp. 9–29). New York: Russell Sage Foundation.

IV

Beyond the Family

12

Neighbors and Friends

Jean M. Ispa and Linda C. Halgunseth

bundant research confirms common knowledge that friendships are important for the psychological well-being of adolescents and young adults (Blieszner & Adams, 1992; Hartup, 1996).
It is typical for individuals in these age groups to seek friends with
whom they share interests, in whom they can confide without fear of
betrayal, and from whom they can derive emotional support (Baxter,
Dun, & Sahlstein, 2001; Fehr, 2000; Tesch, & Martin, 1983). We also
know that social support, including that derived from friendships, is
important for mothers and, indirectly, their children. Mothers' satisfaction with their social networks has been related to their parenting competence, including emotional responsivity, nonpunitive discipline, and
cognitive stimulation (MacPhee, Fritz, & Miller-Heyl, 1996). Most of
the existing research on adolescent and young adult friendships, however, describes the patterns characteristic of childless middle-class European Americans. For this chapter, we explore the friendship ties of
the young mothers in our sample, with particular emphasis on the
ways in which their experiences may be influenced by their poverty,
their responsibilities vis-à-vis their children, and their African American heritage.

An understanding of friendships must take neighborhood context
into account. A substantial body of research supports Bronfenbrenner's
(1986) ecological framework in calling attention to the significance of
neighborhood poverty on the well-being of adolescents and young
adults (also see Chapter 3). We know, for example, that young people
from low-income families are more likely to be drawn into delinquency
and teen pregnancy when they live in high-poverty neighborhoods
rather than more advantaged neighborhoods (Brookes-Gunn, Duncan,
& Aber, 1997; Leventhal & Brookes-Gunn, 2000). In addition, recent
research shows that, unlike in the past, many inhabitants of urban impoverished neighborhoods believe it wise to keep their distance from

neighbors. Crime and other problems exacerbated by poverty tend to make neighbors suspicious and isolated from one another (Barclay-McLaughlin, 2000; Jarrett & Jefferson, 2004). This research is pertinent to our understanding of the friendship patterns of the nine mothers in our study because, with the exception of brief periods, all but one (who part of the time resided with her parents in a middle-income housing development) lived in low-income or inner city neighborhoods during the entire course of our study. We begin then with a look at the mothers' attitudes and experiences regarding their neighbors and follow with an examination of themes that emerged in the young women's conversations about friends.

Our data come from conversations during our interviews and from the Support Wheel we asked the mothers to complete on two occasions. As described briefly in Chapter 3 and as shown in Figure 12.1 below, the Support Wheel consists of four concentric circles divided into four quadrants. In the middle circle, we wrote the mother's name. Each quadrant

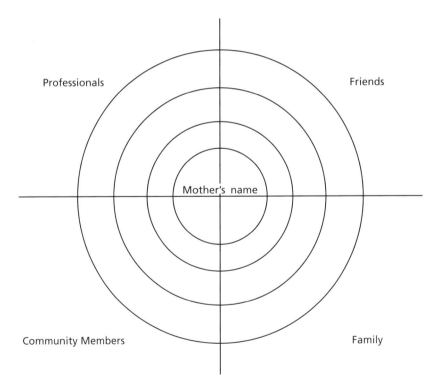

Figure 12.1. The Support Wheel completed by the mothers.

represented family members, friends, community members, or professionals with whom the mother had contact. We asked the mothers to write the names of people in the appropriate quadrant and circle. The names in the second circle showed the people with whom the mothers had positive, supportive relationships. The names in the third circle showed the people who sometimes were helpful and sometimes not. The names in the outermost circle indicated the people who were in the mothers' lives but who did not really contribute anything. Finally, outside the circles, near the edge of the piece of paper, the mothers were to write the names of the people they experienced as mostly hurtful. As the mothers filled in the Support Wheel, we asked them to explain each person's role in their lives.

RELATIONSHIPS WITH NEIGHBORS

Most of the themes that emerged from our analysis of conversations about the mothers' neighborhoods could be broadly categorized as reflecting either feelings of distance from and mistrust of neighbors or, occasionally, perceptions of friendliness and helpfulness.

Social Isolation

We were struck by how many times the mothers said "I keep to myself" in reference to neighbors. When we asked them if they could call on their neighbors for help if they needed it, the predominant answer was that they barely knew them. For the most part, the only neighbors the mothers talked to were also relatives, friends from school days or from work, and/or parents of their children's playmates. Maria captured the feelings most of the mothers had toward their neighbors when she said, "I just kind of feel like they don't know me, I don't know them." Even when she was living with her parents in the house they had lived in for many years, she said she only knew her neighbors well enough to wave to them in passing. Several of the mothers said that they spoke to their neighbors, but really didn't know them. For example, when asked if she could depend on neighbors for support, Chandra replied, "Not really, I know some of them—it's like I speak to them. I mean I don't basically get to know them but, you know, I speak. They speak back. Things like that." This noninteraction did not seem to worry the mothers; most did not seem to feel that they were missing anything. On the contrary, they indicated that they purposefully kept their distance from their neighbors.

It appeared to us that there were two reasons for this *social isolation,* the term used by Wilson (1987) to describe the phenomenon of neighbors having little to do with one another. The first, alluded to by almost all of the mothers, suggested an underlying wariness, a mistrust of people they didn't already know. They thought it best not to befriend others on their blocks or in their apartment complexes because the relationship was likely to sour over too-frequent requests to use or borrow items or over false rumors the other party might start. For example, when we asked Kyierra why she wasn't interested in getting to know her neighbors, she responded, "I think it's better to just . . . you don't need to be best friends with everybody, because then you get people knocking on your door all hours of the night asking to use your phone. We have that problem now. The friends I have is all I need. I've had them since way back, you know, and I don't need to add any more to that collection. 'Cause then I have too many friends, and that be irritating." Tanisha and Andreya likewise wanted to keep some distance between themselves and neighbors because, as Tanisha explained, "People are nosey." Andreya recounted an experience she had once when a neighbor told false "stories" about her to her public housing project manager. Studies by Allison et al. (1999) and Jarrett and Jefferson (2004) similarly indicated that gossip and rumors are a significant source of stress and alienation for low-income urban adolescents and women. Numerous studies have shown that they are often troublesome at higher socioeconomic levels as well (Dunbar, 2004; Rosnow, 2001).

High rates of crime in the mothers' neighborhoods further contributed to distrust and a distancing from neighbors. (See Chapter 15 for a discussion of violence in the mothers' neighborhoods.) Maria remarked when asked about neighbors, "I really don't trust people too much and I'm a little leery," and Kyierra commented, "When I walk out the door I'm scared—not scared, like 'ooh, they're gonna get me'—but nervous." Safety concerns also may have been at the heart of several of the mothers' preference for quiet neighborhoods. As pointed out by McCallum, Arnold, and Bolland (2002), the idea that "good neighbors mind their own business" may be a strategy for survival in high-crime communities. Frequent moving was a second major reason the mothers did not know their neighbors. The mothers moved an average of once a year during the 5 years of our study, and some moved several times a year. We noticed that their vocabulary reflected this instability: They talked about "staying" at their current addresses, not "living" there. Some of the moves occurred when the mothers left their own mothers' homes to live on their own, but most were in response to safety concerns (lead in the paint, arson, city condemnation of the house due to structural instability, fear of street crime) or, less frequently, an inability to pay the rent. Other researchers have found residential mobility to be common among the urban poor (Brookes-Gunn, Duncan,

Leventhal, & Aber, 1997); our sample therefore was not unusual. Little wonder then that our participants did not develop stable relationships with neighbors, especially if neighbors were moving at similarly high rates.

Some Exceptions: Examples of Neighborliness

Although our impression is that the mothers' dominant disposition toward their neighbors was one of disinterest and/or suspicion, sprinkled amongst their comments were a few examples of neighborly cooperation. Even though Andreya said that she didn't want to have anything to do with her neighbors, at various times she also told us that one neighbor had done her hair (for a fee), that another had agreed to get her something at the store, and that a third had given her rides and allowed her to use her phone. Tanisha once mentioned that a neighbor had helped her mow her lawn, and Shardae spoke of a 45-year-old man who repaired things for her mother and cleared Shardae's driveway after a snowstorm. Kyierra's example of neighborly help had a more somber touch. After her first child's father had punched Kyierra, Ms. Guss, an elderly woman who lived downstairs, responded to the commotion by calling the police and then chasing the man away with a bat.

The last two examples reflect the particular standing that some older neighbors had in the mothers' eyes. Tanisha, Kyierra, Andreya, and Maria mentioned having positive interactions with, and even some fondness for, neighbors who were of an older generation. Tanisha described the "older crowd" in her neighborhood as always saying hi and offering advice when her car broke down. Kyierra and Tejon spoke kindly of the aforementioned Ms. Guss, even though Ms. Guss had complained to Kyierra that the rap music on her stereo was too loud. When asked about a neighbor she was talking to on the phone one day when we arrived, Andreya felt the need to qualify by saying, "She's an older lady, though." Maria also mentioned older neighbors who would approach her and her son in a friendly way.

It is important to note that five of the mothers said that they had felt more connected in neighborhoods where they used to live. Andreya and her mother missed the block barbeques and garage sales and being "tight" with neighbors before moving to their current homes. (Their previous house had been condemned.) Breanna recalled that she "knew everybody" in her old neighborhood, and that all the children on her block would congregate at her home. Not surprisingly, she had liked it better there. Similarly, Roneeka said that she had known half of the neighbors on the block where her family had lived before.

Chandra demonstrated that the quality of housing mattered less than access to relatives and friends when she moved from an attractive apartment complex on the outskirts of the city back to a deteriorating building in the inner city. She had been excited when a Section 8 voucher permitted her to move to the newer apartment, but without reliable transportation to see relatives and old friends, she was lonely.

About half of the mothers thus reported that they had at one time in their lives experienced neighborhoods in which they had felt more of a sense of community. It is possible that they were looking at relations with past neighbors through rose-colored glasses. On the other hand, it is quite likely that neighborly relations were indeed more positive when they were younger. Nationally, concentrated urban poverty combined with racial isolation and crime increased significantly during the 1980s and 1990s (Jargowsky, 1997). These conditions have been linked to loss of neighborly trust and exchange (Barclay-McLaughlin, 2000; Korbin, 2001). The friendliness of some older residents in their neighborhoods may be reflections of a former social landscape when neighbors were more open to one another.

Also potentially significant is the fact that the years when the mothers recalled feeling more connected to neighbors were their school years. It is likely that connections through schoolmates who lived nearby were a critical factor. Without such structural support and until families *live* rather than simply *stay* at one address for substantial periods of time, it will be difficult for them to establish the kinds of supportive neighborly relations that could be the "anchor and shield" (Barclay-McLaughlin, 2000) that neighborhoods have the potential to provide.

RELATIONSHIPS WITH FRIENDS

When we asked about friendships in our initial interviews with the mothers, to our surprise, five of the nine first responded that they had no friends, but later revised that number to one or two. Three others said that they had just two friends. Only Shardae listed people whom she saw often. Moreover, as time went on, we learned that for several of the mothers, friendships were quite unstable. Someone who was a friend at the time of one interview might not be considered a friend 4 months later, only to reappear in the mother's life a few months after that.

Our surprise may have been partially due to some miscommunication. We were to learn that the word *friend* had a more specific meaning for the African American community in which mothers lived than it had for us. The mothers distinguished between *friends* and *associates*. We learned that the word *friends* is used to refer to people with whom one can talk about very personal matters and who really listen, who reciprocate emotional support and instrumental aid, who are loyal even in the face of disapproval and negative rumors from others, and with whom one can have a good time. The word *associates,* on the other hand, referred to people one might talk to, but superficially and without feelings of mutual commitment. As Roneeka put it, "If I think they're a friend to me, 'That's my friend,' you know, and 'I don't care what you all say, but that's my friend.' If this is my friend, I *know* she's my friend. If she's my associate, I just socialize with her. We might just talk on the phone about, like, just different things. But it don't be concerning myself and her. We just talk about the old times."

Breanna extended our understanding of the distinction when she explained that contacts with associates happen irregularly or by chance. She was telling us that she had associates but not friends when she said, "I got like, not as far as friends—we don't see each other every day. We run into each other some of the time but as far as an everyday friend or something like that, no. Yeah, just people I went to school with that I may see around."

The everyday vocabularies of some languages (e.g., Russian) convey clear distinctions among relationships based on their levels of closeness. In standard English, one calls people *friends* even when relationships lack depth. The mothers in our study did not seem to be entirely consistent in their use of the words *friend* and *associate.* Sometimes they reserved the word *friend* for people to whom they felt very close. At other times they used the word more loosely. In the sections below, we report on the mothers' replies to our interview questions using their vocabulary at the time.

Friends Aren't Necessarily Peers

The research literature on adolescent and young adult friendships is largely confined to studies about peer relationships—relationships among people of the same age. The mothers in our study, however, did not reserve the word *friend* for age-mates. When asked to tell us about friends, five of the mothers named women and men who were 7 or more years older than they. In Breanna's case, one of her two older friends was the father of her child; she felt that he was a "really good person" and that "If I felt that I needed to talk to him about something, I feel I could." As with others, she also viewed one of her mother's friends as her friend. Breanna loved hearing this friend tell stories from her childhood and her first years in the labor force. She said the stories inspired and comforted her. In other cases, the mothers viewed their children's older child care providers, certain older men and women from church, and specific older female neighbors as friends. Most of these friends were a decade or two older than the mothers.

Friends Help One Another

Our understanding of the mothers' friendships was shaped by conversations about the likable and unlikable qualities of current and former
friends. We have already mentioned the importance of having someone with whom one could have fun and in whom one could confide
without fear of betrayal. Some mothers also noted similarities between
themselves and their friends in terms of personality and preferred activities. These are characteristics that are often cited in the literature on
adolescent and young adult friendship (Akers, Jones, & Coyl, 1998;
Baxter et al., 2001).

About half of the mothers gave high priority to achievement-related
characteristics when describing valued qualities in friends. Four of the
mothers mentioned liking and admiring friends who had graduated
from high school; who worked hard and responsibly at their jobs; and
who in general were independent, determined to succeed, and smart.
Maria noted that respect for such qualities worked both ways in one of
her friendships, "I admire her and she admires me that I'm working
and I'm doing what I gotta do." Determination and hard work may be
especially valued in poverty contexts that pose particular challenges for
school- and employment-related success.

Having an energetic, hard-working friend also could have economic
benefits. Friends told the mothers about openings in their workplaces
and encouraged them to apply. Economists point out that most businesses rely on existing employees to tell friends about job openings because word-of-mouth recruitment is efficient and inexpensive for them.
This practice, however, is a mixed blessing for low-income individuals
because their social networks are unlikely to lead to the better-paying
or more prestigious positions within a company (Schiller, 2004).

Other forms of financial help involved in-kind trading of services
such as hair styling, rides to appointments and shopping, and occasional
child care—for example, when the mothers' regular child care providers
were ill or on vacation, when they had to work evening or weekend
hours, and when they simply needed free time for themselves. We also
learned of instances when friends extended invitations to the mothers
to move in with them when mothers couldn't find or afford their own
housing.

A stellar example of such support was provided by the help Sherryce received when she was on unpaid maternity leave. Noticing that
she was exhausted and that her cupboards were bare, friends from her
church cleaned her house, took her laundry to their own homes to
wash, paid her utilities, and bought groceries for her and her children.
When we went to her house for a visit, she was sorting hand-me-

downs that these friends had brought for her baby daughter and her 4-year-old son. Illustrating the reciprocal nature of this help-giving, she told us that she had already prepared a bag of clothes that her son had outgrown so she could give it to others in need. A year later, Sherryce and her children were living in the home of a friend from church. This woman had a steady job at a telephone company and owned a three-bedroom house in a working-class neighborhood. She had moved her 6-year-old daughter into the smallest bedroom so that Sherryce and her children could have the larger bedroom. She had urged Sherryce to accept her invitation to move in for a year so that she [Sherryce] could save the money she would otherwise have had to pay in rent.

Sherryce's story brings up the role played by friends in encouraging mothers to attend church. As discussed in Chapter 10, mothers saw church affiliation as important for their children. Some thought it important for themselves, too, but wanted to delay joining a congregation until they found a church they felt comfortable in and felt ready to commit to steady attendance. Friends played a role in this when they invited the mothers to go to church with them. One friend had tried to convince Tanisha to become involved in church activities. Tanisha was reluctant because, she said, she was "not right with the Lord" due to her history of drinking and premarital sex, and also because she wasn't comfortable at the friend's church when "everyone was jumping up and down and falling all out and I was getting kind of scared." After one visit to a friend's church, Kyierra similarly declined subsequent invitations because "I'm not into holy rolling." (She also said that she didn't have the right clothes.) However, after another friend took her to a Catholic church, she decided to embrace that form of Christianity and later made plans to have her wedding in that church.

Moreover, as much research shows (Brodsky, 2000) and as Sherryce's experience described earlier illustrates, fellow church members can be good sources of social and instrumental support. Sherryce actively searched for a congregation that would suit her preference for unconventional (nonsexist, humanistic) worship. After she found it during the third year of our study, we noticed a great change for the better in her overall mood and outlook. She attributed this change to the spirituality provided by church membership and to her involvement with this new group of supportive friends.

Impacts of Children on Friendships

Roy, Tubbs, and Burton (2004) reported that because the low-income women they interviewed were so busy with work, household, and family responsibilities, time to talk to friends was viewed as discretionary.

Likewise, in Chapter 10 we noted that the demands of motherhood put severe limitations on the amount of time the mothers could spend with existing friends and restricted their freedom to go out and make new friends. (We also mentioned Maria's contrasting experience: She found that her son was a magnet for peers who thought he was cute.) As we read and reread our transcripts, we found that rearing children had other implications for friendships in addition to the simple issue of finding time to socialize. Three such implications involved feelings about advice giving, reactions to the child-rearing styles of others, and reactions to evaluations by others of one's own parenting behavior and children.

When the mothers talked about their friends, they sometimes mentioned giving or receiving child-rearing advice. During two of our interviews, we specifically asked the mothers what they would do if a friend asked them for advice about child-rearing issues. We noticed that most of the mothers were willing to make suggestions and also were open to receiving advice from others. It seemed that often advice was delivered in a straightforward, blunt manner. Talking about how she often gave child-rearing advice to a 17-year-old friend, Andreya said, "I'm a tell the truth because this girl, she's young." During one visit, Kyierra told us that one of her friends often told her that she had become "motherly." When we asked what "motherly" meant, she replied, "I'm quick to tell her when she's messing up. And I'm upfront with her. I'm not going to bullsh** around about it. And I'll lecture her." Our impression was that, although this kind of "truth telling" (Ward, 1996) sometimes led to hurt feelings or anger, it did not sever relationships. On the contrary, it sometimes strengthened friendships through its intensity and its message of caring. Shardae illustrated this phenomenon when she explained, "She [her friend] doesn't like it when I don't agree with her way of thinking. She doesn't want to hear what I got to say. But we're still friends."

Chandra and Maria were the only mothers to explicitly say that they didn't like to give advice to friends. Chandra explained that "all kids are different" so her experience might not apply to others. Maria said advice giving was "touchy"; she'd rather "play dumb." She said her perspective was based on her own annoyance when a close friend gave her unsolicited parenting advice. For Maria and others like her, advice may be welcomed if it is delivered as a suggestion rather than as a directive. In an article describing relationships among mothers attending a high school program for adolescent parents, Higginson (1998) noted that the young mothers rejected advice worded as orders, but were open to advice that was more indirect, or offered simply as a suggestion. Along these lines, recall that Rickie, one of the Early Head Start home visitors, told us that he was always careful to phrase his advice in terms of possibilities, not commands.

Friendships also could be affected by the mothers' evaluations of the parenting effectiveness of others. Higginson (1998) called attention to the phenomenon of "competitive parenting." She found that the adolescent mothers in her sample made many comments favoring their own parenting dedication and skills over others'. Higginson thought that their competiveness grew out of a need to legitimize their roles as unmarried adolescent mothers. Seccombe, James, and Walters (1998) similarly noted that many mothers receiving public assistance view others in their situation, but not themselves, as deficient in parenting motivation and skills. Five of the mothers in our study made comments along these lines, saying that their friends or associates were too easily frustrated, too harsh, too permissive, too neglectful or "wild," and/or lacked an understanding of their children's perspectives. We are aware of at least two cases in which the mothers curtailed relationships because they disapproved of the mothering practices of friends or associates.

Not surprisingly, friendships were supported when the mothers felt that their friends liked their children or approved of their child-rearing efforts. For example, when we first met Chandra, she described the woman with whom she and Patrick were living as a close friend. When asked to elaborate, she said that they talked a lot and that the woman enjoyed playing with Patrick. Others also spoke happily and proudly of instances when friends had praised their children. It seemed that such comments benefited friendships in addition to making the mothers feel good about their parenting.

Distinctions Between Friends and Relatives

When asked about friendships, four of the mothers talked about relationships with their cousins, aunts, and/or mothers. Shardae mentioned having a friend whom she had known so long and with whom she was so close that the friend was "like a cousin or a sister to me. I think of her more as family." This led us to wonder if and how the mothers distinguished between relationships with relatives and relationships with friends. Our transcripts suggest that most of the mothers felt more obligated to family members than to their best friends and, in turn, they felt more comfortable turning to family members than to friends for certain kinds of help.

Our question concerning to whom the mothers could turn if they needed financial assistance was most revealing. All of them except for

Sherryce listed relatives first and then friends. Kyierra was adamant that she would ask her best friend for money only if she were in dire circumstances.

> Kyierra: If it really came down to it, [friend's name] probably would help. But I really wouldn't ask her. . . . I never ask my friends for anything.
>
> Interviewer: What keeps you from doing that?
>
> Kyierra: I guess pride. Well, maybe not pride. Maybe just not wanting to do that. I don't like asking my friends for financial help at all. 'Cause they're not family, they're my friends. Friends are supposed to be there to have fun with, to talk to. Not to help you with money.

Maria expressed similar sentiments when she complained that a pregnant friend expected her to give her Bryce's crib and baby clothing when he was finished with them. Instead, she had sold it all at a garage sale, "I think she thinks I'm gonna be there more than I plan to be as far as that. I was lucky. I had an aunt and uncle who gave me a lot of their things for free and so I was lucky. I didn't have to buy a lot of things, but you know, she's not my family and she does have a mom and she does have family."

Comments of this nature were in keeping with the high value placed on family interdependence reported by most scholars of African American culture (McAdoo, 1997) and echoed by the mothers in our study (see Chapter 10).

Arguably the most startling comment on this topic came from Denzel, Breanna's boyfriend. He had been talking about a high school business class he'd taken and said that one day he'd like to have his own business. We asked if he'd like to do this with friends. He replied, "With family, not friends," and then went on to explain, "Family always be there. I don't really trust a friend. My brother's best friend killed him so I don't really trust friends. I hang with them to a certain extent but [only with] the friends I been around all my life." We gathered that he considered the friends he'd known all his life to be like family.

Viewing close, trusted, longtime friends as family brings up the phenomenon of godparenting. Recall Shardae's comment that she had known her best friend so long and they were so close that she was "like a cousin or a sister to me." This friend and another close friend were both godmothers to Shardae's daughter. In fact, it seemed to us that asking someone to be a godparent was a way of bringing that person into the family. We knew of six godmothers and two godfathers. (Both godfathers were husbands of godmothers.) Each was a trusted, close friend either of the child's mother or grandmother. They were like part of the family and could be called on to take care of the children when the mothers had to go out. They also took the children on outings, called to see how they were doing, bought things for them, and occasionally gave money to the mothers to help with child-related expenses. The godmother of Roneeka's first child was both her mother's best friend and her best friend's mother. Roneeka's mother called this woman as soon as Roneeka went into labor, and she was present in the delivery room when her goddaughter was born.

Why Some Friendships End (or Do Not Get Started)

When we asked the mothers to tell us how long they had known their friends and associates, all but Andreya and Chandra spoke of relationships that had continued on some level since elementary or middle school. Why then did so many of the mothers feel that they either did not have friends or had very few?

Themes described in earlier sections of this chapter regarding neighborhoods and neighbors, the functions of friendship, and issues related to child rearing help explain why some relationships failed or were unstable. The simplest reason, we found, involved mobility. Friends of Kyierra and Maria had moved away to attend college. For some of the other mothers, lack of transportation made it difficult to get together even if moves were within the same city. (This seemed less of a problem for "best friends"; in those cases, frequent telephone contact was maintained.) Further, many of the jobs that were available to mothers and their friends involved evening and night shifts—times when friends would ordinarily meet. Shardae had a close friend (one of her daughter's godmothers) who worked all night and often came to see Shardae in the morning, when she got off work. This, however, was an unusual arrangement. The demands of child rearing added further obstacles in that there often was little time or freedom for socializing. In addition, friends sometimes "fell out" when they looked down on each other's parenting styles.

Male versus Female Friends

A theme that was not introduced in the earlier sections of this chapter involves the mothers' negative evaluations of *women* (as compared with men) as potential friends. Breanna's first response when asked about her friends was, "I don't have too many female friends because I just don't think I can seem to get along with them. We always end up fighting." This was not an isolated comment: Five of the nine mothers expressed the same sentiment. Chandra once told us, "I don't really hang with girls." Another time, when asked if she liked her new job at a fast food restaurant, she replied that she did and compared it favorably to other jobs in that "some jobs, it's like too many girls, and they keep up a lot of ruckus." Maria said that she had two close girlfriends and didn't want more because she didn't "believe in having too many girlfriends. It's just not possible. It's not easy to be friends with girls or to have too many girlfriends because they turn to fake relationships, I think." Kyierra simply told us, "I don't really have a bunch of girlfriends 'cause I don't really like girls that much." Andreya explicitly related problems between female friends to jealousy.

Andreya: I'm just a person that I rather have male friends than female friends.
Interviewer: Would you?
Andreya: Uh-huh. Because female friends can keep you in trouble. And male friends you can sit back and you could talk to them about your personal problems and y'all won't be arguing or a male won't feel jealous because you got more shoes or more clothes than them. They don't feel jealous.

In their qualitative study of women living in an inner city public housing complex, Jarrett and Jefferson (2004) similarly heard comments about the need for women to be careful in relationships with other women. The issues involved the damage that could come from gossip, the spread of false rumors ("people lying that you said it," p. 143), and jealousies arising when women suspected other women of "messing with" their men—an issue that may be exacerbated in neighborhoods in which the ratio of available men to available women is low (see Chapter 9). Gossip came up in our study as well. Tanisha, for example, wasn't happy that one of her friends would come over just because (according to Tanisha) she wanted to talk about other friends. Andreya told us many stories about one woman or another who was "running her mouth" and "getting stuff started." Underscoring the issues of trust and betrayal, Andreya told us that her mother was her best friend because "that's the only person I can talk to without somebody else knowing it."

As mentioned earlier, numerous studies on gossip have found that it is by no means confined to women in poverty. Gossip and the spread of rumors occur at all socioeconomic levels, in workplaces as well as in informal settings, and among men as well as women (Rosnow, 2001). In a low-income context, however, the tendency to gossip may take on particular strength and maliciousness if, as is often the case, it is rooted in the storyteller's feelings of injustice, powerlessness, and envy (Dunbar, 2004; Wert, 2004).

Another way in which trust and betrayal issues soured friendships occurred when the mothers protected friends from the consequences of their wrongdoing but then felt used. In Andreya's case, Cheryl, a girlfriend, had drunk from Andreya's mother's stash of liquor. Knowing that her mother would never allow Cheryl to come back to the house if she knew what she had done, Andreya told Patricia that she was the guilty one and endured her mother's anger. In the ensuing months, however, Andreya became increasingly resentful toward Cheryl because she felt that her loyalty was not reciprocated.

In Maria's case, Bianka, a friend who had recently smoked marijuana, asked her to "donate" a urine sample so that she could pass a drug test required by a job application. At first, Maria refused because she worried that the urine analysis might detect a prescription drug she was taking and that Bianka would be asked to furnish the prescription number. The friend persisted and Maria finally complied, but only after warning that she would never give Bianka the prescription number because it would identify her as the donor and get her into trouble. Maria was right; Bianka was asked for the prescription number and begged Maria to give it to her. At this point, Maria adamantly stood her ground and thought, "It's time to stop the friendship. She's trying to get me to do things that are illegal." That her friend had asked her to put herself (and her son had she gone to jail) in jeopardy troubled Maria a great deal.

Other situations that resulted in the mothers feeling used involved one-sided emotional support or instrumental assistance that was not reciprocated or paid for in cash. These stories demonstrate the role played by reciprocity in either cementing or dissolving friendships. Stack (1974) wrote about the importance of "swapping" as a survival strategy within a low-income African American community. Friends and relatives did favors for one another knowing that eventually the recipient would pay back. These favors could involve financial assistance or labor (e.g., child care, rides, help with repairs). For the mothers in our study, the concepts of sensitivity and reciprocity seemed intertwined. Friends were expected to buy things for one another (and for one another's children) and to trade needed services. When this did not happen, friendships suffered. Andreya told us about a young woman she'd stopped thinking of as a friend because she felt this person called only when she needed to talk or wanted to borrow something, never just to find out how Andreya was doing. Another former friend of Andreya had borrowed clothing and never returned it and had not paid for or reciprocated the child care Andreya had provided. Tanisha had similar reasons for being annoyed with a friend.

> Tanisha: Dana gets on my nerves. She came over last night. I cooked dinner for her and all of her kids and she borrowed a vacuum and she got a outfit and I did her hair and I'm like, 'I'm glad that's what you came over for.'

Interviewer: And that gets on your nerves?
    Tanisha: Yeah, but it doesn't matter. It's not a big deal because I
              know that I don't use her but I know if it got down to it,
              I could, but I don't, but it's just sad that she is using me.

We might add that during another interview, Tanisha admitted that she
was "using" a male friend who was interested in her so that she could
borrow his car.

Early Head Start's Role in the Mothers' Friendships

Early Head Start affected the mothers' friendships in three ways. First,
home visitors tried to help the mothers develop social skills, including
conflict resolution skills that would be useful for them in their relationships with friends and family members, social service personnel, and
co-workers. Recall from Chapter 5 Rickie's positive influence on Andreya's ability to meet social challenges more calmly than she had before. Second, the Early Head Start parent meetings afforded opportunities to meet other young mothers in like circumstances (see Chapters
7 and 13). Our impression is that the mothers did not take advantage
of these meetings as much as they might have, but some did mention
enjoying the chance to see others who were working on many of the
same issues they were facing.

    Third, at one time or another all but Tanisha and Shardae considered
their home visitors to be their friends. On their Support Wheels, some
of the mothers also listed us, the researchers, as supportive friends. We
were gratified by these demonstrations of trust, affection, and appreciation, but we also worried because we knew that these relationships
were not entirely reciprocal and that they were ultimately temporary.
The nature of home visiting and research is such that home visitors
(and we the researchers) learned much more about the mothers' lives
than they learned about ours. In addition, eventually the children would
"age out" of Early Head Start and a couple of years thereafter our project would end.

CONCLUSIONS

We often think of friendship during adolescence and young adulthood
as involving emotional support and companionship. For young single
mothers living in poverty, neighborly relations and friendships may be
especially important because they also carry the potential for the provision of needed goods and services. Nonetheless, as we have seen, the
mothers in our study reported little contact with neighbors and, with
some important and happy exceptions, some difficult issues in relationships with friends.

The mothers' remarks concerning their neighborhoods, in combination with previous research on the isolation that is increasingly characteristic of urban neighborhoods with concentrated poverty, have policy and service implications. We have long known that when individuals are brought together to work toward common goals, personal relationships improve and the community as a whole benefits (Sherif, 2001). Crime reduction could be one such goal. Programs and policies that result in reduced crime would seem to go a long way toward making neighbors more trusting of one another, especially if community members participated in decision making and informal social control, and if efforts were made to improve relationships between law enforcement officers and neighborhood residents. Community centers and programs that provide safe ways for neighbors to congregate for recreational activities may also help strengthen neighborly relations, as would programs that bring people together to advocate for other neighborhood improvements. In their groundbreaking study of Chicago neighborhoods, Sampson, Raudenbush, and Earls (1997) found that it was not poverty in and of itself that promoted crime so much as the lack of "collective efficacy," or mutual trust and willingness to intervene to maintain public order, that separated low-crime from high-crime neighborhoods. Low collective efficacy was most common in poor neighborhoods, but the fact that there were poor neighborhoods in which collective efficacy was high and crime rates low supported the statistical finding that it was collective efficacy, not poverty (and not race), that best predicted crime rates.

One improvement that is clearly needed is the availability of sufficient numbers of affordable, attractively appointed housing units in good repair. Adequate housing may indirectly benefit relationships among neighbors because families are likely to move less often if they are happy with their living situations. Efforts to repair existing homes and to ensure that families have the option of moving into a new home in their current neighborhoods after their homes have been condemned would also help prevent the weakening of neighborly relations. Finally, increased employment opportunities close to low-income neighborhoods would lessen the need for families to relocate. Supportive relationships with neighbors cannot develop in the absence of residential stability. Our impression on this score is supported by the Sampson et al. (1997) study showing that residential turnover is linked to low neighborhood collective efficacy.

Programs for young families, such as Early Head Start, could be a catalyst in this regard. Because Early Head Start staff are charged with the task of partnering with community agencies as well as working directly with parents and children, they are in a position to facilitate the development of the types of community organizations just mentioned.

For some parents, good-humored coaching in the social skills that sustain long-term friendships also could be of use. In keeping with the qualities the mothers mentioned as important in their friendships, the emphasis might be on behaviors that build reciprocal emotional and instrumental support. Concerted efforts to bring parents together not only for the purpose of learning self-sufficiency and parenting skills, but also for the purpose of making friends and forming support groups, may have long-lasting benefits for the parents and, indirectly, for their children.

REFERENCES

Akers, J., Jones, R.M., & Coyl, D.D. (1998). Adolescent friendship pairs: Similarities in identity status development, behaviors, attitudes, and intentions. *Journal of Adolescent Research, 13,* 178–201.

Allison, K.W., Burton, L., Marshall, S., Perez-Febles, A., Yarrington, J., Kirsh, L.B., & Merriwether-DeVries, C. (1999). Life experiences among urban adolescents: Examining the role of context. *Child Development, 70,* 1017–1029.

Barclay-McLaughlin, G. (2000). Communal isolation: Narrowing the pathways to goal attainment and work in the social contexts of inner-city poverty. In S. Danziger & A. Lin (Eds.), *Qualitative research on the African-American experience* (pp. 52–75). Ann Arbor: University of Michigan Press.

Baxter, L., Dun, T., & Sahlstein, E. (2001). Rules for relating communication among social network members. *Journal of Social and Personal Relationships, 18,* 173–199.

Blieszner, R., & Adams, R.G. (1992). *Adult friendship.* London: Sage.

Brodsky, A.E. (2000). The role of religion in the lives of resilient, urban, African American single mothers. *Journal of Community Psychology, 28,* 199–219.

Bronfenbrenner, U. (1986). Ecology of the family as a context for human development: Research perspectives. *Developmental Psychology, 22,* 723–742.

Brookes-Gunn, J., Duncan, G.J., & Aber, J.L. (Eds.). (1997). *Neighborhood poverty: Context and consequences for children (Vol. 1).* New York: Russell Sage Foundation.

Brookes-Gunn, J., Duncan, G.J., Leventhal, T., & Aber, J.L. (1997). Lessons learned and future directions for research on the neighborhoods in which children live. In J. Brookes-Gunn, G.J. Duncan, & J.L. Aber (Eds.), *Neighborhood poverty: Context and consequences for children, Vol. 1* (pp. 279–297). New York: Russell Sage Foundation.

Dunbar, R.I.M. (2004). Gossip in evolutionary perspective. *Review of General Psychology, 8,* 100–110.

Fehr, B. (2000). The life cycle of friendship. In C. Hendrick & S.S. Hendrick (Eds.), *Close relationships: A sourcebook* (pp. 71–82). Thousand Oaks, CA: Sage.

Hartup, W. (1996). The company they keep: Friendships and their developmental significance. *Child Development, 67,* 1–13.

Higginson, J.G. (1998). Competitive parenting: The culture of teen parents. *Journal of Marriage and the Family, 60,* 135–149.

Jargowsky, P. (1997). *Poverty and place.* New York: Russell Sage Foundation.

Jarrett, R.L., & Jefferson, S.M. (2004). Women's danger management strategies in an inner-city housing project. *Family Relations, 53,* 138–147.

Korbin, J.E. (2001). Context and meaning in neighborhood studies of children and families. In A. Booth & A.C. Crouter (Eds.), *Does it take a village? Community effects on children, adolescents, and families* (pp. 79–86.) Mahwah, NJ: Lawrence Erlbaum Associates.

Leventhal, T., & Brookes-Gunn, J. (2000). The neighborhoods they live in: The effects of neighborhood residence on child and adolescent outcomes. *Psychological Bulletin, 126,* 309–337.

MacPhee, D., Fritz, J., & Miller-Heyl, J. (1996). Ethnic variations in personal social networks and parenting. *Child Development, 67,* 3278–3295.

McAdoo, H.P. (1997). Upward mobility across generations in African American families. In H.P. McAdoo (Ed.), *Black families* (3rd ed., pp. 139–162). Thousand Oaks, CA: Sage.

McCallum, D.M., Arnold, S.E., & Bolland, J.M. (2002). Low-income African-American women talk about stress. *Journal of Social Distress and the Homeless, 11,* 249–263.

Rosnow, R.L. (2001). Rumor and gossip in interpersonal interaction and beyond: A social exchange perspective. In R.M. Kowalski (Ed.), *Behaving badly: A social exchange perspective* (pp. 203–232). Washington, DC: American Psychological Association.

Roy, K.M., Tubbs, C.Y., & Burton, L.M. (2004). Don't have no time: Daily rhythms and the organization of time for low-income families. *Family Relations, 53,* 168–178.

Sampson, R.J., Raudenbush, S.W., & Earls, F. (1997). Neighborhoods and violent crime: A multilevel study of collective efficacy. *Science, 277,* 918–924.

Schiller, B.R. (2004). *The Economics of Poverty and Discrimination* (9th ed.). Upper Saddle River, NJ: Prentice Hall.

Seccombe, K., James, D., & Walters, K.B. (1998). "They think you ain't much of nothing": The social construction of the welfare mother. *Journal of Marriage and the Family, 60,* 849–865.

Sherif, M. (2001). Superordinate goals in the reduction of intergroup conflict. In D. Abrams (Ed.), *Intergroup relations: Essential readings (Key readings in social psychology)* (pp. 64–70). Philadelphia: Psychology Press.

Stack, C.B. (1974). *All our kin: Strategies for survival in a Black community.* New York: Harper & Row.

Tesch, S.A., & Martin, R.R. (1983). Friendship concepts of young adults in two age groups. *Journal of Psychology, 115,* 7–12.

Ward, J.V. (1996). Raising resisters: The role of truth telling in the psychological development of African American girls. In B.J.R. Leadbeater & N. Way (Eds.), *Urban girls: Resisting stereotypes, creating identities* (pp. 85–99). New York: New York University Press.

Wert, S.R. (2004). A social comparison account of gossip. *Review of General Psychology, 8,* 122–137.

Wilson, W.J. (1987). *The truly disadvantaged: The inner city, the underclass and public policy.* Chicago: University of Chicago Press.

13

Home Visitor
Roles and Dilemmas

Sheila J. Brookes, Kathy R. Thornburg, and Jean M. Ispa

As explained in Chapter 1, the Early Head Start program with which we partnered initially used the home visiting model to support parents in their roles as primary caregivers and educators and to help them meet personal goals related to self-sufficiency. Recent evaluations of home visiting programs have shown that we are in the early stages of understanding how to work effectively with parents who live under high-stress circumstances. Researchers have come to the disconcerting conclusion that overall there is little evidence of long-term benefit for either parents or children from most existing home visiting models (Barnard, 1997; Daro & Harding, 1999; Gomby, Culross, & Behrman, 1999; Outreach Partnership, 1999–2000; St. Pierre & Layzer, 1999). Yet, it is important to keep in mind that some home visiting programs and strategies have been relatively more successful than others (see Ispa, 2002, for a review of this literature).

In this chapter, we examine issues related to home visiting through three lenses: the mothers', the home visitors', and our own. The nine mothers we interviewed shared with us their perspectives on home visits and their home visitors, including how they believed they benefited from Early Head Start and the changes they thought the program should make to better assist families in the future. The home visitors, in turn, provided us with their perceptions of their relationships with the mothers.[1] As we conducted our research, we came to genuinely appreciate the complexities and difficulties inherent in a home visitor's job.

---

[1]Over the course of the study, some home visitors left the program and were replaced by others. A total of eight home visitors served our nine families. There were two White females, five African American females, and one White male.

Breanna's story below demonstrates the wide-ranging impact of Early Head Start on her family. It also demonstrates the depth of her appreciation of her home visitor's help. As might be expected, however, given the tentative picture drawn by evaluations of home visiting programs, not all of the mothers were as happy with Early Head Start as Breanna, received as much support from their own home visitors, or were as receptive to learning about parenting.

Breanna

We met shy, soft-spoken Breanna shortly after the birth of her first child Corinna. She had become sexually active at the age of 12, pregnant at 14, and a mother at 15. Her father was unemployed, her mother had a history of substance abuse, and the father of her daughter, 7 years her senior, was uninvolved for the majority of her pregnancy. As we came to know Breanna over the course of the next few years, we realized that her relationship with her Early Head Start home visitor served as an important buffer protecting her from some of the likely consequences of her background.

When Breanna entered Early Head Start, she was attending what was dubbed the "pregnant school,"[2] but soon after Corinna's birth, she dropped out. She told us that she had applied to Early Head Start because "I felt that it would be an opportunity for me to learn more and be doing something. Since I'm so young, I thought that it would probably help me, and just get me somewhere else." While in Early Head Start, Breanna enrolled her daughter in a high-quality early childhood program, earned a high school diploma and a certified nursing assistant certificate through Job Corps, obtained employment, began taking college courses at a local community college, and regularly attended Early Head Start monthly parent meetings with her boyfriend. Breanna credited her Early Head Start home visitor Carrie with helping her to set and achieve these goals. Three years later, as the family prepared to exit from Early Head Start and Corinna was about to enter a new early childhood program, we asked Breanna to tell us about her relationship with Carrie.

"Our usual meetings are every week. She brought me some information [on the transition process] as far as what Corinna might feel and things that I can do, books that I can start reading to Corinna, things that I can start telling her as far as moving to a big girl classroom. . . . She's always offered to give me information I've needed. Like, if I needed to know anything like as far as why was Corinna wetting, she had feedback to give me. It wasn't just, 'Well. I don't know.' I didn't have to figure it out for myself. And she doesn't wait for me to ask. She makes suggestions, 'cause I'm not too outgoing sometimes, so she brings it up to me.

---

[2]An alternative school for students who are pregnant or who have recently had a baby.

She's a very nice person. I trust her. I like her a lot. I think that she likes me. She trusts me. I confide in her sometimes. She's a very good role model, someone that I can look up to. . . . Half of [my] being a good parent is because of Early Head Start."

To understand the themes that emerged from our interviews with the home visitors and mothers about their relationships, the reader must first be acquainted with the duties of home visitors as prescribed by Early Head Start guidelines. We turn now to a brief description.

HOME VISITORS' CHILD AND FAMILY DEVELOPMENT RESPONSIBILITIES

The Early Head Start home visitor's job is multifaceted, involving responsibilities in each of the four cornerstones and requiring them to meet the Head Start Performance Standards as described in Chapter 1. Parents are probably most aware of and most directly impacted by the two cornerstones that require focus on child and family development. The other two cornerstones, community and staff development, are likely to be less obvious to parents, although they were critical for the behind-the-scenes preparation that makes work toward the child and family development goals possible. In the following two sections, we describe home visitors' responsibilities in the child and family development cornerstones—the two that bring home visitors into direct contact with children and parents.

Child Development Services

To address the child development cornerstone, home visitors were required to provide parenting information. This was a complex endeavor because in many cases they were working with new mothers whose understanding of child development and parenting was limited or based on information not currently accepted by early childhood professionals. The topics that home visitors focused on included infant and toddler development, childproofing the home, early childhood milestones, toilet training, appropriate discipline techniques, age-appropriate learning activities, and child care selection criteria.

Some topics, such as childproofing the home, seemed best taught through direct teaching methods. Kyierra told us that "Nicole [her home visitor] told me to put caps on the outlets, use door stoppers so she [her child] can't open the doors, and stoppers for the cabinets. She told me to put the gate at the stairs, to keep chemicals and medicines up high." Roneeka provided another example when she described what she was learning from Nicole about child development and the use of redirection as a way to manage normal toddler curiosity.

"I'd be telling my daughter, 'You know better' and 'You know not to touch that.' Nicole said, 'Roneeka, she really doesn't know better because she's still a child. She's still a baby.' She helps me in all different kinds of ways to deal with my daughter. She has taught me to find Regina something else to do, instead of hollering at her about what I don't want her to do. And I was . . . telling Nicole, 'She's bad. You just don't know her.' And she said, 'She's just curious. She's not bad. She's very smart for her age.' Sometimes she is bad, but I know kids are gonna be kids. Nicole helps me in a lot of ways to try to discipline my kids."

Later, Roneeka told us that she was trying to internalize the information Nicole was giving her. "They [Early Head Start] have helped me a lot . . . like one of my goals was to stop yelling so much at Regina. One day I said, 'Okay, I'm not gonna yell.' I had yelled at her and I told her to bring me something and she just stood there. You know, I guess she was scared. . . . And then I just calmed her down and I was like, 'Would you bring that to me?' And she brought it to me. So, it helps me a lot."

These remarks reflect Nicole's conversations with Roneeka about positive disciplinary techniques. Nicole also had provided Roneeka with printed information about the importance of appropriate discipline. As a result, Roneeka made it one of her goals to try to refrain from raising her voice when speaking to her daughter.

In addition, mothers were given printed information regarding developmental milestones to keep at home to refer to regularly. Kyierra, like some of the other mothers, told us that she found this information helpful, "There were things that they say in the little pamphlets that Nicole gave me to know what to look for when Jalisa's birth to 6 weeks. I noticed that Jalisa was doing everything. Sometimes even more than what the pamphlets were saying that she should be doing."

Other topics seemed best taught through modeling. Several mothers explained how their home visitors taught them about using common household objects as teaching tools. Home visitors presented these items to infants and toddlers, played with them for a short while, and then stepped back so that the mothers could become the teachers.

Home visitors worked directly with the children to determine their developmental skill levels. For some assessments, they used standardized tests; at other times, they relied on their knowledge of normal developmental milestones. "Carrie [her home visitor] was doing an [activity with] Corinna to see if she could do certain things and see if her motor skills were with her age. . . . She talked to me about ways to increase [her skills]," Breanna told us.

Some of the monthly parent meetings also addressed child development topics, including typical infant and toddler physical, social, emotional, cognitive, and language development; toilet training; and effective disciplinary techniques. At some meetings, parents were given appropriate gifts, such as children's picture books.

Family Development Services

Many of the mothers we interviewed were experiencing challenging family development issues when they entered the Early Head Start program. This meant that home visitors had to concern themselves with a variety of psychological and relationship issues troubling the mothers, as well as with practical needs for cash assistance, food stamps, housing, transportation, schooling, job training, employment, medical care, and child care. Helping the mothers identify and work toward personal goals in these areas required home visitors to understand coping styles and relationship patterns and to keep abreast of local resource availability, changing state and federal policies, and the myriad of rules families must follow to apply for and obtain services.

Right after Andreya exited from Early Head Start, we asked her to tell us what she thought she'd gotten from the program. Shifts in attitude were high on her list, reflecting Rickie's (her home visitor's) sensitivity to her aggressive coping style, which he wanted to help her change. Recall (from Section II of this book) how Rickie tried to persuade her to take things more in stride and to problem-solve better solutions. "'Cause I could just not have no ketchup and be mad," she once told us when describing how easily she'd gotten upset about small problems before Rickie had worked with her. "I mean I learned how to be more mature, instead of arguing with people about stuff. It's always another way or another route to go with things in different situations." Recognizing that low self-confidence was behind some of Andreya's poor decisions, Rickie tried to help her see that she had real strengths. Andreya accordingly gave him credit for giving her "more self-esteem than I used to have for myself. He gave me another way to look at life, instead of me being so negative. He gave me a lot of positive things to look at."

Helping the mothers connect with other social services such as Temporary Assistance for Needy Families (TANF), food stamps, and Medicaid also benefited the mothers and their children a great deal. Kyierra, for example, said, "She [Nicole, her home visitor] took me down to apply for welfare and food stamps and stayed down there. She's been real helpful." Andreya told us that Rickie helped her not just in applying for social services, but also in understanding the rules she would have to follow.

Five of the mothers (Andreya, Breanna, Chandra, Roneeka, and Tanisha) dropped out of high school before or during their pregnancies. Home visitors were instrumental in motivating Roneeka, Chandra, and Tanisha to sign up for GED classes. Roneeka told us, "I have a good [home visitor]. She got me in for GED classes. Now I'm looking forward to getting my GED. Setting my goals, you know, what I want to be and what I want to do and what I want to get out of life. It's made a very good impact on me and my kids." Andreya had enrolled in Job Corps before she met Rickie, but his encouragement to stick with it was critical. Without his support, she may well have dropped out.

The mothers also told us about home visitors' help with job searches. Shardae credited her home visitor with "telling me where some of the other mothers work and she was giving me phone numbers [of employers]." Sherryce told us that her home visitor helped her type up and photocopy her resume. Occasionally, dilemmas regarding education and work surfaced for home visitors, as when the goals they wanted the mothers to adopt conflicted with the mothers' own goals. For example, Chandra chose to drop out of a GED program to work full time in a restaurant. Although her hourly wage was low, the tips she made allowed her to get off cash assistance, obtain an apartment of her own, and purchase furniture and a used car. Marissa, her home visitor, thought that the long-term benefits of an education were more important than current employment, but she put aside her own values to serve Chandra's.

Home visitors also helped the mothers find adequate housing. Sometimes they suggested that the mothers might be happier if they had more space or if they moved out of their mothers' homes. Sometimes they explained how to apply for housing assistance (public housing and Section 8) and drove the mothers to look at available apartments and houses. Kyierra, for example, appreciatively reported that "She's [her home visitor] been helping me get that housing straight 'cause I'm wanting to move out of here and she said, 'That's what you guys need to do.' And I agree with her 150%. You know I didn't realize how bad I was gonna need more space 'til after Ciera [her second child] was born."

Home visits were supplemented by monthly parent meetings at the Early Head Start center. Grandparents, fathers, social fathers, and other family members important to the children were invited to attend the meetings with the mothers. The agendas for most of the meetings included dinner (to encourage attendance), presentations on topics such as career options, help that could be expected from various community agencies, infant and toddler development, and recommended parenting strategies. Roneeka told us that she liked hearing about career options from members of the community. "Last time we had one guy that's in our class, his mother, she's an entrepreneur and she came to talk to us," she told us. "She's a caterer. So, we've been having some good topics. They are nice."

Perhaps even more important, parent meetings provided opportunities for the mothers to socialize and compare notes with other mothers and to engage in activities designed to empower them. When asked if she had attended any of the parent meetings, Breanna said, "I like those meetings 'cause they give a lot of information. . . . It's just like people talking and it's fun to see moms and dads and kids just all being together and talking." We asked if her boyfriend attended the meetings and she told us, "Yeah, and Roger [her child's fictive grandfather] too. It's nice, I like those 'cause it brings everybody together. I didn't think Denzel [her child's social father] would like it, but he has, like, maybe one or two people, males, he knows in there with kids."

To empower the mothers, home visitors had them nominate and elect fellow attendees for positions such as chair, vice chair, secretary, and social chair. Roneeka explained, "They are trying to get all the moms involved in being something like a secretary or a social chair. It's different people doing different things. So, they trying to get everybody involved in something instead of us just sitting around listening."

Two other examples of program strategies for empowering mothers and bolstering their self-esteem are contained in Andreya's happy recollections of parent meetings. Recall that while attending one meeting, she was encouraged to speak her mind in front of a group of parents, and at another, she was persuaded to join a group dancing-and-singing activity. Psychological support for the mothers was thus an integral part of the program's efforts in the family development arena.

MOTHER–HOME VISITOR RELATIONSHIP

In the mother–home visitor relationship, six themes emerged as most salient. The first concerned home visitors' struggles to balance the provision of services focused on family development with the provision of services focused more specifically on children's development. A second, related, theme was the pull home visitors felt to spend most of their energy and time on families experiencing crises. In some cases, important but less urgent needs of the mothers and children were ignored. We explore this issue from the perspectives of both the mothers and the home visitors. A third theme centered on the importance of the home visitors' conscientiousness, especially in light of complaints by some mothers that home visitors were not dependable, particularly in the early days of the program. Our fourth theme concerned the individuality of each mother with regard to personality, learning style, and needs. This theme involved the home visitors' efforts to tailor services to meet these individual differences.

A fifth theme involved the tightrope the home visitors walked as they negotiated the line between friend and professional in their relationships with the mothers. As one can imagine, meeting weekly with a young woman and becoming privy to her innermost thoughts and wishes can generate feelings of friendship that may not be entirely appropriate in a relationship that is ultimately service-based and temporary. The mothers, for their part, likewise tended to see their home visitors as somewhere between a professional mentor and close friend.

Our sixth and final theme was closely related to the fifth. It directed our attention to another boundary issue—the risk that mothers will become overly dependent on home visitors. Both the mothers and the home visitors found that it was not always easy to maintain boundaries that would prevent this from happening. Below, we illustrate and elaborate on each of the six themes.

Tensions Between Child Development and Family Support

Recall from Chapter 2 that when the Early Head Start program began, its main focus was on the family development cornerstone; in fact, the job title for the home visitors was Family Development Specialist. When the program emphasis shifted more directly to child development, the home visitor's job title changed to Child and Family Development Specialist. In-service training on child development topics was instituted and considerable staff turnover occurred as new staff members with backgrounds in child development were hired.

As noted by Hebbeler and Gerlach-Downie (2002), especially when families are in a state of crisis, balancing their multiple needs with a focus on child development is a daunting task. This difficulty is exemplified by one home visitor, Nicole, as she described the helpful aspects of Early Head Start for Kyierra. Note that she did not even mention the needs of the child.

"I think that Kyierra seems to really appreciate just having someone to converse with. Also to assist her with those emergency-type needs that I helped her with. I think that kind of popped up quite a bit, especially recently. I think she would have been in dire straits without those emergency services. Although she can at times be kind of shy about asking for help, when she gets it, she's very much appreciative of it. And that has helped her a lot. But we need to really work on her education goals. We went to [community college] and we had filled out the enrollment papers. Everything was set. But it's like she changed her mind. I don't know if she got scared. Another issue was they [the college] wanted some money

up front that she didn't have. We [Early Head Start program] were looking to fund her for that, but I think it was more of an issue of Kyierra getting a little scared about that commitment. Now we're trying to get her back on track with her education. It's definitely something that she wants to do. It's something that she still can benefit from—more skills and training. It can get real depressing if you're not working and you're not going to school. Your self-esteem can go down."

Focusing on Crises Rather than More Routine Events

As explained in Chapter 1, the Head Start Performance Standards for the home-visiting model required the families in Early Head Start to receive four 90-minute visits per month if their children were not in child care. Initially, each home visitor was assigned 14 families, and some families were frequently in a state of crisis and thus required a greater amount of the home visitors' time. (These crises involved everything from job loss and homelessness to partner and child abuse.) It seemed that the families that were more stable received fewer services from their home visitors. A related quantitative research project (also from EHS data) supports that conclusion: The number of minutes the mothers were visited was positively related to their degree of stress-proneness and alienation, as determined by scores on a personality measure (Sharp, Ispa, Thornburg, & Lane, 2003).

As was true of many of the mothers, when Kyierra went to work, she received fewer home visits than she had while she was unemployed, even though her child was not in a center or home-based early childhood program. (Tejon, Kyierra's boyfriend, provided child care while Kyierra was at work.) When asked about her Early Head Start experiences after entering the workforce, she told us, "Well, now I'm always at work so Nicole doesn't really get to come over as much. We see her like every couple of weeks. She doesn't come over that much 'cause I'm always at work." Three months later, when Kyierra was unemployed again, she received more frequent home visits and additional services from Nicole, her home visitor. "She's [Nicole] helped get diapers and things for Jalisa," Kyierra told us. "She took me to the store and that's very good because I really don't have the transportation right now. She's helped in a lot of ways."

Hence, as a family faced a crisis such as unemployment, home visitors provided more services for that family. This inevitably left the home visitor with less time to work with the other families she or he served. Some of the mothers were aware that their home visitors gave much of their attention to families in crisis. "Well, it's all good, but I think you really have to be in a position where you need a lot of help to really get the full benefit of the program," Maria told us when we asked her to evaluate her Early Head Start experience.

For families that were not in crisis but that could have used help to attain goals, the home visitors were often less resourceful. Shardae, for example, had stable housing and reliable transportation and had succeeded in obtaining affordable and suitable child care. Moreover, she worked full time and did not qualify for most public assistance programs. One of Shardae's goals was to return to college, but financial constraints were an obstacle. When Shardae was asked what types of things her home visitor helped her with and if the visits were more child- or family-focused, she replied, "It's more based on Alexis [her child]. Every once in a while we talk about what I might want to do. But my goals are just going back to school, you know. There's only so much you can talk about that until it actually happens."

Before becoming pregnant, Shardae had completed 2 years of college. She dropped out when she was several months pregnant because she had a very difficult pregnancy. Her Early Head Start home visitor did not connect her with appropriate resources to continue her education either part time or full time. Instead, Shardae worked full time from noon to 9:00 P.M. When we asked her how often Marissa (her home visitor) visited her, she consistently downplayed the fact that she did not get very many visits and did not attend the parent meetings. "I don't get off until 9:00 P.M. so I can't [do home visits], and even on Saturdays when they have some of the activities I can't go, I have to work."[3] In a follow-up interview several years after exiting the Early Head Start program, Shardae told us, "Early Head Start was just a job for Marissa. It was just a job." Despite her long and inconvenient working hours, it can be argued that Shardae should have received more attention and services from the program. Marissa could have visited her in the mornings, before she went to work, and could have helped her reenter college to complete her degree. Shardae may then have been in a much better position to find employment that paid a living wage.

The Importance of Being Dependable

We learned that clear and honest presentation of Early Head Start services at the time of recruitment was important for the development of relationships between home visitors and mothers. The mothers in our study were upset when promises were not fulfilled. For example, in the early months of recruitment, when home visitors felt pressure to enroll 150 eligible families (half of whom would be assigned to the compari-

---

[3]A year after Alexis exited Early Head Start because of her age, we learned that Shardae had returned to college at a local campus of a state university. In order to achieve this goal, she returned to living with her mother and applied for and received federal financial aid (Pell grants and work-study funding).

son group), some of the mothers were courted with assurances of slots for their children in an affiliated child care center. When this promise was not fulfilled for many months, the mothers were understandably disillusioned with the program and angry with their home visitors.

Also in the beginning year of program operations, some of the home visitors sometimes missed appointments and did not return phone calls. (Some of these home visitors were among those who were replaced within the first 2 years of the program.) When home visitors did not show up for scheduled home visits, the mothers felt as though they were being stood up. Kyierra, who was dismayed when her home visitor did not come at an appointed time, reported, "I called complaining about [her home visitor]. She didn't come when she said she was going to. She came and she said, 'I am so sorry.' I was like, 'Yeah, right' [sarcastically]." In contrast, the mothers praised the home visitors who were conscientious about keeping their appointments, noting that if they weren't able to come they would call and say so.

The mothers told us that the home visitors' not returning phone calls negatively affected their relationships. They felt that, especially when calls concerned crises, it was important that they be returned in a timely manner. At first, Tanisha was tolerant of her home visitor's lack of responsiveness. She told us that the relationship "could be better, but I guess she's busy and sometimes I do leave messages and she doesn't return them. When I do speak with her she's pretty good with me, but it's hard to catch up with her." In a subsequent interview, however, she made it clear that she was upset by this behavior, "Basically, sometimes when I call her she doesn't return my calls, and that's kind of frustrating because I feel like, okay, they say that they are there for you, so when she doesn't call me back I'm assuming that, 'Are you or are you not there for me?'"

Several months later, Tanisha commented, "She hasn't called me or anything, so I just haven't worried about it." In other words, she had given up trying to get the home visitor to assist her in meeting her needs.

Sometimes, even though the home visitors attempted to keep all of their appointments, it was not possible due to the mothers' high mobility. The mothers took the difficulty in locating them into consideration and were understanding when appointments were not kept because of a recent move or when calls were not received because their phones had been disconnected or their numbers had changed.

Individualizing Approaches to Mothers

Just as excellent teachers vary their teaching methods to suit the learning styles of their students so, too, did the home visitors try to understand the personalities and learning styles of the mothers they worked with to achieve the greatest amount of benefit for them. As they talked to the mothers and played with their children, the home visitors used a variety of techniques to teach the mothers about positive adult–child interactions, appropriate play strategies, disciplinary practices, and a host of other parenting behaviors. Most tried to adjust their intervention strategies to the specific personality and learning styles of the mothers with whom they were working. Research aimed at discovering critical elements of effective home visiting programs strongly supports such individualization (Barnard, 1997; Daro & Harding, 1999; Outreach Partnership, 1999–2000). It is thus appropriate that home visitors used a variety of techniques, including modeling, indirect and direct teaching methods, and provision of printed materials to teach the mothers about child development.

When the relationships between the mothers and their home visitors were new, the mothers seemed to respond best to an indirect, soft approach that allowed them to perceive the home visitor as giving them "food for thought" rather than commands. Commands could be perceived as nagging and/or as intrusive. With time, after the relationships had been solidified, the home visitors could become more directive. Rickie, for example, told us that in the beginning months of his relationship with Andreya, he had been very careful to step lightly—to observe her mood and reactions before deciding what to say. His success in gaining her trust, he told us, was a result of his having been slow, "letting her have her time"—not probing when she did not seem to want to reveal private thoughts—and never being quick to judge or give advice. "Somebody who's quick to say, 'You can't do that; that's wrong' would not work well with her. I mean it has to be more like, you know [softly], 'Well, that didn't work real well, but what do you think about next time?'" In Chapter 4, we saw that he also used affectionate humor as a tool for building his relationship with Andreya.

Earlier we mentioned that Breanna credited Carrie, her home visitor, with having provided her with many examples of good parenting strategies. Carrie used modeling to show Breanna ways to facilitate play. That way she did not have to use a didactic teaching style that Breanna might have perceived as heavy-handed. Breanna explained that Carrie "always brings a toy or Corinna has a toy of her own, or she'll bring a paper. It's got Hide-and-Seek or Peekaboo. Or some game like where you can get two pots and clang them together. Then you sit them down and walk away and Corinna will do the same thing."

Research evaluating strategies for working with parents on child development issues supports Carrie's use of modeling as a tool for teaching. Particularly for mothers with limited education and significant stress, a teaching style that involves simple dispensing of prescriptive information is less effective than more process-oriented and interactive approaches such as modeling and discussion following the mothers' own questions (Barnard, et al., 1988; Booth, Barnard, Mitchell, & Spieker, 1987; Outreach Partnership, 1999–2000).

Varying her teaching methods to suit the learning styles of the mothers, Carrie gave Maria, who had attended some college and whose home life was more stable than Breanna's, pamphlets and articles that she thought would benefit her and her son. Maria did in fact appreciate and learn from these written materials. She told us, "She [Carrie] knows what my strengths and my weaknesses are. She usually gets, like, you know, handouts from books that she's read or will suggest, 'Read this, I think this will help you with prioritizing,' and things like that."

Friend or Professional?

Home visitors' relationships with family members are expected to be professional and temporary rather than personal or friendship-based. However, because home visitors come to know mothers and children intimately in the course of their work, and because they are typically caring people, it is not surprising that it can be difficult for them to maintain a purely professional stance. This is an issue faced by many in the "caring occupations" (DeVault, 1999). While aiming to be a friendly face, a reliable professional, and someone who is trustworthy, the home visitor can find that boundaries are blurred. This can make the "emotional labor" (Hochschild, 1979, 1983) of this occupation challenging. Difficulties exist for both parties. Service providers must be careful to maintain the line between professional and friend. Those being served are also in a delicate position as they must be cognizant that the professional is just that—a *professional*—and not a friend, no matter how warm their relationship becomes.

Understanding when and how much personal information should be shared was an issue for several of the home visitors. When home visitors had personal histories similar to those of the mothers they served, sharing such information seemed to help create a bond between them. One of the home visitors, Marissa, had had her first child when she was a teenager and had personally experienced many of the struggles of the mothers with whom she worked. She told us that she believed her own past helped her to relate to Chandra, "I think we [home visitors] are all good at what we do, but knowing the different staff members . . . I don't, in my opinion, think that that same relationship would have been formed. . . . Chandra and I had some common things in our lives when I was younger and I've shared that with her."

In another instance, Kyierra explained that the kinship she felt with Nicole, her home visitor, was due to the fact that Nicole had recently had her second child, just as Kyierra had, and was dealing with raising two children, just as Kyierra was. "It's just like she can relate a lot, and now she has two children. Me, too," she said. "What makes it easy is that she's going through similar stuff like I am."

Revealing personal information thus had positive consequences for some mother–home visitor relationships. When personal histories did not correspond, however, sharing such information had the potential to push the mother and home visitor apart. What the mothers knew about the home visitors' personal lives could damage their confidence in the validity of the information imparted by the home visitors. For example, Sherryce's view of her home visitor's knowledge was diminished by the fact that her home visitor did not have children of her own. When asked if her home visitor had given her good information about child development, she answered, "Not really, 'cause she don't have any children so it's kind of, she don't know nothin'."

Helping versus Enabling

There is a fine line between *helping* and *enabling*. Helping involves showing support or doing something for someone when there is a problem or task at hand that the person being helped cannot handle. Enabling involves doing something for someone when that person could—and *should*—be doing it herself. One of the beliefs behind this Early Head Start program's family development approach is that although it is important to provide services to families, it is also important to teach parents how to obtain needed services on their own. The idea is to help the parents transition from dependency on the program into becoming comfortable advocates for themselves and their children. Despite the centrality of this belief, the difference between enabling and helping was a challenging issue for home visitors. Examination of the limited literature on emotional labor among home visitors reveals that this problem is not unusual in such programs; staff are often pulled into parents' dependency and have difficulties determining where their responsibility for needy families ends (Ware, Osofsky, Eberhart-Wright, & Leichtman, 1987).

Rickie's recollection of a conversation with his wife regarding Andreya's request to teach her how to drive demonstrates well how hard it can be to make judgments about the line between helper and enabler, "I said to my wife, 'I hate to say this but, you know, your car's small enough . . . it'd be easy to maneuver.' I said, 'Maybe Andreya and I could just go practice driving like two hours on a Sunday or something.'

And my wife said, 'Well, is that kind of stepping over the boundary? Are we going a little bit too far?' And I'm like, 'Well, I don't know because I don't want her to buy a car unless she's got a license. Because then no telling what will happen. And you got tags and insurance.'"

Other home visitors also found it difficult to maintain boundaries. As illustrated in the preceding excerpt, transportation was often an issue for families. Several home visitors told us that they used their own cars to transport mothers to and from parent meetings, to GED classes, and to other places such as social services agencies. Although some of these transportation activities were regular duties of the job, in some cases they seemed to enable mothers rather than help them. For example, Marissa's picking up Chandra and Patrick each morning to take her to GED classes and him to his early childhood program may have crossed the line between helping and enabling. It might have been better to help Chandra learn how to use the public transportation system.

In fact, Chandra, a teenager when she entered Early Head Start, provided a sobering example of what can happen when the home visitor allows the mother to become too dependent. As noted in the vignette below, Marissa described their relationship as "mother–daughter." Although a true mother–daughter relationship was nonexistent in Chandra's life, it was not within the program's mission to provide such a relationship. We would argue that it was also not in Chandra's best long-term interests because of the temporary nature of the mother–home visitor relationship. The following vignette describes Chandra's background and her transition out of Early Head Start as her child, Patrick, reached his fourth birthday.

Chandra

When we met Chandra she was the 17-year-old mother of 10-month-old Patrick, she was homeless, and she had a tenth-grade education. Her second stepmother had tolerated life with Chandra's father for a while so that she could help provide a home for Chandra. Once Chandra turned 17, however, this marriage ended. Not wanting to stay alone with her father, Chandra and her infant son moved into a friend's apartment.

During the 5 years we knew her, Chandra alternately showed a strong desire to be self-sufficient and a responsible mother balanced by a yearning for an unfettered adolescence. There was palpable tension between her love for and enjoyment of Patrick and her feeling that parenting was a burden. She also demonstrated that she felt at a loss as to how to manage many basic tasks. She had a desire for independence and at the same time a desire for someone to hold her hand and arrange for the resources she needed.

Chandra joined Early Head Start at the advice of a cousin soon after Patrick's birth. Marissa, her home visitor, initially thought of her as a "rabbit" because she was so hard to catch, but the more she got to know Chandra, the more determined she was to work with her. In her view, Chandra had two major related issues: the fact that no one seemed to be constant in her life and her low self-esteem.

When we asked Marissa how she would characterize her relationship with Chandra, she chose to describe it as a "mother–daughter" relationship, saying, "I think that it's something that she missed in her life." Thinking that Chandra needed "covering," the home visitor gave her rides to GED classes and child care, took her to get papers signed so that she could get public assistance, drove her to her many attempts to pass the learner's permit test for a driver's license, and even went without her to get her TANF benefits reinstated when Chandra was sanctioned for missing GED classes.

As Marissa provided all of those services for Chandra, she worried that she was enabling her, allowing her to become too dependent. "How do I wean her?" she once asked at a case conferencing session. One example she related had to do with Chandra coming in to the Early Head Start office and asking Marissa to make phone calls for her. "She would come into our office and she would sit at the desk and say, 'Marissa would you call? Will you call for me?' And eventually I told her, 'No, Chandra you need to make this phone call,' you know, and so I would sit right there as she made the call."

Inevitably, the time came for Patrick to "transition out" of Early Head Start. Chandra, alone with Patrick in her apartment, confronted with employers who wanted employees who could work evenings and weekends, wanting to be free to be the teenager she felt herself to be, and no longer buoyed in her mothering by the excitement of the Early Head Start staff about her son, decided that parenting was too much for her. "It's too hard," she told us. "It's too hard emotionally." She asked her second ex-stepmother to take her son. She said he was better off there, getting lots of attention from her half-siblings, going to church, and going to pre-school— all things he wasn't getting with her. She thought that in 2 years, after she had "gotten my life together," she would ask him if he wanted to come back to her. If he refused, she said she would understand. Although Chandra never suggested it, we think the loss of Early Head Start support was a factor in her decision to give up her child. (Patrick was back with Chandra a year later. Her ex-stepmother had grown tired of caring for him and told Chandra to take him back. "I didn't lie in that bed," the stepmother told us.)

CONCLUSIONS

Our interviews made it clear that Early Head Start was an important part of the bioecological system (Bronfenbrenner & Ceci, 1994) of most of the mothers we interviewed. The home visitors provided the mothers with information about child development, helped them to set and achieve personal and family development goals, and guided them in navigating the social services system. As they worked toward those goals, the home visitors had to attend to influences on themselves and on families at several levels: their own and family members' individual characteristics, the mothers' home and child care contexts, the mothers' work situations, cultural expectations, societal norms and policies, and changes over time. We looked at the challenges that became apparent to us at the site we studied as manifestations of the tensions that must be resolved when social service providers try to help their clients within and across these levels. Attention to family development needs had to be balanced with attention to child development needs. The pull to help families in crisis had to be balanced with time for working with more stable families. Problems managing workloads (i.e., balancing all the demands of the job) may have been at the root of some of the problems with dependability. The individual personalities, coping styles, and needs of the different mothers in the home visitors' caseloads had to be considered and appropriately matched with the home visitors' repertoire of skills. Finally, the home visitors walked a fine line between friend and professional in their relationships with the mothers whom they saw often and knew well. Training, resources, and support will help home visitors who are often forced to walk that fine line.

Because this particular program was new and administrators and home visitors were still finding their way, their struggles probably appeared in sharper relief than they would have in a more mature program. We have written this chapter in the hope that awareness of these issues will be instructive, informing the administrators and staff of some of the challenges they are likely to meet as they search for strategies to effectively help children and families living in poverty.

REFERENCES

Barnard, K.E. (1997). Influencing parent–child interactions for children at risk. In M.J. Guralnick (Ed.), *The effectiveness of early intervention* (pp. 249–268). Baltimore: Paul H. Brookes Publishing Co.

Barnard, K.E., Magyary, D., Sumner, G., Booth, C.L., Mitchell, S.K., & Spieker, S. (1988). Prevention of parenting alterations for women with low social support. *Psychiatry, 51*, 248–253.

Booth, C.L., Barnard, K.E., Mitchell, S.K., & Spieker, S.J. (1987). Successful intervention with multiproblem mothers: Effects on the mother–infant relationship. *Infant Mental Health Journal, 8*, 288–306.

Bronfenbrenner, U., & Ceci, S.J. (1994). Nature–nurture reconceptualized in developmental perspective: A bioecological model. *Psychological Review, 101*, 568–586.

Daro, D.A., & Harding, K.A. (1999). Healthy Families America: Using research to enhance practice. *The Future of Children, 9*(1), 152–176.

DeVault, M.L. (1999). Comfort and struggle: Emotion work in family life. In A.W. Heston & N.A. Weiner (Series Eds.) & R.J. Steinberg & D.M. Figart (Vol. Eds.), *The annals of the American Academy of Political and Social Science: Vol. 561. Emotional labor in the service economy* (pp. 39–51). Thousand Oaks, CA: Sage.

Gomby, D.S., Culross, P.L., & Behrman, R.E. (1999). Home visiting: Recent program evaluations—Analysis and recommendations. *The Future of Children, 9,* 4–26.

Hebbeler, K.M., & Gerlach-Downie, S.G. (2002). Inside the black box of home visiting: A qualitative analysis of why intended outcomes were not achieved. *Early Childhood Research Quarterly, 17,* 28–51.

Hochschild, A.R. (1979). Emotion work, feeling rules, and social structure. *American Journal of Sociology, 85,* 551–575.

Hochschild, A.R. (1983). *The managed heart: The commercialization of human feeling.* Berkeley: University of California Press.

Ispa, J.M. (2002). Working with parents: Applying lessons from home visiting evaluations to center-based programs. *International Journal of Early Childhood Education, 8,* 173–193.

Sharp, E.A., Ispa, J.M., Thornburg, K.R., & Lane, V. (2003). Relations among mother and home visitor personality, relationship quality, and amount of time spent in home visits. *Journal of Community Psychology, 31,* 591–606.

St. Pierre, R.G., & Layzer, J.I. (1999). Using home visits for multiple purposes: The Comprehensive Child Development Program. *The Future of Children, 9,* 152–176.

Ware, L.M., Osofsky, J.D., Eberhart-Wright, A., & Leichtman, M.L. (1987). Challenges of home visitor interventions with adolescent mothers and their infants. *Infant Mental Health Journal, 8,* 418–428.

14

Child Care Arrangements

Sheila J. Brookes and Kathy R. Thornburg

Interviewer: Do you feel like her [Tanisha's daughter] child care center is a pretty good place? Do you feel like it is high quality?

Tanisha: It's not high, high quality. . . . I pay $50.00 a week for her day care. It was the cheapest day care I could find.

The government's economic support of child care has increased dramatically since the creation of the Child Care and Development Block Grant in the Omnibus Budget Reconciliation Act of 1990 (Omnibus Reconciliation Act of 1990, 1990). The Personal Responsibility and Work Reconciliation Act of 1996 changed that program by combining all of the previously existing child care entitlement programs (Committee on Ways and Means, 1996). The combined funding stream, the Child Care and Development Fund (CCDF), provides funding to states to help pay child care subsidies for families with low incomes (Archer, 2000). Parental responsibility through choice is one of the key premises behind this block grant (Cohen, 2001). Despite the increased funding and regulations allowing parental choice, parents with low incomes are still faced with few options when it comes to choosing child care arrangements for their young children.

Federal CCDF regulations require child care programs that accept child care subsidies to comply with all state and local licensing requirements (Archer, 2000). These requirements, including adult-to-child ratios, group size limitations, teacher education requirements, and other quality measures, vary from state to state (Cohen, 2001). In fact, parents may choose unlicensed facilities or providers if their state (like the one in which our study families lived) does not impose stricter standards.

Unfortunately, according to two large in-depth observational studies of center and family/relative early childhood programs, the quality of child care is on average poor to mediocre across the United States

267

(Cost, Quality, and Child Outcomes [CQCO] Study Team, 1995; Galinsky, Howes, Kontos, & Shinn, 1994; National Institute on Child Health and Development [NICHD], 2001, 2002). Although a lack of high-quality programs affects all families with children, families with low-to-moderate incomes are affected the most (Helburn & Bergmann, 2003). High-quality programs that do exist are often inaccessible to families because of limited transportation options and an inability to pay for the higher-quality care. Further, there is an availability issue, as there often is a limited supply of high-quality programs in low-income communities.

The well-being of children is affected by the quality of nonparental care they experience (CQCO Study Team, 1995; Galinsky et al., 1994; [NICHD] Early Child Care Research Network, 1999; Shore, 1997), and children from families with low incomes are especially vulnerable to the negative effects of poor-quality child care (Michel, 1999). (For recent reviews of research on child care, see Lamb, 1998; Love, Schochet, & Meckstroth, 1996; Marshall, 2004; National Research Council and Institute of Medicine, 2003.) This "silent crisis" (i.e., the lack of high-quality child care programs in the United States) is likely to explode into a very serious societal problem (Helburn & Bergmann, 2003). Lost productivity for a generation of children spending their early years in poor-quality early childhood programs will no doubt impact the U.S. economy for many years (Blau, 2001; Blau & Tekin, 2001).

In this chapter, we discuss the child care preferences of and options available to the mothers in our study. Understanding what they believe to be the ideal child care arrangement will help us to shape policy to fit the needs of the mothers and their children.

THEMES RELATED TO CHILD CARE PREFERENCES AND OPTIONS

Using the constant comparative approach (Glaser & Strauss, 1967), we analyzed several themes that emerged from the data. These themes included 1) advances and constraints in Early Head Start's influence on the mothers as child care consumers; 2) "mothering" my baby and "schooling" my toddler; and 3) special concerns about health, safety, and consistency.

Advances and Constraints in Early Head Start's Influences on Mothers as Child Care Consumers

Recall from Chapter 2 that Early Head Start regulations changed during the 5 years of our study. Our interviews were conducted before current regulations went into effect requiring Early Head Start children to be in a *high-quality* early childhood setting if they were enrolled in non-parental care while their parents were in school or at work.

Research on child care quality focuses on structural and process indicators (Marshall, 2004). Structural indicators of child care quality include adult-to-child ratios, group size, and teacher training or education. Process indicators of quality include the warmth and sensitivity of the caregivers, the emotional tone of the child care classroom and program, the activities to which children have access, and the developmental appropriateness of those activities.

Early Head Start home visitors spent a great deal of time helping families become acquainted with these indicators so that they could be informed child care consumers. During home visits, the mothers were given both written and verbal information about what to look for when considering an early childhood program for their children. Nicole, Roneeka's home visitor, told us, "Roneeka's goals are to get quality child care for the children. I'm gonna take her a packet on choosing quality child care which has a parent checklist."

Some parents were more receptive to this information than others. Those who credited Early Head Start with teaching them what to look for when they visited early childhood programs tended to choose higher-quality programs than other parents.

Making Do: Settling for Low-Quality Child Care When we first asked the mothers about their child care arrangements, their children ranged in age from newborn to 12 months. At that time, seven of the nine mothers were engaged in work or school, and the other two began school within the following 6–12 months. Of the seven mothers initially using child care, only two had licensed family child care, and both were receiving child care subsidies. The remaining five were using relatives or boyfriends as child care providers and were not receiving child care subsidies even though they may have qualified for this benefit. Perhaps they were put off by state regulations requiring child care providers paid with child care subsidies to undergo criminal background checks. In another study, parents and social workers indicated that this was one reason some individuals who provide child care in their homes discourage parents from applying for state funding. They do not want government agencies "messing in their business" (Brookes, 2002).

Home visitors' efforts to steer parents toward high-quality child care were not always successful. Kyierra, for example, told us that her home visitor, Nicole, "took me downtown. We went to, like, four or five different day care centers one day trying to find day care for the girls." Despite the fact that Nicole had spent a day taking Kyierra to several high-quality child care centers, Kyierra chose to use a license-exempt child care facility of questionable quality. Home visitors expressed their frustration as they attempted to help the mothers choose good programs, only to find out that the mothers continued to leave their children in programs the home visitors considered to be inadequate.

Often, when the mothers chose care that was of questionable quality, it was because access to higher-quality care was too difficult. Roneeka, like other mothers, found transportation to be an obstacle. "Only reason why I didn't wanna really put 'em [her children] up there [Early Head Start child care facility] was because I would have to take the bus all the way, you know, from here to all the way around there, make double trips and then come back this way [to go to school]."

Chandra also told us how important the location of her child care arrangement was. "And the day care is like maybe . . . it's not even that far from [her job]," she said. "So I can still take the highway and take him to day care, and still make it to work on time. My friend takes her kids there, so he [her child] knows some kids there. So I'm just waiting to get a car, and that's it."

Almost all child care centers are open only during typical weekday working hours. This means that for parents working evening, night, or weekend shifts, finding center care is close to impossible. As Sherryce explained, even finding a family child care provider willing to work on the weekends was difficult, "I have to work the weekend now. I might have to change it where I can work my five days just Monday through Friday, because it is hard for me to find somebody to keep him, because nobody wants to stay home on weekends to watch somebody's child."

Further, we were dismayed to discover that despite their low incomes, several of the mothers did not qualify for child care subsidies. The very low income threshold for child care subsidies in the state in which these mothers lived disqualified them from receiving child care subsidies once their income reached 120% of the federal poverty level. This meant that when a mother with one child made more than $6.90 per hour working full time ($14,350 annually), she did not qualify for child care subsidies. Sherryce understood this reality because she earned just over the income cutoff, "Well, to go through the state, to get them to pay for child care and stuff, you have to make six dollars or under. And I don't think that's fair." This limitation forced some mothers to choose child care that was substandard because they could not afford high-quality care. Moreover, the regulations within this state allowed parents receiving subsidies to use care that was unlicensed; even the mothers benefiting from subsidies could choose substandard care.

The mothers who knew that the program they were using was mediocre—or worse—continued to have high expectations of caregivers. They also understood that more money could buy better care.

For example, Tanisha, constrained by severe financial limitations but still unable to qualify for child care subsidies, responded as follows when asked about her daughter's child care center.

Interviewer: Do you feel like [child care] is a pretty good place? Consistent? Do you feel like it's high quality?

Tanisha: It's not high, high quality, but it's, I know, like, I say I pay $50 a week for her day care. It was the cheapest day care I could find. It's in the bottom of a church, but there are good people. They care about the kids and that's all that I was looking for. . . . So I'm comfortable with her being [there]. She is real filthy when she comes home but I know that she had fun. The ideal child care place is a bunch of people, a bunch of staff that wants to be there because they like kids, not just basically for the money. . . . I just prefer them to be more professional as far as looking at the business more professional than what they do.

Interviewer: What about how expensive they are—is that a concern?

Tanisha: That's a problem. I feel that it's expensive, but the more expensive they are the more they care because the more they push the staff to be there for the kids because the parents are paying so much for the kids to go there. Paying more I think is better sometimes in some ways. I'm going to try to see if I can pay more.

Mothers such as Tanisha realized the limitations placed on them by financial constraints, but despite these limitations, they continued to search for programs that reflected at least some level of professionalism. Andreya observed a program for days before placing her child there, thus seeming to give her decision careful thought and consideration. When we observed in the center, however, we saw children wandering aimlessly about the classrooms, teachers yelling at children, children hitting one another, and children eating from one another's plates with teachers seeming to be unaware of what children were doing. Was this program her last resort? It is possible that Andreya noticed these negative qualities but was forced to settle for a lower-quality child care program than she desired. Resignation to low-quality care may be especially true for mothers who have transportation constraints and who must choose centers on the bus route or within walking distance of their homes.

Perhaps the mothers, when forced to settle for child care programs of substandard quality, rationalized the situation and began to see what they wanted to see. Researchers studying the child care evaluations of middle-class parents also found that they tended to overestimate the quality of care their children were receiving (Britner & Phillips, 1995;

Erdwins, Casper, & Buffardi, 1998; Hofferth, Brayfield, Diech , & Holcomb, 1991). These researchers have concluded that parents either do not know how to judge child care quality or cannot admit to themselves that their children are in programs that are less than satisfactory (Cryer & Burchinal, 1997; Hofferth, 1999).

Thus, despite increased funding for child care subsidies and the education parents received via Early Head Start regarding the importance of choosing high-quality child care, many children remained in care that was poor to mediocre, often because of limited options. Ensuring that high-quality care is available in the neighborhoods in which families live and work, and during the hours they work, is vital to making sure that parents have the option to choose high-quality early childhood programs for their young children.

"Mothering" My Baby—"Schooling" My Toddler

We asked the mothers to tell us about the criteria they used when choosing child care and when judging the quality of the child care their children were receiving. The mothers' decisions to use informal care by relatives, friends, or neighbors while their children were infants reflected their belief that nurturing and one-on-one care is essential during the first year of life. Previous studies have similarly shown that parents who use this form of care prefer the intimate familiarity of the caregiver to the benefits associated with regulated care (Brown-Lyons, Robertson, A., & Layzer, 2001; Galinsky et al., 1994).

The woman next door or around the corner, a friend, a cousin, a brother, a grandmother, or a boyfriend—these were the people the mothers preferred as caregivers for their youngest children because, as one mother put it, "I just don't trust anybody." The predominant belief of mothers of infants was that someone they knew was more trustworthy than a stranger who was employed as a professional early childhood teacher. As Tanisha told us, "My boyfriend's been taking care of my daughter and he's been doing a real good job." When asked what makes it hard to find high-quality child care, Tanisha told us, "Finding the right people. I mean, it's the people that you want your child to be watched by, finding the right person to watch your child, [one] that loves kids."

Tanisha thus expressed the same frustrations that many working parents of all socioeconomic statuses experience—finding a provider whom they can trust (Helburn, 1999). As mentioned earlier, the mothers' concerns about the quality of care that was available were well warranted. According to studies of informal care, mothers also have reason to be concerned about the care provided by friends and relatives (Brown-Lyons, Robertson, & Layzer, 2001; Galinsky et al., 1994). We were concerned that initially some mothers preferred care by familiar persons over care in formalized, licensed settings, even when others may have questioned the character or ability of the familiar persons.

However, often as early as the child's second year of life, and definitely before the third year, the mothers shifted their focus to education and, therefore, their preferences began to lean toward more formalized care arrangements. It seemed that they wanted someone familiar to provide a warm, home-like atmosphere for their infants but a professional to "educate" their toddlers to "get them ready for school." As the children entered their second year of life, the mothers went from saying, for example, "I don't let her go without no relatives. She ain't never been without no relative," to expressing a desire for their children to attend formal child care settings. As Shardae told us,

"Lord knows, this lady [current child care provider] that keeps her, she's licensed but she just doesn't keep any other kids. And she does real good with Alexis [Shardae's daughter] and her grandbabies. And she's always teaching them. She has learning activities, but I'd rather have her more like in a classroom atmosphere like my aunt [who has a licensed child care home]. Aunt Ann has them all learning, seated at a table. They take turns. I just want her around a lot more kids too. I can tell she's already getting selfish. She needs to get around other kids." [At the time of the interview, Alexis was 12 months.]

The mothers consistently expressed a desire for their children to begin formal education before or near their second birthday. They feared that their children would fall behind their age-mates if not exposed to other children and given formal instruction by teachers. Sherryce explained the reasoning behind changing her child care arrangements as Michael turned 2.

"So I'm thinking about when Michael turns, you see he ain't turn 2 until next month. But when he turns 2, I want him in a center. I don't want him to be in an in-home [child care] anymore. Because it's [child care center] a lot more kids, and I just feel like they learn better. I mean I'm not saying he's not learning, he's learning a lot where he is, it's just. . . . I just want him to be around a lot more kids because then he'll learn to share more. He is so selfish. He doesn't like to share. There he don't have a choice because it's more than just him."

As these comments from Shardae and Sherryce illustrate, it was not just academic learning that the mothers wanted from child care. As noted in Chapter 10, they also wanted their children to learn social skills—most notably how to share—and they thought that these skills were best learned in child care centers in which there were more peers per classroom than was likely in informal care.

As their children entered formal child care settings, the mothers often attributed typical developmental milestones to their new child care arrangements. Breanna told us, "Everybody in her class is older than her, so I feel she's learning from them. She's talking more. She can climb up things now. Before she started at the day care she couldn't. I think she likes going every day. . . . I think it's nice, it's real nice." (At the time of the interview, Corrina was 19 months.)

When Corrina was 30 months old, Breanna told us, "Miss Delores and Miss Helen are Corrina's teachers. They're like professional. . . . When I look at her, I see how much they've helped her. . . . Like when I've been at work, they're teaching my child." As demonstrated by the mothers' remarks, it was obvious that they perceived child care programs to be a major and positive influence on their children's social and cognitive development. Parents also seemed to believe that the programs were more able or prepared to strengthen the social and cognitive skills of their children than the parents themselves. It was common to hear parents say, "They'll probably teach her more than we're teaching her here."

Some mothers had expectations that were not age-appropriate— for example, they expected child care providers to teach their 12-month-olds to share or their 18-month-olds to be toilet trained. In addition, parents who use poor-quality child care may have had expectations that were unattainable for that care arrangement. After enrolling his daughters in a child care program of questionable quality, Kyierra's boyfriend Tejon told us, "We are sending her to school, they spending a lot of time there, there's a lot of kids. They play, they teach 'em, don't they? In day cares they teach 'em. It's just like school, it's just little school."

It was our impression that the mothers may have given too much credit and/or responsibility to child care teachers and programs. Practitioners who work with low-income families should inform parents of the reality of child care programs (i.e., that most programs in the United States are of poor to mediocre quality, as discussed earlier in this chapter). In addition, it is important for those who work with parents to dispel the myth that parents are less effective teachers than child care providers. Parents should know that regardless of the extent of their education, they are their children's first teachers.

Special Concerns about Health, Safety, and Consistency

Time and again, the mothers made it clear that attention to such special concerns as nutrition, cleanliness, safety, and consistency weighed heavily in their evaluations of the child care programs attended by their toddlers.

Nutritious Meals When the mothers were asked what they looked for in a child care program, meals were consistently mentioned, often as the most important item. LeVine (1988) and his colleagues (LeVine et al., 1994) theorized that when risks to children's health are high, as, unfortunately, is the case in impoverished U.S. inner cities, parents give high priority to "pediatric" goals and strategies—those that protect health and safety. Kyierra exemplified this theory as she explained, "[I want to] make sure that she's eating like she should be." Other questions the mothers consistently asked providers are "How much are you feeding my kid?" "What are you feeding my kid for a snack?" "What types of meals do you provide?"

Yet, after observing several meals in the children's homes, we found it interesting that child care providers in formal settings often were expected to uphold nutritional standards that were higher than those kept at home. In the interview below, Maria indicates her satisfaction with the fact that the food served at the child care center is more nutritionally balanced than the meals served at home.

Maria:	Yeah, I'm very satisfied [with my child care].
Interviewer:	Really? What do you like about it?
Maria:	Because they get good meals. He's getting his breakfast and his lunch, you know, they feed him there. They're not cold lunches, they're hot meals and so the food's really important to me. I like to get his menus. I wanna know what he's eating for lunch. And I really don't have to worry about it because they have an excellent cook there and he makes good breakfasts. I mean, I think Bryce eats better there than he does at home. See Bryce eats a lot of fast food and a lot of, you know, just spaghetti, macaroni, grilled cheese, you know, stuff like that here. But he eats really good there. I mean they give 'em like vegetables, mixed fruit, juice, bread and butter, spaghetti. I'm like, "Gosh, Bryce, I wanna go to school." You know they eat everything. They make 'em Oriental rice with chicken and mixed vegetables.

The contrasting emphasis on nutrition in the home and child care contexts requires further investigation. There may be several reasons for the discrepancy. Some of the young mothers may not have had much experience preparing family meals. Also, it may be that some of the mothers, as was the case with Andreya, were not in charge of their own food stamps and did not have control of food purchases in the home because they lived with relatives who made those choices for them.

Cleanliness   Also in accord with LeVine's thesis (LeVine, 1988; LeVine et al., 1994), when asked what they would look for in a child care program, the mothers consistently mentioned cleanliness.

> Kyierra: [I look at] the neatness of the classroom. [I want to] see
>   if the facility is clean and see if the staff is clean and neat.
>   See if they're ghetto fabulous or not.
> Interviewer: What's that—"ghetto fabulous"?
> Kyierra: Tore up. If they're looking dirty and scrounge. I don't want
>   them kind.

Roneeka also told us that cleanliness was important, "We was looking at the [center] next door to the [school] but they're nasty. And somebody told me that they had roaches. It just really didn't look right, you know. Before I had any kids, I had went and visited. And it just didn't look right as no child care."

After visiting many child care programs in the neighborhoods in which the mothers lived, we began to understand why cleanliness was one of the first things that the mothers looked for when choosing a program. Many of the places were neither clean nor safe. Obviously, an early childhood program site with an insect infestation is neither a clean, nor a safe environment for young children.

Safety   Another part of the reality of the communities in which the mothers lived was neighborhood violence (see Chapter 15). Several mothers mentioned concerns about the safety of children playing outdoors. These concerns are exemplified by the questions Maria told us she asked when she visited child care facilities: "Is there an outside playground? Is it fenced in? Can the kids run out into the street? And say, if there's a drive-by shooter, you know, [can they shoot] into the playground? I mean at [child's] school, the playground's on the inside of the school. I mean it's really neat. So if anything happened on the outside it would not even affect the children. You know, people are shooting outside or cars crashing or anything. That's what I really liked about that center. I was like, 'Oh, this is so safe.'"

Issues of safety were also involved in some mothers' attention to providers' knowledge of first aid and in their evaluations of the physical condition of the child care facility and equipment. Maria explained that she asked potential child care providers to answer the question, "If my child was choking, what would you do? Would you know what to do?" She went on to tell us, "Just safety, I mean I'd look around and make sure there's nothing that will harm my child."

Consistency in Daily Routines   The mothers expressed an understanding of the need for young children to have consistent and regular daily routines in the early childhood setting. When we asked what they looked for in a child care setting, they relayed the importance of daily routines and set activities.

Roneeka: They did activities. They did drawings every day. They did creative activities as far as drawing every day.

Interviewer: At child care, do they do the same thing at certain times of the day?

Roneeka: Yeah. They have her on a schedule.

Interviewer: Did she [provider] keep them in a routine?

Roneeka: Yeah. They napped all at the same time. She had a list of what they did at each time—a daily schedule.

At home, many of the families did not have regular mealtimes or bedtimes for their young children. The mothers told us that they often kept their young infants up until very late at night. Sometimes toddlers did not have regular bedtimes or mealtimes. Thus, the children's schedules in their early childhood settings may have been considerably more consistent than their schedules at home.

Consistency in Child Care Staffing   Another aspect of child care consistency that the mothers greatly valued was consistent staffing. With the high teacher turnover rates that plague child care programs in the United States (Center for Family Policy and Research, 2004; Cohen, 2001; CQCO Study Team, 1995), parents are often faced with a revolving door of caregivers. As one mother told us, "It was always a different person watching her every time I had dropped her off. Or every other week it was always, they hired someone new. I seen different faces and I didn't like that."

CONCLUSIONS

Policy makers can learn much from the thoughts and actions of the mothers we studied. As this is being written, funding for the CCDF is being debated in Congress. How much funding should be allocated? Should there be an increase in funding if TANF (Temporary Assistance for Needy Families) reauthorization requires more welfare recipients to work and to work longer hours? What about the near-poor? Should funding be increased to assist that income group?

High Cost and Little Support

In 26 states there is a waiting list for child care subsidies (Mezey, 2003); moreover, states are serving only one in seven children who qualify for child care subsidies (Ewen & Hart, 2003). According to a recent study, in most areas of the country, families must make twice the federal poverty level ($36,800 for a family of four) in order to have enough income to provide their households with the basic necessities of food, shelter, and health care (National Center for Children in Poverty, 2003). Therefore, many families that do not qualify for child care subsidies are spending an enormous portion of their incomes on child care, *or* they are choosing to use care that is not regulated and perhaps of questionable quality. Low-income families would have a hard time choosing between paying the premium for employer-provided health care and paying for child care.

Increased Parent Education or More Restrictive Regulations?

Would increased parent education regarding the benefits of high-quality early childhood programs help more parents make better choices for the nonparental care of their children? Or, would more restrictive regulations help to solve the child care crisis? According to Helburn and Bergmann (2003), if child care subsidies could only be used for licensed care, more programs would become licensed. This would increase the quality of early childhood programs available to all families and not just families with low incomes. Parents, of course, could still choose unregulated care; but that care could not be paid for with public funds.

Justification for making regulations more stringent and decreasing parental choice could come from the examples set by other government assistance programs. For example, the Special Supplemental Program for Women, Infants, and Children (WIC) provides vouchers only for certain foods that meet specific nutritional requirements, which limits parental choice. Medicaid will pay only for care by physicians licensed to practice medicine, which also limits parental choice. CCDF funds should pay only for child care that meets certain standards. This would limit parental choice, but it also would support future opportunities for children raised in poverty because high-quality care leads to enhanced cognitive and social-emotional development (Lamb, 1998; Marshall, 2004; National Research Council and Institute of Medicine, 2000; NICHD, 2001, 2002).

REFERENCES

Archer, B. (Chairman). (2000). *2000 green book 106th Congress.* Washington, DC: Department of Health and Human Services (WMCP: 106-14).

Blau, D.M. (2001). *The child care problem: An economic analysis.* New York: Russell Sage Foundation.

Blau, D., & Tekin, E. (2001). *The determinants and consequences of child care subsidy receipt by low-income families.* New York: Joint Center for Poverty Research.

Britner, P.A., & Phillips, D.A. (1995). Predictors of parent and provider satisfaction with child day care dimensions: A comparison of center-based and family child day care. *Child Welfare, 74,* 1135–1168.

Brookes, S. (2002). *Welfare reform: How it shapes the lives of infants and toddlers, their families, and their communities.* Columbia: University of Missouri–Columbia, Center for Family Policy and Research.

Brown-Lyons, M., Robertson, A., & Layzer, J. (2001). *Kith and kin—informal child care: Highlights from recent research.* New York: National Center for Children in Poverty.

Center for Family Policy and Research. (2004). *Who's educating Missouri's youngest children?* [Policy brief]. Columbia, MO: Author.

Cohen, S.S. (2001). *Championing child care.* New York: Columbia University Press.

Committee on Ways and Means, U.S. House of Representatives. (1996). *Summary of welfare reforms made by Public Law 104-193: The Personal Responsibility and Work Opportunity Reconciliation Act and associated legislation (WPICP: 104-15).* Washington, DC: U.S. Government Printing Office.

Cost, Quality, and Child Outcomes (CQCO) Study Team. (1995). *Cost, quality, and child outcomes in child care centers, technical report.* Denver: University of Colorado at Denver.

Cryer, D., & Burchinal, M. (1997). Parents as child care consumers. *Early Childhood Research Quarterly, 12,* 35–58.

Erdwins, C.J., Casper, W.J., & Buffardi, L.C. (1998). Child care satisfaction: The effects of parental gender and type of care used. *Child and Youth Care Forum, 27,* 111–123.

Ewen, D., & Hart, K. (2003). *State budget cuts create a growing child care crisis for low-income working families.* Washington, DC: Children's Defense Fund.

Galinsky, E., Howes, C., Kontos, S., & Shinn, M. (1994). *The study of children in family child care and relative care.* New York: Families and Work Institute.

Glaser, B.G., & Strauss, A.L. (1967). *The discovery of grounded theory: Strategies for qualitative research.* Chicago: Aldine.

Helburn, S.W. (Ed.). (1999). *The silent crisis in U.S. child care.* Thousand Oaks, CA: Sage.

Helburn, S.W., & Bergmann, B.R. (2003). *America's child care problem: The way out.* New York: Palgrave Macmillan.

Hofferth, S.L. (1999). Child care, maternal employment, and public policy. In S.W. Helburn (Ed.), *The silent crisis in U.S. child care* (pp. 20–38). Thousand Oaks, CA: Sage.

Hofferth, S.L., Brayfield, A., Diech, S., & Holcomb, P. (1991). *The national child care survey, 1990.* Washington, DC: Urban Institute Press.

Lamb, M.E. (1998). Nonparental child care: Context, quality, correlates. In W. Damon, I.E. Sigel, & K.A. Renninger (Eds.), *Handbook of child psychology: Vol. 4. Child psychology in practice* (5th ed., pp. 73–134). New York: Wiley.

LeVine, R.A. (1988). *Human parental care: Universal goals, cultural strategies, individual behavior.* In R.A. LeVine, P.M. Miller, & M. Maxwell (Eds.), *Parental behavior in diverse societies* (pp. 3–12). San Francisco: Jossey-Bass.

LeVine, R.A., Dixon, S., LeVine, S., Richman, A., Leiderman, P.H., Keefer, C., & Brazelton, T.B. (1994). *Child care and culture: Lessons from Africa.* Cambridge, UK: Cambridge University Press.

Love, J.M., Schochet, P.Z., & Meckstroth, A.L. (1996). *Are they in any real danger? What research does—and doesn't—tell us about child care quality and children's well-being.* Princeton, NJ: Mathematica Policy Research.

Marshall, N.L. (2004). The quality of early child care and children's development. *Current Directions in Psychological Science, 13,* 165–168.

Mezey, J. (2003). *GAO finds state child care assistance limits disproportionately impact low-income, working, non-TANF families and children.* Washington, DC: Center for Law and Social Policy.

Michel, S. (1999). *Children's interests/Mother's rights: The shaping of America's child care policy.* New Haven, CT: Yale University Press.

National Center for Children in Poverty. (2003). Low-income children in the United States. Retrieved September 2003, from http://www.nccp.org/pub_cpf03.html

National Institute of Child Health and Development (NICHD) Early Child Care Research Network. (1999). Child outcomes: When child care center classes meet recommended standards of quality. *American Journal of Public Health, 89,* 1072–1077.

National Institute of Child Health and Development (NICHD) Early Child Care Research Network. (2001). Nonmaternal care and family factors in early development: An overview of the NICHD study of early child care. *Applied Developmental Psychology, 22,* 457–492.

National Institute of Child Health and Development (NICHD) Early Child Care Research Network. (2002). Child-care structure process outcome: Direct and indirect effects of child-care quality on young children's development. *Psychological Science, 13,* 199–206.

National Research Council and Institute of Medicine, Committee on Integrating the Science of Early Childhood Development, Board on Children, Youth, and Families. (2000). *From neurons to neighborhoods: The science of early child development* (J.P. Shonkoff & D.A. Phillips, Eds.). Washington, DC: National Academies Press.

National Research Council and Institute of Medicine, Division of Behavioral and Social Sciences and Education, Board on Children, Youth, and Families, Committee on Family and Work Policies. (2003). *Working families and growing kids: Caring for children and adolescents* (E. Smolensky & J.A. Gootman, Eds.).

Washington, DC: National Academies Press. Retrieved July 1, 2004, from http://www.nap.edu/openbook/0309087031/html/R1.html

Omnibus Budget Reconciliation Act of 1990, PL 101-508, 42 U.S.C. §§ 1395cc *et seq.*

Shore, R. (1997). *Rethinking the brain: New insights into early development.* New York: Families and Work Institute.

15

Violence

Kathy R. Thornburg and Sheila J. Brookes

The News
On hearing
that twelve
children
die
by handguns
each day
in the U.S.A.
my son,
aged six,
says, "I'm
glad we
don't
live there."

© *Maxine Chernoff*

The families that participated in our study, unlike the child in the poem above, spend their everyday lives in the urban core. This is an environment that has more murders, more burglaries, more domestic violence, more arson, more child maltreatment, more rapes—more violence overall—than is found in rural and suburban areas.

Homicide is the leading cause of death for African American males ages 15–34 (Anderson, 2002). According to predictions based on mortality data from the nation's counties with the largest number of African American citizens, the percentage of African American males who will be murdered before the age of 45 ranges from 2% to 8.5% (U.S.

Census Bureau, 1999). With statistics such as these, neighborhood violence undeniably affects many families living in these communities.

In the large midwestern city in which the families in our study lived, there were between 84 and 116 murders annually during the years we conducted this research (Police Department Reports, 1996–2002). Between 47% and 62% of those murdered during these years were African American males, yet African American males made up only 14% of the population (U.S. Census Bureau, 2004).

This chapter is divided into two sections in order to examine both the etic ("outsider") and the emic ("insider") perspectives. First, we will examine the outsiders', or etic, point of view relating to community violence and the impact it has on children, families, and communities. An *outsider* is defined as one who does not live in the community and/or who does not experience the societal issues, including violence, associated with poverty. These individuals do not have the lived experience of dealing with the community's violence in the same manner as the families who reside there. Our analyses led us to one major conclusion about the role played by the outsiders: They were striving to make a difference.

Then we will explore the effects of community violence on families from the emic, or insiders', perspectives. *Insiders* are those who have the lived experience dealing with violence within the community on a daily basis. The emic point of view came from mothers, fathers, grandparents, other relatives, and friends. As the data were analyzed, three themes regarding insiders emerged: 1) violence was relatively pervasive in their lives, 2) they tended to downplay the seriousness of violence, and 3) they were very protective of their sons and daughters.

VIEWS OF OUTSIDERS

Below, we review the theme that emerged from our data pertaining to outsiders' views of violence. The outsiders in this analysis were police department administrators, city officials, and other at-large community leaders. In addition, for several years we collected local daily newspapers, analyzing the content related to the specific neighborhoods in which the mothers in our study lived.

Striving to Make a Difference

Community leaders, including neighborhood association officers, clergy, and police, were concerned about crime in the urban core and were aware that a systemic change was needed.

"We can't throw police at the situation and hope that things get better. Unless we can give those young people some reassurance, then we are just spinning our wheels."

—president of a neighborhood association, April 1997

Our analysis of newspaper stories found that this city was actively working to help impoverished neighborhoods become safer places to raise children. As Corrina, Patrick, Regina, Bryce, and Michael were turning 1 year old, city officials were taking advantage of public and private dollars and partnerships to decrease crime in their neighborhoods and to foster positive development such as economic growth and cultural/recreational activities. Samples of newspaper headlines at the time read

- Loan Programs Aimed at Black Entrepreneurs (February 1997)

- Over 150 Community and Neighborhood Activists, Police, Prosecutors, and Gang Members Met to Develop Solutions (April 1997)

- Neighborhoods Join Together to Fight Against Residential Crime by Taking Part in a Night Out Against Crime (July 1997)

- Restored Movie House Helps Breathe New Life into 63rd and Lancaster (August 1997)

- University Will Offer Practical Help to City's Core (September 1997)

Crime-Reducing Initiatives

During this period, many urban areas across the country were developing new programs to reduce crime, and our study city was no exception. In 1998, police and city-sponsored programs helped cut crime in many areas. In fact, this midwestern city was one of just a few that received federal grant monies to support new program initiatives and activities, including

- Police and teen basketball teams

- Crime Stoppers

- Neighborhood associations working with police and businesses

- Community policing

- Antidrug programs

- Prosecutors and parole officers in police patrol divisions

- A city and light company agreement to double the number of streetlights in 4 years

- Support to clean up vacant lots
- City officials conducting neighborhood assessments to determine what residents wanted in their communities
- Federal money to complete a downtown civic mall

It was obvious to us that city officials and community members wanted to make their city a better place for all to live. Other proposed solutions included closing liquor stores on Sundays, replacing multifamily housing with single-family homes, forcing landlords to repair housing that had code violations, and encouraging stronger ties between the police and the community.

VIEWS OF INSIDERS

In this section, we present the three themes related to insiders' views of violence. The insiders in this analysis are, of course, the parents, brothers, boyfriends, other relatives, and friends of the nine mothers.

The Pervasiveness of Violence

The public hears about murders in large American cities, about innocent people being killed by stray bullets from gang shootings, and about children killing children. In communities with high rates of violence, family members experience chronic stress and worry, often leading to posttraumatic stress disorder (PTSD; Goguen, 2004; Linares, 2004).

Breanna's Story: Shootin' Down at the Crowd

There was some girls about to start fighting. One of the girls was about to fight her boyfriend and kicked the dude. But they were about to start fighting . . . and then somehow they broke up. And the dude stepped on the girl's foot and this girl got to talking crazy to this dude. And, then everybody started walking away from that. And [then] the dude got on top of his truck and start shooting down at the crowd. Just shootin'. He was shooting at her. I was not too far from all of this and like . . . we was all right here. The dude started shooting from right here where the car was [and shot an innocent bystander]. It was sad [describing the crowd's reaction to the scene]. . . . As he [the victim] was laying down on the ground, people was going in his pockets, taking his money. . . . They were grown men taking stuff out of his pockets . . . 'cause when they first went up, they laid him on his back . . . he got shot somewhere in his head. And he got to choking on his blood. . . . I thought it was a friend of mine, so I went back over there but I seen that it wasn't. But they were like screaming and hollering and I'm like, 'Well, hey, everybody. . . . Be quiet everybody. Talk to him. What's his name?' And so one of his friends came over there. He was panicking. I'm telling him, 'Well, call his name. Talk to him. Ask him questions. See if he's all right.' He wasn't saying nothing, but he was trying and he was on his [the victim's] side. . . . [The] friend was going to go get the cell phone and call the police. When we left [the victim] was dead and they were just waiting on the ambulance to come and get him, 'cause he died right there. We seen him. I seen him die. We seen him die.

Recall that the nine mothers in our study were part of a larger study. When their children were about to enter kindergarten, 76 mothers in the same community responded to a questionnaire about violence in their lives. Of the 76, 24% reported that they had been hit, kicked, or pushed by a boyfriend. While pregnant, Kyierra was severely beaten by her boyfriend (her child's father). She was not alone, as 5% of the mothers in our study had also been badly beaten by a boyfriend or husband. Because of past abusive relationships, Kyierra placed great value on the fact that her current boyfriend Tejon never threatened her physically. Her mother, who had experienced abuse from a former boyfriend, also did not take domestic peace for granted. She seemed to think this quality was reason enough to love Tejon, "I'll tell you why Kyierra told me she's with him. She says she loves him, which I honestly believe she does love him. She says she's used to him. She don't have to put up with no beatings. If he has something to say, he leans out the door and says it. Kyierra's told me that. If he has a problem or if he feels like it he gets up off the couch and goes out the door. I mean what more could you ask. He doesn't lay a hand on my daughter."

As noted previously, Andreya had been sexually assaulted as a child by one of her mother's boyfriends. Again, this was an all-too-common occurrence, with 9.2% of the mothers reporting that they had been sexually assaulted at some time in their young lives. The stories of violence continued until our last interviews, with some mothers reporting additional episodes when they were threatened or attacked with a weapon, or witnessed the assault of others. Andreya reflected the regrets and fears that come with living in a neighborhood in which violence is pervasive, "I wish I never would have brought no kids up in this world. So many crazy things be happening. . . . There's so many crazy people out here, you don't know who to trust. You hear so much stuff on the news; it's just crazy. You are scared to open your door at night."

Breanna, who moved more often than any of the other mothers, described some of the areas in which she lived. Although the houses were in the same general vicinity, some of the neighborhoods were more violent than others. In describing the neighborhoods she liked best, Breanna often referred to safety conditions. She liked 65th Street because it was not like "56th street where you hear arguing, you see fighting, guns, and drugs." One house was close to a park and that was not necessarily a good thing because, according to Breanna, "The park over there is really dirty. You'd see beer bottles and needles on the ground and stuff when I took Corrina over there to swing on the swings. You see lots of drunks walking around here. . . . I feel unsafe at night."

Breanna was satisfied with a house on East 44th Street. She liked it "a lot better, that's why we're gonna stay out here." Once again, she thought it was a better place to live because she could not hear the firing of guns and no one was "out there fighting."

At the time Andreya's sons Lavell and Kevon were born, violent crime was on the decline in the study city. In fact, since the boys' births, the community had seen a 31.8% decrease in violent crime, including a 25% decrease in the number of murders of African American males. Statistics were meaningless, however, to Andreya, Lavell, and Kevon when Andreya's younger brother, Tony (age 22), was murdered on April 30, 2002. One of the saddest moments of our study came on the day we visited Andreya's mother Patricia a month after her son was killed. It was about 3:00 in the afternoon when we visited, but Patricia was still in her nightgown, sitting in the living room with blinds drawn, no lights on—the very picture of despair.

Tony was not just a statistic, he put a face on the statistics. Patricia and Andreya loved him. He was Patricia's youngest son, the one she so wanted to keep out of jail because that was where her other son was. Nevertheless, Patricia and Andreya had both known for a few years that he was "hanging with the wrong crowd." Patricia had made many attempts to stop him from going out at all hours with questionable associates, but the lure of the streets and a fast buck, and the influence of so-called friends, brought him closer and closer to danger. His progression downward began with expulsion from school, followed by time served in a juvenile detention facility. Finally, and fatally, he was in the wrong place at the wrong time.

Many fathers and uncles were not available to the children in our study because they were in jail or prison for drug offenses, robbery, assault, and attempted murder. The children also were victims because they missed out on contact with their fathers and uncles. Breanna, Roneeka, and Andreya shared a common bond although they had never met: They each had two male siblings in prison at the same time. And Breanna and Andreya both lost brothers to murder within months of each other. Statistics showing a decline in murders in the community that year did not ease the reality that Breanna and Andreya faced: the traumatic loss of a loved one at a young age.

Downplaying the Seriousness of Violence

We noted a tendency among some of the mothers to minimize or downplay the seriousness of the violence they experienced or witnessed, perhaps because it was their way of coping. Maria's thoughts regarding an incident when her son's father, Marcus, assaulted her is illustrative.

"I was doing a regular visit with Bryce's father . . . and he got upset because he had wanted me to stay longer and it was getting late for me. I wanted to go home, I was tired. He got upset and you know . . . some violence took place. His mom, and she had a niece and nephew there, saw the whole thing and they didn't help me. So, when I came home I called the police and the police went ahead and arrested him that night. They charged him with adult abuse. . . . But he didn't hurt Bryce or anything like that."

Despite reporting the assault to the police and pressing charges against Marcus, Maria requested that the court be lenient, "I had requested no jail time . . . [but] a judge is going to decide what he wants to do anyway. So this judge was like, 'You're going to jail for 3 months for what you did.'" Maria reported that after the sentencing, and despite the assault and even though she had a restraining order against Marcus, she began to bring Bryce over to see Marcus again.

"I feel like I'm putting myself in a [bad] position, but he hasn't threatened me physically and I'm not scared of that anymore. I think I scare him more than I'm afraid of him now. . . . I was with him for 2½ years and I didn't expect any kind of an action like he took. . . . He's been really, like, harassing me, [saying], 'I want to see my son. Please, please, please.' He had court-ordered visitations but they were supervised. He didn't want to do that and he said, 'I don't feel I need to be supervised. I would never hurt the baby.' He didn't want my mom to supervise. Because he's like, 'Well, your parents hate me and I just can't stand to be in the same room as them.' So against my better judgment and the better judgment of my [family], I went over there with somebody else. I didn't go by myself."

Thus, Maria downplayed the assault and continued to place herself and Bryce in a tenuous situation.

Tanisha provided another example of downplaying when asked about her boyfriend's imprisonment. "He is in jail," she said. "I mean it wasn't anything bad. He had just got into some trouble as far as a shooting incident I'm thinking with someone on a highway. He was shooting someone and they were shooting. Well, he was riding with someone in his car but one of his friends was shooting somebody on the highway. They all got in trouble . . . he had to do time for that."

These incidents point out that the mothers' definition of safety and concerns about violence were surprisingly different from ours, contributing to our initial difficulty finding the right questions to ascertain their lived experiences. Before conducting this research, we had read about murders, drive-by shootings, rapes, and so forth in the local newspaper, and we had seen reports on urban core crime on the nightly newscasts. We knew the crime statistics associated with this community. Nevertheless, when we first asked the mothers about the effects of violence on their lives, almost unanimously they responded that violence did not affect them. We asked, "Do you have any violence in your life?" and we were repeatedly told that they did not. When we asked, "Have you ever lived where you think the neighborhood has been unsafe?" we were told, "Nowhere that I felt unsafe."

When we explored the topic of violence further over time, we discovered that the mothers' definition of a safe neighborhood was far different from ours. For example, a safe neighborhood to them might mean that nightly shootings did not occur on *their* block or that they did not hear gunshots *every* night. For example, in one of our first interviews, Andreya told us how she went to the store via a certain street, not via another street that seemed dangerous to her. These streets were mere blocks away from each other. Was she really safer or was this a misperception?

When we asked Shardae how safe she felt, she responded that she felt safe because of the places she went. She said that the majority of her outings were to child care settings and to work. The only other places that she frequented were the grocery store, the Laundromat, and, every once in a while, a restaurant. Chandra described a party that she attended, the details about what she wore, how she fixed her hair, and the cost of the party ($5.00). Her final statement was, "It was real fun, there was no fighting or shooting."

The mothers often perceived that they were safe when there were no direct threats to themselves or their children. When drug dealing, drive-by shootings, and prostitution are a daily reality within one's community, the scope of one's "neighborhood" seems to be more discretely delineated in order to have the perception that those crimes do not occur in one's own neighborhood. According to Garbarino, Dubrow, Kostelny, and Pardo, there are "two senses of the term danger" (1998, p. 4): objective and subjective. Objective danger refers to the real likelihood that an event will occur, whereas subjective danger refers to the perception of imminent harm (i.e., the feeling that harm may come). It seems that there was a higher level of objective danger than the mothers admitted to us or to themselves. People tend to misperceive the threat of danger when the objective threat is high and the threat seems clear (Garbarino et al.). Thus, because the mothers had lived their entire lives within communities riddled with violence, the threat was neither mysterious nor low, and they grew to be comfortable within what others would define as an uncomfortable setting.

Responsibility of the Victim The mothers and family members tended to view their murdered loved ones as victims. Yet they also told us that their children were "mixed up with the wrong crowd," were "in the wrong place," or were "with the wrong people." It could be argued that being in the wrong place or with the wrong people is not purely happenstance. When someone is murdered, he is likely to be with people he knows or has had some connection with at the time of the murder. Thus, the murders of the brothers of Andreya and Breanna were not random, accidental shootings but crimes purposefully committed.

The tendency of family members to whitewash their loved ones' involvement in their own deaths seemed to be related to the perhaps universal inclination to idealize those who have died. In a telephone conversation, Andreya told us that she thought the police were not attempting to find and prosecute her brother's killers because they were always lax when it came to "Black on Black crime." The police had told her mother that they viewed the murder as due to a "dispute between the boys." (As of November 2003, approximately 1½ years after the murder, the police had not arrested any suspects for Tony's murder.) Andreya, however, did not agree with that assessment because although her brother had had his gun with him, he did not shoot at the killers and "Tony would never hurt anybody."

We were touched by the coping strategy Lavell and Kevon (Andreya's sons) created for themselves. A few months after the shooting, they told us that their uncle was on the moon. Andreya explained that her boys had made up this story, and that it was comforting to them. In the evenings, they would sometimes all go outside to look up at the moon and remember the good times they had with Tony.

Protecting Their Sons and Daughters

"There's worry and great pain in being the mother of a boy in the urban core," Andreya once told us. There is no doubt that Andreya's son Lavell was influenced by what he saw in his own home and neighborhood.

When looking at a picture of a fire truck, he asked, "Where is it going to take me?" When it was explained to him that it would go to a fire, he said, "No, take me to jail."

Coping with community violence while parenting a young child was a daily experience for all of the mothers, and for several of them, surviving the loss of loved ones due to homicide was an additional burden. As their children approached school age, the mothers of boys expressed the fear that, despite their attempts to protect their sons, they would, for example, "meet a friend in school and get around their neighborhood or something." Recall from Chapter 10 that some of the mothers had an almost fatalistic attitude toward their sons' futures, expressing concern that they would not be able to protect them through their adolescence.

When pregnant, a few of the mothers had hoped to have boys. We heard comments such as "I think it would be much easier 'cause I'd rather have a boy bouncing off the walls than a girl coming home telling me she's pregnant." Nevertheless, within the next few years all expressed anxiety about raising boys. We heard the same thoughts expressed by grandparents. Both generations realized that it was difficult to raise boys when male role models were not available. As Patricia, who had two sons in jail, told us, "Boys will be boys, and if you try to tame them, they'll just go wilder. They have to learn from their mistakes" (see Chapter 5). The mothers in our study started worrying about their sons before the boys turned 2. Roneeka commented that "Boys are gonna be boys. They gonna do what they want to do regardless of what their mother says or if it has to be sneaky you know. I'll bring him up the best way I can . . . try not to get out there and live that fast lane, drug life or you know jail life. All it's gonna do is wind you up in one of two places—death or jail. So I will try my best to teach him." (Roneeka had three brothers, all of whom were in and out of prison during the 5 years we interviewed her.)

Raising boys and girls in African American families was a topic at one of the Early Head Start meetings. Rickie, Andreya's home visitor, explained to us how he presented culturally sensitive information to mothers to help them break the cycle of violence for their sons.

"We've had a lot of talks about culture. We had talked about how African American families feel about their sons and their daughters. And we were talking about that one day and I was explaining about how [mothers believe] the son can do no wrong and whatever they do is okay just as long as they're still alive and making it through the day. I was saying that and how moms are so hard on their daughters because they have to also help with those sons to make sure those sons do right, and I mean, Andreya, it just like a big lightbulb went

*off. She's like, 'That's my mom!' And then she just said many, many times,
'That's my mom! That is exactly what she did with Quintus and what she's
doing with Tony.' She really sees that and she doesn't want to blame her mom.
Yet she knows that her mom learned from her mom. And that it's just a cycle, and
Andreya wants so bad not to raise sons that will end up in any type of system. I
think that's why she is so willing to listen to what I have to say about . . . however touchy the subject may be. I just keep speaking about it."*

It is easy to understand why all of the mothers were worried about their
sons. The despair they experienced over the murders of their brothers,
the fathers of their children, and their uncles and cousins was all too
common.

"If I ever have a baby, God, please let me have a girl," Roneeka
once said. And although the mothers also worried about their daughters, their violence-related concerns centered not on violence that the
girls might perpetrate, but on the possibility that they might become
the victims of violence. They worried about the violence in public
schools, which were considered to be unsafe. As one mother told us, "I
don't want her in an inner-city school. It's too rough." In addition, several mothers had been witnesses or victims of domestic violence during
childhood and worried that their daughters might experience this as
well. As noted in Chapter 10, the mothers' fears for their daughters'
safety led many to teach their daughters to be independent and self-
sufficient so that they could better protect themselves.

We also were aware of female family members who participated in
illegal or violent activities. One female cousin of a mother was in jail for
selling drugs, and Andreya told us of a physical fight that she had had with
Sonya, a girlfriend of the father of her children. Although there were fights
and drug usage among some of the females, it seemed that women were
far less likely than men to have guns or engage in drug dealing. According
to a study city police report, on average, during the 5 years of this study,
14% of the murder victims in the city were African American females,
but few of the murders were committed by African American females.

Parenting While Coping with Tragedy

Breanna's brother Terral, who was just one year younger than she, was murdered
a few blocks from their house late on a Saturday night. Was it drug-related? We
never found out because when we tried to find out if the case had been solved,
the police could not locate Terral in their database.

A very important person in the life of Breanna's daughter Corrina, the man she
had known as "Daddy" from birth, was there to help her through the terrible days,
weeks, and months after her Uncle Terral was murdered. When we asked Breanna

who the most important men in Corrina's life were, she always listed Denzel first. And when we asked about the relationship between Denzel and Corrina, Breanna told us, "Well, Denzel, he's been there ever since Corrina was born. Yeah, ever since I was pregnant, he was there. . . . He loves her. He takes care of her. He's her dad. He's her father."

Breanna and Denzel were romantic partners for 3 years. Even after they were no longer romantically involved, Denzel saw Corrina almost every day.

Nine months after Uncle Terral was murdered, we called Breanna. "I am so sad," she told us. "I have a funeral this afternoon—Denzel was stopped at a light on Tuesday and someone put a gun to the back of his head and killed him. . . . Why did Corrina have to lose the two most important men in her life?"

On November 18, 2003, we learned that a suspect had been charged with Murder One in the death of Denzel Travis. The last time we talked to Breanna she was still recovering from her losses, which occurred just prior to Corrina entering kindergarten. That first year of school was hard for Corrina—she couldn't concentrate and was often absent. That year was hard for Breanna too. Often, she just could not get up in the morning and face another day.

CONCLUSIONS

Violence has a direct effect on its victims, but most of the children in our study were no less victimized, even if indirectly. Violence has been shown to affect cognitive, social, and emotional functioning, and even when children are not the direct victims, they are affected by community violence (Margolin & Gordis, 2004). Community violence threatens the very core of what we as a society believe that children need to grow up to be healthy, productive adults. Childhood is considered a special period in which children feel protected and safe. This sense of safety begins during the prenatal period when children are safe from outside elements and continues into infancy and early childhood when the home provides a safe haven, allowing the child to grow and develop and to feel loved and nurtured. As children grow up, their safe havens should include their neighborhoods, early childhood settings, and schools (Garbarino et al., 1998). However, when chronic danger is a part of the community, children's ability to explore their world, to grow, and to develop is affected. Growing up in a community plagued by chronic violence uproots the quintessential safety that children need.

The safety of their children was of the utmost importance to all of the mothers in our study. And although violence affected their lives almost on a daily basis, it was clear to us that the mothers coped and were careful without overly alarming their children.

It is a regrettable reality that children in the United States are exposed to or are victims of violence at alarming rates. Each year, between

3.3–17.8 million children witness a physical assault between their parents (Carlson, 2000), 1.1 million children are substantiated victims of child maltreatment (Prevent Child Abuse America, 2004), 22% of all victims of violent crime in the United States are children, and 71% of all sex crime victims are children (Children's Defense Fund, 2001). Furthermore, 1 in 18 victims of violent crime and 1 in 3 victims of sexual assault are under the age of 12. Children who experience violence are more likely to commit violent crimes in adolescence and adulthood. Therefore, early intervention in conjunction with increased efforts to decrease community violence is needed. Professionals working with young children and their families must be adept at helping families cope with the violence that permeates their lives in order to help them overcome the negative impact of this exposure. PTSD, depression, poor school achievement, anxiety, anger, and substance abuse have all been linked to exposure to violence (Berkowitz, 2003). Vulnerable children living in impoverished communities are already at increased risk and are thus more likely to be affected by exposure to community violence. At the same time, it is unrealistic to think that early intervention alone can be effective for children who continue to live in objective or subjective danger. We must focus efforts on both helping the children and families to cope with the very real dangers in their community *and* working to ameliorate these dangers by improving the safety of urban core communities.

REFERENCES

Anderson, R.N. (2002). *Deaths: Leading causes for 2002. National vital statistics report, 50*(16). Hyattsville, MD: National Center for Health Statistics.

Berkowitz, S.J. (2003). Children exposed to community violence: The rationale for early intervention. *Clinical Child and Family Psychology Review, 6* (4), 293–302.

Carlson, B.E. (2000). Children exposed to intimate partner violence: Research findings and implications for intervention. *Trauma, Violence, and Abuse, 1*(4), 321–340.

Chernoff, M. (2002). The news. In V. Suarez & R.G. Van Cleave (Eds.), *Like thunder: Poets respond to violence in America.* Iowa City: University of Iowa Press.

Children's Defense Fund. (2001). *The state of America's children.* Washington, DC: Children's Defense Fund.

Garbarino, J., Dubrow, N., Kostelny, K., & Pardo, C. (1998). *Children in danger: Coping with the consequences of community violence.* San Francisco: Jossey-Bass.

Goguen, C. (2004). *The effects of community violence on children and adolescents.* Retrieved July 20, 2004, from the U.S. Department of Veterans Affairs: National Center for PTSD Web site: http://www.ncptsd.org/facts/specific/fs_child _com_viol.html

Linares, L.O. (2004). *Community violence: The effects on children.* New York: NYU Child Study Center.

Margolin, G., & Gordis, E.B. (2004). Children's exposure to violence in the family and community. *Current Directions in Psychological Science, 13*(4), 152–155.

Prevent Child Abuse America. (2004). *Frequently asked questions about child abuse.* Retrieved July 21, 2004, from Prevent Child Abuse America web site: http://www.preventchildabuse.com/abuse.htm

U.S. Census Bureau. (1999). *Population estimates program, population division, "Counties ranked by Black population in 1998"* (Table CO-98-16). Washington, DC: Author.

U.S. Census Bureau. (2004). *American factfinder.* Retrieved July 16, 2004, from http://factfinder.census.gov

V

Implications for Researchers, Practitioners, and Policy Makers

16

Improving the Lives of Children and Families Living in Poverty

Kathy R. Thornburg, Linda C. Halgunseth,
Sheila J. Brookes, Jean M. Ispa, Mark A. Fine, and Elizabeth A. Sharp

In this book, we have used bioecological (Bronfenbrenner, 1999) and feminist (Thompson, 1992; Wuest, 1995) frameworks to understand and describe the lives of nine young mothers and their relationships with family members, romantic partners, friends, and neighbors.

Bronfenbrenner's theory allowed us to acknowledge and balance the many contexts influencing the mothers' lives: macro-level influences, such as state and national policy, as well as the interplay of community, family, and individual variables. Over a 5-year period, we asked questions of and learned from the mothers themselves; their biological and social parents; their aunts, uncles, and cousins; their children; their children's biological and social fathers; their Early Head Start (EHS) home visitors; their friends and neighbors; their teachers; and their community leaders. Our quest to understand both direct and indirect influences on the lives of the nine participating families included interviews with and observations of more than 100 individuals.

Our data collection also was guided by feminist theory. We were interested in learning about the daily, lived experiences of a group of individuals who are marginalized in U.S. society—African American, single young mothers living in poverty—and we wanted to hear how they interpreted the circumstances and events that occurred in their lives. We also were mindful of the fact that feminist theory prompts researchers to consider the practice and policy applications of their findings.

In this chapter, we draw on the themes identified in preceding chapters to arrive at implications for practice, policy, and future research.

We focus on nine components of the experiences of the mothers and family members that seemed to have particular relevance for their well-being: employment, Temporary Assistance for Needy Families (TANF), child care, transportation, housing, health care, food and nutrition services, EHS, and child-rearing practices. In the following sections, we have grouped the components into three broad categories: Supports for Work, Supports for Basic Needs, and Supports for Child and Family Development. For each component, we first briefly present key family needs that became clear to us as we conducted our study and that have often been corroborated in other research. We then offer suggestions for practitioners and identify programs in need of evaluation. Finally, we briefly describe current relevant governmental policies and propose, when appropriate, modifications and evaluation. As illustrated in Figure 16.1, we conceptualize research, practice, and policy as interlinking mechanisms essential for improving conditions for families in poverty. Each must inform the others.

SUPPORTS FOR WORK

Work issues discussed below include employment, TANF, child care, and transportation. Ideas to support practice, policy development, and evaluation and research are suggested.

Employment

Employment and unemployment played major roles in the lives of the nine families. Parents[1] in our study were striving to improve their families' quality of life and wanted to work and be economically self-sufficient. Yet, the mothers were still unable to make ends meet, even when, as was the case with Sherryce, they worked two jobs. The fathers of the children also were frustrated in this regard. Tejon, for example, complained that the jobs he was offered paid only minimum wage, and he knew he could not support his family on such an income. Low wages thus presented the families with persistent challenges. Partially for this reason, employment status seemed to be in a continual state of transition for our participants. Several had a different job almost every time we interviewed them.

The employment problems we observed were similar to those reported by other researchers (Cauthen & Lu, 2003; Morris, 2002). Although employment rates increased temporarily following the initiation

---

[1]Includes biological mothers and residential and nonresidential social and biological fathers.

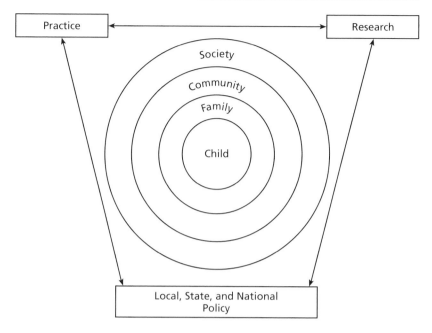

Figure 16.1   A model interrelating research, practice, and policy.

of TANF (Morris, 2002), welfare-to-work policies have not been effective in sustaining employment rates nor in reducing the number of families living in poverty (Sherman, Fremstad, & Parrot, 2004). The federal minimum wage ($5.15/hour), which was last modified in 1997 and which is not indexed to inflation, has eroded in value over time. In fact, a single parent working full time at a minimum wage job will not receive an earned income above the poverty line—a line that is determined by using an index established 40 years ago and that falls short of meeting the needs of most working families today (Zedlewski, 2002).

Male unemployment was important not only in terms of the fathers' economic self-sufficiency, but also because it impacted their relationship with their children and their children's mothers. The mothers in our study felt that it was essential for their partners to have steady employment before they would commit to them through marriage (see Chapter 9). According to the U.S. Department of Labor (2004), however, African American men have higher unemployment rates (10.6%) than African American women (9.9%), European American men (3.9%), and European American women (4.6%). The importance of employment for cohabiting couples was illustrated by Kyierra's frustration with Tejon when he was not employed—even as she recognized the difficulty African American men experience accessing stable employment. Father unemployment also caused friction between the mothers and the nonresidential fathers, which, in turn, led the fathers to feel less comfortable visiting their children (see Chapters 6 and 11). Paternal unemployment may have further negative impacts on the father–child relationship because employment status tends to be integral to men's self-concepts (see Chapters 5 and 11).

Practice Suggestions   The EHS site with which we partnered gave considerable attention to the mothers' educational and employment needs. Given the particular difficulty the fathers experienced in acquiring and maintaining employment that paid a livable wage, we recommend that family support programs such as EHS expand services to link residential and nonresidential fathers with job training and placement programs. Regular evaluations would be needed to assess the quality and effectiveness of these programs. In addition to assessing the success of such programs in terms of job placement, it would be important to find out if they led to enhanced relationship quality between fathers and their children and between fathers and their children's mothers. If employment is related to better relationship outcomes and/or to increased financial contributions to their families, it would make considerable sense for EHS to devote more resources to helping fathers with low incomes secure stable, adequately paying employment.

Moreover, our observation that parents moved frequently from one low-paying job to another suggests that pay is not the only issue. Recall Andreya's dilemma when she was reprimanded by her supervisor for rushing her child to the emergency room during one of his asthma attacks (see Chapter 5). Recall, too, that Shardae often struggled to find child care during nights when she was scheduled to work. We suspect that jobs that allow flexible hours in periods of family emergencies and that arrange for mothers to work when child care services are generally available would contribute to an increase in job satisfaction and retention. Research on the costs and benefits of flexible scheduling for employers as well as for families is imperative. Some research, for example, suggests that flexible scheduling results in improved morale and, therefore, retention of already-trained employees, which in turn saves employers considerable time and money (Ayree, Luk, & Stone, 1998).

Policy Suggestions   As indicated above, the parents in our study could not support their families when working full time at or slightly above minimum wage. To be economically self-sufficient, most working families today would need to earn incomes that are approximately twice that of the official poverty standard, which was $20,000 for a family of four in 2006). It would require two full-time, year-round jobs at a little over $9.00 an hour to reach this income level (Cauthen & Lu, 2003; U.S. Department of Health and Human Services, 2004a). Thus, it is no wonder that the families in our study often struggled to pay their basic bills (e.g., rent, utilities, child care). According to the Children's Defense Fund (2004), modest incremental raises in the minimum wage would, over time, greatly benefit the families of the 1.8 million minimum-wage workers who are parents raising children.

An argument against increasing the federal minimum wage is that such raises would result in higher rates of unemployment because employers may not be able to meet these increased financial demands. However, although this view merits consideration, we also are reminded that higher rates of unemployment are usually caused by large minimum wage increases. Modest increases in the minimum wage have not increased unemployment in the past (Bernstein, 1998; Card & Krueger, 1995). Considering how much the purchasing power of the minimum wage has eroded over time, many policy makers argue that an increase in the minimum wage will only recover lost ground and will not cause a loss in the number of jobs (Bernstein, 1998; Card & Krueger, 1995; Children's Defense Fund, 2004). One study found that a minimum wage increase in New Jersey increased employment and productivity rates due to lower turnover (Card & Krueger, 1995).

The federal government could also help many working families raise their incomes above the poverty line by expanding the Earned Income Tax Credit (EITC; Zedlewski, 2002). The purpose of this refundable federal tax credit is to increase the value of low-wage work, because by definition only families with earnings are eligible. We saw that the mothers waited eagerly for this "tax money" because it helped them buy large-item necessities such as furniture and used cars. Unfortunately, however, working families whose incomes are between $10,000 to $15,000 a year rapidly lose eligibility for the federal EITC, as well as for other supplemental support (e.g., food stamps, subsidized child care and housing, health care) because their incomes exceed the low cutoff levels (Cauthen & Lu, 2003). Thus, individuals such as Shardae who worked low-wage jobs and received a raise at work as a reward for her hard work, or who started a slightly higher-paying job, ultimately saw a decrease in their annual incomes.

A solution recommended by Cauthen and Lu (2003) and Zedlewski (2002) would involve raising money through more equitable Social Security taxation (commonly referred to as FICA taxation) and applying the increased revenue to higher EITC benefits. Currently, federal payroll taxes include a deduction of 7.65% of earnings from FICA. Amounts over $87,000, however, are taxed at a rate of only 1.45%.

Dropping the FICA rate to 1.45% at a higher income ceiling (i.e., above $87,000) and using these new funds to expand the EITC (Cauthen & Lu, 2003) could help "make work pay" (Zedlewski, 2002, p. 125) with no additional cost to the government. As with any change in policy, research should be conducted to determine the effects of this change on families.

Temporary Assistance for Needy Families

The PRWORA replaced Aid to Families with Dependent Children (AFDC) (Committee on Ways and Means, 1996) with TANF, a program that introduced time limits on cash assistance and imposed work activity requirements on recipients (Morris, 2002). Problems with TANF surfaced for several of the mothers in our study. Chandra and Tanisha were unaware that they were eligible for certain services (e.g., child care subsidies, job training) while on TANF. Roneeka and Andreya were unclear about some of the TANF rules such as the 60-month lifetime limit for cash assistance and the requirement to find work within 24 months of receipt. Some mothers were also unaware that they and their children were eligible for certain services (e.g., food stamps, health care) when transitioning off TANF. We also noted that some mothers were reluctant to apply for TANF because they knew that doing so meant revealing the names of their children's fathers, which would lead to pursuit of the fathers by the state's child support enforcement agency.

A lack of knowledge about existing welfare rules and services is not limited to the families in our study. In a national survey of welfare recipients, nearly 40% did not know when their benefits would end. Sixteen percent said that they had not been informed of any time limit, while 21% were aware that their benefits would end but were uncertain as to when that would happen (Zedlewski & Holland, 2002). Zedlewski (2001) found that 57% of families who left welfare were not receiving food stamps, even though they were eligible. Furthermore, only 13%–36% of qualifying families leaving welfare receive child support (Brauner & Loprest, 1999).

At the same time, the mothers' reports about TANF services were not all negative. The PRWORA allows states to try new solutions to old problems. One success story involved Andreya's employer's participation in a welfare-to-work initiative (see Chapter 7). Employers often believe that it is a risk to hire those with little or no work experience. To encourage employers to take that risk, many states choose to spend some of their TANF funds on incentives for employers. Andreya's employer received reimbursement for a portion of her hourly wage in exchange for employing her, a TANF recipient. Andreya thus obtained a job at a higher wage, $6 per hour instead of $5.15. After she had been employed for 6 months, she received a bonus. The bonus was also supported by TANF funds.

Practice Suggestions EHS and other family support programs should educate parents regarding their rights and responsibilities while receiving and transitioning off TANF. Regular, accurate, and up-to-date information would help parents advocate for their families. For example, the mothers in our study were unaware that receiving partial monthly TANF assistance benefits when they were transitioning from welfare to work counted against their lifetime limit of 60 months of cash assistance in the same fashion as receipt of a full month of TANF assistance. So, when Breanna went to work part time and continued to receive TANF benefits of $50 per month for the next 6 months, she used 6 months of her lifetime limit of 60 months of TANF even though the total amount of money was only equivalent to less than 2 months of her full TANF benefits. If she had known the consequences of receipt of this partial benefit, perhaps she would have decided to forego the assistance to "save" part of her lifetime benefits.

Practitioners should also be aware of other benefits families may be eligible for while they are receiving or as they transition off TANF. It is difficult to navigate the myriad rules and regulations of public assistance. In an ideal world, TANF caseworkers would inform the parents of these rules and regulations, as well as their rights and responsibilities. It may be possible, however, that some caseworkers did not provide adequate information to parents because at the outset of PRWORA, the rules were ever changing and social service caseworkers were encouraged to do what they could to reduce TANF rolls.

Furthermore, EHS and other family support programs may be able to help fathers understand the importance of providing regular child support and help mothers feel less apprehensive about applying for TANF benefits even if they must reveal the paternity of their children. Mothers need to be reminded that formal support is not a punishment for fathers, but rather a right of children who should be supported by both parents. Evaluation research should accompany these new practices so that we may better understand their implications—both intended and unintended.

Policy Suggestions Some state governments supplement federal TANF funds (Zedlewski, 2002). Federal TANF policies impose a 5-year lifetime limit on cash assistance, but state-funded TANF programs can be designed without such a time restriction. States could move working families from federally funded TANF into state-funded TANF programs so that the time during which mothers like Breanna are earning income is not deducted from their federal lifetime limit (Zedlewski, 2002). Several states such as Delaware, Illinois, Maryland, and Rhode Island transfer working families to state-funded TANF programs (State Policy Documentation Project, 2002). We are aware that in the current economic climate, most states can ill afford to implement their own TANF programs. This solution may not be feasible until the economy is strong enough to support it. In the meantime, economic impact analyses should be conducted in those states that have already instituted such policies.

Child Care

"No other developed nation would allow such an uneven hodgepodge of [early childhood] programs for children birth to age 5. The nation *truly* is at risk" (Hodgkinson, 2003, p. 5).

The lack of available, accessible, and high-quality child care in the United States, especially for infants and toddlers, has been well documented (Brauner, Gordic, & Zigler, 2004; Helburn & Bergmann, 2002; Paulsell et al., 2002). As noted in Chapter 14, the child care-related concerns of the mothers in our study reflected these scarcities. Early childhood programs[2] often were located outside the mothers' immediate communities and were too expensive for their limited budgets. As a result, several mothers enrolled their children in care that they could afford and access, but that was not of desirable quality.

All children in nonparental child care should receive the best possible care. Studies have shown that children in high-quality child care have higher cognitive and language scores, better school achievement, and greater social competence than children in poor-quality child care (Burchinal, Roberts, Nabors, & Bryant, 1996; Howes, Matheson, & Hamilton, 1994; Lamb, 1998; National Institute of Child Health and Development Early Child Care Research Network [NICHD], 2000; Peisner-Feinberg & Burchinal, 1997; Peisner-Feinberg et al., 1999). In addition, children in poor-quality child care programs display more aggression and defiance as well as delays in reading (Hausfather, Toharia, LaRoche, & Engelsmann, 1997).

The average cost of child care ranges from $4,000 to $10,000 per year. In many states across this nation, child care can cost more than tuition at state universities. For the one third of families with young children earning below $25,000, this cost is prohibitive (Almanac of Pol-

---

[2]The terms *child care* and *early childhood program* are used interchangeably. Each refers to nonparental care used by parents in order to attend school, work, or a work-related activity.

icy Issues, 2004). Too many parents cannot afford the cost of even poor-quality child care, much less the prohibitive cost of high-quality care.

Furthermore, as family earnings increase and child care subsidy-eligibility cutoffs are surpassed, access to quality child care is often even more limited. Recall from Chapter 14 that Shardae and Sherryce were ineligible for child care subsidies because their incomes were too high. In their state, *too high* was defined as a full-time wage of $6.90 per hour or $14,350 annually for a family of two.

The mothers in our study faced numerous additional challenges because of the lack of available and accessible good quality child care and the high cost of such care. These challenges included finding transportation to the early childhood programs and finding a program with extended hours of operation. For example, limited transportation options played a major role in Andreya's early childhood program choice (see Chapters 5 and 6), and Sherryce struggled to find care when she worked weekends.

Practice Suggestions   It is important for EHS and other parent and family education programs to continue to teach parents about the characteristics and benefits of high-quality child care. Informed parents may make wiser child care choices, and perhaps persevere to overcome obstacles such as transportation in order to place their children in the best child care.

EHS and other early intervention programs should continue to partner with and provide training to community early childhood programs. This will increase the quality of care for both EHS children and non-EHS children who attend the same facility. More research is needed to evaluate the curricular elements of early childhood education that are most important for children living in poverty. Furthermore, EHS programs must assess the need for and, if necessary, work to increase the availability of care during nontraditional working hours.

Policy Suggestions   Some people are opposed to government funding for early childhood programs. They believe that child care is a family responsibility and that further government intervention is not needed (Public Agenda, 2000). Others believe that encouraging business involvement in child care financing is a solution to the problems of availability, accessibility, and affordability (Blank & Poersch, 1999). We respond by reminding the reader that child care is not merely a family or business issue, it also is a societal issue, just as building roads to get to and from work is a societal issue, not merely a business issue, and K–12 public education is a societal issue and not merely a family issue. Research shows that investing in high-quality early childhood

education yields a benefit–cost ratio of 1:7.16 of the program investment returned to the public (Schweinhart, 2003). Given that the government saves $7 for every dollar spent on high-quality early educa-
tion, it pays to invest in such programs for children.

In fiscal year 2004, 4.8 billion federal dollars were available to the
states for the Child Care Development Fund (CCDF). In addition, some
states chose to transfer a portion of their TANF block grant to help families pay for child care assistance, increasing the amount spent on child
care subsidies by another $3.5 billion (U.S. General Accounting Office,
2003). Despite these large expenditures, however, fewer than 15% of
eligible children received subsidized child care (Ewen & Hart, 2003), 32
states made cuts to their child care programs (Parrott & Wu, 2003), and
23 states had waiting lists for child care subsidies (Mezey, 2003). We
therefore suggest a short-term goal to increase allocations for the CCDF
so that the parents of at least 25% of eligible children receive child care
subsidies. Furthermore, we suggest gradually continuing to increase
federal CCDF allocations so that within the next decade, all children
eligible for such assistance can be served. Indexing this funding to in-
flation must also be a priority so that progress is not lost incrementally.

Research is needed on the individual and cumulative effects of
providing greater financial subsidies for the cost of child care, locating
high-quality early childhood programs in the neighborhoods in which
families with low-to-moderate incomes reside, and providing care during nontraditional working hours. Exploring parents' reactions to new
policies and how their child care choices might be affected also would
be informative.

As suggested in Chapter 14, policies and regulations that affect child
care *quality* must also be examined at both the federal and state levels.
Despite the fact that for almost four decades, experts have affirmed and
reaffirmed the need for federal child care regulations, none exist
(American Academy of Pediatrics, 2002; Brauner et al., 2004; Cohen,
2001). National standards should set a minimum level of quality for all
states. This would ensure that children such as Jalisa, Ciera, Lavell, and
Tierra, who were all enrolled in programs of low quality, could attend
high-quality programs. Federal standards could be set in accord with the
National Association for the Education of Young Children's (NAEYC)
accreditation standards (NAEYC, 2004), the National Health and Safety
Standards (American Academy of Pediatrics, 2002), the U.S. Department of Defense standards for military child care (U.S. Department of
Defense, 2004), and/or the Head Start Performance Standards (U.S.
Department of Health and Human Services, 2004b). When improvements in child care affordability, accessibility, and quality are made,

evaluative activities ascertaining the effects that these policies have on children's outcomes and their readiness for school should follow.

Transportation

Transportation emerged as an issue for all of the families in our study in that some of the mothers did not have driver's licenses, did not own or have access to a reliable automobile, could not always count on family or friends for rides, and/or did not have ready access to dependable public transportation. Recall Andreya's difficulties getting her sons to their child care center and herself to school or to work. When offered child care at the EHS site, she had to refuse because she did not want to wait at bus stops in the cold with two asthmatic children (see Chapter 6). Kyierra wanted to work as a cashier or secretary and proudly told us that she could type 70 words per minute; however, those kinds of jobs were outside her community. She did not own a car and did not have the money to pay for bus fare on a regular basis. She explained, "Two dollars [for one round-trip bus fare] doesn't seem like much, but it's a whole lot when you don't have it." Tejon would also look through the newspaper for jobs, but the ones he wanted, such as janitorial or maintenance jobs, were outside the inner city. Like Kyierra, he did not have a car and could not afford the daily bus fare.

Some of the parents owned cars, yet this was not a solution without problems. Some could not afford safe, reliable cars that would pass inspection and others could not afford the tax, or licensing, or insurance costs required for cars. Chandra, who persevered by taking the driver's license exam 10 times before passing, succeeded in obtaining her own car only to struggle with car maintenance problems. Then, when her car tags expired, she was arrested for driving without a properly licensed vehicle. Shardae and Tanisha also faced car maintenance problems. For example, one day Tanisha's car broke down on the way to work, and she could not afford to have it fixed or moved from the side of the road. After a few days, the city towed her car to a lot and she never saw it again. Several months later, she used EITC money to buy another used car. She tried hard to pick a newer model car with low mileage. On the way home from the used car lot, however, even this car broke down.

Such situations led several EHS home visitors to give family members rides so that they could get to EHS services such as parent meetings and other places they needed to go (see Chapter 13). Over time, it concerned us and some home visitors that this transportation assistance could inadvertently keep parents from learning how to solve their transportation problems themselves. Because EHS is a time-limited program, the mothers needed to develop these skills in order to continue managing their families after graduation from the program. The home visitors had to keep a balance between supporting the families and helping them develop the skills to solve these issues themselves.

Practice Suggestions It is crucial that EHS home visitors and other human service professionals help parents become familiar with available transportation services. These professionals could partner with public transportation programs and receive training on options available to families with low incomes.

In addition, EHS may be interested in determining if taxicab vouchers and tokens for free and/or reduced bus fares would allow parents to hold better jobs, use higher-quality child care, and/or attend more EHS meetings. It also would be important to find out if holding informational meetings within the families' immediate neighborhoods (e.g., at community centers or in neighborhood homes) versus at EHS facilities would influence attendance. This practice might mean that for every topic, EHS home visitors would have to conduct multiple meetings in several neighborhoods; however, increased attendance and reduced transportation costs might make this option worthwhile.

Policy Suggestions Several grant opportunities for transportation research and pilot programs are made available each year through the Federal Transit Administration (FTA), an agency within the U.S. Department of Transportation. FTA research grants could support the investigation of alternative solutions to transportation problems, which could enhance overall program effectiveness. In addition, state governments could allocate a portion of their TANF funds to support transportation aid for families in poverty. Down payments, subsidies, or no-interest loans for the purchase of cars have already been initiated for qualifying workers in states such as New Mexico, Kansas, Michigan, Pennsylvania, Virginia, and Tennessee (Sweeney et al., 2000; Zedlewski, 2002).

The question arises as to whether greater investment in the infrastructure of public transportation would result in improved outcomes for parents and children. Such investment could include funding for enhanced public transportation, extended service hours, more reliable schedules, bus stop shelters that shield families from bad weather, and/or door-to-door van services that could lessen the burden of carrying groceries and small children. Before these services begin, however, an evaluation of usage patterns and preferences for various forms of transportation would be needed to ensure cost-efficiency. Although some may argue that the costs of financing an efficient, dependable mass-transit system are prohibitive, our hypothesis would be that this investment would yield benefits exceeding the original expenditures because access to decently paying jobs would be significantly enhanced. Of course, empirical research using a large and diverse sample would be needed to substantiate this claim.

SUPPORTS FOR BASIC NEEDS

Suggestions for supporting housing needs, health care, and food and nutrition assistance for families with low incomes are discussed in this section.

Housing

Housing affordability, stability, and safety were major issues for the families in our study. Shardae moved back in with her mother twice because of the high cost of housing. Breanna was never able to afford her own place and regularly moved from one biological or fictive relative's home to another. The fair market rent for a two-bedroom apartment in the city in which our families lived was $587 per month in 2000 (Twombly, Pitcoff, Dolbeare, & Crowley, 2000) and $713 in 2003 (Pitcoff et al., 2003). The general standard used to determine affordability of housing is that families should not spend more than 30% of their gross income on rent (Pitcoff et al.). In 2000, the families in this study, making minimum wage, needed to work 89 hours per week to afford the fair market rent of a two-bedroom apartment (Twombly et al.); in 2003 that same family needed to work 106 hours at minimum wage (Pitcoff et al.). The reality was that most of the mothers in our study did not earn enough to pay that much rent without falling victim to what is considered a high-rent burden (paying more than 50% of one's income for housing; Pitcoff et al.).

Most of the families did, however, qualify for housing assistance from the U.S. Department of Housing and Urban Development. Andreya, for example, was delighted when she and her children moved into an apartment in a new housing project (see Chapter 7). Several other mothers received vouchers from the Housing Choice Voucher Program, commonly known as Section 8. Federal money pays for these rental vouchers via the U.S. Department of Housing and Urban Development (U.S. Department of Housing and Urban Development, 2004). Because recipients must locate landlords who are willing to accept the vouchers, this often leaves parents with few housing or neighborhood options, because many of the landlords who are willing to accept Section 8 rental assistance vouchers often manage or own dilapidated properties in run-down, high-crime neighborhoods.

Due to lengthy waiting lists, some of the mothers waited for long periods of time before receiving housing assistance. Sherryce, for example, told us that her "lottery number" for Section 8 housing was 2,000, denoting that there were 1,999 families waiting ahead of her. (Just as Andreya did while living with her mother [see Chapter 7], Sherryce told the housing authority that she was homeless so that she could move up on the waiting list.) Nationwide, only about 12% of those who qualify for any form of housing assistance receive help because the funding for these programs is insufficient (Nelson, Treskon, & Pelletiere, 2004).

Another issue that affects families is income eligibility cutoffs. Shardae, for example, moved into her own apartment in a subsidized apartment complex, only to lose the assistance when her income increased, forcing her to return to living with her mother.

Housing instability, often interconnected with the desire to find a safe and affordable place to live, was also typical for the mothers in our study (see Chapters 1 and 12). When asked about their residence, most of the mothers replied, "I'm stayin' here" rather than "I live here," or "This is my home," indicating the transient nature of their housing arrangements. Although 18% of all African Americans move annually, the rates for young African American children (ages 1–4) and adults (ages 20–29) are much higher at 28% and 27%, respectively (Schachter, 2004).

Furthermore, according to Lee and Burkam (2002), 48% of the poorest children in America have lived in more than three different homes by the age of 5, whereas 80% of the nation's children from the richest fifth of the population have lived in only one or two homes by that age. The mothers in our study moved an average of 5 or 6 times; Chandra and Breanna, who "stayed with" multiple biological and fictive kin, seemed to have no clear permanent residence during the 5-year period of this study.

Safety was another factor affecting the lives of the families in our study. In fact, almost all of the families lived in high-crime neighborhoods. As reported in Chapter 15, one way the mothers coped with community violence was by denying that it existed "on their street," but the reality of its existence was all too real for Tony, Denzel, and Terral, who were murdered within short distances of their homes.

Practice Suggestions   Some of the EHS home visitors made concerted efforts to help families find affordable and safe housing. This should continue to be a goal of this and other family support programs.

Program staff should also make a point of informing parents of the income cutoffs of the various housing assistance programs so that they can prepare to lose financial assistance when their income increases to a certain level.

In addition, parents should be informed about programs that support home ownership. Examples include Habitat for Humanity, local programs that offer reduced mortgage interest, and state savings accounts that match family savings if they are used to purchase homes. Home ownership may be desirable because it helps protect families from increases in housing costs due to market fluctuations and their own increases in income (and attendant losses of housing assistance).

Family support programs may be able to help parents work with others in their communities to make their neighborhoods safer. Obviously, this is a huge undertaking and must involve collaboration with many individuals in the community, not just the parents enrolled in EHS. Neighborhood watch programs seem to increase involvement and therefore improve community safety (Salcido, Ornelas, & Garcia, 2002). Revitalization of older neighborhoods is critical because the solution to the need for affordable and safe housing cannot always lie in moving families out of their native neighborhoods. Recall Chandra's feelings when she found a nice new apartment in a quiet suburban area that accepted Section 8 rental vouchers (see Chapter 12). She was thrilled to move there, but the excitement quickly waned as she began to miss her support network; 9 months later, she moved back to her old neighborhood to be closer to her extended family.

Policy Suggestions   The exceptionally long waiting lists make it obvious that local, state, and federal funding for housing assistance does not meet the needs of families with low incomes. Additional allocations must include not only more funding for Section 8 rental assistance vouchers, but also the building of additional low-income housing units because the number of affordable housing units continues to decline.[3] Fifty-six percent of those living in extreme poverty (i.e., with incomes below 30% of the local Area Median Income [AMI; Nelson et al., 2004, p. 2]) pay more than one half of their income for rent and utilities. It is estimated that across the nation there is a need for 4.9 million more affordable rental units for families with the lowest incomes (Nelson et al., 2004). We suggest that income cutoff levels be gradual so that housing assistance is lost incrementally rather than abruptly as family income increases. Research is needed to determine the costs of these sugges-

---

[3]Between 1990 and 2000, state level shortages of available housing for low-income renters grew by 15% (Nelson et al., 2004).

tions to local, state, and federal governments and the effects the incremental cutoff policy would have on family residential stability.

Because of the paucity of employment opportunities within urban core communities, however, policies that encourage revitalization of housing in the urban core will need to be coupled with renewed efforts to bring employers back into these areas. Community centers and family programs may play positive roles in the development of supportive relationships among neighbors. As noted in Chapter 12, such programs may help neighbors connect with one another to create the mutual trust that Sampson and his colleagues found to be critical for the reduction of crime in low-income neighborhoods (Sampson, Raudenbush, & Earls, 1997).

Health Care

In the last half of the 20th century, even though the overall health of those living in the United States improved, African Americans died from disease, accident, and homicide at twice the rate of European Americans. These racial differences have continued to either widen or remain unchanged. Differential socioeconomic status has been a major reason for these disparities, but racism, differential access to health care, and the quality of care all affected (and continue to affect) racial differences in health (Daniels, 2004).

Health and health care are important issues for all families with young children. Families with low incomes are likely to find access to care especially challenging. All of the mothers in the study were on Medicaid when their children were born. As a part of the PRWORA, federal incentives encouraged states to provide transitional Medicaid for parents and their children moving from welfare to work (Cauthen & Lu, 2003). When parents in this study transitioned from welfare to work, they could continue to receive Medicaid for 6 months after beginning employment, even if they were no longer income-eligible. Shardae, like the other mothers, appreciated this benefit, as it helped her while she waited to become eligible for health benefits from her employer. Unfortunately, when Shardae became eligible for her employer's health insurance, she could not afford the monthly insurance premiums. Therefore, she had to go without health care coverage for a period of time.

Through the Balanced Budget Act of 1997, Congress created Title XXI, the State Children's Health Insurance Program (CHIP). This program was developed to address the growing number of children without health insurance (Cauthen & Lu, 2003). CHIP provides federal incentives for states to extend health insurance coverage to children in families with incomes up to 200% (or higher) of the federal poverty level (Cauthen & Lu, 2003). Nonetheless, in 2003, 11.4% (8.4 million) of all children were uninsured. The percentages among African American and poor children were even greater, 14.5% and 19.2%, respectively (U.S. Census Bureau, 2004).

All but one of the children in our study were either on Medicaid or enrolled in CHIP for the entire 5-year period of the study. The parents were very appreciative of Medicaid and CHIP, mentioning that they were allowed to choose their child's pediatrician and that prescription drug benefits were especially helpful. Although Andreya mentioned concerns about long waits at the hospital when she had to take her children to the emergency room, it was not clear whether this was due to shortages of hospital staff, her enrollment in Medicaid, racism, or other factors.

Although children from low-income families may be covered by CHIP (Zedlewski, 2002), most low-income working parents in the United States do not qualify for public health benefits (Cauthen & Lu, 2003). For example, in the state in which this study was conducted, once a family's income reaches 77% of the federal poverty line, parents no longer qualify for Medicaid (other than transitional Medicaid when they are moving from welfare to work). Moreover, many working parents who qualify for government assistance with health care do not avail themselves of the opportunity. Researchers have found that within 12 months of leaving welfare, 30%–60% of eligible working families are not enrolled in public health insurance plans (Zedlewski, 2001). Acquiring employer-provided insurance cannot entirely explain this finding, however, because past studies have revealed that more than half of all mothers leaving welfare are uninsured one year later (Garrett & Holahan, 2000; Pollack, Davis, Danziger, & Orzol, 2002).

Practice Suggestions The EHS home visitors worked hard to ensure that all of the eligible EHS children were enrolled in either Medicaid or CHIP. They also were careful to remind the mothers to make appointments for well-baby check-ups and immunizations. Nonetheless, given that 19.2% of the nation's children living in poverty remain uninsured (U.S. Census Bureau, 2004), there is much work left to be done before all children are insured. Social services professionals must continue to proactively seek to enroll children eligible for CHIP. It is critical that parents of minority children and adolescents and immigrant families be targeted, as they are overrepresented among those without health care coverage (Lewit, Bennett, & Behrman, 2003). The Centers for Medicare & Medicaid Services, a federal agency in the U.S. Department of Health and Human Services, provide the use of an outreach information clearinghouse for social service agencies across the country to increase the enrollment of eligible uninsured children. However, little is understood about why some parents do not enroll their children or the best methods of reaching eligible children. Research is needed to determine effective methods and to guide enrollment practices and outreach programs.

Policy Suggestions   As the number of uninsured children and adults continues to rise (U.S. Census Bureau, 2004), there is mounting evidence that there is a health care crisis in America. Currently, a debate exists over how Medicaid should be funded. The federal government is deliberating over two options: whether states should be offered the choice every decade to receive block grants[4] (with a fixed 8.5% growth rate per year) or whether to continue the existing policy of matching funds[5] provided by the federal government. The federal government may prefer the certainty of a fixed growth rate, although some states would welcome the increased control of serving their constituents the way they feel is best. We, along with others (Holahan & Weil, 2003), argue for a matching policy and against a block grant policy. A matching formula program encourages expansion and spending on public benefits during all economic times because states must meet maintenance of effort (MOE) requirements (i.e., states are required to fund social services at the same level, maintaining the efforts they have made in the past) before they can receive federal funds. Under a block grant policy, on the other hand, states would likely expand their health care services and implement innovative ideas only during good economic times. Moreover, a block grant policy would put states at economic risk. In general, states are less equipped than the federal government to deal with unexpected financial downturns in the economy because, in such downturns, there may be an increased demand for public health care services. A block grant policy does not prepare states for times of sudden increases in the number of clientele, although matching funds provide some flexibility. Finally, a block grant policy would not consider the variability in financial demands across states, while a matching formula policy would provide federal funds depend-

---

[4]A block grant is a lump sum of funds given by a governing agency (in this case, the federal government), based upon a formula. A block grant typically has few restrictions and the purposes for which the funding can be allocated are broad (Holahan & Weil, 2003).

[5]Matching funds are funds given by a governing agency (in this case, the federal government) that require the agency receiving the allocation (in this case, state governments) to match the funding with its own money. Agencies can be required to match funds based on a fixed dollar amount or a percentage basis (Holahan & Weil, 2003).

ing on the amount of money the state is willing to devote to health care coverage (Holahan & Weil, 2003).

Programs such as Medicaid and CHIP have been implemented so that children from both nonworking and working-poor families can receive health care coverage; however, no provisions have been made to extend coverage to working parents who do not have access to employer-provided health insurance (or those who cannot afford the premiums for employer-provided health insurance). While their daughters continued to have health care coverage, Shardae and Tanisha lost their coverage after returning to work because they earned an income slightly above the threshold rate (i.e., 77% of the federal poverty line). Several of our working mothers, in fact, did not have health care insurance because they were either not eligible for public health insurance or could not afford to pay the premiums for the programs their employers offered.

Recognizing that many adults do not have health care coverage, various proposals have been developed for extending public health care to universal coverage. Although some proposals would require that all employers be mandated to provide health care coverage to employees (Pauly, 1994), others advocate different social insurance solutions (Steuerle, 2003). It is unclear to us what is the best way to improve the health care of all families. What is clear, however, is that universal coverage is necessary to reduce the large number of uninsured parents.

Food and Nutrition Services

All of the mothers in our study received assistance from the Special Supplemental Nutrition Program for Women, Infants, and Children (WIC). In the United States, almost 50% of infants and 25% of children ages 1–4 receive WIC (Oliveira, Racine, Olmsted, & Ghelfi, 2002). The mothers appreciated the WIC vouchers, especially when their children were infants, because infant formula is costly. Evaluations have shown that WIC has a positive effect on children's diets (Rose, Habicht, & Devaney, 1998; U.S. General Accounting Office, 1992), immunization rates, cognitive development (U.S. Department of Agriculture Food and Nutrition Service, 1987), and growth rates (Edozien, Switzer, & Bryan, 1979; Heimendinger, Larid, Austin, Timmer, & Gershoff, 1984).

Most of the mothers received food stamp benefits during at least a portion of this 5-year study. Nationwide, 12% of children are members of families receiving food stamps (Child Trends, 2004). One problem that surfaced for our participants was connected to the federal policy tying food stamp eligibility to household rather than to individual income. If the household qualifies for food stamps, only the head of the household receives the food stamps. As evidenced by Andreya and Roneeka's situations, young mothers who reside with their parents are not eligible to directly receive food stamps; instead, the household allotment is increased. Recall in Chapter 6 that Andreya felt that she would make wiser food purchasing decisions than her mother if she were in charge of her own food stamps.

Another problem that some families faced was access to supermarkets. According to research, their plight is not uncommon. Forty percent of food stamp recipients do not shop in their own neighborhoods because there are no supermarkets available. Another 48% look for stores outside their own neighborhoods because of the high prices at their neighborhood stores (Ohis, Ponza, Moreno, Zambrowski, & Cohen, 1999). Due to limited access to supermarkets, some mothers in our study were forced to buy groceries at local convenience stores in which the prices often were high and the availability of nutritious products low.

Practice Suggestions Unfortunately, WIC vouchers did not cover jarred baby foods, which became a concern for the mothers when their infants began to eat solid foods. Practitioners should teach parents about the economic and health benefits of home-prepared baby food. Furthermore, although WIC educators do provide information on the benefits of breastfeeding, only one of the mothers in this study chose to breastfeed for an extended period of time. Practitioners, including the EHS home visitors, should provide additional information and support to encourage mothers to breastfeed. This is the preferred form of feeding for infants, offering unique benefits such as reductions in ear, urinary tract, and upper and lower respiratory track infections; diarrhea; asthma; and eczema (American Academy of Pediatrics, 2002). As with any new or revised method of service delivery, evaluation research to determine the effectiveness of these educational components (i.e., preparing homemade baby food, breastfeeding) would be needed to determine their efficacy.

Another suggestion for community practitioners is to form a task force to solve problems associated with family access to nutritious foods. The task force should include parents, grocers, EHS and other family support professionals, and community leaders.

Policy Suggestions It is unclear whether the mothers' lack of control over their own food stamps interfered with their children's nutrition. Research is needed to examine the most effective ways to ensure that low-income families receive the food they need. If food stamp eligibility were not tied to household income, a mother with an income below the food stamp eligibility cutoff would qualify for food stamps even if she lived with parents who earned higher incomes. This could lead to more individuals qualifying for food stamps and, in turn, an increase in government cost; however, decoupling food stamps from the household income would allow young mothers to make food choices on their own and could reduce family conflict that arises because of limited control over food purchases.

A policy suggestion with regard to food stamps is the provision of nutrition education for recipients. Mandatory nutrition education on application for and renewal of food stamps may increase parents' knowledge of proper nutrition for their children and themselves. Furthermore, mandatory education on stretching the food dollar may be of great benefit to mothers while they are using food stamps and when they are no longer eligible to receive them. To determine the effectiveness of these suggested educational components, evaluation research would need to be conducted. Evaluations could measure parental knowledge of nutrition, actual provision of nutritious foods, and the health of adult family members and children.

SUPPORTS FOR CHILD AND FAMILY DEVELOPMENT

This last section presents practice, policy, and research suggestions for Early Head Start and for child-rearing practices to support the development of young children and their families.

Early Head Start

In this subsection, we highlight a few issues from Chapter 13 that emerged as most salient for the families in our study. Overall, the mothers described their experiences with EHS as positive. Andreya, Kyierra, and Chandra had especially close relationships with their home visitors and felt that they could tell them "anything." Shardae, Breanna, and Kyierra reported that they would like regular weekly home visits with their home visitors, while Kyierra and Breanna wished their home visitors would call them three or four times a week. Kyierra was impressed with how Nicole, her home visitor, sensitively responded after they discussed the relationship difficulties Kyierra was having with Tejon. Kyierra, Breanna, and Andreya indicated that they appreciated the child development information they received from EHS meetings and home visits. Several mothers valued their home visitors' help in finding high-quality child care, enrolling in Job Corps, acquiring housing, navigating social services agencies, dealing with interpersonal conflicts, and managing time, given their multiple responsibilities.

However, some of the mothers had complaints about and suggestions for improving the EHS program. Although Sherryce and Shardae were the most independent and economically self-sufficient mothers in this study, they also felt the most neglected by their home visitors. For example, Sherryce, who worked full time, participated in most of the evening parent meetings, yet her home visitor missed numerous scheduled appointments and provided her with minimal-to-no assistance in enrolling her child in a high-quality child care program. It was Sherryce's belief that the program rewarded unemployed mothers with more attention than employed mothers. Roneeka also complained that her home visitor was apt to miss appointments or show up late for home visits. She understood that her home visitor had a large caseload and strongly recommended that EHS expand the number of home visitors. (We should note, however, that due partially to their many moves, it was often difficult for the mothers themselves to keep home visit appointments. In fact, Tanisha was eventually dropped from the program because she had missed too many of her home visits and could not be located.)

The mothers also complained about misleading EHS recruitment strategies. Sherryce enrolled in EHS after hearing a radio advertisement she interpreted as offering families free high-quality child care. After she enrolled, she was told that her son Michael could not receive these child care services because Sherryce earned an income slightly more than the threshold for state aid. These policies eventually changed; however, by then, there were no immediate openings for her child. It was many months before Michael got a spot in the early childhood program with which this EHS program partnered. Sherryce told us repeatedly how angry she was over the inaccurate information she had understood to be a promise when she was recruited into the program.

Practice Suggestions   According to several mothers, the EHS program would benefit from improved communication between home visitors and EHS participants. Needless to say, home visitors should return phone calls and notify mothers if they are running late or need to reschedule appointments; however, we also understand that some mothers in our study did not have phones, making communication difficult. Perhaps scheduling standing weekly appointments could help structure the home visitor's schedule, ensure regular communication between home visitor and mother, and reduce the uncertainty that many of the mothers felt regarding when they would next see or talk to their home visitor. In addition, EHS sites could implement program policies that hold participants and home visitors accountable for keeping appointments. Such a practice could include having home visitors and participating mothers sign and date forms at the completion of each visit. These forms would verify that the current appointment was kept by both parties. One copy could be left with the participant, one with the EHS home visitor, and one with the EHS site supervisor. This tracking method could help monitor the actual number and length of visits for each participating parent, which, in turn, could strengthen the validity of evaluation studies.

It also is important that potential participants be properly informed of the services EHS programs do and do not provide. Several home visitors were unsure about some EHS policies and procedures. Before a family support program begins recruiting participants, it is essential that recruiters (in this case, the EHS home visitors) be thoroughly trained so that they know which services are and are not included. Radio and television advertisements for EHS and related programs must not overstate program services. Although recruiters may feel pressure to meet enrollment quotas that often determine the program's very existence, it is imperative that they convey to parents its limitations as well as its benefits. Trust in the program and its representatives depends on this clarity.

Lastly, EHS participants regularly face the need to manage their families on limited resources. During home visits, EHS home visitors should help mothers build skills in household budgeting and in accessing requisite family resources. Home visitors already help link parents to needed programs or agencies; we recommend that programs expand this activity to include learning how to set up monthly budgets and how to navigate the social services system on their own. Tanisha's daughter Tierra was without health insurance coverage for many months because her mother did not understand how to enroll her daughter in Medicaid. Roneeka did not know that missing 2 days of her job training program would result in sanctions, causing a significant reduction in her receipt of social services and cash assistance. EHS programs could collaborate with other social services agencies in their communities to develop a handbook of the community's social welfare programs and policies if there is not one already available. As with child development literature (see child-rearing section below), parents may benefit from having a printed resource to which they can refer.

Policy Suggestions   As explained in Chapter 13, miscommunication between EHS recruiters and participants in part stemmed from the fact that recruiters were mandated to enroll, in a limited time frame, twice the number of families that they would eventually serve. (For the evaluation component, participants were needed for both the program and comparison groups. This requirement of the original EHS programs included in the national evaluation is not characteristic of EHS programs developed since then.) In addition, the EHS evaluation began without sufficient time for the development of policies and the training of home visitors. It is our recommendation that the evaluation of new programs begin *after* programs have been in operation for at least one year. Recruiters, of course, also need to be given reasonable time to find participants.

Due to a lack of funding, only 5% of eligible children can participate in EHS (Hodgkinson, 2003). Evaluative data thus far suggest that EHS is associated with cognitive, social, and emotional benefits for children and that intervention during the first 3 years of life can positively affect the development of children in families with low incomes (Raikes, 2004). Every effort to expand early intervention services such as EHS to all eligible children is therefore warranted. Although this expansion would increase costs substantially in the short run, we are also reminded that in the long run, schools save approximately $11,000 per child when low-income children participate in high-quality early childhood programs and therefore are less likely to need special or remedial education (Masse & Barnett, 2002).

Child-Rearing Practices

Throughout the years of our study, we saw much evidence of the mothers' dedication to the well-being of their children. Breanna, for example, said that she would read "everything" to her daughter, including the backs of cereal boxes, because her EHS home visitor informed her that reading to children was good for them. Several mothers stated that they were interested in learning about children's development and were grateful for the information they received from EHS in this regard. Kyierra mentioned that her favorite benefit of EHS participation was the information her home visitor provided regarding child development. Tanisha told us that she appreciated the written information given to her by her home visitor and would find herself referring back to it in between home visits.

As indicated in Chapter 10 (and illustrated in Chapters 5–7), there were some child-rearing issues that were of particular concern for parents. Most were specific to the ages of the children or the neighborhood contexts in which they lived. Tanisha often felt frustrated by her daughter's tantrums; she did not understand why Tierra had them or what she could do about them. It bothered Chandra, Kyierra, and Andreya to see their children obey them less frequently than they obeyed other family members (e.g., fathers, grandparents). Kyierra, Andreya, and Roneeka mentioned that they feared they would not be prepared to steer their children away from the pressures in their neighborhoods to engage in drug use and sales, early sex, and gang activity. They were also uncertain as to how they would teach their children to understand and protect themselves from the racial discrimination they themselves had experienced as children. These areas of concern often left the mothers feeling ineffective in their parenting or upset with their children.

Practice Suggestions   The fact that the mothers often mentioned child development information as a benefit of participating in EHS speaks highly of this early intervention program. One reason this component may have been successful is because home visitors provided child development information in a variety of ways, including verbally and through written material and videos. This multifaceted approach allowed mothers with various learning styles to process new information and should be considered by all parent educators. We suggest that parent educators make sure that all written materials given to parents are at an appropriate reading level and in their preferred language.

We also would underscore the importance of helping parents understand the principles underlying typical infant and toddler development and behavior. We think such understanding would have helped some of the mothers transition from the parenting of dependent infants to parenting toddlers striving for autonomy. Moreover, parent educators should help parents understand *why* certain parenting strategies are recommended. Breanna read to Corinna because her home visitor encouraged her to do so, but when asked why this was important, Breanna admitted that she did not know. Kyierra knew that her home visitor was encouraging her to babyproof her home, but without a complete understanding of why this practice was necessary, she continued to delay implementing this task.

In addition, early childhood parent educators working in low-income communities should be knowledgeable about topics that might seem important only for parents of adolescents but that weigh heavily on the minds of parents of very young children. Parents clearly want to learn strategies they can use as their children grow older and are confronted with pressures to associate with "the wrong crowd" or to join gangs or engage in drug use or early sex. Although their children were still very young, the parents in our study worried about these issues because they knew that their children would face them in the future. Recall, for example, Andreya's speech to other EHS parents about her fears regarding raising sons in today's environment (see Chapter 7).

We also recommend that parent educators broaden their conceptions of "parenting" to include more than just mothers. Several of the parents in our study lived with extended family members, many of whom served as caregivers for their children. As indicated in Chapters 8 and 10, Maria and Andreya experienced conflict with their mothers over child-rearing strategies. They felt that their sons were receiving mixed messages from their mothers and grandmothers. A few grandmothers were included in the EHS home visits and attended parent meetings, but a more intentional approach may be helpful. Perhaps, just as there were some father-only meetings in EHS, there also should be special meetings or events for grandparents and other caregivers.

Moreover, six biological or social fathers were incarcerated at least one time during the study, and none had received parenting education even though their children were enrolled in EHS. Learning about child development and parenting while incarcerated may have helped the fathers prepare to care for their children once they returned to the community. Past research has indicated that there are positive benefits to offering parent education to incarcerated fathers (Harrison, 1997; Wilczak & Markstrom, 1999). However, there is limited research on the effects of these programs on children's well-being. EHS should consider extending services to incarcerated parents and evaluating the effectiveness of such services on parents and children.

Policy Suggestions   Although some home visitors in this EHS program provided the *how* and the *why* of the child-rearing practices they taught parents, many were not well versed in child development knowledge, having instead a background in social work. It is suggested, therefore, that policies change to explicitly require EHS home visitors to have both child- and family-development expertise.

Parents also expressed concern about how they would help their children understand and cope with racial discrimination. As children, both Andreya and Roneeka had been hit by soda cans and bottles by adults who yelled racial slurs. Kyierra remembered children calling racial slurs as she walked home from school one day. Tejon recalled a White man spitting at his father and commenting on their race as they were walking into a store. Other parents recounted feeling mistreated in stores or at their place of employment because of the color of their skin. A plenitude of research supports the claim that racial socialization benefits children's development (Caldwell, Zimmerman, Bernat, Sellers, & Notaro, 2002; Caughy, O'Campo, Randolph, & Nickerson, 2002). Much research has examined the need for and benefits of cultural competence on the part of practitioners (Hernandez & Isaacs, 1998; Lynch & Hanson, 2004). We recommend, therefore, that policies require parent educators who work with families from a variety of cultures to be well trained in the areas of racial socialization and cultural sensitivity.

INTRODUCING THREE EXPERTS

The research, practice, and policy ideas in Chapter 16 were generated to improve the lives of young children and their families who daily face issues related to poverty and racial minority status. Our suggestions for future research, practice, and policies were derived from past studies, conversations with experts and social services personnel, and interviews with nine mothers and their many family members and friends.

We wanted to hear from other professionals as well and invited three of the best to comment on our ideas and conclusions. The final chapter of the book, "Commentaries," includes the thoughts of three professionals who care about improving the lives of all families living in poverty. For sharing her views with us, we thank Dr. Gina Barclay-McLaughlin, whose qualitative work has contributed to our knowledge of social relationships in inner-city neighborhoods, of early intervention programs, and of parent–child relationships in African American families. In addition, we are privileged to hear from Gayle Cunningham, a highly regarded practitioner who positively affects the lives of hundreds of children and their families on a daily basis. Ms. Cunningham's comments come from the perspective of having directed a Head Start program for many years. Today, she is executive director of a committee for economic opportunity. Finally, we give a heartfelt thanks to Dr. Deborah Phillips, who shares with us a policy perspective. Dr. Phillips has worked to improve policies for thousands of children—children like Lavell and Jalisa.

Our hope is that the practices and polices of programs for young children in our nation will improve when more people learn from the many families who welcomed us into their lives for 5 years, as well as from the ideas presented by Dr. Barclay-McLaughlin, Ms. Cunningham, and Dr. Phillips.

REFERENCES

Almanac of Policy Issues. (2004). *Child care.* Retrieved August 5, 2004, from http://www.policyalmanac.org/social_welfare/childcare.shtml

American Academy of Pediatrics. (2002). *Caring for our children: National health and safety performance standards: Guidelines for out of home child care* (2nd ed.). Elk Grove Village, IL: American Academy of Pediatrics.

Ayree, S., Luk, V., & Stone, R. (1998). Family-responsive variables and retention-relevant outcomes among employed parents. *Human Relations, 51*(1), 73–97.

Balanced Budget Act of 1997. PL 105-33, 111 Stat. 251.

Bernstein, J. (1998). *Another modest minimum wage increase: Clinton proposal would help close gap between current and historic value.* (Issue Brief No. 124). Washington, DC: Economic Policy Institute.

Blank, H., & Poersch, L. (1999). *State developments in child care and early education.* Washington, DC: Children's Defense Fund.

Brauner, J., Gordic, B., & Zigler, E. (2004). Putting the child back into child care: Combining care and education for children ages 3–5. In L. Sherrod (Ed.), *Social policy report: Giving child and youth development knowledge away, Vol. 18*(3), 3–5. Ann Arbor, MI: Society for Research in Child Development.

Brauner, S., & Loprest, P. (1999). *Where are they now? What states' studies of people who left welfare tell us.* (Assessing the New Federalism Series, No. A-32, table 8). Washington, DC: Urban Institute.

Bronfenbrenner, U. (1999). Environments in developmental perspective: Theoretical and operational models. In S.L. Friedman & T.D. Wachs (Eds.), *Measuring environment across the life span: Emerging methods and concepts* (pp. 3–28). Washington, DC: American Psychological Association.

Burchinal, M.R., Roberts, J.E., Nabors, L.A., & Bryant, D.M. (1996). Quality of center child care and infant cognitive and language development. *Child Development, 67,* 606–620.

Caldwell, C.H., Zimmerman, M.A., Bernat, D.H., Sellers, R.M., & Notaro, P.C. (2002). Racial identity, maternal support, and psychological outcomes among African-American adolescents. *Child Development, 73*(4), 1322–1336.

Card, D., & Krueger, A. (1995). *Myth and measurement: The new economics of the minimum wage.* Princeton, NJ: Princeton University Press.

Caughy, M.O., O'Campo, P.J., Randolph, S., & Nickerson, K. (2002). The influence of racial socialization practices on the cognitive and behavioral competence of African American preschoolers. *Child Development, 73*(5), 1611–1625.

Cauthen, N., & Lu, H. (2003). *Living at the edge: Employment alone is not enough for America's low-income children and families.* New York: National Center for Children in Poverty.

Child Trends. (2004). Food stamp receipt. Retrieved July 29, 2004, from http://www.childtrendsdatabank.org/indicators/56FoodStampReceipt.cfm

Children's Defense Fund (2004). Increasing the minimum wage: An issue of children's well-being. Retrieved July 24, 2004, from www.childrensdefense.org/familyincome/minimum_wage_report_2004.pdf

Cohen, S.S. (2001). *Championing child care.* New York: Columbia University Press.

Daniels, L.A. (2004). *The state of Black America 2004: The complexity of Black progress.* New York: National Urban League.

Edozien, J., Switzer, B., & Bryan, R. (1979). Medical evaluation of the Special Supplemental Food Program for Women, Infants and Children. *American Journal of Clinical Nutrition, 32,* 677–692.

Ewen, D., & Hart, K. (2003). *State developments in child care, early education, and school-age care.* Washington, DC: Children's Defense Fund.

Garrett, B., & Holahan, J. (2000). *Welfare leavers, Medicaid, and private health insurance* (Assessing the New Federalism Series, No. B-13, p. 3). Washington, DC: Urban Institute.

Harrison, K. (1997). Parental training for incarcerated fathers: Effects on attitudes, self-esteem, and children's self perceptions. *Journal of Social Psychology, 137*(5), 588–593.

Hausfather, A., Toharia, A., LaRoche, C., & Engelsmann, F. (1997). Effects of age of entry, day-care quality, and family characteristics on preschool behavior. *Journal of Child Psychology and Psychiatry and Allied Disciplines, 38,* 441–448.

Heimendinger, J., Larid, N., Austin, J., Timmer, P., & Gershoff, S. (1984). The effects of the WIC Program on the growth of infants. *American Journal of Clinical Nutrition, 40,* 1250–1257.

Helburn, S.W., & Bergmann, B.B. (2002). *America's child care problem: The way out.* New York: Palgrave.

Hernandez, M., & Isaacs, M.R. (Eds.). (1998). *Promoting cultural competence in children's mental health services.* Baltimore: Paul H. Brookes Publishing Co.

Hodgkinson, H.L. (2003). *Leaving too many children behind: A demographer's view on the neglect of America's youngest children.* Washington, DC: Institute for Educational Leadership.

Holahan, J., & Weil, A. (2003, May 27). Block grants are the wrong prescription for Medicaid. In *Health policy online: Timely analyses of current trends and policy options* (No. 6, pp. 1–12). Washington, DC: Urban Institute.

Howes, C., Matheson, C.C., & Hamilton, C.E. (1994). Maternal, teacher, and child care correlates of children's relationships with peers. *Child Development, 65,* 253–263.

Lamb, M.E. (1998). Nonparental child care: Context, quality, correlates, and consequences. In W. Damon, I.E. Sigel, & K.A. Renninger (Eds.), *Handbook of child psychology, Vol. 4: Child psychology in practice.* New York: Wiley.

Lee, V., & Burkam, D. (2002). *Inequality at the starting gate.* Washington, DC: Economic Policy Institute.

Lewit, E.M., Bennett, C., & Behrman, R.E. (2003). Health insurance for children: Analysis & recommendations. *Future of Children, 13*(1), 1–24.

Lynch, E.W., & Hanson, M.J. (Eds.) (2004). *Developing cross-cultural competence: A guide for working with children and their families* (3rd ed.). Baltimore: Paul H. Brookes Publishing Co.

Masse, L.N., & Barnett, S. (2002). Benefit cost analysis of the Abecedarian Early Childhood Intervention. Retrieved September 20, 2003, from http://www.childcarecanada.org/research/complete/benefit_cost_quality.html

Mezey, J. (2003). *Making the case for increasing federal child care funding: A fact sheet.* Washington, DC: Center for Law and Social Policy.

Morris, P.A. (2002). The effects of welfare reform policies on children. In L. Sherrod (Ed.), *Social policy report: Giving child and youth development knowledge away, Vol. 16*(1). Ann Arbor, MI: Society for Research in Child Development.

National Association for the Education of Young Children (NAEYC). (2004). Accreditation criteria and procedures of the National Association for the Education of Young Children. Retrieved July 29, 2004, from http://www.naeyc.org/accreditation/naeyc_accred/draft_standards/intro.asp

National Institute of Child Health and Development (NICHD) Early Child Care Research Network. (2000). The relation of child care to cognitive and language development. *Child Development, 71,* 958–978.

Nelson, K.P., Treskon, M., & Pelletiere, D. (2004). *Losing ground in the best of times: Low income renters in the 1990's.* Washington, DC: National Low Income Housing Coalition.

Ohis, J.C., Ponza, M., Moreno, L., Zambrowski, A., & Cohen, R. (1999). *Food stamp participants' access to retailers.* Princeton, NJ: Mathematica Policy Research.

Oliveira, V., Racine, E., Olmsted, J., & Ghelfi, L.M. (2002). *The WIC program: Background, issues, and trends* (Food Assistance and Research Report No. 27). Washington, DC: U.S. Department of Agriculture Economic Research Service.

Parrott, S., & Wu, N. (2003). *States and cutting TANF and child care programs.* Washington, DC: Center on Budget and Policy Priorities.

Paulsell, D., Cohen, J., Stieglitz, A., Lurie-Hurvitz, E., Fenichel, E., & Kisker, E. (2002). *Partnerships for quality: Improving infant-toddler child care for low-income families.* Princeton, NJ: Mathematica Policy Research.

Pauly, M.V. (1994). A case for employer-enforced individual mandates. *Health Affairs, 13,* 21–33.

Peisner-Feinberg, E.S., & Burchinal, M.R. (1997). Relations between preschool children's child-care experiences and concurrent development: The Cost, Quality, and Outcomes Study. *Merrill-Palmer Quarterly, 43,* 451–477.

Peisner-Feinberg, E.S., Burchinal, M.R., Clifford, R.M., Culkin, M.L., Howes, C., Kagan, S.L., Yazejian, N., Byler, P., Rustici, J., & Zelazo J. (1999). *The children of the Cost, Quality, and Outcomes Study go to school* (Tech. Rep.). Chapel Hill: University of North Carolina: Frank Porter Graham Child Development Center.

Personal Responsibility and Work Opportunity Reconciliation Act of 1996 (PRWORA). PL 104193, U.S.C. §§ 1601 *et seq.*

Pitcoff, W., Pelletiere, D., Crowley, S., Schaffer, K., Treskon, M., Vance, C., & Dolbeare, C.N. (2003). *Out of reach 2003: The growing gap between housing costs and income of poor people in the United States.* Washington, DC: National Low Income Housing Coalition.

Pollack, H.A., Davis, M.M., Danziger, S., & Orzol, S. (2002). *Health insurance coverage and access to care among former welfare recipients.* Ann Arbor, MI: Economic Research Initiative on the Uninsured.

Public Agenda. (2000). *Necessary compromises: How parents, employers and children's advocates view child care today.* New York: Public Agenda.

Raikes, H. (2004). Infant–toddler intervention on the road to school readiness: Lessons from EHS. *The Evaluation Exchange, 10*(2), 22–23.

Rose, D., Habicht, J-P., & Devaney, B. (1998). Household participation in the food stamp and WIC programs increases the nutrient intakes of preschool children. *Journal of Nutrition, 128,* 548–555.

Salcido, R.M., Ornelas, V., & Garcia, J.A. (2002). A neighborhood watch program for inner-city school children. *Children and Schools, 24*(3), 175–187.

Sampson, R.J., Raudenbush, S.W., & Earls, F. (1997). Neighborhoods and violent crime: A multilevel study of collective efficacy. *Science, 277,* 918–924.

Schachter, J.P. (2004). *Geographic mobility: 2002–2003 Population characteristics.* Washington, DC: U.S. Census Bureau.

Sherman, A., Fremstad, S., & Parrott, S. (2004). *Employment rates for single mothers fell substantially during recent period of labor market weakness.* Washington, DC: Center on Budget and Policy Priorities.

State Policy Documentation Project. (2002). *The state policy documentation project.* Washington, DC: Center for Law and Social Policy and the Center on Budget and Policy Priorities. Retrieved July 15, 2004, from http://www.spdp.org

Steuerle, C.E. (2003). A workable social insurance approach to expanding health insurance coverage. *Covering America: Real remedies for the uninsured, Vol. 3.* New York: Economic and Social Research Institute.

Sweeney, E., Scott, L., Lazere, E., Fremstad, S., Goldberg, H., Guyer, J., Super, D., & Johnson, C. (2000). *Windows of opportunity: Strategies to support families receiving welfare and other low-income families in the next stage of welfare reform.* Washington, DC: Center on Budget and Policy Priorities.

Thompson, L. (1992). Feminist methodology for family studies. *Journal of Marriage and the Family, 54,* 3–18.

Twombly, J.G., Pitcoff, W., Dolbeare, C.N., & Crowley, S. (2000). *Out of reach 2000: The growing gap between housing costs and income of poor people in the United States.* Washington, DC: National Low Income Housing Coalition.

U.S. Census Bureau. (2004). Income stable, poverty up, numbers of Americans with and without health insurance rise. Census Bureau Reports. Retrieved August 30, 2004, from http://www.census.gov/PressRelease/www/releases/archives/income_wealth/002484.html

U.S. Department of Agriculture Food and Nutrition Service. (1987). *The national WIC evaluation: An evaluation of the Special Supplemental Food Program for Women, Infants, and Children* (Vol. 1: Summary). Alexandria, VA: U.S. Department Agriculture.

U.S. Department of Defense. (2004). Military family resource center. Retrieved July 26, 2004, from http://www.mfrc-dodqol.org/MCY/index.htm

U.S. Department of Health and Human Services. (2004a). Computations for the 2004 annual update of the U.S. Department of Health and Human Services poverty guidelines for the 48 contiguous states and the District of Columbia. Retrieved August 1, 2004, from http://aspe.hhs.gov

U.S. Department of Health and Human Services. (2004b). Head Start performance standards. Retrieved July 27, 2004, from http://www.acf.gov/programs/hsb/performance/

U.S. Department of Housing and Urban Development. (2004). Renting. Retrieved August 26, 2004, from http://www.hud.gov/renting/index.cfm

U.S. Department of Justice. (2004). *Prison statistics.* Retrieved July 29, 2004, from http://www.ojp.usdoj.gov/bjs/prisons.htm

U.S. Department of Labor. (2004). *Employment status of the civilian population of race, sex, and age.* (Table A-2). Washington, DC: Bureau of Labor Statistics.

U.S. General Accounting Office. (1992). *Early intervention: Federal investments like WIC can produce savings* (Document HRD 92-18). Washington, DC: Author.

U.S. Government Accounting Office. (2003). *Child care: Recent state policy changes affecting the availability of assistance for low-income families* (GAO-03-588). Washington, DC: Author.

Wilczak, G., & Markstrom, C. (1999). The effects of parent education on parental locus of control and satisfaction of incarcerated fathers. *International Journal of Offender and Comparative Criminology, 43*(1), 90–102.

Wuest, J. (1995). Feminist grounded theory: An exploration of the congruency and tensions between two traditions in knowledge discovery. *Qualitative Health Research, 5,* 125–138.

Zedlewski, S.R. (2001). *Former welfare families and the Food Stamp program: The exodus continues.* (Assessing the New Federalism, Policy Brief B-33). Washington, DC: Urban Institute.

Zedlewski, S.R. (2002). Family economic resources in the post-reform era. *The Future of Children, 12*(1), 121–145.

Zedlewski, S.R., & Holland, J. (2002). *How much do welfare recipients know about time limits?* (Assessing the New Federalism, Snapshots 3, Report No. 15). Washington, DC: Urban Institute.

17

Commentaries

A Research Perspective

Gina Barclay-McLaughlin

*K*eepin' On: The Everyday Struggles of Young Families in Poverty offers compelling evidence of the complicated, dynamic nature of relationships and the ways in which individuals and families experience and make sense of them. It provides a picture of micro- and macro-level trends shaping healthy and unhealthy functioning that have important consequences for young children, parents, and communities.

Multiple research methods and techniques together with systematic and long-term, in-depth interviews afforded an extraordinary opportunity to make sense of the many transitions the participants experienced over time and the meanings those transitions had for their daily encounters, goals, choices, decisions, and outcomes. Interviews with members of the mothers' social networks permitted a comprehensive view beyond the parent-child dyad, the traditional focus of much child development and intervention research.

A book of the sweep of *Keepin' On* brings many questions and directions for future study to the researcher's mind. Given the limitations of space, this commentary centers on three observations and recommendations for future research. First, I comment on the researchers' willingness to share how they changed during the data collection and interpretation phases of the study. Second, I call attention to a theme in virtually every chapter—the back-and-forth captured in the mothers' thoughts about their relationships and living situations. In my view, studies that examine these oscillations will broaden the depth and range of our understanding of participants' lives. Finally, I discuss the need for research examining the intersections of adolescent development, intergenerational relationships, and African American valuing of interdependence.

CROSSING THE BOUNDARIES OF RACE, CULTURE, CLASS, AND GENDER

As Collins (2000) argued, African American family life cannot be understood without an in-depth understanding of racism and oppression and the positioning of the dominant group throughout history. Researchers must be aware of the range of ways participants may perceive them and how and why participants share their experiences and stories (Barclay-McLaughlin & Hatch, 2005). Behar (1993) said, "We ask for revelation from others, but we reveal little or nothing of ourselves; we make others vulnerable, but we ourselves remain invulnerable" (p. 273). Research ers studying racial minority women with low incomes are faced with the task of talking to people who have often been socialized to repress true feelings and ideas, especially when in conversation with Whites of higher socioeconomic status (Reinharz, 1992). This can make for a researcher–researched partnership that is not an easy one for either side.

The *Keepin' On* researchers revealed their struggles and growth in the process of understanding values and perspectives often foreign to their own way of thinking and understanding. They acknowledged their fears on entering the world of the participants, as well as the challenges they faced in looking beyond their limited experiences to examine the lived experiences of the participants. The honest acknowledgement of their anxieties gave meaning to the process. For example, Dr. Ispa's first encounter with one of the mothers generated a range of emotions related to acceptance, comfort, and safety. The immeasurable learning process that transformed the researchers' own understanding and work through entering the world of the mothers underscores the significance of a focus on crossing the boundaries of differences (Hatch & Barclay-McLaughlin, 2006).

I am often approached by scholars and professionals who want to know whether researchers can effectively study across boundaries such as gender, race, socioeconomic status, sexual orientation, and nationality. There is no linear response to this question. Yet, from the perspective of critical race and feminist theories, differences such as race and social class are fundamental for understanding poverty and the lived experiences of individuals and groups influenced by oppression. *Keepin' On* demonstrates the centrality and importance of connecting with and understanding the lives of participants. Equally significant for understanding are the roles and responsibilities of the researchers. As one participant said to me years ago, you have to "do time" (Julion, Gross, & Barclay-McLaughlin, 2000). "Doing time" is a process for gaining increased competence and understanding from the perspective of a participant. The process contributes to the development of a close relationship between the interviewer and the research participants. As the participants begin to trust the researchers, they feel more comfortable in dropping their guard, sharing experiences, and revealing more intimate information, unavailable to those outside the inner circle.

SWINGS AND SEESAWS

As stated in my introduction, I was struck by the fact that in almost every chapter of *Keepin' On,* we see what appear to be swings and seesaws in feelings and evaluations about living situations and relationships. Such swings in people's emotions and thoughts are often missed in studies based on data gathered at single-time points. The longitudinal nature of the *Keepin' On* project afforded opportunities to see many examples of changes of heart, as when the mothers and grandmothers complained about one another during one interview but showed great solidarity and love during the next (e.g., Chapters 6, 7, and 8), or when Chandra expressed excitement about a new apartment in what might be perceived by others as a more attractive and safer neighborhood but moved back to her old neighborhood a few months later because she was lonely (Chapter 12). What do these ups and downs and changes of mind mean? Are they simply "contradictions" that can be dismissed as evidence that people give hasty or superficial attention to decisions, or are they ephemeral reflections of true feelings? I don't think so. Instead, I assert that in the next wave of research, we need to dig in and study the sources and consequences of the multiple perspectives reflected in these seemingly apparent contradictions. Research with such a focus will greatly enrich our understanding of participants' values and the range and depth of the meanings they attach to them.

THE INTERSECTIONS OF DEVELOPMENTAL STAGE, LIFE DEMANDS, POVERTY, AND INTERGENERATIONAL CONNECTIVITY

This brings me to my point about the need for research examining the intersections of adolescent development, African American culture, poverty, and intergenerational relationships. Some of the back-and-forth in the *Keepin' On* mothers' relationships was conceivably due to their developmental stage, a time when testing boundaries is typical, compounded by the demands of parenting and seeking a fulfilling relationship with a partner. Any one of these factors alone would be expected to present challenges. In the context of multigenerational poverty, their associated stresses are surely multiplied.

Keepin' On illustrates the intergenerational landscape in which many young African American parents live. We must understand the dimensions of support (and conflict) that are part and parcel of these tight connections across generations. When we see the nuclear family as the ideal family model, we accentuate the negative aspects of families that lack adult male support. How and to what extent does extended family involvement make up for inconsistent father presence? The message of the mothers of *Keepin' On* is that father involvement is still essential. In Andreya's story and in Chapters 8, 9, and 11, we learn of the mothers' unwavering belief that children need their fathers. This valuing of father involvement is all the more poignant because most of the mothers described few positive relationships with men.

Bronfenbrenner's bioecological model of human development points to the importance of the macrosystem. We must take into consideration the macro-level barriers that serve to discourage many African American men from being consistently available to their children, and we must come to understand what grandparents and other extended kin give to their grandchildren when their fathers are not available. In what ways can other kin replace fathers, and in what ways are fathers' contributions unique and irreplaceable? In what ways do the contributions of extended kin *supplement* fathers' contributions, bringing something different and valuable, but not the same, to children's lives?

Moreover, we must ask how societal expectations of fathers affect fathers, mothers, and children. As Sherryce said, our societal norms require men to "bring something to the table." We expect men to provide financial and emotional support to their women and children. How is the men's limited availability to their children linked to the tensions created by the felt need to "bring something to the table" juxtaposed with the lack of opportunity for well-paying employment? And what does all of this mean for children? In the case study of Andreya, we see how Lavell and Kevon missed their father. How early do children construct the meaning of fathers, and when and under what circumstances do they begin to see their fathers' unavailability as a void?

Finally, we need to learn about grandparents' perspectives. How do they view their roles as they try to help their children find their way in a larger culture that dismisses the importance of the young learning from their elders?

I believe that researchers studying young African American parents and their family members must take all of these components into account—the developmental aspects of participants' behaviors, thoughts, and emotions and the complexities of their multiple sources (at multiple levels) of social support and conflict within a context of multigenerational poverty.

REFERENCES

Barclay-McLaughlin, G. (2000). Communal isolation: Narrowing the pathways to goal attainment and work in the social contexts of inner-city poverty. In S. Danziger & A. Lin (Eds.), *Coping with poverty: The social context of neighborhood, work, and family in the African-American community* (pp. 52–75). Ann Arbor: University of Michigan Press.

Barclay-McLaughlin, G., & Hatch, J.A. (2005). Studying across race: A conversation about the place of difference in qualitative research. *Contemporary Issues in Early Childhood, 6*(3), 216–232.

Behar, R. (1993). *Translated woman: Crossing the border with Esperanza's story.* Boston: Beacon.

Collins, P. (2000). *Black feminist thought: Knowledge, consciousness, and the politics of empowerment* (2nd ed.). New York: Routledge.

Johnson, J.M. (2001). In-depth interview. In J.F. Gubrium & J. Holstein, *Handbook of interview research: Context and method.* (pp. 103–120). Thousand Oaks, CA: Sage Publications, Inc.

Hatch, J.A., & Barclay-McLaughlin, G. (2006). Qualitative research: Paradigms and possibilities. In B. Spodek & O. Saracho (Eds.), *Handbook of research on the education of young children* (2nd ed.). Mahwah, NJ: Lawrence Erlbaum Associates.

Hicks-Bartlett, S. (2000). Between a rock and a hard place: The labyrinth of working and parenting in a poor community. In S. Danziger & A. Lin (Eds.), *Coping with poverty: The social context of neighborhood, work, and family in the African-American community* (pp. 27–51). Ann Arbor: University of Michigan Press.

Julion, W., Gross, D., & Barclay-McLaughlin, G. (2000). Recruiting families of color from the inner city: Insights from the recruiters. *Nursing Outlook, 48,* 230–237.

Olesen, V. (2000). Feminism and qualitative research at and into the millennium. In N.K. Denzin & Y.S. Lincoln (Eds.), *Handbook of qualitative research* (2nd ed., pp. 215–255). Thousand Oaks, CA: Sage Publications, Inc.

Reinharz, S. (1992). *Feminist methods in social research.* New York: Oxford University Press.

A Practice Perspective

Gayle Cunningham

I enjoyed this book immensely. Ever since I finished reading it, I have been quoting from it and referring to it because it so brilliantly records insights about the lives of families served by so many of our programs at the Jefferson County Committee for Economic Opportunity (JCCEO), the community action agency I direct. JCCEO administers Head Start, Early Head Start, and a number of other programs for people with low incomes who need help meeting fundamental needs and achieving self-sufficiency. For example, we help with needs for education and training, job placement, decent and affordable housing and home ownership, child care, care for elderly relatives, enrichment opportunities for youth, substance abuse treatment, and so forth. In Early Head Start and Head Start alone, we serve 1,579 infants, toddlers, and preschoolers and their families. It is rare for the people we serve to get the in-depth attention each chapter of this book gives them. More often than not, they are just seen as people with problems—as statistics.

As I read *Keepin' On*, I thought about all the young parents who need families they can lean on, but instead have families who can't help them much because they themselves have few resources. I thought about how overwhelming the circumstances of their lives too often are, how brave they often are, and how many of them have so much spirit and so much intelligence and yet have such a hard row to hoe. The young women portrayed in this book fiercely resist potential dangers to themselves and their children, but it is overwhelmingly difficult, in our society, to manage without basic academic skills and without the credentials to get a job that pays a decent salary. Add to that the dwindling support of the government and society—for example, the reduction of housing and food subsidies. And once they are in the maze of poverty, it is difficult for them to escape because there are too many obstacles, too many dead ends. It seems so wrong, and the authors of this book did an excellent job capturing all of this.

There are so many things that we Black folks don't talk about much, and especially not with anyone outside the Black community—issues, for example, related to the troubling phenomenon of multiple relationships that result in children who are not, who cannot be, supported by their fathers. Or the raw racism, such as an incident documented in the book, that is still experienced occasionally by members of our community. Such indignations and insults continue to happen in a society that claims to be far beyond that kind of racism. All of this is compounded in too many communities by terrible housing, poor transportation, unsafe neighborhoods, poor child care and especially poor infant care, chaos and disorganization within households, chaos within communities, and programs that are supposed to help but instead punish the person who seems to be getting ahead.

I was a member of an advisory committee that helped develop Early Head Start. When we envisioned this program, we knew it would take a long time before it would reach many of the people who need it, but we were optimistic. We thought it would eventually make a huge difference in the lives of parents and children. I came away from this book thinking that as important as Early Head Start is, it is not nearly enough for those who need help. It can make things better, but *by itself* it cannot dramatically change lives, given the resources that we presently have. We need to figure out how to do more. Let us be realistic. It will take significantly more resources to make a difference in the lives of families living in poverty. I have been thinking that it would be wonderful if we could build a program that provided a living and learning situation—something like a college dorm—where families could obtain what they need and see positive examples of day-to-day living. Children would be in good child care while parents took classes that would help them move toward self-sufficiency and family success.

I was disturbed by the difficulties several of the families in the book had with child care. Of course, the research for this book began when the Early Head Start program serving the families was new and having growing pains, and when national Early Head Start policies did not yet oblige staff to ensure high-quality care for all infants and toddlers in the program. These policies are now in place. *Keepin' On* shows how important it is that these policies be maintained. High-quality child care that is readily accessible, consistent, and affordable is crucial to helping families become successful. It is something we can give these young women and their children so that they will have one less thing to worry about. It will allow parents to deal with the other issues in their lives and prepare for brighter futures. It will make a real difference for them, for their families, for their communities, and ultimately for our nation.

Administrators who run social services programs and staff who work directly with mothers and children must read this book. It will give them greater insights into the lives of the families they serve. I am impressed that the researchers who wrote this book got to know some aspects of the mothers' lives better than service providers ordinarily do. We need to hear these stories. Many of our staff come from the same communities as the families they serve, but they need to understand what has made their circumstances different. This will help them become more sensitive to the situations of the young children and parents they are trying to help. They need to understand how important it is to support the mothers—to help them find resources and make good decisions about education and training. These supports will make a difference in their futures.

Policy makers—people who can affect the systems and service delivery in low-income communities—also need this book. The families described in *Keepin' On* are living in inner-city neighborhoods, but the problems they face also can be applied to rural areas. The rural underclass is often overlooked.

And finally, I think that those who are not directly involved in service delivery or policy should read this book. So many people have no idea how others in their own cities and towns live and the struggles they face. *Keepin' On* will show them how they might contribute to creating better communities for all.

A Policy Perspective

Deborah A. Phillips

This account of a five-year longitudinal, qualitative study of nine young African American women adjusting to single motherhood, conducted just as dramatic changes in the welfare system were being implemented, provides both sobering portrayals of the adversities that these women face and inspiring stories of their courage, commitment, and endurance. It deserves a place alongside the work of Kotlowitz (1992), Kozol (1991), and Edin and Lein (1997), offering as it does an essential complement to large-scale empirical studies that necessarily skim the surface of real lives as they unfold day by day. I was particularly struck by three themes that have been bypassed by quantitative research on families living in poverty: 1) the heartbreaking tone of fatalism that the mothers expressed regarding their children's transition into adolescence—including their odds for survival—as it affected their *early* child-rearing practices and attitudes, 2) the extent to which negative attitudes about men affected the mother's goals for their young daughters (to be self-sufficient and independent) and sons (to be different from most of the men they knew), and 3) the virtual absence of female friendships and the ensuing loneliness that characterized the young mothers. My broader comments address three issues: the value of juxtaposing the perspectives of research, practice, and policy; the expectations placed on Early Head Start (EHS) to meet the needs of the families it serves; and the intersection of policies guiding EHS, child care, and welfare reform.

A SHARED AGENDA FOR RESEARCH, PRACTICE, AND POLICY

Keepin' On: The Everyday Struggles of Young Families in Poverty represents an unusual blend of research, practice, and policy perspectives. As such, it begins the task of building bridges across these "three related, but distinct cultures" (Shonkoff, 2000, p. 181) in the service of creating a shared agenda. As scientists, the authors embed their insights in bioecological and feminist theories and offer ideas about the research questions that emerge from their work. They also overlay their findings with commentary about the changes in policy and practice that impinged on the lives of the women they followed. The confusion and staff turnover that arose from the shift in priorities for EHS home visitors, the interruptions in benefits that occurred when Medicaid and welfare benefits were decoupled, and the precipitous loss of benefits that affected the mothers who were able to obtain jobs that paid decent wages are just a few examples of policy-driven disruptions that compounded the tumultuous quality of these women's lives. There are messages in this for researchers who attempt to capture the synergistic effects of multiple levels of turbulence in the lives of young mothers living in poverty, for practitioners who are the front line of connection between program policies and clients, and for policy makers who need to be cognizant of the unintended consequences that arise from policy provisions that work against these young women's efforts to be the best mothers and the best providers they can be.

The authors also balance their thoughts about what we have yet to understand with recommendations for what we should do with what we have learned. This is a leap that many investigators are reluctant to take, but, as a result, the book will be equally valuable to those who study and to those who seek to affect the lives of low-income, single mothers. Perhaps it takes an intimate look at the lives of those who are simultaneously research subjects, program clients, and individuals who are eligible for public benefits to set aside disciplinary differences and instead to weave together lessons learned from science, practice, and policy.

EXPECTATIONS OF EARLY HEAD START

One of the most prominent lessons in the book concerns the centrality of EHS as a source of support and connection in the young women's lives. The authors' research joins other empirical studies of the EHS eligible population in its effort to examine links between this program and child care, transportation, welfare reform, employment, nutrition, and child welfare policies. The legislation creating the EHS program emphasizes a comprehensive model of service delivery that includes strengthening child development, family development, staff development, and community building. And EHS practitioners—whether home visitors or center-based teachers—stretch themselves to address each of these goals. In this spirit, from chapter to chapter the authors present a

growing list of ways in which EHS could extend the reach of its services—for example, by

- linking fathers to job training and placement programs

- educating parents regarding their rights and responsibilities while
  receiving and transitioning off TANF

- intervening in families to ensure that more children receive regular
  child support payments

- partnering with and providing training to community early childhood programs, increasing the availability of care during nontraditional working hours

- determining if taxicab vouchers and tokens for reduced bus fares
  would allow parents to better fulfill their multiple responsibilities

- helping parents find affordable and safe housing, ensuring that all
  enrolled children receive Medicaid or Child Health Insurance Program (CHIP) benefits and reminding mothers to make appointments
  for well-baby visits and immunizations

- participating in local task forces to solve problems associated with
  family access to nutritious food

- developing a handbook of community social welfare programs and
  policies

- educating parents about adolescent development, as well as early
  childhood development

The fundamental question this list raises is whether we are expecting
too much from EHS. Are we expecting the program to compensate for
weaknesses in virtually every other realm of policy that touches the
lives of young mothers and children growing up in poverty? At what
point does the capacity of EHS to promote children's development become diluted by additional demands on its staff to respond to virtually
every need faced by participating families? As a case in point, I was troubled to learn that EHS performance standards, as revised during the
span of this study, reduced in half the number of home visits required
for working mothers. At what point does the early childhood community call upon welfare and workplace policies to accommodate the goals
of EHS rather than comply with requests to adjust the program to accommodate the demands of welfare reform and inflexible employment?
At what point do we stop accepting funding shortfalls, gaps in coverage,
and inadequate information and outreach that characterize other domains of child policy (i.e., housing, transportation, health care, child care,

employment, child support policies) and hold policy makers accountable for better addressing these basic needs and rights?

The authors clearly recognize this source of tension. They are quick
to acknowledge that "we are in the early stages of understanding how
to work effectively with parents who live under high-stress circumstances" (Chapter 13, p. 1), and they also highlight the "complexities and
difficulties inherent in a home visitor's job" (Chapter 13, p. 1). They describe home visitors who took mothers to welfare offices and stayed
with them while they completed applications, helped them type and
photocopy their resumes, drove them to apartments and houses for
rent, filled out community college enrollment forms for them, and took
them shopping for diapers. Not surprisingly, their observations and
those of others reveal that mothers experiencing crises receive a dis-
proportionate share of home visiting time and services, to the frustration of home visitors and the more stable mothers alike. While family
stress is associated with poorer parenting, there is no evidence to suggest that children benefit from fewer rather than more home visits focused on their developmental needs. Indeed, the evidence on home
visiting is highly cautionary regarding the low dosage of services that
many families receive and the negative consequences for program outcomes (Margie & Phillips, 1999; Sweet & Appelbaum, 2004).

The authors do a thorough job of providing recommendations for
virtually all of the policy areas that touch the lives of the women they
followed, and, as such, make it clear that EHS fits within an array of
other policies and services. The next stage of this discussion needs to
confront the short- and long-term benefits and costs to the families who
rely on EHS when this program is expected to compensate for the failures of—rather than complement—other service arenas and providers.
Knowing that child development is profoundly affected by stresses arising from factors as far-flung as poor public transportation and lengthy
application forms for public benefits should not translate into pressures
upon a small, fledgling program to address all of these problems.

EARLY HEAD START AND CHILD CARE

A natural place to begin confronting these issues lies at the intersection
of EHS and child care policy. One of the more striking findings from this
qualitative study concerns the juxtaposition of the mother's high expectations for how their children's child care experiences would ad-
vance the social and cognitive development of their children with their
acceptance of arrangements they knew to be sub-optimal. Equally interesting was the mothers' awareness that high teacher turnover is
cause for concern. Not surprisingly, *trust* plays a salient role in the moth-

ers' selection of child care arrangements, even if assurance in this arena comes at the cost of using the more formal arrangements that the mothers preferred after the first year of life.

The authors, as well as substantial research, documented the barriers to obtaining high-quality child care that confront low-income, inner-city parents, particularly those struggling with long commutes and nontraditional work hours. Imagine the added challenges to low-income parents—represented by Andreya and far from uncommon—who are raising a child with a disability or a special health care need.

Today, it is impossible to consider these issues outside the context of welfare reform. The EHS evaluation has highlighted the large extent to which this program touches the lives of families participating in welfare reform, with 12% to 66% of families participating in both programs depending on the study site (Administration for Children and Families, 2001, 2002). Other related evidence concerns the growing share of EHS programs that are changing from home-based to center-based options, shifting home visits to evenings and weekends, and experiencing a loss of parent volunteer time (which reduces the programs' capacity to meet their mandated non-federal share of costs). Still other evidence suggests that Head Start eligible families are trading off enrollment in Head Start for reliance on child care arrangements that better meet their work-related needs (Gassman-Pines, 2003; Gennetian, Huston, Crosby, Change, & Weisner, 2003). It is clear that the confluence of changes in welfare policy, child care policy, and EHS practices poses a significant challenge to policy makers and practitioners alike.

In response to these challenges, the authors call upon practitioners to inform parents of the "reality" of child care programs, presumably in hopes that they will figure out a way to place their children in higher-quality, more stable arrangements. They also call upon EHS practitioners to increase the availability of care during nontraditional working hours, and upon policy makers to increase funding for the Child Care and Development Fund and to pass federal child care regulations. These are, of course, laudable and useful recommendations. But, as far-reaching as they may seem, I fear that they are insufficient to address the crisis in child care that now confronts our nation.

In *From Neurons to Neighborhoods* (Shonkoff & Phillips, 2000), we chose not to reiterate the many child care recommendations that have emerged from various panels, commissions, and task forces—and that have not been implemented. Rather, we took the approach of asserting a clear set of priorities for the nation's early care and education system and calling for a comprehensive reassessment of current investments insofar as they address these priorities. The three priorities are

1) that young children's needs are met through sustained relationships with qualified caregivers; 2) that the special needs of children with developmental disabilities or chronic health conditions are addressed; and 3) that the settings in which children spend their time are safe, stimulating, and compatible with the values and priorities of their families. Efforts to increase income eligibility thresholds for subsidies, apply sliding fee formulas, reward families who use higher-quality arrangements with higher-reimbursement rates, add hours to training requirements for child care providers, and other similar actions are all good ideas. But these incremental steps are unlikely to lift existing services above the thresholds needed to address the three priorities.

Absent serious efforts to improve the qualifications and salaries of the early childhood workforce, tinkering with the existing system is unlikely to ensure sustained relationships, equitable care for children with disabilities, and safe and stimulating environments for all children. Absent efforts to decouple public support for child care from poverty and welfare policies, it is unlikely that the developmental needs of young children will rise to the top of the list of priorities for government child care benefits—the place they rightfully hold within the Early Head Start and Head Start programs. And, absent efforts to adjust private and public policies that affect the conditions of work for all parents of young children, but perhaps especially for parents struggling with the myriad stresses exemplified by the mothers in this book, we will continue to find the majority of young children in early childhood programs that constitute lost opportunities for fostering the children's optimal development.

REFERENCES

Administration for Children and Families. (2001). *Building their futures: How EHS programs are enhancing the lives of infants and toddlers in low-income families, Volume 1: Technical report.* Washington, DC: U.S. Department of Health and Human Services.

Administration for Children and Families. (2002). *Making a difference in the lives of infants, toddlers, and their families: The impacts of EHS, Volume 1: Final technical report.* Washington, DC: U.S. Department of Health and Human Services.

Edin, R., & Lein, L. (1997). *Making ends meet: How single mothers survive welfare and low-wage work.* New York: Russell Sage Foundation.

Gassman-Pines, A. (June 2003). *The effects of welfare and employment policies on child care use by low-income young mothers. Working Paper No. 19.* New York: MDRC.

Gennetian, L.A., Huston, A.C., Crosby, D.A., Change, Y.E., & Weisner, T.S. (August 2003). *Making child care choices: How welfare and work policies influence parents' decisions.* New York: MDRC.

Kotlowitz, A. (1992). *There are no children here: The story of two boys growing up in the other America.* New York: Anchor Books.

Kozol, J. (1991). *Savage inequalities: Children in America's schools.* New York: Crown Publishers.

Margie, N.G., & Phillips, D.A. (1999). *Revisiting home visiting: Summary of a workshop.* Washington, DC: National Academies Press.

Shonkoff, J.P. (2000). Science, policy, and practice: Three cultures in search of a shared mission. *Child Development, 71,* 181–187.

Shonkoff, J., & Phillips, D. (Eds.). (2000). *From neurons to neighborhoods: The science of early childhood development.* Washington, DC: National Academies Press.

Sweet, M.A., & Appelbaum, M.I. (2004). Is home visiting an effective strategy? A meta-analytic review of home visiting programs for families with young children. *Child Development, 75*(5), 1435–1456.

Index

Page numbers followed by *f* and *t* refer to figures and tables, respectively.